PREFACE

By Dr. Herbert Lockyer

Digging into the biography and books of Dr. John Owen, a phrase arrested my mind and is worthy of repetition. . . "He counted it a higher honor to be John Owen, a servant of Jesus Christ than a Doctor of Divinity by human creation." Apart from his vast learning and pulpit talents, John Owen preached and wrote for Eternity . . .

> "Ambitious, not to shine or to excell,
> But to treat justly, what he loved so well."

This mighty man of God enjoyed an extraordinary measure of spiritual power, producing in him a life of faith, of self-denial, and of heavenly tranquility. Describing, as he often did, the mortification of sin, he emphasized what he himself daily practiced. Deep humility of disposition was characteristic of this man of eminent talents. Gifted and honored beyond degree, John Owen sought to be unconscious of his own superiority. The prominent feature of his character was the recognition of the supreme authority of the Bible and his ability to expound it. From his *Epitaph* over his grave in Bunhill Fields we take the sentences . . .

> "His publications were the effulgent lamp of evangelical truth
> to guide their step to immortal glory.
> He was a scribe in every way instructed in the mysteries of
> the Kingdom of God."

His character and qualifications made him the most powerful expositor of his time. Says William Orme, "Of the learning, knowledge of the Scriptures and piety, the grand requisites of the Gospel ministry, it is scarcely necessary to say anything, after what has been brought forward. The languages of the Cross were familiar to John Owen as his mother tongue. He was well skilled in the tongues, Rabbinical learning, and Jewish Rites and customs, as his work on "Hebrews" reveals.

Owen's ability to present the Truth has been described by one of his contemporaries, Dodwell . . . "This personage was proper and comely and he had a very graceful behavior in the pulpit, an eloquent elocution, a winning and instinuating deportment, and could, by the persuasion of his oratory, in conjunction with some other outward advantages, move and win the affections of his audiences almost as he pleased.

There are many commendable aspects of John Owen's life and labors we could dwell upon. Over 125 years ago, William Orme wrote his "Memoirs of Owen's Life and Writings" and he has given us a deep insight into the unique character of this renowned Puritan theologian and preacher.

The exposition before us is the most outstanding of Owen's Works, and is a condensation of eight volumes occupying his attention for sixteen years. His own delight in the preparation of this great work is expressed thus . . . "I found the excellency of the writing to be such, the depth of the mysteries contained in it to be so great, the compass of the truth asserted, unfolded, and explained so extensive and so diffused through the whole body of the Christian religion, the usefulness of the things contained in it, so important and indispensably necessary, that I was quickly satisfied that the wisdom, grace and truth treasured in this sacred storehouse, are far from being exhausted by the endeavors of all that are gone before us. So far did these truths then, seem from being all perfectly brought to light by them; that I was assured there was left a sufficient ground, not only for renewed investigation after rich ore in this mine, for the present generation, but for all them that shall succeed to the consumation of all things."

Here is a nugget gathered at random from this mine of truth. In Chapter 2, John Owen dealing with the phrase, "He is able to succor" gives these four aspects . . .

1. "He hath a sufficiency of *care*, wisdom and faithfulness to observe and know the seasons wherein succor is necessary.

2. He hath a sufficiency of *tenderness*, mercy and compassion to excite Him thereunto.

3. He hath a sufficiency of *power* to afford succor that shall be effectual.

4. He hath a sufficiency of *acceptation* at the throne of grace to prevail with God for suitable supplies and succor."

Another popular preacher of Owen's day was another, John, John Bunyan, whom Owen often heard preach when he came to London. Charles II expressed his astonishment to Owen that a man of his learning should listen to a tinker preach. John Owen replied, "Had I the tinker's abilities, please your Majesty, I would most gladly relinquish my learning."

The end of this gifted expositor of "The Epistle to Hebrews" was as triumphant as his life. John Owen spent his closing days in writing his "Meditations on the Glory of Christ." What a spiritual treasure this is! On the morning of the day he died, a friend called to tell him the work was put to press. "I am glad to hear it," said the dying expositor; and lifting up his hands and eyes as if transformed with joy, he exclaimed, "But O! the long wished-for day is come at last, in which I shall see that glory in another manner than I have ever done, or was capable of doing in this world."

HEBREWS

THE EPISTLE OF WARNING

by

John Owen, D. D.

Author of *The Holy Spirit, His Gifts and Power*

Preface by Herbert Lockyer, D.D.

KREGEL PUBLICATIONS
Grand Rapids, Michigan 49501

Library of Congress Catalog Card Number: 68-57719
ISBN 0-8254-3407-6 (Paper)
ISBN 0-8254-3406-8 (Cloth)

HEBREWS: The Epistle of Warning is an abridgement by M. J. Tyron of John Owen's *Exposition of the Epistle to the Hebrews* originally published in eight volumes.

First American Edition 1953
Reprint Edition 1968
Reprinted 1973
Reprinted 1977

PRINTED IN THE UNITED STATES OF AMERICA

HEBREWS

THE EPISTLE OF WARNING

CHAPTER ONE

Vs. 1, 2. *God, who at sundry times and in divers manners spake in time past unto the fathers by the prophets, hath in these last days spoken unto us by [His] Son, whom He hath appointed heir of all things, by whom also He made the worlds.*

"**God, who at sundry times and in divers manners spake in time past unto the fathers by the prophets, hath in these last days spoken unto us by His Son.**" God, even the Father, by way of eminency was the peculiar author of both law and gospel; and the Apostle proceeds at once to give various instances of the difference there was between the law and the gospel as to their revelation from God. He spake in "*time past*," that is "of old," "formerly;" this denotes some space of time, which comprises the whole space of time from the giving out of the first promise unto that end which was put unto all revelations of public use under the Old Testament. But more especially the Apostle hath respect unto the period of time commencing with the giving of the law by Moses in the wilderness. He had no contest with the Jews about the first promise, and the service of God in the world built thereon, nor about their privilege as they were the sons of Abraham; but only about their then present church privilege and claim under the law of Moses. "*He spake unto the fathers:*" that is unto all the faithful of the Judaical church, from the days of Moses unto the ceasing of prophecy in the days of Malachi.

But "*in these last days*" God hath spoken to us. These "last days" have special reference to the last days of the Judaical church and state, which were then drawing to their period and abolition. This was the time when God specially spoke by His Son. That this is the time intended by the Apostle is clear if we consider to whom God spoke: He hath spoken "*unto us*;" that is to the members of the Judaical church who lived in the days of the personal ministry of Christ, and afterwards under the preaching of the gospel unto that day (c. ii. 3). The Jews were very apt to think that if they had lived in the times of the former prophets, and had heard them delivering their message from God, they would have received it with cheerful obedience. But the Apostle reminds them that, in the revelation of the gospel, God had actually spoken to themselves, the very thing they so much desired.

In former days God spoke to them at "*sundry times*," that is, "by many parts." God gradually discovered His mind and will, by the addition of one thing after another, as the Church could bear the light of them. There were four principal times in which God spoke: 1. Unto Adam, in the promise of "the Seed;" subservient to this were the particular revelations made to Seth, Enos, Enoch, Lamech, and others before the flood. 2. Unto Noah after the flood, in the renewal of the covenant and establishing of the Church in his family; subservient to which were the revelations made to Melchisedec and others before the call of Abraham. 3. Unto Abraham, in the restriction of the promise to his seed, confirmed in the revelations made to Isaac, Jacob, Joseph, and others of their posterity. 4. Unto Moses, in the giving of the law and the erection of the Judaical church in the wilderness; unto which there were three principal subservient revelations: to David and Solomon, which was particularly designed to perfect the revelation of the will of God concerning the Old Testament worship; to the prophets, after the division of the kingdom unto the captivity; and to Ezra, with the prophets that assisted in the reformation of the church after its return from Babylon. In opposition to this gradual revelation, the Apostle intimates that now, by Jesus the Messiah, God had *at once* begun and finished the revelation of His will, according to their own hopes and expectations.

But God spake not only at sundry times, but in "*divers manners*." Now this hath respect to the various ways God had of revealing Himself to the prophets: by dreams, visions, inspirations, voices, angels, every way, with an equal evidence of being from God. Also to the ways of His dealings with the fathers by the prophets: by promises, by threats, by gradual discoveries of His will, by special messages, by public sermons, and the like. In opposition to this the Apostle intimates that the revelation of God and His will by

Christ was accomplished in one way only, and in one manner only, namely, by His preaching the gospel, who was anointed by the Spirit without measure.

The last difference or instance in the comparison insisted on by the Apostle is this : that of old God spake " *in the prophets*," but now " *in the Son*." The prophets were but instruments to give out what they had received from God. The word of the Lord was "in the hand" of this or that prophet. That which made any revelation to be prophecy was that inspiration of the Holy Ghost which implanted in the minds of the prophets, and gave forth by their tongues or pens, that which God would utter in them and by them. In answer unto this speaking of God in the prophets, it is asserted that in the revelation of the gospel God spake " *in His Son*." This is the main hinge on which all the arguments in the whole epistle do turn. There is a difference between the Son of God revealing the will of God in *His Divine Person* to the prophets, and the Son of God as *incarnate* revealing the will of God immediately to the Church. This is the difference here insisted on by the Apostle. The principal comparison is between God speaking *in* Moses and God speaking *in* Christ. (See chap. iii. 5, 6.) The just privileges belonging to Moses above all other prophets lay in three things : 1. He was the lawgiver or mediator by whom God gave that law, and revealed that worship in the observation of which the very being of the Judaical church did consist; 2. That God dealt with him in a more familiar and clear manner as to the way of His outward dealing than with any other prophet ; 3. In that the revelation made unto him concerned the ordering of the whole house of God, when the other prophets were employed only about some particulars built on his foundation.

But the revelation of the mind of God in and by the Son, is compared with and preferred before that of Moses, and that because—1. The Lord Jesus Christ, by virtue of the union of His Person, was from the womb filled with a perfection of gracious light and knowledge of God and His will ; 2. The commission, mission, and furnishing of the Son as incarnate and Mediator, with abilities for the declaration of the mind and will of God unto the Church, were peculiarly from the Father. For the whole work of mediation He received command from His Father, and what He should speak, according to which command He wrought and taught. That blessed " tongue of the learned," whereby God spake in Him and by Him the refreshing word of the gospel unto poor weary sinners, was the gift of the Father; 3. That Jesus Christ in His Divine nature as He was the eternal Word and Wisdom of the Father, not by a voluntary communication, but eternal generation, had an omnisciency of the whole nature and will of God, as the Father Himself hath, their will and wisdom being the same; 4. The Lord Christ discharged His office and work of revealing the will of His Father in and by His human

nature, that nature wherein He "dwelt among us;" for although the
Person of Christ—God and man—was our Mediator, yet His human
nature was that wherein He discharged the duties of His office; 5. The
human nature of Christ, as He was in it "made of a woman, made
under the law," was from the instant of its union with the Person
of the Son of God "a holy thing"—"holy, harmless, undefiled,
and separate from sinners"—and radically filled with all that perfection of habitual grace and wisdom which was or could be
necessary to the discharge of that whole duty which He owed unto
God; 6. There was a peculiar endowment with the Spirit, without
and beyond the bounds of all comprehensible measures, that He
was to receive as the great Prophet of the Church, in whom the
Father would speak and give out the last revelation of Himself.

In these, and sundry other things of the like importance, had
the Father's speaking in the Son the pre-eminence above His
speaking in Moses and the prophets. Observe, 1. That the authority
of God speaking in and by the penmen of the Scriptures is the
sole bottom and foundation of our assenting unto them with faith
divine and supernatural; 2. God's gradual revelation of Himself,
His mind and will unto the Church, was a fruit of infinite wisdom
and care towards His elect; 3. We may see the absolute perfection
of the revelation of the will of God by Christ and His apostles, as to
every end and purpose whatever for which God ever did or ever will
in this world reveal Himself, or His mind and will. Having
declared the Son to be the immediate revealer of the gospel, the
Apostle now proceeds to declare His glory and excellency—both that
which He had in Himself before He entered upon the office of
Mediator, and that which He received upon His investiture with
that office.

"**Whom He hath appointed heir of all things, by whom
also He made the worlds.**" There are three things intended by
this word "*heir*:" 1. Title, dominion, lordship; 2. Possession:
Christ is made actual possessor of that which He hath a title unto;
3. That He hath this title and possession by grant from the Father.
He is appointed heir of "*all things.*" He the author of the gospel
—being heir and lord of all things whatever, the sovereign disposal
of all the rites and ceremonies of worship about which the Jews
contended must needs be in His hand, to change and to alter them
as He saw good. Also, He being Lord and heir of all things, it was
easy for them to conclude that if they intended to be made partakers of any good in heaven or earth, in a way of love and mercy,
it must be by an interest in Him. The next words evince this
sense: "*by whom also He made the worlds.*" He made all, and it
was meet He should be lord of all. Jesus Christ was "appointed"
heir of all things. This was according to the eternal purpose of
God; to the covenant of old between the Father and the Son for
the accomplishment of the great work of redemption; to the

promises made Him in the types; to the promises left on record in the Old Testament; to the solemn proclamation of Him to be the great heir and lord of all at His first coming into the world. " *By whom also He made the worlds;* " not as an instrument, or an inferior, but as God's own eternal Word, Wisdom, and Power.

V. 3. *Who being the brightness of* [*His*] *glory, and the express image of His Person, and upholding all things by the word of His power, when He had by Himself purged our sins, sat down on the right hand of the Majesty on high.*

" **Who being the brightness of** [**His**] **glory.** " The Apostle reminds the Jews that God had promised to dwell among them by His glorious presence; hence the very name of Jerusalem is called, " The LORD is there." Now He who in and under that name was with them as sent by Jehovah (Zech. ii. 8) was the Son, in whom He had now spoken in these latter days. And this must needs be of weight with them, that He who had revealed the will of God unto them was none other but He who had dwelt among them from the beginning, representing in all things the Person of the Father, being typically revealed unto them as the " *brightness of His glory.*"

" **And the express image of His Person.** " As is the Father, so is the Son. What the Father is, doth, hath, that the Son is, doth, hath; or else the Father could not be fully satisfied in Him, nor represented by Him. By the " *express image,*" or " express character," we are to understand that the whole nature of God is in Him, as also that by Him God is declared and expressed unto us. Observe, 1. That all the glorious perfections of the nature of God do belong unto and dwell in the Person of the Son; 2. That the whole manifestation of the nature of God unto us, and all communications of His grace, are immediately by and through the Person of the Son. There are some signal instances wherein God reveals Himself and communicates from His own infinite fulness unto His creatures, and in all of them He doth it immediately by His Son. He does so in the creation of all things, in their providential rule and disposal; in the revelation of His will, and institution of ordinances; and in the communication of His Spirit and grace.

The whole end of the gospel is to give us " the knowledge of the glory of God in the face of Jesus Christ; " that is, the glory of the invisible God, whom none hath seen at any time. That is to be communicated to us, as it is in the Person of Jesus Christ manifested and represented unto us, for He is " the image of God." The expressions of God in all other things besides the Son, Christ Jesus, are all of them partial, revealing only something of Him—not all that is necessary to be known, that we may live unto Him here, and enjoy Him hereafter. And hence it is that all who have attempted to come unto God by the light of that manifestation which He hath made of Himself any other way than in and by Christ Jesus, have all failed and come short of His glory. But now the Lord Christ being the "*brightness of His glory*," in whom His glory shines out of the thick darkness that His nature is enwrapped in unto us, and beams out of that inaccessible light which He inhabits ; and "*the express image of His Person*," representing all the perfections of His person fully and clearly unto us ; it is in Him alone we can attain a saving acquaintance with God.

" And upholding all things by the word of His power." We may learn from these words that our Lord Jesus Christ hath the weight of the whole creation upon His hand, and disposeth of it by His wisdom and power. Such is the nature and condition of the universe, that it could not subsist a moment, nor could anything in it act regularly unto its appointed end, without the continued supportment, guidance, influence, disposal, of the Son of God. " All things were created by Him and for Him, and He is before all things, and by Him all things consist." When we name a creature, we name that which hath a derived and dependent being. From this we may see the vanity of expecting anything from creatures, but only what the Lord is pleased to communicate unto us by them. He alone hath an absolute sovereignty over us in all things ; this should teach us our constant dependence on Him, and our universal subjection unto Him. And this abundantly discovers the vanity and folly of those who make use of the creation in an opposition unto the Lord Christ and His peculiar interest in the world. His own power is the very ground on which they stand in their opposition unto Him ; and all things which they use against Him consist in Him ; their very lives are at the disposal of Him whom they oppose.

"When He had by Himself purged our sins." This purging of our sins, which the Apostle declares to have been effected before the ascension of Christ, consisteth not in the actual sanctification and purification of believers by the Spirit, in the application of the blood of Christ unto them, but in the atonement made by Him in the sacrifice of Himself, that our sins should not be imputed unto us. He is said, therefore, to purge our sins, and not to purge us from our sins. This He did "*by Himself.*" He Himself was priest, sacrifice, altar, incense—as we shall see in our progress —and He perfected His whole sacrifice at once in and by His death, as the Apostle declares (chap. ix. 12—14). So great was the work of freeing us from sin, that it could no otherwise be effected, but by the self-sacrifice of the Son of God. This should teach us to live in a holy admiration of this mighty and wonderful product of the wisdom, righteousness, and goodness, which had found out and appointed this way of delivering sinners, and gloriously accomplished it in the self-sacrifice of the Son of God.

This is the great *hidden* mystery which is *revealed* in the gospel, and is there alone to be learned and attained unto ; this we cannot do in our own strength and by our most diligent endeavours, unless we receive from God the spirit of wisdom, knowledge, and revelation, enabling us to discover these depths of the Holy Ghost in a spiritual manner. Let us consider the unspeakable love of Christ in delivering us from sin. We were "sinners," "lost," "children of wrath," "under the curse ;" and He delivered us from "wrath," and "curse," and "vengeance eternal ;" and this by "the sacrifice of Himself," by "laying down His life for us"—and greater love can no man manifest than by so doing. In all this we see His infinite condescension in putting Himself into that condition wherein He by Himself might purge our sins, and this He did that He "might bring us unto God"—unto His love and favour here, and the eternal enjoyment of Him hereafter.

"**Sat down on the right hand of the Majesty on high.**" Two things are intended : 1. The security of Christ from all His adversaries, and all sufferings for the future ; 2. His majesty and glory inexpressible. How little can our weak understandings apprehend of His majesty. By the words "*sat down*," a contrast is drawn between Christ and Aaron. Aaron *stood* with all humility and holy reverence ministering before the Lord, when he entered the most holy place on the day of atonement, after he had offered the sacrifice of expiation. He did not sit down between the cherubim, but, worshipping at the footstool of the Lord, he departed. But it is not so, saith the Apostle, with Christ. After His one offering He entered into heaven itself ; into the real, glorious presence of God ; not to minister in humility, but to a participation of the throne of majesty and glory. Thus the Apostle closes the general proposition of the whole matter, which he intends further to dilate and treat upon.

V. 4.   *Being made so much better than the angels, as He hath by inheritance obtained a more excellent name than they.*

The Lord Christ, who in respect of His divine nature was always infinitely and incomparably Himself more excellent than all the angels, after His humiliation in the assumption of human nature, with the sufferings and temptation that He underwent, upon His resurrection was exalted into a condition of glory, power, authority, excellency, and entrusted with power over them, as the Apostle here informs us. How "*much better*" He is "*than the angels*" we shall see in the instances given of it in the verses ensuing. When God said to Him, "Thou art My Son," He thereby declared His state and condition to be far above that of the angels ; He gave Him a *"more excellent name than they."* This name He inherited—He obtained it *" by inheritance."* As He was made heir of all things, so He inherited a more excellent name than the angels. He had this " name," denoting His glory and excellency, by " inheritance " —a heritage designed for Him and given unto Him in the counsel, will, and good pleasure of God.

V. 5. *For unto which of the angels said He at any time, Thou art My Son, this day have I begotten Thee ? And again, I will be to Him a Father, and He shall be to Me a Son ?*

The Apostle insists upon the peculiar assignation of this name " Son " unto the Lord Jesus ; also upon the reason thereof, " *This day have I begotten Thee.*" The appropriation of this name to Him in the manner expressed proves His dignity and pre-eminence over the angels. Had He not been so the Son of God, as never any angel or other creature was, He had never been called so in such a way as they never are called.

"And again, I will be to Him a Father, and He shall be to Me a Son." These words are taken from the answer returned from God unto David by Nathan, upon his resolution to build Him a house. Both Solomon and the Lord Christ are intended in these words ; Solomon literally and typically, the Lord Christ principally and mystically. They express the eternal, unchangeable love which the Father bore unto the Son, grounded on the relationship of Father and Son. The declaration of Christ to be the Son of God is the care and work of the Father ; He said it, He recorded it, He revealed it. It is His design in all things to glorify His Son.

V. 6. *And again, when He bringeth in the First-begotten into the world, He saith, And let all the angels of God worship Him.*

"And again . . . He saith ; " this is another proof of the excellency of Jesus Christ above the angels. He saith again, **"When He bringeth the First=begotten into the world."** Into the habitable world or earth, with them that dwell therein. Into this world Christ was brought by His Father, by whose appointment He is intrusted with the whole inheritance of heaven and earth, and authority to dispose of it, that He might give out portions to all the rest of God's family of whom He is, and is called *" the Firstborn."*

" And let all the angels of God worship Him." This is the command of God. " He saith." Observe, 1. That the authority of God speaking in the Scripture is that alone which Divine faith rests upon, and is to be resolved into " He saith ; " 2. That for the begetting, strengthening, and increasing of our faith, it is useful to have fundamental truths confirmed by many testimonies of Scripture —" He saith again ; " 3. That the whole creation of God hath a great concernment in God's bringing forth Christ into the world, and His exaltation in His kingdom ; 4. That the command of God is the ground and reason of all religious worship. The angels are to worship the Lord Christ, the Mediator, and the ground of their doing so is God's command : He saith, " Worship Him all ye angels; " 5. Great is the Church's security and honour when the Head of it is worshipped by all the angels in heaven ; 6. That it can be no duty of the saints of the New Testament to worship angels, who are their fellow-servants in the worship of Jesus Christ.

V. 7. *And of the angels He saith, Who maketh His angels spirits, and His ministers a flame of fire.*

The Apostle shows us the dignity, honour, and employment of the angels, on which account he preferreth Christ before them. He maketh them speedy, spiritual, agile, powerful, quickly and effectually accomplishing the work appointed them. This is the testimony of the Holy Ghost concerning angels ; but now, saith the Apostle, consider His testimony concerning the Son. He calls Him God, and ascribes to Him a throne and a kingdom. Observe, 1. That all our conceptions of the angels—their nature, office, and work—is to be regulated by Scripture ; this will keep us to that becoming sobriety in things above, which the Scripture greatly commends ; and this alone can bring us unto any certainty and truth ; 2. That the glory, honour, and exaltation of angels lies in their subserviency to the providence of God. It lies not so much in their nature, as in their work and service. Their readiness and ability to serve the providence of God is their glory. This service they perform, either in the communication of protection and blessings to the Church, or in the execution of the vengeance and judgments of God against His enemies ; and this in a very glorious manner, with great power, wisdom, and uncontrollable efficacy. Now if this be the great glory of the angels, and we poor worms of the earth are invited, as we are, unto a participation with them therein, what unspeakable folly will it be if we be found negligent in labouring to attain thereunto. Our future glory consists in this, that we shall be made *like unto angels* ; and our way towards it is to do the will of our Father on earth as it is done by them in heaven. But we must treat again of these things when we come to the last verse of this chapter.

Vs. 8, 9. *But unto the Son [He saith], Thy throne, O God, [is] for ever and ever : a sceptre of righteousness is the sceptre of Thy kingdom. Thou hast loved righteousness, and hated iniquity ; therefore God, [even] Thy God, hath anointed Thee with the oil of gladness above Thy fellows.*

"**But unto the Son He saith, Thy throne, O God, is for ever and ever.**" We must keep in view the design of the Apostle, which is to show that He whom they saw for a time made "lower than the angels" (chap. ii. 9) was yet in *His whole Person*—and as He discharged the office committed unto Him—so far *above* them that He had power to alter and change those institutions which were given out by the *ministry of angels*. It is, then, Christ the Son that is spoken to and denoted by that name, "O God," as being the true God by nature ; though what is affirmed of Him here be not as God, but as the King of His Church and people ; as in another place God is said to redeem His Church with His own blood.

"**A sceptre of righteousness is the sceptre of Thy kingdom.**" A kingdom is assigned unto Him with royal insignia. 1. There is a "*throne*," which is "*for ever and ever.*" A throne is the seat of a king, and is often used to represent the kingdom itself. Being on His throne, He is in the height of His glory. Because God manifests His glory in heaven, He calls that His throne, as the earth is His footstool. So that the throne of Christ is His glorious kingdom. To His throne *eternity* is attributed—it is "*for ever and ever.*" It will continue until all the *ends of rule* be perfectly accomplished ; that is, until all the enemies of it be subdued and all the Church be saved, and the righteousness, grace, and patience of God be fully glorified ; 2. There is His "sceptre." This sceptre denotes both the laws of the kingdom and the efficacy of the government itself. The means whereby Christ carrieth on His kingdom are His Spirit and His Word, with a subserviency of power in the works of His providence to make way for the progress of His Word. This sceptre is said to be a "*sceptre of righteousness,*" or uprightness. All the laws of Christ's kingdom are righteous, holy, just, full of benignity and truth ; and all His administrations of grace, mercy, justice, rewards and punishments, according to the rules, promises, and threats of it in the conversion, pardon, sanctification, trials, afflictions, chastisements, and preservation of His elect ; as also in His convincing, hardening, and destroying of His enemies ; are all righteous, holy, unblamable and good, and as such they will be gloriously manifested at the last day, though in this present world they are reproached and despised.

"**Thou hast loved righteousness, and hated iniquity.**" This is the habitual frame of the heart of Christ. The laws of His rule are righteous, and His administrations are righteous, and they all proceed from an habitual love to righteousness, and hatred of iniquity in His own Person.

"**Therefore God, even Thy God, hath anointed Thee with the oil of gladness above Thy fellows.**" God is said to be the *God of the Son* on a threefold account : 1. As He is His Father, so His God ; 2. In respect of His human nature, He was "made of a woman, made under the law ; " 3. In respect of His whole Person, God and man, as He was designed by His Father to the work of mediation ; in which sense Jesus Christ calls God His God, and His Father. The privilege conferred upon Him by His Father was anointing " *with the oil of gladness.*" He was the anointed Prophet, Priest, and King. That which the Apostle seems here to express with the Psalmist is the glorious exaltation of Jesus Christ when He was solemnly instated in His kingdom. This is that which is called the making of Him " both Lord and Christ ; " this was when "God raised Him from the dead and gave Him glory." This "oil of gladness" denotes triumph and exaltation, freedom from trouble and distress ; whereas before this anointing He was a " man of sorrows, acquainted with grief," and exposed to innumerable evils and troubles. But now He is anointed *"above His fellows ;"* this may be taken generally for all those who partake with Him in this unction, that is, all believers who are co-heirs with Him and thereby "heirs of God" (Rom. viii. 17) ; or, more especially, those who were employed by God in the service, building, and rule of His Church, in subordination to Him ; such as were the prophets of old, and after them the apostles. The Apostle presently gives an especial instance in Moses (chap. iii.), affirming the Lord Christ to be partaker of more glory than he.

Vs. 10—12. *And, Thou, Lord, in the beginning hast laid the foundation of the earth ; and the heavens are the work of Thy hands : they shall perish, but Thou remainest ; and they all shall wax old as doth a garment ; and as a vesture shalt Thou fold them up, and they shall be changed : but Thou art the same, and Thy years shall not fail.*

"**And Thou, Lord.**" The word "and" relates to "But unto the Son He saith " (v. 8) ; it is as if he said : " But unto the Son He said, Thy throne, O God, is for ever and ever ; and to the Son He said, Thou, O Lord, in the beginning hast laid the foundation of the earth." The Apostle affirms two things unto the Lord :

1. "**Thou, Lord, in the beginning hast laid the founda- tion of the earth, and the heavens are the work of Thy hands.**" These had their being and existence from the Lord ; of old they were not, but in Thy season Thou gavest being or existence to them ;

2. "**They shall perish, but Thou remainest ; and they all shall wax old as doth a garment ; and as a vesture shalt**

Thou fold them up.'' It is enough for the purpose of the Apostle to show that the work which was of old in the creation of the world, and that which shall be in the change or abolition of it —which is no less an effect of infinite power than the former— are ascribed unto the Lord Christ.

"But Thou art the same, and Thy years shall not fail." " Thou remainest ; " " Thou art the same ; " " Thy years fail not." One and the same thing is intended by these expressions, even His eternal and absolutely immutable existence. Observe, 1. That the Lord Christ—the Mediator, the Head and Spouse of the Church— is infinitely exalted above all creatures whatever, in that He is God over all, omnipotent and eternal ; 2. The whole world—the heavens and the earth—being made by the Lord Christ, and being to be dissolved by Him, is wholly at His disposal, to be ordered for the good of them that do believe ; 3. That such is the frailty of the nature of man, and such the perishing condition of all created things, that none can ever obtain the least stable consolation but what ariseth from an interest in the omnipotency, sovereignty, and eternity of the Lord Christ.

V. 13. *But to which of the angels said He at any time, Sit on My right hand, until I make thine enemies thy footstool ?*

"Unto which of the angels said He at any time ? " A vehement negation is implied in this question—He said not at any time to the angels. It is implied, that whilst He did not say to the angels, **"Sit on My right hand till I make thine enemies thy footstool,"** He did say so to His Son. The Person speaking is the LORD : " The LORD said unto my Lord, Sit Thou on My right hand "—it is God the Father who speaks. The Person spoken to is the Son—the Lord. It is the Lord Christ who is here spoken to, not in respect of His Divine nature only, which is not capable of exaltation or glory by the way of gift ; nor in respect of His human nature only, which is not the Head and King of the Church ; but in respect unto His whole Person, wherein the Divine nature, exerting its power in the will and understanding of the human nature, is the principle of those God-man acts whereby Christ ruleth over all in the kingdom given Him of His Father. As He was God, He was David's Lord but not his son ; as He was man, He was David's son, and so absolutely could not be his Lord ; in His Person, as He was God and man, He was David's Lord and David's son—which is the intention of our Saviour's question (Matt. xxii. 45).

The thing spoken about is Christ's sitting at the right hand of God. In brief, this is the exaltation of Christ unto the glorious administration of the kingdom granted unto Him with honour, security, and power; it is His reigning (1 Cor. xv. 25). The duration of His reigning is "*till I make Thine enemies Thy footstool.*" Now the kingdom of Christ may be considered two ways. First, in respect of the internal spiritual power and efficacy of it in the hearts of His subjects; and second, with respect unto the outward glorious administration of it in the world. In the first sense, of converting and sanctifying and saving His elect, Christ hath many enemies. The *law* is an enemy unto Christ in His kingdom; not absolutely, but by accident and by reason of the consequences that attend it where His subjects are obnoxious unto it—it slays them, is contrary unto them, and contributes strength unto their adversaries (1 Cor. xv. 56); all which discovers the nature of an enemy. *Sin* is universally and in its whole nature an enemy unto Christ; so also is *Satan* a sworn enemy, the adversary that openly, constantly, avowedly opposeth Him in His throne; the *world* also is the professed enemy of the kingdom of Christ; *death* also is an enemy; the *grave*, and lastly, *hell*, are enemies to Christ and His kingdom. Now all these, as far as they oppose the spiritual internal carrying on the work of Christ, must be made the footstool of His feet. He is to have an absolute, complete conquest over them; and their being made His footstool implies their perpetual and unchangeable duration in that condition.

Then secondly, the kingdom of Christ respects His administration of it in this world, in the profession and obedience of His subjects unto Him; and this also with the opposition made unto it. The world understands not His right, hates His government, and would not have Him to reign. Kings, rulers, counsellors, the multitude, have set themselves against Him. They are and have been, many of them, His enemies. The aim and design of all these is to dethrone Him, by the ruin of His kingdom which He hath set up in this world. In every age they have hoped to accomplish this, and continue to do so unto this day, but in vain.

"*Until I make Thine enemies Thy footstool.*" It is God the Father who saith this unto Him. There are sundry reasons why that work which is immediately wrought by the Son may, by the way of eminency, be ascribed unto the Father. Power and authority to subdue and conquer all His enemies is given unto the Lord Christ by the Father, in the way of reward of the travail of soul which He underwent in His work on the earth. Observe, 1. That the exaltation of Christ to the right hand of God is the great pledge of the acceptation of the work of mediation performed in the behalf of the Church. Now saith God, "Sit Thou at My right hand;" the work is done, wherein My soul is well pleased; 2. Christ hath many enemies unto His kingdom: saith God, "I will deal with all of them;" 3. The kingdom and rule of Christ is perpetual and abiding, nothwithstanding all the opposition that is made against it. His enemies rage, as though they would pull Him out of His throne, but altogether in vain ; He hath the faithfulness and the power, the word and the right hand of God for the security of His kingdom ; 4. The end whereunto the Lord Jesus Christ will assuredly bring all His enemies, let them bluster whilst they please, shall be unto them miserable and shameful ; to the saints, joyful ; to Himself, victorious and triumphant.

V. 14. *And are they not all ministering spirits, sent forth to minister for them who shall be heirs of salvation ?*

"**Are they not all ministering spirits?** " Angels are *created* spirits, and therefore not to be compared with Him who made and created all things. In their ministry they are waiting on God in a readiness to do His will.

"**Sent forth to minister.**" They are daily sent out, continually being sent forth—sometimes some, sometimes others— always those that are sufficient for His work.

"**For them that shall be heirs of salvation.**" For their sakes, for their good, in their behalf who shall inherit salvation. This privilege, amongst others innumerable and inexpressible, we have by our adoption ; being admitted into the family of God, those blessed angels, whose special ministry respects that family, have us under their constant care. Observe, 1. The highest honour of the most glorious spirits in heaven is to minister unto the Lord in the service whereunto He appoints them ; 2. Such is the love and care of God towards His saints labouring here below, that He sends the most glorious attendants on His throne to minister unto them in taking care of them.

CHAPTER TWO

V. 1. *Therefore we ought to give the more earnest heed to the things which we have heard, lest at any time we let [them] slip.*

"**Therefore ;** " seeing the gospel hath such a blessed Author, we ought to take heed that we forfeit not our interest therein.

"**We ought.**" This expression is to be regulated by the words that follow : "All we who have heard the gospel preached and made profession thereof."

"**To give the more earnest heed.**" The Apostle informs

them that they have abundant cause to take heed to the things
spoken and heard, because of Him that spake them ; for concerning Him alone came that voice from the excellent glory, "This is
My beloved Son, hear Him."

"To the things which we have heard." Herein doth the
Apostle magnify the great ordinance of preaching, as everywhere
else he maketh it the great means of begetting faith in men.　He
insists on and commends unto them, not only the things themselves,
but also the way by which they were communicated to them,
namely, by preaching, as he further declares (v. 3).

" Lest at any time we let them slip." The design of the
Apostle in this, as in verses 2 and 3, is to show that they shall
assuredly and deservedly perish who neglect the gospel.　It is our
duty to retain the word we hear ; and therefore it is not said that
the word flows out, but that we, as it were, pour it out.　Diligent
attendance unto the word of the gospel is indispensably necessary
unto perseverance in the profession of it ; such a profession, that
is, as will be acceptable unto God, and useful unto our own souls.
To *" give the more earnest heed"* implies a due valuation of the
grace tendered in *" the things heard ;"* it is giving such an attention
as proceeds from an estimation of the things answerable to their
worth.　Also it is needed that we mix faith with what we hear, and
that we labour to express the word received in a conformity of heart
and life unto it.　There are sundry times and seasons wherein, and
several ways and means whereby, men are in danger to lose the
word that they have heard, if they attend not diligently unto its
preservation.　Some lose it in a time of *peace and prosperity ;* others
in a time of *persecution ;* others in a time of trial by *temptation ;*
some lose it by the *love of this present world :* others by the *love of
sin ;* and others by *false doctrines,* errors, heresies, and false worship.
These break the vessel, and at once pour out all the benefits of the
word that ever were received.

Observe from this, 1. That the word heard is not lost without
the great sin as well as the inevitable ruin of the souls of men ;
2. It is in the nature of the word of the gospel to water barren
hearts, and to make them fruitful unto God ; 3. The consideration
of the revelation of the gospel by the Son of God is a powerful
motive unto the diligent attendance unto it.　This is the inference
that the Apostle makes from one proposition he had made as to the
excellency of the Son of God—*" therefore ;"* 4. This word is final :
" Last of all He sent His Son," and " Hath spoken unto us by
Him."　Never more will He speak in the world with that kind of
speaking ; 5. The true and only way of honouring the Lord Jesus
Christ as the Son of God, is by diligent attendance and obedience
unto His word.

Vs. 2, 3.　*For if the word spoken by angels was stedfast,*

and every transgression and disobedience received a just recompense of reward; how shall we escape if neglect so great salvation, which at the first began to be spoken by the Lord, and was confirmed unto us by them that heard [Him]?

"**For if the word spoken by angels was stedfast.**" The word is the doctrine of the law; that is, the law itself spoken, declared, and published. This law was given from God, but it was given by angels. He who spake on Mount Sinai in the name of God was none other than God Himself, the second Person in the Trinity. It is nowhere said that the law was *given* by angels, but that the people received it "by the disposition of angels," and that it was "ordained by angels," and here "spoken by them." From hence it is evident that not the original authoritative giving of the law, but the ministerial ordering of things in its promulgation, is that which is ascribed unto angels. The Apostle affirms concerning the word thus published, that it was "stedfast," that is, an assured covenant between God and the people.

"**And every transgression and disobedience received a just recompense of reward.**" "*A just recompense of reward,*" is that which is just and equal according to the judgment of God. The Apostle refers especially to the temporal punishment of cutting off from the land of the living, which respected that dispensation of the law which the Israelites were subject unto. He is comparing the law in the dispensation of it on Horeb unto the Jews with the present dispensation of the gospel; and from the penalties wherewith the breach of it was then attended, he argues unto the "sorer punishment" that must needs ensue upon the neglect of the dispensation of the gospel. For otherwise, the penalty assigned unto the transgression of the moral law is the very same, in the nature and kind of it, with that which belongs unto despisers of the gospel, even death eternal.

"**How shall we escape if we neglect so great salvation, which at the first began to be spoken by the Lord, and was confirmed unto us by them that heard?**" The subject-matter here spoken of is "*so great salvation.*" It is the gospel which is intended by this expression, as is evident from the preceding verse, where it is called "the word which we have heard." This gospel "*began to be spoken by the Lord.*" The great reason why the Hebrews so pertinaciously adhered to the law. was the glorious publication of it; it was the "word spoken by angels"— they received it "by the disposition of angels." "If," saith the Apostle, "there were a sufficient cause why the law should be attended unto, and that the neglect of it should be so sorely avenged, then consider what is your duty in reference unto the Gospel, which is not only a word of life and great salvation, but was spoken, declared, and delivered by the Lord Himself, whom we have manifested to be exalted so exceedingly above all angels whatever." This "great salvation" was "*confirmed unto us by them that heard Him.*" The gospel was delivered unto those that heard it, infallibly by the ministry of the apostles; this was from their Divine inspiration.

Vs. 4. *God also bearing [them] witness, both with signs and wonders, and with divers miracles and gifts of the Holy Ghost, according to His own will.*

God Himself bore witness with and unto the witness and testimony of the apostles; by miracles and wonders and mighty works and distributions of the Holy Ghost, He signified His approbation and confirmation of the doctrine they taught; and stirred up, by them, the minds of the hearers to a diligent attention to the things that they heard. The gospel being of this nature, thus taught, thus delivered, thus confirmed, there is a neglect of it supposed (v. 3)—"*If we neglect.*" This word intimateth an omission of all those duties which are necessary for our retaining the word preached unto our profit, and that to such a degree as to utterly reject it. There is a punishment intimated upon this neglect of the gospel— "how shall we escape" a just retribution, "a just recompense of reward?" The breach of the law had so: a punishment suitable unto the demerit of the crime was by God assigned unto it, and inflicted upon them that were guilty. So is there unto neglect of the gospel, even a punishment justly deserved by so great a crime; so much greater and more sore than that designed unto contempt of the law, by how much the gospel, upon the account of its nature, effects, Author, and confirmation, was more excellent than the law. There are three things intended in this question, "How shall we escape?" 1. A denial of any means or way of escape; 2. The certainty of the punishment; 3. The inexpressible greatness of this unavoidable evil.

The observations for our instruction which these four verses offer unto us are these: 1. Motives unto a due valuation of the gospel and perseverance in the profession of it, taken from the penalties annexed unto the neglect of it, are evangelical, and of singular use in the preaching of the word. Some would fancy that all threatenings belong unto the law, as though Jesus Christ had left Himself and His gospel to be securely despised by profane and impenitent sinners; but as they will find to the contrary to their eternal ruin, so it is the will of Christ that His ministers should let them know it. These threatenings belong to the gospel, they are recorded in the gospel, and by it His ministers are commanded to make use of them (Matt. x. 28; xxiv. 50, 51; xxv. 41; Mark xvi. 16; John iii. 36; 2 Cor. ii. 15, 16; 2 Thess. i. 8, 9), and other places innumerable.

If the dispensers of the word insist not on them they deal deceitfully with the souls of men and detain from the counsels of God. Let not men think themselves more evangelical than the Author of the gospel, more skilled in the mystery of the conversion and edification of the souls of men than the apostles—in a word more wise than God Himself, which they must do if they neglect this part of His ordinance. These threatenings become the gospel, and it is meet that it should be armed with them, and that on the part of Christ Himself its Author. A sceptre in a kingdom without a sword, a crown without a rod of iron, will quickly be trampled on. They also become the gospel on the part of sinners. It is meet that unbelievers, hypocrites, apostates, impenitent neglecters of the great salvation should by them be kept in fear and awe, that they may not openly break out in contempt of Christ; also that they may be inexcusable, and the Lord Christ be justified in His proceedings against them at the last day. They also become the gospel on the part of believers, that by them there may be kept up in their hearts a constant reverence of the majesty of Jesus Christ with whom they have to do; also they tend unto their consolation under all their afflictions and sufferings for the gospel; they also give them constant matter of praise and thankfulness when they see in them, as in a glass, a representation of that wrath from which they are delivered. And, lastly, these threatenings of eternal punishment unto gospel neglecters do become the gospel with respect to them that are the preachers and dispensers of it, that their message be not slighted nor their persons despised; and this will appear fully clear if we consider that the threatenings of future penalties on the disobedient are far more express in the gospel than in the law; also that the punishment threatened in the gospel is as unto degrees greater and more sore than that which was annexed to the transgression of the first covenant; hence the Apostle calls it "death unto death," by reason of the sore aggravation which the first sentence of death will receive from the wrath due unto the contempt of the gospel. A fond conceit hath befallen some that all denunciations of future wrath are legal, which therefore it doth not become the preachers of the gospel to insist upon; so would men make themselves wiser than Jesus Christ and all His apostles, yea, they would disarm the Lord, and expose Him to the contempt of His vilest enemies.

2. All punishments annexed unto the transgression either of the law or gospel are effects of God's vindictive justice, and consequently just and equal. "A just recompence of reward." God's justice in constituting and in inflicting the reward of sin is essential unto Him; and this justice is inseparably accompanied with infinite wisdom, and it is He alone who knows what is the true desert and demerit of sin. Shall we make ourselves judges of what sin against God doth deserve? What a folly, what a madness is it, to make

light of Christ, unto which an eternity of punishment is a just and meet recompence of reward.

3. Every transaction between God and man is always confirmed and ratified by promises and threatenings; "every trespass"— covenant transgressions are attended with unavoidable penalties.

4. The gospel is great salvation, which whoso neglecteth shall therefore unavoidably perish. It is "great salvation" *declaratively*, in that the salvation is of God by Christ, as declared, taught, and revealed in the gospel (Rom. i. 16, 17). But it is "great salvation" *efficiently*, as it is the great means by which God bestows salvation upon His elect; it is the "power of God" in regeneration, in the gift of the Lord Jesus Christ; in all the promises by which believers are made actually and really partakers of the Spirit; in our justification, in which there must be a righteousness before God, on the account whereof the person to be justified is pronounced and declared righteous. This is no other but the Lord Christ Himself and His righteousness; and faith in Him is wrought in us by the word of the gospel, for "faith cometh by hearing, and hearing by the word of God." It is "great salvation," as we may see if we consider the eternal contrivance of it, the way and the means by which it was wrought and accomplished according to the infinite wisdom and goodness of God, in the incarnation, sufferings, death and resurrection of His dear Son. It is "great" salvation, and we shall see it to be so if we consider what by it we are delivered from, and what we are interested in and made partakers of.

And "*How shall they escape who neglect so great salvation?*" Let believers learn to admire the riches of the grace of God which hath provided so "great salvation" for poor sinners. When Divine wisdom, goodness, love, grace, and mercy set themselves to work, what will they not accomplish? And the effect of them doth the Scripture set forth in such expressions as "God so loved the world;" "God commendeth His love toward us;" "Riches of grace;" "Exceeding greatness of power," and the like. Were our minds fixed on these things as they ought, how would the glory of them cast out our cares, subdue our fears, sweeten our afflictions and persecutions, and take off our affections from the fading, perishing things of this world, and make us in every condition rejoice in hope of the glory that shall be revealed.

To stir us up, let us remember the excellency of the things themselves that are included in the "great salvation;" also our interest and propriety in them; also the profit and advantage we shall have thereby. In this exercise we shall find the profit of, 1. Intense prayer for the Spirit of wisdom and revelation, to give us an acquaintance with the mystery and grace of this great salvation; 2. Diligent study of the Word; 3. Sincere love unto and delight in the things that are by the Spirit of God revealed unto us; 4. A spirit of thankfulness; thankfulness for the things themselves, thankfulness for the revelation of them, thankfulness for the love of God and the peace of our Lord Jesus Christ. Some neglect the gospel, some despise it, some persecute it, some look upon it as foolishness, and some as weakness ; but unto them which believe it is "the power and the wisdom of God."

The excellence of the gospel ariseth from its first Revealer, that is, the Lord Christ, the Son of God. "It was begun to be spoken by the Lord ; " hence the Apostle prefers it before the law. It is that word which the Son came from the bosom of the Father to declare, and surely He deserves to be attended unto. Hence the gospel is called "the word of Christ" and "the gospel of Christ," not only because it treateth of Him, but it proceedeth from Him, and on that account is "worthy of all acceptation." To neglect the gospel is to neglect and despise the Son of God who is the author of it ; so the Lord tells them that preach the gospel, "He that despiseth you, despiseth Me; and he that despiseth Me, despiseth Him that sent Me." This gospel was witnessed unto and confirmed by mighty works and miracles which attended the dispensation thereof, and though we saw not those miracles, yet we have an infallible record of them given to us, that we might thereby be stirred up to value and attend to the Word in a due manner. God hath so ordered things in His holy providence that none can neglect the Word without shutting his eyes against such light and evidence of conviction as will abundantly leave him inexcusable at the last day.

Vs. 5—9.   *For unto the angels hath He not put in sub-jection the world to come whereof we speak. But one in a certain place testified, saying, What is man that Thou art mindful of him, or the son of man that Thou visitest him ? Thou madest him a little lower than the angels ; Thou crownedst him with glory and honour, and didst set him over the works of Thy hands. Thou hast put all things in sub-jection under his feet. For in that He put all in subjection under him, He left nothing [that is] not put under him. But now we see not yet all things put under him. But we see Jesus, who was made a little lower than the angels for the suffering of death, crowned with glory and honour ; that He by the grace of God should taste death for every man.*

"For unto the angels hath He not put in subjection the world to come whereof we speak." The Apostle con-tinues his argument in the above testimony ; it is to this purpose : The " *world to come* " is not in subjection " *unto angels,*" but it was made subject unto Jesus, therefore He is exalted above them. This he proves from the testimony of the Psalmist, to this purpose all things were made subject to man, who for a little while was made lower than the angels; but this man was Jesus. And this assumption he proves from the event: First, on the part of man absolutely considered, 'We see that all things are not made subject unto him,' therefore he cannot be intended; secondly, on the part of Jesus, 'All things in the event agree unto Him, for He was made for a little while lower than the angels, and then He was crowned with glory and honour, all things being made subject unto Him;' from all which it appears, that it is He and not angels unto whom the world to come is put in subjection. This is the series of the Apostle's discourse, wherein are many things difficult and "hard to be understood," which must be particularly considered.

By the expression, "*the world to come*," is intended no other but the promised state of the Church under the gospel. This will appear from the following considerations: 1. From the limitation, "*of which we speak.*" This is the world whereof the Apostle treats throughout this epistle; it is the gospel state of the Church, the worship whereof he had in the words immediately foregoing pressed them into the observation of; 2. We cannot understand this expression, "the world to come," to refer to heaven, the state of future glory, as some have done, for the Apostle treats of that which is already done, in the crowning of Jesus with glory and honour; now this was upon His ascension, so that then the state of glory was not made subject unto Him, because it was not then nor is yet in being. The world whereof the Apostle treats was immediately made subject unto Jesus—that is, the Church of the New Testament —when God anointed Him King upon His holy hill of Zion; 3. The Apostle in these words insists upon the antithesis which he pursueth in his whole discourse between the Judaical and the evangelical Church state. Now it is not heaven and glory that he opposeth to the Judaical church state and worship, but that of the gospel, as we shall find in the progress of the epistle, which is therefore necessarily here intended.

The Apostle denies that this "world to come" is made subject to angels; he seems to grant that the old church and worship were in a sort made subject to angels; but this "world to come" is immediately in His power who in all things is to have the pre-eminence. This will further appear if we consider: 1. That the Church was not put in subjection unto angels in its erection or institution; the work was not committed to them, as the Apostle shows in the opening verses of this epistle; 2. It is not put in subjection unto angels as to the rule and disposal of it. Their office in this world is a ministry (chap. i. 14), not a rule or dominion; 3. As to the power of judging and rewarding at the last day, it is openly manifest that God hath not put this "world to come" under angels, but under Jesus alone. The great privilege of the "world to come "—the Church of the gospel—is, that it is made subject unto and immediately depends upon the Lord Jesus Christ, and not on any other, angels or men. He is the Head of the Church, and its only Head; the Head of all vital influence to the whole Church and every member of it, the Head of all rule and government unto every member of the Church; we have immediate dependence upon Him, and immediate access unto Him. Thus the " *world to come* " is made subject to Jesus.

"But one in a certain place testified, saying, What is man that Thou art mindful of him, or the son of man that Thou visitest him?" In verse 7 all things whatsoever are said to be put in subjection unto man, that is, unto human nature in one or more persons, in opposition unto angels or the nature of angels. Now this privilege was never absolutely or universally made good in or unto the nature of man, but in or with respect unto the Person of Jesus Christ, the Messiah. The testimony of the Psalmist, as quoted by the Apostle, consists in a contemplation of the infinite love and condescension of God towards man, which is set out, 1. In the expression, " *What is man*," by way of admiration; yea, he cries out with a kind of astonishment; 2. He expresses his admiration at the condescension of God in the words that he useth, " *What is man*," intimating the low and mean state of man in his own nature; 3. He expresses this condescension of God in the affections and actings of His mind towards man, "Thou art mindful of him," Thou rememberest him. In these words is couched the whole counsel and purpose of God concerning the salvation of mankind, in and by the humiliation, exaltation, and whole mediation of " the man Christ Jesus "; 4. He expresses the effects of this act of condescension, " *He visitest him*." " He hath visited and redeemed His people " (Luke i. 68).

"Thou madest him a little lower than the angels, Thou crownedst him with glory and honour, and didst set him over the works of Thy hands." The special instances of God's visitation of men are contained in these words; they are referred to under two heads. First, man's depression and humiliation; second, man's exaltation and glory. His depression and humiliation are expressed in these words, " *Thou madest Him a little lower than the angels*." It was God who made Him lower than the angels; the measure of His humiliation here spoken of is in reference unto angels, with whom He is compared by the Apostle. He speaks not now of this humiliation absolutely, which was far greater than here expressed, as he afterwards declares, but only in respect of the angels. He was made a " *little lower than the angels*," that is, lower than the angels for a little time; it was but for a short time that the Person of Christ in the nature of man was brought into a condition more indigent than the state of angels is exposed unto; neither was He for that reason made a little, but very much lower than the angels.

The other effects of God's visitation of man is his exaltation ; expressed in the dignity whereunto He advanced him, and in the rule and dominion that He gave unto him. As to the dignity, " *He crowned him with glory and honour.*" To be crowned is to be invested with sovereign power, or with right and title thereunto. To be crowned with glory and honour is to have a glorious and honourable crown, or rule and sovereignty. But this dignity is attended with actual rule : " *Thou didst set him over the works of Thine hands*; " and as we may see from the next verse, this rule was universal : **"Thou hast put all things in subjection under his feet,"** an expression setting forth a dominion every way unlimited and absolute.

"For in that He put all in subjection under him, He left nothing that is not put under him. But now we see not yet all things put under him." We see by our own observation that this word respects not the first man or his posterity, for we see not as yet after this long space of time since the creation that all things are put into subjection under him. It can only be true of the man Christ Jesus. And so the Psalmist says of Him, " O LORD our Lord, how excellent is Thy name ; " and from thence doth he proceed to a consideration of His condescension in His regard and love to man. He speaks of the heavenly bodies which we behold, and which are in themselves exceedingly glorious ; they show forth the infinite glory of Him that made them ; they proclaim His greatness, His infinite self-sufficiency, His eternal power, His wisdom and His goodness. He it is who remembers man—man who is made out of the dust of the earth, whose frailty is inexpressible ; and more, he hath made himself inexpressibly vile by sin. Let the result of such thoughts be a holy admiration of God's infinite love, care, grace and condescension in having any regard unto us. So doth the Psalmist teach us to do.

"But we see Jesus, who was made a little lower than the angels for the suffering of death, crowned with glory and honour, that He by the grace of God should taste death for every man." In these words we have the sum of the gospel and the doctrine of it, concerning the Person and office of the Messiah, asserted and vindicated from the prejudiced opinions of the Jews under two heads : 1. That the salvation and deliverance that God had promised and intended to accomplish by the Messiah was *spiritual and eternal*, from sin, death, Satan, and hell, ending in everlasting glory ; not temporal and carnal, as they vainly imagined ; 2. That this salvation could be no otherwise brought about but by the incarnation, suffering, and death of the Messiah. So the Apostle says here, " *But we see Jesus made a little lower than the angels for the suffering of death.*"

The Apostle knew that he had now fixed upon that which of all things the Jews most stumbled at, the low, mean, and despised condition of Jesus. He was so humbled that He might suffer death, and this by the "*grace of God*"; He tasted death for all, that is, for all those many sons which God by His death intended to bring unto glory (v. 10); those sanctified by Him, whom He calls brethren and children, given Him by God (vs. 11, 12, 13), and whom by death He delivers from the fear of death (vs. 14, 15), even all the seed of Abraham (v. 16).

Let us observe some of the things that are tendered to us for our instruction in these words : 1. That the care, love, and grace of God unto mankind, expressed in the Person and mediation of Jesus Christ, is a matter of singular and eternal admiration. All God's regard for man is a fruit of mere sovereign grace and condescension ; there was no consideration of anything without God Himself that moved Him thereunto. The assumption of our nature into personal union with the Son of God was an act of mere free, sovereign, inconceivable grace ; 2. Had not God been mindful of man and visited him in the Person of His Son incarnate, every one partaker of that nature must have utterly perished in their lost condition ; 3. That God is more glorified in the humiliation and exaltation of the Lord Christ, and the salvation of mankind thereby, than in any of or all the works of the first creation ; 4. That such was the inconceivable love of Jesus Christ, the Son of God, unto the souls of men, that He was free and willing to condescend unto any condition for their good and salvation. "His delights were with the sons of men," and He delighted in the counsel of redeeming and saving them by His own humiliation and suffering. "Unto Him that loved us and washed us from our sins in His own blood, and hath made us kings and priests unto God and His Father ; to Him be glory and dominion for ever and ever. Amen "; 5. That the blessed issue of the abasement of Jesus Christ in His exaltation unto glory and honour is an assured pledge of the final glory and blessedness of all that believe in Him, whatever difficulties and dangers they may be exercised withal in the way ; 6. Jesus Christ as the Mediator of the new covenant hath absolute and supreme authority given unto Him over all the works of God in heaven and earth ; 7. The Lord Jesus Christ is the only Lord of the gospel state of the Church, called here "the world to come "; and therefore He only hath power to dispose of all things in it relating unto that worship of God which it is to perform and celebrate ; 8. The Lord Jesus Christ did in His death undergo the penal sentence of the law, in the room and stead of them for whom He died. Death was that which, by the sentence of the law, was due to sinners. He died for them, and in His death tasted of the bitterness of that death which they were to have undergone, or else the fruit of it could not have redounded unto them ; for what was it towards their discharge if that which they had deserved was not suffered ? But this being done, certain deliverance and salvation will be the

lot and portion of them—all of them—for whom He died, and that
upon the rules of justice and righteousness on the part of Christ,
though on theirs of mere mercy and grace.

V. 10. *For it became Him, for whom [are] all things,
and by whom [are] all things, in bringing many sons unto
glory, to make the Captain of their salvation perfect through
sufferings.*

"**For it became Him, for whom are all things, and by
whom are all things.**" It was the design of God to bring many
sons unto glory; in order to do so He made the "*Captain of their
salvation perfect through sufferings,*" and all this in a way becoming
to Himself. Now the description of God in these words is plainly
of Him as the first cause and the last end of all things. God is
the supreme Governor and Judge of men, and in the righteousness
of His government it became Him to bring many sons to glory by
the sufferings of the Captain of their salvation. From whence we
may learn that such is the desert of sin, and such the immutability
of the justice of God, that there was no way possible to bring
sinners unto glory but by the death and sufferings of the Son of
God, who undertook to be the Captain of their salvation. All the
saints of God admire, and all the angels desire to look into, this
great and astonishable mystery, that the Son of God, who knew no
sin, should suffer and die, and that under the sentence and curse of
the law.

Various are the conceptions of men about this mystery; but let
it suffice us to know that it became God, who is the supreme Ruler,
Governor, and Judge of all, that sin should be punished with death
in the sinner or in his surety; and therefore if God would bring
many sons to glory, the Captain of their salvation must undergo
sufferings and death, to make satisfaction for them. It became the
righteous God to make the "*Captain of salvation perfect through
sufferings.*" In the cross of Christ God gave an eminent instance of
His righteousness and the desert of sin. Sin being imputed unto
the only Son of God, He could not be spared. If He be made sin,
He must be made a curse; if He will take away our iniquities, He
must make His soul an offering for sins, and bear the punishment
due unto them. Nothing but undergoing the wrath of God will
effect an end to sin; how then can God spare sin in His enemies
who could not spare it in His only Son? Had it been possible this
cup should have passed from Him; but this could not be, and God
continue righteous.

"**In bringing many sons unto glory.**" This work of
"*bringing many sons*" is here signally assigned by the Apostle unto
God the Father, whose love, wisdom and grace, believers are

principally to eye in the whole work of their salvation, wrought out and accomplished by Jesus Christ. This work is assigned unto the Father because: 1. The *eternal designation* of the sons unto glory whereunto they are to be brought is of Him. He "predestinates them to be conformed unto the image of His Son." The electing love of God, the eternal purpose of His good pleasure, is the fountain and spring of all other immediate causes of our salvation; 2. He was the spring and fountain of that covenant that was of old between Himself and His Son about the salvation and glory of the elect; 3. He signally gave out the first promise, that great foundation of the covenant of grace, which was afterwards declared, confirmed, and ratified by His oath. He is the Author of the covenant, the Son being considered as the Surety or Mediator of it; 4. He gave and sent His Son to be a Saviour and Redeemer, so that in His whole work, in all that He did and suffered, He obeyed the command and fulfilled the will of the Father; 5. He draws His elect, and enables them to come to the Son, to believe in Him, and so obtain life, salvation, and glory by Him; 6. Being reconciled unto them by the death of His Son, He reconciles them unto Himself, by giving them pardon and forgiveness of sins in and by the promises of the gospel, without which they cannot come to glory; 7. He quickens and sanctifies them by His Spirit, to make them "meet for the inheritance of the saints in light"; 8. As the great Father of the family He adopts them and makes them His sons, that so He may bring them to glory; 9. He confirms them in faith, establisheth them in obedience, preserveth them, and in manifold wisdom keepeth them through His power unto the glory prepared for them; 10. He gives them the Holy Ghost as their Comforter, with all the blessed and unspeakable benefits that attend that gift of His.

"To make the Captain of their salvation perfect through sufferings." To understand this we must observe that the Apostle speaks not here of the redemption of the elect absolutely, but of the bringing them unto glory in an especial manner; he treats here of that part of Christ's office of Mediator which especially concerns the leading of the sons unto glory. The word to "make perfect" signifies to consecrate, to dedicate, to sanctify unto some special office, or part of that office. By all the sufferings of Christ in His life and death—by which sufferings He wrought out the salvation of the elect—did God consecrate and dedicate Him to be a Prince, a Leader, a Captain of salvation unto His people. The whole work of saving the sons of God, from first to last, is committed unto the Lord Jesus; God hath set Him as a Lord over His whole house, and placed Him in trust as a faithful Captain. This office He dischargeth with care and watchfulness, also with great tenderness and love, and with power, authority, and majesty.

As the Captain of salvation He goes before the sons of God. He went before them *in obedience:* "I have given you an example, that ye should do as I have done." The utmost perfection which we are bound to aim at in holiness and obedience, is nothing but conformity unto Jesus Christ—to mark His footsteps and to follow Him. He went before them *in sufferings*, and therein is a Leader unto them by His example. Peter saith, "Christ hath suffered for us, leaving us an example, that we should follow His steps"; that is, be ready and prepared unto patience in sufferings when we are called thereunto. The Apostle makes all the afflictions of the Church to be the "afflictions of Christ" (1 Col. i. 24), who both before underwent them in His own Person, and led the way to all that should follow Him.

But He hath gone before the sons in *passing through death and entering into glory.* In His resurrection He hath showed us that death is not the end of our course, but a passage into another more abiding condition. Jesus as our Forerunner hath entered heaven, and as the Captain of salvation He guides and directs the sons in their way to glory. As that way is revealed in the Word of God He enables them by His Spirit to see, discern, and know it in such a holy and saving manner as to bring them unto the end of it. He not only directs them in their way, but He supplies them with *strength by His grace* that they may be able to *pass on in their way.* He *subdues their enemies.* "Be of good cheer," He says, "I have overcome the world." He not only subdues their enemies *for them* but also *in them.* "Thanks be unto God, who giveth us the victory through our Lord Jesus Christ," so that, "in all things we are more than conquerors." And then the "Captain of salvation" provides *a reward, a crown* for these sons of God. He is gone before them to "prepare a place for them," and "He will come again and receive them unto Himself, that where He is there they may be also."

And these things should teach us to betake ourselves unto Him, and to rely upon Him, and in all things to look to Him for guidance and direction. Let us observe, 1. That the Lord Jesus Christ being Priest, sacrifice, and altar Himself, the offering whereby He was consecrated unto the perfection of His office was of necessity part of that work which He, as our Priest and Mediator, was to undergo and perform; 2. The Lord Christ being consecrated and perfected through sufferings, hath *consecrated the way of suffering* for all that follow Him on their way to glory. Believers are "predestinated to be conformed to His image," and no small part of their conformity consists in their sufferings and afflictions; 3. The consecration of the Lord Christ by suffering hath made all sufferings for the gospel honourable; not only so, they are useful and profitable; mixing His grace and love and wisdom with these bitter waters, He hath made them sweet and wholesome.

Vs. 11—13. For both He that sanctifieth and they who are sanctified [are] all of one, for which cause He is not ashamed to call them brethren, saying, I will declare Thy name unto My brethren, in the midst of the Church will I sing praise unto Thee. And again, I will put My trust in Him. And again, Behold I and the children which God hath given Me.

" **For both He that sanctifieth and they who are sanc= tified [are] all of one.**" Now, in further description of the Captain of salvation and of the sons, the Apostle intimates a further necessity of His sufferings—because they were to be sanctified by Him, which could no otherwise be done but by His death and blood-shedding. The Lord Christ is the great sanctifier of the Church; He sanctifies every son whom He bringeth unto glory. He will never glorify an unsanctified person. It is utterly impossible that any soul not washed in the blood of Christ, not sanctified by His Spirit and grace, should stand in the sight of God. None can serve Him here unless their consciences be purged from dead works by the blood of Christ; nor can they come to Him hereafter unless they are washed from all their defilements. Jesus Christ—the Sanctifier—is the Head, and they, the members of His body. He is holy, so must they be also; a living Head and dead members, how uncomely would it be. " Christ loved the Church, and gave Himself for it, that He might sanctify and cleanse it with the washing of water by the Word, that He might present it to Himself a glorious Church, not having spot or wrinkle or any such thing, but that it should be holy and without blemish."

There is surely a woful mistake in the world. It is grown amongst us almost an abhorrency unto all flesh to say that the Church of God is to be holy. If men be baptised whether they will or no, and outwardly profess the name of Christ, though not one of them be truly sanctified, yet they are, so it is said, the Church of Christ. But let none deceive themselves; sanctification is a qualification indispensably necessary unto them who will be under the conduct of the Lord Christ unto salvation. He will lead none to heaven but whom He sanctifies on earth. The holy God will not receive unholy persons; this living Head will not admit dead members, nor bring men into the possession of a glory which they neither love nor like.

The Sanctifier and the sanctified " *are all of one.*" He and they are of one nature, of one mass, of one blood; and hereby He became meet to suffer for them, and they to be in a capacity of enjoying the benefit of His sufferings. The agreement of Christ and the elect in one common nature is the foundation of His fitness to be an undertaker on their behalf, and of the equity of their being made partakers of the benefits of His mediation; but this will occur again more fully, verse 14.

"For which cause He is not ashamed to call them brethren." That is because they are one, partakers of one common nature. He calls them brethren; He not only declares them to be so, but He owns them and avouches them as such. This is a wonderful expression of His condescension and love. He is not ashamed to call them brethren, though considering what Himself is, and what they are, it should seem that He justly might be so. Four things may be noticed as to the distance between Christ and us which make His condescension so marvellous : 1. The immunity of the nature wherein He was of one with us in His Person from all sin ; 2. His owning of us as brethren made Him obnoxious to all the miseries, the guilt whereof we had contracted upon ourselves. He who was rich, for our sakes became poor; 3. He is inconceivably distanced from us in respect of that place and dignity which He was designed unto. Thoughts of His glorious exaltation as King of kings will put a lustre on His condescension in owning us as His brethren ; 4. He is infinitely distanced from us in respect of His Divine nature wherein He is, and was, God over all, blessed for evermore. He did not so become man as to cease to be God. He who calls us brethren, who suffered for us, who died for us, was God still in all these things.

" Saying, I will declare Thy name unto My brethren, in the midst of the Church will I sing praise unto Thee." This is the name of God which the Lord Jesus " manifested unto the men given Him out of the world," which is the same with His declaring the Father whom " no man hath seen at any time." He made known the name of His Father in *His own Person*, and that both before and after His sufferings; also by *His Spirit* whom He gave unto His disciples, enabling them to preach the gospel unto men of their own generation, and in the inspiration of some of them enabling them to commit the truth into writing for the instruction of the elect unto the end of the world.

" In the midst of the Church will I sing praise unto Thee." This explains what went before. There is no way whereby the praise of God may be celebrated like that of declaring His grace, goodness, and love unto men, whereby they may be won to believe and trust in Him, whence glory redounds unto Him. The Lord Christ in His own Person, by His Spirit in His apostles, by His Word, and by all His messengers unto the end of the world, setting forth the love, grace, goodness, and mercy of God in Him the Mediator, sets forth the praise of God in the midst of the congregation. That which was principally in the heart of the Lord Jesus upon His sufferings, was to declare and manifest the love, grace, and goodwill of God unto men, that they might come to an acquaintance with Him, and to an acceptance before Him. He rejoiced greatly in doing this,

because thereby He manifested and exalted the *glory of God*. He came to do the will of His Father, and thereby to set forth His glory. The salvation of the sons to be brought unto glory depended upon this work of His ; and how much He sought that, His whole work declares. For their sakes He came down from heaven, and " was made flesh and dwelt among them ; " for their sakes did He undergo all the miseries that the world could cast upon Him ; for their sakes did He undergo the curse of the law, and wrestle with the displeasure and wrath of God against sin.

Now after He had done all this for them, unless He had declared the name of God unto them in the gospel, they could have had no benefit by it, for if they believe not they cannot be saved. They could not of themselves have known anything of that name of God which is their life and salvation. His *own glory* depended upon this work of declaring the name of God. The gathering of His Church, the setting up of His kingdom, the establishment of His throne, the setting of the crown upon His head, depend solely on His declaring the name of God in the preaching of the gospel.

" And again, I will put my trust in Him." What the Apostle intends to prove is that He was really and truly of one with the sons to be brought unto glory, and so He shows from these words how Jesus Christ was made and brought into that condition wherein it was necessary for Him to trust in God, and act in that dependence upon Him which the nature of man whilst exposed unto troubles doth indispensably require. In all the troubles and difficulties He had to contend with He put His trust in God, and this evinceth Him to have been truly and really one of the children— His brethren, seeing it was His duty, no less than theirs, to depend upon God in troubles and distresses.

" And again, Behold I and the children which God hath given me." The Apostle still further confirms his testimony that Jesus Christ and the sons who are to be brought unto glory " *are all of one*." Being of the same nature with them, and so meet to become a common parent unto them all, God, by an act of sovereign grace, gives them unto Him for His children. From these things we may observe, 1. That God gives all the sons that are to be brought to glory to Jesus Christ. He says, " Thine they were, and Thou gavest them Me ; " 2. God gives them to Him as His children to be provided for, and to have an inheritance purchased for them, that they may become heirs of God and co-heirs with Himself ; 3. That the Lord Christ is satisfied with, and rejoiceth in, the portion given Him of His Father—His portion is His children, His brethren. Such was His love, such was His grace ; for we in ourselves are " a people not to be desired ; " 4. That the Lord Christ assumes the children given Him of His Father unto the same condition with Himself, both as to time and eternity—" I and the children." As

He is, so are they; His lot is their lot; His God is their God; His Father is their Father; and His glory shall be theirs.

Vs. 14, 15. *Forasmuch then as the children are partakers of flesh and blood, He also Himself likewise took part of the same; that through death He might destroy him that had the power of death, that is, the devil; and deliver them who through fear of death were all their lifetime subject to bondage.*

"**Forasmuch then as the children are partakers of flesh and blood, He also Himself likewise took part of the same.**" The Apostle in the first place expresseth the *natural* condition of the children whom God designed to bring unto glory; those who were given unto Christ, they were in common partakers of flesh and blood. It is as though he said: The children are men subject unto death, and as much as this was the condition of all the children—liable to sufferings, sorrows, and death—He was so also. But in the second place the Apostle expresseth the *moral* condition of the children; they were subject to death, and this wrought fear in them and brought them into bondage during the whole course of their lives. They were subject to death as it is penal; the fear of death, as it is penal, is inseparable from sin, before the sinner be delivered by the death of Christ; and this fear of a penal death brings men into bondage. Now the Apostle shows us two things: 1. That Jesus Christ partook of their *natural condition*; 2. That He delivered them from their *moral condition*.

Let us observe here, 1. That the Lord Christ, out of His inexpressible love, willingly submitted Himself unto every condition of the children to be saved by Him, and to everything in every condition of them, sin only excepted. Though He was in the "form of God," equal unto Him, yet "that mind," that love, that affection towards us was in Him, that to be like unto us, and thereby to save us, "He emptied Himself, and took upon Him the form of a servant," our form, and became like unto us. He would be like unto us, that He might make us like unto Himself; He would take our flesh, that He might give unto us His Spirit; He would join Himself unto us, and become "one flesh" with us, that we might be joined unto Him, and become "one Spirit" with Him.

2. It was only in flesh and blood, the substance and essence of human nature, and not in our personal infirmities, that the Lord was made like unto us. He took to Himself the *nature* of all men, and not the *person* of any man. We have each one of us particular infirmities and weaknesses, following our common human nature as existing in sinful persons. Such are the sicknesses and pains of our bodies from inward distempers, and the disorders and passions

of our minds. Of these the Lord Christ did not partake. It was
not needful, it was not possible that He should do so; not *needful*,
because He could provide for their cure without assuming them;
not *possible*, for they can have no place in a nature innocent and
holy. He took our nature by a miraculous conception in a virgin,
whereby He had truly our nature, yet not subject on its own account
unto any of those evils whereunto it is liable as propagated from
Adam in an ordinary course. And thus, though He was joined
unto our nature, yet as He was "holy, harmless, and undefiled " in
that nature, He was separate from sinners; so that although our
nature suffered more in His Person than it was capable of in the
person of any mere man, yet, not being debased by any sinful
imperfection, it was always excellent, beautiful, and glorious.

3. That the Son of God should take part in human nature with
the children is the greatest and most admirable effect of Divine love,
wisdom, and grace. This is the mystery that atheists scoff at,
deluded Christians deny it; but the angels adore it, the Church
professeth it, and believers find the comfort and benefit of it. In
this assuming of human nature into personal subsistence with Himself, the scattered beams of light are gathered into one Sun, giving
out the most glorious beams, unto the manifestation of His most
glorious excellencies far above all other things; and this surely was
not done but for the greatest end that can be conceived, and such
is the salvation of sinners.

**"That through death He might destroy him that had
the power of death, that is, the devil, and deliver them
who through fear of death were all their lifetime subject
to bondage."** All sinners out of Christ are under the power of
Satan. They belong unto that kingdom whereof he is the prince
and ruler. However men may flatter themselves that they are free,
as the Jews of old did, yet if they are not freed by an interest in
the death of Christ, they are in bondage unto this beastly tyrant,
and as he works effectually in them here, he will ragingly inflict
vengeance on them hereafter. But the Lord Christ destroyed "*him
that had the power of death.*" "Now is the judgment of this world,
now is the prince of this world cast out." That which is here
called destroying is there called casting out. It is the casting him
out of his power, from his princedom and rule. The destruction
here intended is the dissolution and removing of that power which
he had in and over death, with all the consequences of it.

It was "*through death*" that Jesus Christ destroyed the devil.
The death of Christ is here put as the *end* of one thing and the
means or cause of another—the end of His own incarnation and the
means of the children's deliverance. The first and principal end of
the Lord Christ's assumption of human nature was not to reign in
it, but to suffer and die in it. He was indeed from of old designed
unto a kingdom; but He was to " suffer," and so to enter into His

glory. Glory was to follow, a kingdom to ensue; but suffering and dying were the principal work He came about. He need not have been made a partaker of flesh and blood to have been a King, for He was the King eternal, immortal, invisible, the King of kings, and Lord of lords, the only Potentate from everlasting; but He could not have died if He had not been made partaker of our nature.

The *means* whereby Satan was destroyed was by "His death." The power of Satan in reference unto death was all founded in sin. The obligation of the sinner unto death was that which gave Satan all his power; the taking away of that obligation must needs be the dissolution of his power. Now this, in reference unto the children for whom Christ died, was done in His death—*virtually* in His death itself, *actually* in the application of His death unto the children. The first branch of the devil's power consisted in bringing sin into the world. This is dissolved by Christ's "taking away the sin of the world," which He did as the "Lamb of God," by the sacrifice of Himself in His death. When contending with Christ for the continuance of his sovereignty, he was conquered, the ground whereon he stood, even the guilt of sin, being taken away from under him, and his title defeated; and actually believers are translated from under his rule, from the powers of darkness into the kingdom of light and of the Son of God.

The final execution of the sentence of death is utterly taken out of the hands of the devil by the death of Christ, inasmuch as they for whom He died shall never undergo death penally. And thus was Satan, as to his power over death, fully destroyed by the death of Christ. By this dissolution of the power of Satan, deliverance was procured for the children. The fear of death being taken away, the bondage that ensueth thereon vanisheth also. And these things, as they are done *virtually and legally* in the death of Christ, so are they actually accomplished in the children upon the application of the death of Christ unto them when they do believe. From all which we may learn that the death of Christ, through the wise and righteous disposal of God, is victorious, all-conquering, and prevalent. Men and devils were ignorant of the great work God had in hand, and whilst they thought they were destroying the Christ of God, God was in and by Him destroying them and their power. *Whilst His heel was bruised He brake their head.* Faith in the death of Christ is the only way and means of obtaining a conquest over Satan. He will fly at the sign of the cross rightly made.

V. 16. *For verily He took not on [Him the nature of] angels, but He took on [Him] the seed of Abraham.*

The Apostle in these words confirms what he had before affirmed concerning the Lord Jesus being made partaker of flesh and blood together with the children. He is here said to take the "*seed of Abraham*," because in the Scripture it is so plainly foretold that He should do so, when not one word is spoken anywhere that He should be an angel or take their nature upon Him. We may observe, 1. That the Lord Jesus Christ is truly God and man in one Person, and this is fully manifested in these words. There is in them supposed His *pre-existence* in another nature than that which He is here said to assume. He was before, He subsisted before, or He could not have taken on Him what He had not. The nature He took to Himself was "of the seed of Abraham" according to the promise. So, continuing what He was, He became what He was not. For He took this to be His *own nature*. He took it so entirely as to become truly the seed of Abraham, to whom and concerning whom the promise was given (Gal. iii. 16), and was Himself made "of the seed of David according to the flesh" (Rom. i. 3), and "as concerning the flesh came of the fathers" (Rom. ix. 5), and so was "the son of David, the son of Abraham" (Matt. i. 1). And this could be done no otherwise but by taking that *nature* into *personal subsistence* with Himself. The nature He assumed could not otherwise become His. If He had by any ways or means taken the person of a man to be united unto Him in the strictest union that two persons are capable of—a Divine and a human—the nature had still been the nature of that other person and not *His own*. But He took it to be *His own nature*, and He is therefore a true and perfect man, for no more is required to make a perfect man but the entire nature of man subsisting, and this is in Christ as a man, the human nature having a subsistence communicated unto it by the Son of God. And therefore this is done without a multiplication of persons in Him, for the human nature can have no personality of its own, because it was taken to be the nature of another Person who was pre-existent unto it, and by assuming of it prevented its proper personality. Neither did hence any mixture or confusion of natures ensue, or of the essential properties of them ; for He took the seed of Abraham to be His human nature, which if mixed with the Divine it could not be.

2. The redemption of mankind, by the taking of our nature, was a work of mere sovereign grace. He took the seed of Abraham, and for what cause or reason ? Can any be assigned but the sovereign grace, love and pleasure of God ? nor doth the Scripture anywhere assign any other. And this will better appear if we consider, That for a *sinning nature* to be saved it was indispensably necessary for that nature to be assumed. Those who fancy a possibility of saving sinners any other way but by satisfaction made *in the nature that had sinned*, seem not to have considered aright the nature of sin and the justice of God. Also, that we were carrying away all human nature into endless destruction, whence Christ's assumption of it is expressed by His putting forth His hand and taking hold of it to

stop it in its course of apostacy and ruin. Of angels only some individuals fell from God, but our whole nature in every one to whom it was communicated from and by Adam was running headlong to destruction. As to angels, "He spared them not," and "He spared not His Son" for us.

Vs. 17, 18. *Wherefore in all things it behoved Him to be made like unto [His] brethren, that He might be a merciful and faithful High Priest in things [pertaining] to God, to make reconciliation for the sins of the people. For in that He Himself hath suffered being tempted, He is able to succour them that are tempted.*

"**Wherefore in all things it behoved Him to be made like unto His brethren.**" God having designed Him unto the office of a High Priest, it was indispensably necessary for Him to be made like unto His brethren in all things. He was made like unto His brethren in the essence of human nature—a rational, spiritual soul, and a mortal body quickened by its union therewithal. But that He should take this nature upon Him by natural generation, after the manner of the brethren, this was not necessary; this would have rendered Him incapable of being such a priest as He was to be, for He must be "holy, harmless, undefiled, separate from sinners." It was also necessary that, in and with His human nature, He should take upon Him all the properties and affections of it, that so He might be made like unto His brethren. His soul was the subject of those affections, such as love, joy, fear, sorrow, shame, and the like, that belong to a rational human soul; so also was His body subject unto hunger, thirst, pain, cold, death itself. But now whereas these things in the brethren are attended with irregular perturbations for the most part, and whereas all the individuals of them have their proper infirmities in their own persons, partly from inordinate inclinations from their various tempers, &c., partly in weaknesses and sicknesses proceeding either from their original constitutions or other following inordinances; it was no way needful that in any of these He should be made like unto His brethren.

He was also made like unto His brethren in temptations, for the reason given in the last verse of this chapter. Our temptations arise from within us, from our unbelief and lusts; and in the case of those that are from without, there is somewhat within us to take part with them, which always makes us fail in our duty of resistance, and sometimes leads to further miscarriages. But from these things He was absolutely free, for as He had no inward disposition or inclination unto the least evil, so when the prince of this world came unto Him he had no part in Him, nothing to close with his suggestions or to entertain his terrors. He was also made like unto His brethren in sufferings—they were of the same kind as those which the brethren underwent, yet they had far different effects on Him from what they would have had on them. He was perfectly innocent and righteous, no way deserving sufferings in His own Person.

"That He might be a merciful and faithful High Priest in things pertaining to God." He was made man, that He might be a High Priest; He suffered being tempted that He might be merciful and faithful. In order to His being a High Priest, it was necessary that He should partake of the nature of them for whom He was to administer in the things of God; that in this nature He should be perfectly holy, and exactly discharge His duty according unto the mind and will of God, was all that was required of Him as a High Priest. But this was not all that the state and condition of His brethren required. Their condition was such, through the infirmities of their nature, with their manifold temptations and sufferings, that He as the High Priest was furnished with qualifications for His office, and this by His own sufferings and temptations. He was a *" merciful and faithful High Priest."*

" Merciful." Mercy in Christ is a compassion, a condolency, and hath a moving of pity and sorrow joined with it. And this was in the human nature of Christ a grace of the Spirit in all perfection. *" Faithful."* His faithfulness as a High Priest consists in His exact, constant, careful consideration of all the concernments of the brethren under their temptations and sufferings. This He is excited unto by His own experience of what it is to serve God in such a condition.

Let us here observe, 1. That the promised Messiah was to be the High Priest of the people of God. He was made a High Priest by the oath of Jehovah (chap. vii. 20, 21). He alone had somewhat of His own to offer unto God; other priests offered the beasts that were brought unto them by the people, but the Lord Christ had a body and soul of His own prepared for Him to offer. He alone was set over the whole spiritual house of God—the whole family of God in heaven and earth. He alone abides for ever, and He alone did and can do the true and proper work of a priest, namely, to make *" reconciliation for the sins of the people."*

2. The assumption of our nature, and His conformity unto us therein, were principally necessary unto the Lord Jesus on the account of His being a High Priest unto us. Without the assumption of our nature He had nothing to offer; and " of necessity," saith the Apostle, " He must have somewhat to offer unto God."

3. Such was the unspeakable love of Christ unto His brethren, that He would refuse nothing, no condition, that was needful to fit Him for the discharge of the work which He had undertaken. Their High Priest He must be; this He could not be unless He were made like unto them in all things.

" In things pertaining unto God, to make reconciliation for the sins of the people." The *" things pertaining to God "* are either the things to be done for God with men, or the things toward God which on the part of the people were to be performed ; and this latter is here intended, as we may see from the next clause of the text : *" To make reconciliation for the sins of the people."* In this word " reconciliation " there is understood, 1. An *offence, crime*, guilt, or debt to be taken away ; 2. A *person offended* to be pacified, atoned, reconciled ; 3. A *person offending* to be pardoned, accepted ; 4. A *sacrifice*, or other means of making atonement. The Jews knew the great work of the high priest was to make atonement, and the Apostle now instructs them in the substance of what before they had attended to in types and shadows.

" For in that He Himself hath suffered being tempted, He is able to succour them that are tempted." He suffered in His temptations. Temptation comprises any thing, state, or condition, whereby a man may be tried, exercised, or tempted. This will give us light on the temptations of Christ, for although they were all external and by impressions from without, yet they were not confined unto the assaults of Satan. Some of His temptations we may briefly recount :

1. His state and condition in the world. He was poor, despised, persecuted, reproached, especially from the beginning unto the end of His public ministry. Herein lay one continued temptation, that is, a trial of obedience by all manner of hardships. He says to His disciples, " Ye have continued with Me in My temptations," or in the work that He carried on in a constant course of temptation, arising from His outward state and condition. In this temptation He suffered hunger, poverty, weariness, sorrow, reproach, shame, contempt, wherewith His holy soul was deeply affected.

2. Temptations from His relations in the flesh, being disregarded and disbelieved by them ; from His followers, being forsaken by them upon His preaching the mysteries of the gospel ; from His chosen disciples, all of whom left Him—one denied Him and another betrayed Him ; from the anguish of His mother when " a sword pierced through her soul " in His sufferings ; from His enemies of all sorts, all of which are related in the gospel, from all of which His sufferings were inexpressible.

3. Satan had a principal hand in the temptations from which He suffered. He set upon Him in the entrance of His ministry, immediately in his own person, and followed Him in the whole course of it by the instruments he set on work. He had also a season—an hour of darkness—allowed unto him, when he was to try his utmost strength and policy against Him ; under which assault from him He suffered, as was foretold from the foundation of the world, the bruising of His heel, or the temporal ruin of all His concernments.

4. God's desertion of Him was another temptation from which He suffered. As this was most mysterious, so His sufferings under it were His greatest perplexity. These are some of the heads and springs of those various and innumerable temptations that the Lord Christ suffered in and under. They for whose sakes He underwent this condition of suffering are those whom He reconciled unto God, by His sacrifice as a High Priest. Notwithstanding their reconciliation unto God by the death of Christ, they have a course of obedience prescribed unto them. In this course they meet with many difficulties, dangers, and sorrows, all proceeding from the temptations that they are exercised with. Hence is this description of them—"*them that are tempted*"—the tempted ones. It is reconciled persons who emphatically are the tempted ones; they are the mark of Satan and the world, and besides this they maintain a continual warfare within them against temptations in the remainder of their own corruptions. This is the proper name of believers. As Satan from what he doth is called the tempter, so they from what they endure are called the tempted ones.

The High Priest having suffered the like things with them, they have an assured ground of consolation in all their temptations and sufferings, which the Apostle declares when he says that the High Priest "*is able to succour them that are tempted.*" His ability to succour is not an executive power—a power of working, a power of the hand, but is a power of the heart and will, an ability in readiness of mind, that is here assigned unto Him. Observe then,

1. That He had particular experience of the weakness, sorrows, and miseries of human nature under temptations. *He tried it, felt it, and will never forget it.*

2. His heart is thereby inclined unto compassion, and is acquainted with what it is that will afford relief. In His throne of eternal peace and glory He sees His poor brethren labouring in that storm which, with so much travail of soul, He Himself passed through, and is intimately affected by their condition.

3. This compassion moves and excites Him unto their relief and succour—this is the ability ascribed unto our High Priest, compassion and mercy arising from an experience of the sufferings and dangers of human nature under temptations.

4. That from this ariseth a great advantage unto all the brethren in the succour He is able to afford unto them. They need *strength* to withstand temptations that they prevail not against them; *consolation* to support their spirits under temptations; *seasonable deliverance* out of their temptations. And their High Priest ministers succour to them by His Word and promises, by His Spirit, by communicating unto them supplies of grace and strength, by giving them strong consolation, by rebuking their tempters and temptations, and by His providence disposing of all things to their good and advantage in the issue.

5. That the principal work of the Lord Christ as our
High Priest, and from which all other actings of His in that office
do flow, was to make reconciliation or atonement for sin. "We
have an Advocate with the Father . . . and He is the propitiation for our sins." What He doth in heaven as our Advocate
depends on what He did on earth when He was the propitiation.
They who weaken, oppose, or take away this reconciliation are
enemies to the salvation of men, the honour of Christ, and the glory
of God. From men they take away their hope and happiness, from
Christ His honour and office, from God His grace and glory. I
know they allow of a reconciliation in words, but it is of *men to
God*, not of *God to men*. They would have us reconcile ourselves
by faith and obedience, but for the reconciliation of God unto us by
sacrifice, satisfaction, and atonement, that they deny. But reconciliation by blood is the only relief of a guilty soul.

6. The Lord Christ suffered under all His temptations, sinned
in none. He suffered being tempted, He sinned not being tempted.
He had the heart of a man, the affections of a man, and that in the
highest degree of sense and tenderness. No sorrows, no sufferings
were like unto His ; He made bare His breast unto their strokes,
and laid open His soul that they might soak into the inmost parts
of it. He left nothing in the whole nature of sorrow or suffering
that He tasted not and made experience of.

7. The great duty of tempted souls is to cry unto the Lord
Christ for help and relief. He is every way " able to succour them
that are tempted." He hath a sufficiency of *care*, wisdom, and
faithfulness to observe and know the seasons wherein succour is
necessary unto us; a sufficiency of *tenderness*, mercy, and compassion
to excite Him thereunto ; a sufficiency of *power* to afford succour
that shall be effectual ; a sufficiency of *acceptation* at the throne of
grace to prevail with God for suitable supplies and succour.

CHAPTER THREE

Vs. 1, 2. *Wherefore, holy brethren, partakers of the
heavenly calling, consider the Apostle and High Priest
of our profession, Christ Jesus ; who was faithful to Him
that appointed Him, as also Moses [was faithful] in all His
house.*

"**Wherefore, holy brethren.**" He calls them "*brethren*"
as spiritually interested in the same family of God with himself ;

also with respect unto their new relation in Christ. By "*holy*" he means "sanctified ones." He accounted them holy not upon the account of an external separation, but also of internal, real sanctification and purity. By this compellation of "holy brethren" doth the Apostle manifest his high regard of them or respect unto them, looking upon them as persons sanctified by the Spirit and word of Christ, and a dear affection for them as his brethren. By this treatment of them he gives a great evidence of his sincerity in dealing with them, for they might not fear that he would impose anything on them whom he honoured as holy and loved as brethren. And hereby he smooths the way to his ensuing exhortation.

"Partakers of the heavenly calling." This calling he first describes by its quality: it is "*heavenly;*" it is the "calling that is from above." It is called "heavenly" because God the Father is the fountain and principal cause of it; also in respect of the means whereby this calling is wrought, which are spiritual and heavenly, namely, the Word and the Spirit, both from above. The Apostle calls the gospel "the voice of Him that speaketh from heaven." Also it is called a heavenly calling because of the *end* to which they are called, which is to heaven and heavenly things. The Apostle assigns unto these Hebrews a participation in this heavenly calling. They were partakers of it, had an interest in it; together with himself were so called. And this he doth that he might manifest unto them wherein their *great privilege* consisted, and which, as such, they were to value. The call of Abraham, which was the foundation of all their privileges in Judaism, was but an earthly call, on the earth and to the earth; but this was in every way more excellent, being heavenly.

Also to set forth the *grace of God* towards the Jews and his own faith concerning them, that they were not all rejected of God, notwithstanding the hardness and obstinacy of most of them; and, on the other hand, he insinuates that they were not to make an enclosure of this privilege, like those wherewith of old they were entrusted. The Gentiles being fellow-heirs with them, they were "partakers" with others in this "heavenly calling." Also he declares his own *communion* with them in this great privilege, whereby they might understand his intimate concernment in their state and condition. Also he minds them of their *duty* from their privilege. Being "partakers of the heavenly calling" unto Christ, it must needs be their duty to "consider" Him, which he exhorts them unto.

Observe then, 1. That dispensers of the gospel ought to use holy prudence in winning upon the minds of them whom they are to instruct. 2. Believers are all related one to another in the nearest and strictest bond of an equal relation; they are all "holy brethren." 3. All true and real professors of the gospel are sanctified by the Holy Ghost, and made truly and really holy. 4. No man comes unto a useful, saving knowledge of Jesus Christ in the gospel, but by virtue of an effectual heavenly calling. 5. The effectual heavenly calling of believers is their great privilege, wherein they have cause to rejoice, and which always ought to mind them of their duty unto Him that hath called them.

"**Consider the Apostle and High Priest of our profession, Christ Jesus.**" "*Consider.*" Presently (chap. v. 11, 14) the Apostle blames them for their remissness and backwardness in learning the doctrine of the gospel ; so here he seems to intimate that they had not sufficiently weighed and pondered the nature and quality of the Person of Christ and His offices, and were thereupon kept in their entanglements unto Judaism.

"*The Apostle.*" The Lord Jesus is the one sent of God upon His great errand unto the children of men—His Apostle. "He whom God hath sent" is His own description of Himself. This is His authority for the work He had to do ; He came not of Himself, but was sent of God, even the Father, and therefore spake in His Name, and fed the Church "in the strength of the Lord, in the majesty of the Name of the Lord His God." His work as "the Apostle" was to reveal and declare the will of the Father unto the children of men ; to declare the Father Himself (John i. 18), and His Name (John xvii. 6, 26) ; that is, the mystery of His will concerning our obedience and salvation. I leave unto consideration whether there may not be some especial respect unto His peculiar mission intended in this name and title here only given Him. He was in His own personal ministry on the earth "a minister of the circumcision for the truth of God, to confirm the promises made unto the fathers."

"*And High Priest.*" To manifest unto these Hebrews how the Lord Christ hath the pre-eminence in all things, he instructs them that both the offices—that of an Apostle which of old was executed by Moses, and that of a High Priest committed unto Aaron—were now vested in Him alone, intending afterwards to evince how far He excelleth them both, and how excellent were His offices in comparison of theirs, though they came under the same name.

"*Of our profession.*" The words may be taken objectively and passively. The Apostle and High Priest whom we profess, that is, believe, declare, own to be so. Or they may denote the Author of our profession—the Apostle and High Priest who hath revealed and declared the faith which we profess. Our profession is the gospel, with the worship and obedience required therein. The word "*our*" is used by way of discrimination ; whatever by others He be esteemed, to us He is the Apostle and High Priest of our profession, and it is our inestimable privilege and honour that He is so. From all this we see that the business of God with sinners could be no way transacted but by the negotiation and embassy of the Son.

There was a threefold greatness in this matter, which none was fit to manage but the Son of God : 1. A greatness of *grace, love and condescension*. That the great God should send to treat with sinners for the ends of His message, for peace and reconciliation, is a thing that all creation must admire, and that unto eternity.

2. There is a *greatness in the work itself* that is incumbent on the Apostle of God, which required that the Son of God should be engaged therein. He alone could perfectly represent the Father unto us. This an ambassador has to do ; he bears and represents the person of him by whom he is sent. But who could represent the Person of the Father unto sinners ? Surely, none but He who is in Himself " the brightness of His glory, and the express image of His Person ;" He who is " the image of the invisible God." The greatness of the work required that He who undertook it must be intimately acquainted with all the secret counsels of God, that lay hid in His infinite wisdom and will from all eternity. Now, who shall manage the whole treaty between God and sinners ? " The only begotten Son, who is in the bosom of the Father, He hath declared Him." The nature of this work required that the Apostle of God to sinners should be able to make His message to be believed and received by them. Without this the whole work and undertaking might be frustrated. And this He doth by the effectual working of His Spirit, the dispensation whereof is wholly committed unto Him.

3. There is a *greatness in the end of this work* ; this was no less than to establish peace between God and man. " He is our peace," and " He came and preached peace ; " hence He is called " the Word of God," " the Counsellor," " the Angel or Messenger of the covenant," and here " the Apostle of our profession."

" Who was faithful to Him that appointed Him, as also Moses was faithful in all His house." The chief qualification of an apostle or ambassador is, that he be " *faithful*." He was faithful ; the Apostle states this absolutely ; then comparatively, " faithful as was Moses." His being " faithful " is annexed unto the mention of two offices, apostolical and sacerdotal, yet, as appears from the ensuing discourse, it relates only unto the former. Faithfulness consists of two things, a trust committed and a discharge of that trust. Our Lord had a trust committed unto Him, for it pleased the Father to lay up in Him " all the treasures of wisdom and knowledge," to commit unto Him the whole mystery of His will and grace, and sent Him to make known the last full declaration of His mind and will as to His worship with the obedience and salvation of the Church. This trust He discharged faithfully. He sought not His own glory, but the glory of Him that sent Him ; He ever declared His message not to be His own, but His Father's ; and He declared the whole will or word of God that was committed unto Him.

In all this He **" was faithful to Him that appointed**

Him." This appointment consists of a fivefold act of God in reference to His being made an Apostle : 1. In His eternal designation to this work and office, " He was foreordained before the foundation of the world." 2. In the solemn promise made from the beginning to send Him. 3. In the sending of Him actually into the world to be the light of men. 4. In the declaration He made of Him to be His Apostle and Ambassador by a visible sign ; this was done in the descending of the Holy Ghost upon Him in the likeness of a dove. 5. Unto these acts of appointment God added His command, and published it from heaven unto all, to hear and obey Him, as the great Teacher sent from God, as His Apostle, speaking in His name.

"*As also Moses was faithful in all His house.*" Although Moses failed personally in his faith, there is no impeachment of his faithfulness in the especial office intended—an apostle of God. " According to all that the LORD commanded, so did he." And Moses was faithful in all God's house ;—in His household, in His family. Thus doth the Apostle enter upon his intended proof of the pre-eminence of Christ above Moses ; he grants that they were both prophets, both Apostles of God, sent by Him to declare His mind and will ; that they were both faithful in the discharge of their office and trust ; and that this trust extended to the whole Church, and all that was to be done therein in the worship of God. Wherein the difference lay he declares in the next verse.

Vs. 3, 4. *For this [man] was counted worthy of more glory than Moses, inasmuch as He who hath builded the house hath more honour than the house. For every house is builded by some [man]; but He that built all things [is] God.*

" For this man was counted worthy of more glory than Moses." The Apostle grants and supposeth that Moses was worthy of honour. His honour consisteth principally in the *work wherein he was employed*—God singled him out from all the posterity of Abraham to be the sole mediator between Him and the people ; and in *his fidelity* in the discharge of his work and office. The Apostle would not give the Jews the least cause for suspicion that he would detract from the honour and praise due to Moses. The unbelievers among them boasted of Moses to the contempt of the Lord Christ. " We know that God spake unto Moses ; as for this fellow, we know not whence he is." But these things did not move the Apostle to deal partially with the truth. He allows unto Moses his due glory and honour, and yet asserts the excellency of Christ above him. "*This man—the God-man—was counted worthy of more glory than Moses.*" The glory here spoken of is not that which is due to His Person (as afterwards shall be more fully declared), but that which belongs to Him in His office, the office which He discharged towards the Church.

"**Inasmuch as He who hath builded the house hath more honour than the house.**" In these words we learn, 1. That Christ built the house—the Church of God; 2. That He was worthy of glory and honour on that account; and, 3. That His glory and honour was incomparably greater than that of Moses. When we remember what is said in the Word of God as to the materials of which this house was built—"dead in trespasses and sins," "enemies," "children of wrath"—we may see a little how Jesus Christ—the Builder—was incomparably more glorious than Moses, or any of the sons of men.

"**For every house is builded by some man, but He that built all things is God.**" By "*all things*" we are to understand all things belonging to this building—the Church of God. Now, He who "*built all things is God.*" That it is the Lord Christ who is intended here is plain, for the Apostle is proving that He is more honourable than Moses, and that upon account of His building the house of God; the house could only be built in such a glorious manner because its Builder is God.

Vs. 5, 6. *And Moses verily [was] faithful in all His house, as a servant, for a testimony of those things which were to be spoken after; but Christ as a Son over His own house; whose house are we, if we hold fast the confidence and the rejoicing of the hope firm unto the end.*

"**Moses verily was faithful in all His house as a servant.**" The office ascribed unto Moses is that of a "servant," —a minister, an officer in holy things. This was his place, honour and dignity. Moses was faithful as a servant in "*all His house.*" Other servants were used in various parts of the house, but the glory of Moses was that he was used in the whole house, in every part of it. All things, for the use of all ages, until the time of reformation should come, were ordered by him. But as we shall see, this left him incomparably inferior to the Lord Christ.

"**For a testimony of those things which were to be spoken after.**" By what Moses did in the service of the house of God, he gave testimony to those things—the gospel—which were to be spoken after; he ordered all things by God's direction in the typical worship of the house, so that they might be a pledge and testimony of what God would afterwards reveal and exhibit in the gospel. Herein was Moses faithful; and here the Apostle taketh leave of Moses; he treats not about him any more; and therefore he gives him, as it were, an honourable burial. He puts this glorious epitaph on his grave: "Moses, a faithful servant of the Lord in His whole house."

" But Christ as a Son over His own house." The term " faithful " is here to be understood. Christ was faithful as a Son. Every word proves the pre-eminence of Christ that is asserted. He is a *Son*, Moses a *servant* ; He *over* the house, Moses *in* the house ; He over *His own house*, Moses in the house of another. Absolute and supreme authority over all persons and things is intended in this expression, " *over His own house.*"

" Whose house are we. " That is, believers who worship Him according to the gospel. Believers are the house of God ; in them He dwells really by His Spirit. Hence they are said to be " living stones," and to be built on Christ into "an holy temple ; " and as such God dwells in them.

" If we hold fast our confidence, and the rejoicing of the hope firm unto the end." These words are a description of the persons who are the house of Christ, from a certain effect or adjunct of that faith whereby they became so to be. They are such, and only such, as " hold fast their confidence and rejoicing of the hope firm unto the end," whereby they are distinguished from temporary professors, who may fall away. The " confidence " here intended doth refer unto our " hope " no less than the " rejoicing " that followeth. This is evident from the construction of the words, for the word " firm " agreeth not with " hope " or " rejoicing," but with " confidence." The genuine sense of these words will best appear from a consideration of the state and condition of the Hebrews at this time. Their condition was one of persecution, and therefore of danger of backsliding.

Now a hope in us of a blessed immortality and glory by Jesus Christ requireth two things from us : 1. A free, bold, and open profession of that truth upon which our hope is built, and that against all dangers or oppositions, for we know that this hope will never make us ashamed. This is the " *confidence* " here mentioned—a confident, open profession of our hope. 2. An open opposing of our hope, or that which is hoped for, unto all difficulties, dangers, and persecutions, with a holy boasting and glorying, or rejoicing in our lot and portion, because the foundation of our hope is sure, and the things we hope for are precious and excellent, and that to the contempt of everything that ariseth against them. This is the " *rejoicing of the hope* " here intended.

The Apostle shows us how such "confidence and rejoicing of the hope " are to be secured : " *if we hold fast . . . firm unto the end.*" By the expression, " if we hold fast," is represented to us the *great opposition* that will arise against this duty, against our firmness and constancy in profession ; also that *great care*, diligence and endeavour are to be used in this matter, or we shall fail and miscarry in it. The meaning of the word " *firm* " the Apostle explaineth, c. x. 23 : " without wavering," without declining from it, or shaking in it. And in this we must continue "unto the end," as long as we live in this world, until we come unto the end of our faith, even the end of our lives and the salvation of our souls.

Observe then, 1. That the building of the Church of God is so great and glorious a work as that it could not be effected by any but He who was God. "He that built all things is God."

2. The greatest and most honourable of the sons of men, that are employed in the work of God in His house, are but servants, and themselves part of the house. "Moses verily was a servant." They are servants because no man hath anything to do in His house but by virtue of commission from Him who is the only Lord and Ruler of it. This bespeaks them servants. Also because it is required of them, as servants, to observe and obey the commands of their Lord. Also because, as servants, they are accountable for all that they do in the house unto their Lord. And because, as servants, they shall receive their reward ; they serve a good, just, great and gracious Lord, who will not forget their labour, but will give unto them a crown at His appearing.

3. The great end of all Mosaical institutions was to represent, or prefigure, or give testimony unto the grace of the gospel by Jesus Christ.

4. It is an eminent privilege to be the house of Christ or a part of that house, "Whose house are we," and that because this house is "*God's building*," a house that He built, and that in a most admirable manner. The house is so built that none is employed in a way of authority in the building of it but the Lord Christ alone, the Son and Lord over His own house. And also in this house God dwells by His Spirit. "Ye are builded together for an habitation of God by His Spirit." Unspeakable then is this privilege, and so are the advantages which depend upon it.

5. The greatness of this privilege requires an answerableness of duty. Because we are this house of God, it becometh us to "hold fast our confidence unto the end." On account of our being the house of God, many duties are incumbent upon us, as, *Universal holiness*, especially *purity of body and soul* becoming the habitation of the Holy Spirit ; endeavours to fill up the place, state, condition and relation that we hold unto the house, for the good of the whole.

6. In times of trial and persecution, freedom, boldness and constancy in profession are a good evidence unto ourselves that we are living stones in the house of God. In the discharge of this duty the glory of God is greatly concerned. Other way of giving glory unto God we have not, but by bearing witness unto His excellencies; that is, glorifying Him as God. Again, by these means, the souls of the saints have a trial and experiment of their own grace, of what sort it is ; as Abraham had of his own faith and obedience in the great experiment which God gave him of it by His command for the sacrificing of Isaac. *Tried graces* are exceeding precious, and are evidences that those in whom they are do belong to the house of God.

7. Interest in the gospel gives sufficient cause of confidence and rejoicing in every condition. " Hold fast the rejoicing of your hope."

8. So many and great are the difficulties and temptations that lie in the way of profession, so great is the number of them that decay in it, or apostatise from it, that the principal evidence of its truth and sincerity is to be taken from its endurance unto the end. " Whose house are we, if we hold fast the confidence and the rejoicing of the hope firm unto the end."

Vs. 7—11. *Wherefore (as the Holy Ghost saith, To-day if ye will hear His voice, Harden not your hearts, as in the provocation, in the day of temptation in the wilderness; when your fathers tempted Me, proved Me, and saw My works forty years. Wherefore I was grieved with that generation, and said, They do alway err in [their] heart; and they have not known My ways. So I sware in My wrath, They shall not enter into My rest).*

" **Wherefore.** "   That is, seeing the Lord Christ, who is the Author of the gospel, is in His office as an Apostle preferred far above Moses, let us consider what duty is incumbent upon us, especially how careful and watchful we ought to be, that we be not by any means diverted or turned aside from that obedience which He requires, and which on all accounts is due unto Him.

" **As the Holy Ghost saith, To-day.** "   Consider, saith the Apostle, that these are the words of the Holy Ghost, so that you may submit yourselves to His authority.   The Holy Spirit spake to them of old in and by David, so He continues to speak unto us " to-day " in the Scripture, which is not only His word, but His voice,—His speaking, living, powerful voice.   Whatever was given by inspiration from the Holy Ghost, and is recorded in the Scripture for the use of the Church, He continues therein to speak it unto us unto this day.

" **If ye will hear His voice.** "   The voice of God is the signification of His will, which is the rule of all our duty and obedience.   The Psalmist speaks to the people as if the voice of God were then sounding in their ears.   For that which was once the voice of God unto the Church (being recorded in the Scriptures) continues still to be so, that is, it is not only materially His revealed will, but it is accompanied with that special *impression of His authority* with which it was at the first attested.   " To hear His voice," is the act of the whole soul, in understanding, choosing, and resolving to do the will of God as declared by His voice.

" **Harden not your hearts.** "   The Apostle enforceth his exhortation unto obedience, in the words of the Psalmist, by a caution against or a prohibition of the contrary.   The word "heart" is that whereby the principle of all our moral actions and the respective influence of all the faculties of our souls in them is expressed. It appears that unto this sinful hardening of the heart which the people in the wilderness were guilty of, and which the Apostle here warns the Hebrews to avoid, there are three things that do concur: 1. A *sinful neglect,* in not taking due notice of the ways and means whereby God calls any unto faith and obedience. 2. A *sinful forgetfulness and casting out* of the heart and mind such convictions as God by His word and works, His mercies and judgments, His deliverances and afflictions, at any time is pleased to cast into them and fasten upon them. 3. An *obstinate cleaving of the affections* unto carnal and sensual objects, practically preferring them above the motives unto obedience that God proposeth unto us. Where these things are so, the hearts of men are so hardened, that in an ordinary way they cannot hearken unto the voice of God. Such is the nature, efficacy, and power of the voice or word of God, that men cannot withstand or resist it without a sinful hardening of themselves against it.

Everyone to whom the word is duly revealed, who is not converted to God, doth *voluntarily* oppose his own obstinacy unto its efficacy and operation. If men will add new obstinacy and hardness to their minds and hearts, if they will fortify themselves against the word with prejudices and dislikes, if they will resist its work through a love to their lusts and corrupt affections, God may justly leave them to perish, and to be filled with the fruit of their own ways. This state of things is variously expressed in Scripture. As, 1. By *God's willingness* for the salvation of those to whom He grants His word as the means of their conversion (Ezek. xviii. 23, xxxiii. 11; 2 Peter iii. 9; 1 Tim. ii. 4). 2. By His *expostulations* with them that reject His word, casting all the cause of their destructions upon themselves (Matt. xxiii. 34). The gospel is proposed unto the *wills* of men (Isa. lv. 1; Rev. xxii. 17). Hence it is that the miscarriage of men under the dispensation of the word is still charged upon some *positive actings of their wills* in opposition unto it (Isa. xxx. 15; Matt. xxiii. 37; John iii. 19, v. 40). They perish not, they defeat not the end of the word towards themselves, by a mere abode and continuance in the state wherein the word finds them, but by rejecting the counsel of God made known unto them for their recovering and healing.

Many previous sins make way for the great sin of finally rejecting the voice or word of God. Hardening of the heart goes before final impenitency and infidelity, as the means and cause of it. Things do not ordinarily come to an *immediate issue* between God and them to whom the gospel is preached. He finds men in a state of nature, that is, of enmity against Him; in this state He offers them terms of peace, and waits thereon, during the season of His good pleasure, to see what the event will be. The Apostle enforces his exhortation by the words " *To-day.*" It is now " to-day " with you, it was once to-day with them of old ; but you see what a dark sad evening befell them in the close of their day ; take heed that it be not so with you. The " to-day " in the text has a special reference to the season enjoyed by the people in the wilderness who neglected it ; to those " spoken unto " by the Psalmist typically who were exhorted to use it ; and unto the present Hebrews whose gospel day was therein foretold and prefigured. ·Thus we see that Old Testament examples are New Testament instructions.

At the first preaching of the gospel some were converted, and the rest were hardened ; a signal work passed upon them all, and those who dispensed the word became a " sweet savour in them that are saved, and in them that perish." The consciences of men will discover their times. If the gospel make them not better, they will be worse, and this they may find by the search of themselves. The especial duty incumbent on men in such a day is in all things to hearken unto the voice of God.

"As in the provocation, in the day of temptation in the wilderness ; when your fathers tempted Me, proved Me, and saw My works forty years." God in His dealings with their *fathers* laid instruction for their posterity. It is a dangerous thing for children to boast of the privilege of their fathers, and to imitate their sins ; and it is a great aggravation of sin when multitudes join in it. Their sin consisted in their provoking ; the sin intended, as is evident from the story, was unbelief, acting itself by murmurings and complaints. Their murmurings, which were the fruit of their unbelief, provoked God. And this was specially so " *in the day of temptation* "—the day of Massah—where they first murmured for water and tempted God by the discovery of their unbelief. This day began upon the temptation at Massah, and continued through the whole course of their wanderings in the wilderness— their multiplied temptings of God made this whole time " a day of temptation." The people chode with Moses, but when God came to call them to account, He says they " *strove with Him and provoked Him.*"

We see from this that the sinful actings of men against those who deal with them in the name of God, and about the works or will of God, are principally against God Himself. The Lord applies this rule unto the dispensers of the gospel. He saith, " He that heareth you heareth Me ; and he that despiseth you despiseth Me ; and he that despiseth Me despiseth Him that sent Me." The preachers of the gospel are sent by Christ, and therefore to despise them is to despise Christ, and through Him God Himself. And the reason thereof is, that they act in His name and stead, as His ambassadors. The violation of an ambassador among men is always esteemed to redound unto the dishonour of him by whom he is employed. By these things God is provoked, and let us notice

that there is commonly a day, a time, wherein unbelief ariseth to
its height in provocation. This time is *uncertain*; men know not
when their provocations will come unto this height; it is also unalterable and irrecoverable. When the provocation of unbelief
reaches this height, there is no space or room left for repentance,
either on the part of God or the sinner. Let persons, let churches,
let nations take heed lest they fall unawares in this evil day.

"*When your fathers tempted Me, proved Me, and saw My works
forty years.*" When men are engaged in any way of God, according
to their duty, and meeting with difficulty and opposition therein,
if they give way to despondency and unbelief, after having received
signal pledges of His faithfulness in former effects of His wisdom,
care and power, they tempt God, and are guilty of the sin here
condemned. The most eminent instances of tempting God in the
Scripture, and which are most frequently mentioned, are these of
the Israelites in the wilderness. "They tempted the Lord, saying,
Is the Lord among us or not?" "They turned back and tempted
God, and limited the Holy One of Israel; they remembered not His
hand, nor the day when He delivered them from the enemy."
Alas! how frequently do we contract the guilt of such sins, both in
our personal, family, and public concernments.

They saw the "*works of God for forty years in the wilderness,*"
and by their unbelief they provoked God. The wilderness was the
place wherein they were brought unto liberty after the sore bondage
of Egypt; it was the place where they lived solely and visibly
upon God's extraordinary daily provision for them; it was also the
place where they had none to tempt them, to provoke them, to
entice them into sin, for the people "dwelt alone, and were not
reckoned among the nations;" and it was the place where they
continually saw the works of God, and that for forty years. All
these things greatly aggravated their guilt; they provoked God.
From their history we may learn that no place, no retiredness, no
solitary wilderness, will secure men from sin or suffering, provocation or punishment.

The principle of men's unbelief and disobedience is in themselves, and in their own hearts, which leaves them not upon any
change of their outward condition; and therefore no outward state
of things, whether voluntarily chosen by ourselves, or we be
brought into by the providence of God, will either cure, or conquer,
or restrain the inward principles of unbelief and sin. Let us
learn to look for all help against sin *merely from grace*. A wilderness will not help us, nor a paradise. In the one Adam sinned, in
whom we all sinned; in the other Israel sinned, who were an
example unto us all.

"*They saw My works forty years.*" The greater evidence God
gives of His power and goodness in any of His works, the louder is
the voice in them, and the greater the sin in those that neglect them.

God is ofttimes pleased to grant great outward means unto those in whom He does not work effectually by His grace. Outward means are granted unto men in a way of bounty, grace and favour. Their ends, singly considered, are good, holy, and righteous. Moreover, they are all of them properly effectual in that they always attain unto the end designed. And that men are not bettered by them, or more advantaged than they are, is merely from their own depravity and obstinacy. And those who approve not of this dispensation seem to have a great mind to contend with Him who is mightier than they are. There are determinate bounds fixed unto God's patience and forbearance towards obstinate sinners; so here He appointed *forty years* for the consumption of this provoking generation.

"Wherefore I was grieved with that generation, and said, They do alway err in their heart, and they have not known My ways." When God says He *"was grieved,"* He means that He was burdened, vexed, displeased beyond what forbearance could extend unto. This includes the judgment of God concerning the greatness of their sin with all its aggravations, and His determinate purpose to punish them. Men live, speak and act as if they thought God very little concerned in what they do, especially in their sins; that either He takes no notice of them, or if He do, that He is not much concerned in them; or that He should be grieved at His heart—that is, have such a deep sense of man's sinful provocations—they have no mind to think or believe. They think that, as to thoughts about sin, God is altogether as themselves. But it is far otherwise, for God hath a *concernment of honour* in what we do; He made us for His glory and honour, and whatsoever is contrary thereunto tends directly to His dishonour. And this God cannot but be deeply sensible of; He cannot deny Himself. He is also concerned as a God of *justice.* His holiness and His justice is His nature, and He needs no other reason to punish sin but Himself.

He tells us plainly why He was "grieved;" it was because *"they do alway err in their hearts, and My ways have they not known."* God places the original of all their miscarriages in their error, the *error of their hearts.* Through the power of their lusts and darkness, their temptations and obstinacy, they did in many instances judge that sin and rebellion were better for them than faith, submission and obedience; so they erred in their hearts. Not only so, they *always* erred; in all instances, whenever it came to a trial, they practically chose the wrong side, and having erred they continued in their error.

"And My ways have they not known." As they erred in their hearts because they liked the ways of sin, so they disliked the ways of God, because they knew them not, and from both they rushed into all manner of provocations and miscarriages. Let us here

observe, 1. In all the sins of men, God chiefly regards the principle, that is, the heart, or what is in it.   2. The error of the heart in preferring the ways of sin before obedience, with its promises and rewards, is the root of all great provoking sins and rebellions against God.

3. A constant persistency in a course of sin is the utmost, highest, and last aggravation of sin ; for it includes a neglect and contempt of all times and seasons of amendment.   God gives unto men, especially those who live under the dispensation of His word, many peculiar times or seasons for their recovery.   They have their day, their special day, wherein they ought in an especial manner to look after the things of their peace ; and it may be this day is often revived, often returned upon them, but it is as often despised and neglected by them.   It also includes a rejection of the means of repentance which God is pleased graciously to afford unto them.   During the season of His patience towards sinners, God is pleased to grant unto them sundry means and advantages for their amendment, and that in great variety ; but they are all rejected and rendered fruitless in an unchanged course of sinning. It also includes a contempt of the whole work of conscience, from first to last ; many assistances does conscience receive in its work— convictions from the word, warnings by judgments, mercies, dangers, deliverances, but all its actings are baffled.   And what more can be done against God ?   What can add to the guilt of such sin and sinners ?   And this may serve to justify God in His severity against those who do " alway err in their hearts," that continue in a course of sinning.

4. None despise nor desert the ways of God but those who know them not.   They had seen the works of God in the wilderness, they had heard Himself proclaim His own law, yet they were unbelieving and obdurate, " they knew not the ways of God."

" **So I sware in My wrath, They shall not enter into My rest.** "   This is the issue of the sin before declared ; this sentence of God against this people, after all their temptations and provocations, is *irrevocable*, He confirmed it by His oath.   From this we may see the greatness of their sin, in the great offence that God took at it ; He sware in His wrath, in great indignation.   The sentence was that they should not enter the land of Canaan, no, not so much as put one foot within its borders.   In the wording of this sentence there is a great aggravation of the punishment inflicted.   He doth not swear that they shall not enter into the land of Canaan, the promised land, but " they shall not enter into My rest."   He saith, " It is My rest, the place where I will dwell, where I will fix My worship and make Myself known, but you shall not enter therein."

We may observe, 1. When God expresseth great indignation in Himself against sin, it is to teach men the greatness of sin in themselves. 2. God gives the same stability unto His threatenings as unto His promises. Men are apt to think the *promises* are firm and stable, but as for the threatenings, they suppose some way or other they may be evaded. 3. When men have provoked God by their impenitency to decree their punishment irrevocably, they will find severity in the execution. 4. It is the presence of God alone that renders any place or condition good or desirable. " They shall not enter into My rest." This " My rest " makes heaven to be heaven, and the Church to be the Church; everything answers the manner and the presence of God. Without this, Moses expressly preferred the wilderness before Canaan.

Vs. 12—14. *Take heed, brethren, lest there be in any of you an evil heart of unbelief, in departing from the living God. But exhort one another daily, while it is called To-day ; lest any of you be hardened through the deceitfulness of sin. For we are made partakers of Christ, if we hold the beginning of our confidence stedfast unto the end.*

" **Take heed, brethren.** " The Apostle renews his former (v. 1) affectionate compellation. By this form of addressing them he would remove all jealousies, and let them know that the best of saints have need to be cautioned against the worst of evils. To " take heed " is to use great care, heedfulness, circumspection, with respect to danger and opposition. To "take heed " is to duly consider our danger, with a due consideration of the especial nature of those snares and dangers unto which we are exposed ; it is so to take heed as to endeavour to avoid them, and that in all their occasions, causes, advantages in their whole work and effects. It is to consider, so as to oppose them, and this consisteth in being always ready and standing upon your guard ; in calling in help and assistance ; and in improving the supplies granted with faith and diligence.

" **Lest there be in any of you an evil heart of unbelief.** " The Apostle speaks unto them collectively, to take care that there be none such found amongst them—none with such a heart as he cautions them against. And this consequently falls on each individual, for where all are spoken unto, each one is concerned. Observe, 1. That godly jealousy concerning, and watchfulness over the whole body, that no beginnings of backsliding from Christ and the gospel be found amongst them, is the duty of all churches of believers. 2. That it is the duty of each individual believer to be intent on all occasions, lest at any time, or by any means, there should be found in him an " evil heart of unbelief."

" **In departing from the living God.** " The Apostle, in earnestly cautioning against these evils, points out the *principle* of them—" *an evil heart of unbelief,*" and then the work or effect of that

principle—"*departing from the living God.*" Not an unbelieving
heart, but an "evil heart of unbelief," that is, a heart under the
power of unbelief and principled by its actings. Unbelief is spoken
of as negative and privative, that is, positive. The former is when
men believe not, never having had the means of believing granted
unto them. In this sense all those persons who have never as yet
heard the gospel are unbelievers ; they believe not, but cannot be
said to have an "evil heart of unbelief."

It is privative, that is, positive, when men believe not, although
they enjoy the means of believing. And herein consist the highest
actings of the depraved nature of man. And on many accounts it
is the greatest provocation of God that a creature can make himself guilty of. Hence the gospel, which is a declaration of grace,
mercy, and pardon, though it condemns all sin, yet it pronounceth
the final condemnation of persons only against this sin : "He that
believeth shall be saved ; but he that believeth not shall be
damned." This unbelief either refuses to believe when it is
required ; or it rejects the faith after it hath been received.

As to the first of these, three things do render the unbelief of
men positive : 1. A revelation of the things to be believed made
known in the way of God. 2. Sufficient evidence given unto the
thing proposed. 3. A just assertion of the authority of God
requiring faith and obedience. Now as this unbelief hath its root in
the natural darkness and blindness of the minds of men, so it is
acted out not without new sinful prejudices and stubbornness of
the will, refusing to attend unto and consider the evidences that are
given unto the truth proposed.

Some instances may clear these particulars. 1. The root of
unbelief is the original depravity of our natures, with that spiritual
impotency and enmity to God wherein it doth consist. There is
such an impotency in us by nature, that no man of himself, by his
own strength, can believe, can come to Christ. None can believe
except they are specially taught of God (John vi. 44, 45). Men in
a state of nature neither can nor will believe the gospel.

2. Besides this general cause of unbelief, when it comes to
special instances, and the gospel is proposed unto this or that man,
for his assent and submission unto it, there is always *some especial
corruption of the mind or will*, voluntarily acted, if the soul be kept
off from believing; and on the account there of principally, and not
merely of original impotency and enmity against God, is the guilt
of unbelief reflected upon the souls of sinners. Some are kept off
believing the gospel by *inveterate prejudices in their minds* ; this shut
up most of the Jews in unbelief. This manifested itself in an
especial obstinacy of will, strengthened by those prejudices. So our
Saviour saith to the Pharisees, "Ye will not come to Me that ye
might have life." They put forth a positive act of their wills in
rejecting Him, and on this account the guilt of their unbelief is

absolutely resolved unto their own wills. And whether it be discovered or no, this is the condition with many in all times and seasons.

3. *Love of sin* is with some the immediate cause of their actual unbelief. The light of the gospel comes into a place; they come so near it as to discover its aims and tendency, but so soon as they find that it aims to part them and their sins, they will have no more to do with it. And on this account doth condemnation follow the preaching of the gospel, though its own proper end be salvation, and that only. And this is the common way of ruin of souls; they like not the terms of the gospel, because of their love of sin, and so perish in and for their iniquities.

4. *Stupid ignorance*, arising from the possessing of the minds of men with other things, inconsistent with the faith and obedience of the gospel, through the craft and subtilty of Satan, is another cause of positive unbelief. How is the gospel hindered from shining into the hearts of men? It is by the *darkness and blindness* of their minds. But what darkness is this—that which is common and natural unto all men? No, but that which is in a peculiar manner brought into the minds of some men by the craft and deceits of the god of this world. And these things fully clear the holiness and righteousness of God (I have only mentioned a few of the many instances that might be given) in His judgments against final and impenitent unbelievers to whom the gospel is preached; for as that *impotency* which is in them naturally is culpable—and it is no excuse for them not believing, because of themselves they could not do so, seeing it is by their own default they are brought into this condition—so everyone in his own person who believeth not, doth, by a voluntary act of his will, reject the gospel, and that on such corrupt principles as none can deny to be his sin.

But there is an unbelief that consists in a rejection of the truth of the gospel after it hath been admitted, acknowledged and professed. Hereof is frequent mention made in the gospel, and no less frequent caution against it. And this in general is the highest aggravation of this sin. There is great difficulty in being recovered out of this condition. He who hath made a trial of the gospel, and then casts contempt upon it, who declares that he valueth it not, renders his recovery difficult, almost impossible. Again, there is a degree of this unbelief which puts a soul absolutely into an irrecoverable condition. This is the sin against the Holy Ghost; there must be a renunciation of truth known and professed, or the guilt of that sin cannot be contracted. This sin is peculiar to them who have made a profession, and from this ariseth an especial aggravation of their punishment at the last day. (2 Peter ii. 21.)

There may be a partial rejection of the gospel as to some degrees. Of this the Apostle treats in this place, also chap. iv. 11-13, and chap. xii. 15, 16. There may be a total rejection of the gospel ; of this the Apostle treats in chap. vi. 4-6, chap. x. 26, 27. It is of the former the Apostle here speaks—declension of the heart from Christ and the gospel in various degrees and on various accounts.

Such partial rejection of the gospel *consists in the soul's receiving impressions from arguments and reasonings against profession,* in the whole or some degrees of it. Innumerable are the inclinations, objections, temptations, that lie against the profession of the gospel, especially in times of difficulty, and particularly against stedfastness and preciseness in profession. That the whole of it be laid aside, or the degrees of it be remitted, is the great design of Satan, the world, and the flesh. It also consists in a secret dislike of something in the gospel ; unbelief dislikes the purity, simplicity, and spirituality of gospel worship ; also the severity and universality of obedience which the gospel requireth ; also the grace and mystery of the gospel.

And these things have been spoken unto to discover the nature and the work of that unbelief which the Apostle here warns all professors concerning. The root of all apostacy, of all back-sliding, whether it be gradual or total, lies in unbelief ; this unbelief tends to "*departing from the living God.*" It is plain that it is apostacy from the profession of the gospel that is intended. In a recession from the gospel or doctrine of Christ, God Himself is forsaken. He then that rejects Christ in the gospel, let him pretend what he will of adhering unto one God, he hath forsaken the "living God," and cleaves unto an idol of his own heart. Therefore, whosoever departs from the observation of the gospel and the institutions thereof, doth in so doing depart from the living God ; or an apostate from the gospel is an apostate from God. Let us all know what care and reverence becomes us in the things of the gospel. God is in them, even the living God. Otherwise He will neither be known nor worshipped.

" But exhort one another daily, while it is called To-day ; lest any of you be hardened through the deceitfulness of sin." To "*exhort*" is to persuade with good, meek and comfortable words, upon grounds of consolation, and unto that end that men may be comforted. The season of doing this is " To-day," that is daily, and every day. The exhortation implies a *constant readiness* of mind inclining, inducing and preparing one for the discharge of this duty ; also an *actual discharge* of it on all just occasions, which are to be watched for, and willingly embraced. Be sedulous in the discharge of this duty, whilst the season of it doth continue. The Apostle declares to these Hebrews the great day, the great season of old shadowed out unto their forefathers, was now really and actually come upon them. The Apostle saw that this day of the Hebrews was almost ready to expire. It continued but a few years after his writing this epistle.

He says, "Lest any of you"—believing Hebrews—"be hardened." He states the cause of the evil that is to be feared, and that is "the deceitfulness of sin," the habitual deceit that is in indwelling sin, whereby it seduceth men and draweth them off from God. The design of the Apostle is to prescribe a duty unto them, whereby they might be preserved from being hardened through the deceitfulness of sin. Observe, 1. That sedulous mutual exhortation is an eminent means to obviate and prevent the design of the deceitfulness of sin. 2. Gospel duties have an especial efficacy in them in their special seasons, "while it is called To-day." 3. We have but an uncertain time for the due performance of most certain duties. How long it will be called "To-day" we know not. The day of our life is uncertain; so is the day of the gospel, as also of our opportunities therein. 4. The deceit which is in sin, and which is inseparable from it, tends continually to the hardening of the heart. This is that which is principally taught us in these words, and it is a truth of very great importance unto us.

"**For we are made partakers of Christ, if we hold the beginning of our confidence firm unto the end.**" A present state is here declared, that which is already wrought and partaken of. How then are we made partakers of Christ? It is by our having an interest in His nature, by the communication of His Spirit, even as He had in ours by the assumption of our flesh. It is then union with Christ that is intended, whereby we are made "members of His body, of His flesh, and of His bones." "*If we hold the beginning of our confidence firm unto the end.*" It is by all agreed that, for the substance of it, the same is here intended as in v. 6. But the expression here used is difficult, and hath left an impression of its difficulty on most translations and expositions. We have just shown that our partaking of Christ is our being *united* unto Him, and the confession, which on that union we are bound to hold fast, is our subsistence in Christ, our abiding in Him, as the branches in the vine. Our subsistence in Christ is twofold, either by *profession* only, or by *real union;* and the trial of which it is of these we are partakers of depends on our perseverance. I shall only add here that the Apostle, by joining himself with these Hebrews—"if we hold fast"—shows that this is a general and perpetual rule for professors, and the touchstone of their profession, by which it may be tried at the last day.

Observe, 1. That union with Christ is the principle and measure of all spiritual enjoyments and expectations. Our union with Christ, our participation of Him, consists in the inhabitation of the same Spirit in Him and in us, and the work of this Spirit given unto us is to form Christ in us, whereby our union is completed. 2. Constancy and stedfastness in believing is the great touchstone, trial, and evidence of union with Christ. We are "partakers of

Christ "—that is declared, manifested so to be—" if we hold fast the beginning of our confidence stedfast unto the end." 3. Persistency in our confidence in Christ unto the end is a matter of great endeavour and diligence, and that unto all believers. It is true that our persistency in Christ doth not, as to the issue and event, depend absolutely on our own diligence. The *unalterableness of our union with Christ*, on the account of the faithfulness of the covenant of grace, is that which doth and shall eventually secure it. But yet our own diligent endeavour is such an indispensable means for that end as that without it it will never be brought about. Hence are many cautions given us in this and other epistles that we should take heed of apostacy and falling away ; and these cautions and warnings are given unto all true believers, that they may know how indispensably necessary, from the appointment of God, and the nature of the thing itself, is their watchful diligence and endeavour unto their abiding in Christ.

V. 15. *While it is said, To-day if ye will hear His voice, harden not your hearts, as in the provocation.*

These words are to be taken as a repetition of the former testimony (vs. 7, 8), and their improvement unto some further end. He makes use of the history to enforce his exhortation. Every circumstance of Scripture history is instructive. In the case in hand the Apostle shows who they were that sinned and provoked God ; " some " of them that came out of Egypt but " not all," and we shall see presently what use he makes of this. He shows also what became of those that sinned, " Their carcases fell in the wilderness ; " he also presseth in the consideration of the oath of God, and manifests its exact accomplishment; and lastly he shows what was evidently the direct and special sin that procured so great a destruction, and excluded that people out of the rest of God—it was their " unbelief."

V. 16. *For some, when they had heard, did provoke : howbeit not all that came out of Egypt.*

What they heard is declared before; it was, " *the voice of God.*" Their great provocation lay in this, that they had heard the word, law,٠voice of God. Great provocations have a "bitterness" in them which causeth God to loathe the provokers. By these considerations doth the Apostle enforce his exhortation, before insisted on, that they would diligently attend unto the word of the gospel, and stedfastly continue in the profession thereof. As people provoked God in that dispensation of law, so may they also now who hear His voice in the gospel provoke Him, therefore doth it highly concern them to take diligent heed that this be not the event of their mercy therein.

"**Howbeit not all.**" It is certain that the special reference is to Caleb and Joshua; these men eminently believed and obeyed the voice of God; and this could not be said of all those "under twenty years of age" who perished not in the wilderness. Let us observe, 1. Many hear the word of God to no advantage, but only to aggravate their sin. Their hearing renders their sin provoking unto God, and destructive unto their own souls. They—the Israelites—heard the voice of Him that spake on earth; we, His who speaks from heaven. And what is the issue with us? Plainly some neglect the word, some corrupt it, some despise it; few mix faith with it, or yield obedience unto it. The dispensers of the gospel may for the most part take up the complaint of the prophet, "Who hath believed our report?" or the Apostle's appeal unto the unbelieving Jews, "Behold, ye despisers, and wonder and perish." Most of them that heard our Saviour preach perished. They got nothing by hearing His doctrine, through their unbelief, but an aggravation of their sin and a hastening of their ruin. His presence and preaching "lifted them up to heaven," but their unbelief brought them into a worse condition than that of Sodom—they "were brought down to hell." It is, I confess, a great privilege for men to have the word preached unto them, but privileges are as men use them. Hence the gospel becomes to some "a savour of death unto death."

2. In the most general and visible apostacies of the Church, God still preserves a remnant unto Himself, to bear witness unto Him and for Him by their faith and obedience. "*They provoked; howbeit not all.*"

3. God lays a few, sometimes a very few, of His secret ones in the balance against the greatest multitude of rebels and transgressors. They that provoked God were about six hundred thousand men, and upon this particular matter two only opposed them. But in the language of the Holy Ghost, that great multitude were but "some"—some, not "all"—the principal part was preserved in those who were obedient. They were His portion, inheritance, jewels, dear unto Him as the apple of His eye, and deservedly preferred unto the greatest heap of chaff and rubbish.

Vs. 17, 18.   *But with whom was He grieved forty years? [was it] not with them that had sinned, whose carcases fell in the wilderness? And to whom sware He that they should not enter into His rest, but to them that believed not?*

There were three sorts of sins of which the people were guilty in the wilderness. 1. They were universally guilty of *personal sins;* 2. Of *especial provocations* wherein numbers, but not the whole congregation, were engaged ; and 3. *General sins* of the whole congregation, and it is this last kind of sin in the guilt of which the whole congregation was involved, that the Apostle here intends by the words, "*them that sinned.*" Public sins, sins in societies, are great provocations of God. God help cities and nations, especially such as hear the voice of God, well to consider it, and all of us to take heed to national sins.

"**Whose carcases fell in the wilderness.**" He doth not say, "they died," but their "carcases fell," which intimates contempt and indignation ; God sometimes will make men who have been wickedly exemplary in sin, righteously exemplary in their punishment. The Apostle saith, "They sinned, and provoked God," and their "carcases fell in the wilderness." To what end is this reported ? It is that we may take heed that we "fall not after the same example of unbelief" (chap. iv. 11). There is then an example in the fall and punishment of unbelievers.

"**And to whom sware He that they should not enter into His rest, but to them that believed not ?**" This " believed not "—unbelief—hath principally to do with the promise of God to give them the land of Canaan, and His power to effect it ; they would *not believe* that He could or would bring them into that land ; but yet because they were under the command of God to go up and possess it, their unbelief was accompanied with disobedience and rebellion. This was sufficient to justify God in His severity against them in His oath, and the execution of it. Two things concur in unbelief : first, an *unpersuadableness of mind*, and that against evident convincing reasons ; and second, *a positive act of the will* in opposition unto and rejection of the things proposed unto it. Now, if among the arguments used to persuade the mind, that of supreme authority be one, then *rebellion* is added unto disobedience and stubbornness. (Rom. x. 21.)

Objections against believing may arise, 1. On the part of Him that is the author of the things to be believed, and that either as unto His power and faithfulness or as unto His will, goodness and grace. Or, 2. They may arise on the part of the things themselves proposed to be believed, and that either that they are not good and desirable in themselves ; or, that they are not needful ; or, that they are not adequate or suited unto the end for which they are proposed. Or, 3. They may arise on the part of the persons themselves required to believe, and that either because they are too hard and difficult to attain ; or because they are too good for them to expect ; or because they are too far above them to understand. But all these objections are obviated and prevented in the gospel. And no ground is left unto any sinner, whereon he may manage any of them, against the exhortations and commands of the gospel to believe.

"*And to whom sware He.*" The oath of God is engaged against no sin but unbelief. These things belong unto us, and they may be improved unto the use of all sorts of persons, as, 1. Unto them that have never much considered their duty or concernment in this matter. I intend not now, open and profligate sinners, but I aim at those whose consciences are so far awakened, that they abstain from sin and do good with respect unto their latter end. They would be saved from the "wrath to come;" but as to believing the gospel, or mixing the promise of the gospel with faith, they have not endeavoured after it, or do not at all understand it. But with whom is God provoked? Concerning whom doth He swear that they shall not enter into His rest? Is it not against you, and such as you who believe not, whilst you continue in this state and condition?

2. Unto those who are in doubt as to whether they should believe or no, not notionally and indefinitely, but practically and in particular. This is the state of many; which causeth them to fluctuate all their days. But what is it that they doubt of in this matter? Is it whether it be their duty to believe or no?—this is indispensably required of them by the command of God, so that not to do so is the greatest act of disobedience of which they can be guilty. Is it whether they may do so or no, and whether they shall find acceptance with God in so doing?—this calls the righteousness and faithfulness of God in question. Is it because of the many objections which they find rising up within themselves, which leave them no hope of a participation of the good things promised? But what are all these objections before those evidences which are tendered in the gospel unto the contrary? The truth is, if men will not believe, it is out of love to sin and a dislike of the design of God to glorify Himself by Jesus Christ; and what will be the issue thereof hath been declared; the oath of God is engaged that you shall not enter into His rest.

3. Unto believers. Meat may be taken for them out of this eater. All this terror and dread of God's severity speaks peace and consolation unto their souls; for as the oath of Jehovah is engaged against the entrance of unbelievers into His rest; so also is it engaged for the eternal security of them that do believe.

V. 19. *So we see that they could not enter in because of unbelief.*

It is evident **"that they could not enter in;"** and it is evident that the reason was **" because of unbelief."** This is a sin that men are very unapt to charge upon themselves; but it is that which above all others will be charged upon them by God. From this let us observe, 1. Whatever we consider in sin, God principally considers the root and spring of it in unbelief, as that which maketh the most direct and immediate opposition against Him.

2. Unbelief is the immediate root and cause of all provoking sins. As our obedience follows in proportion to our faith, so do all our sins and irregularities answer the working and prevalency of unbelief in us.

3. Unbelief deprives men of all interest in or right unto the promises of God. There was a promise given this people of their being brought into the land of Canaan; but yet they entered not into it—they died in the wilderness. How came this to pass? The Apostle here declares that they disinherited themselves, and lost all interest in the promise by their unbelief. And let not others entertain better hopes of their condition hereafter, whilst here they follow their example, for—

4. No unbeliever shall ever enter into the rest of God; which, if the Lord will and we live, shall be confirmed in our considerations on the next chapter.

CHAPTER FOUR

Vs. 1, 2. Let us therefore fear, lest, a promise being left [us] of entering into His rest, any of you should seem to come short of it. For unto us was the gospel preached, as well as unto them : but the word preached did not profit them, not being mixed with faith in them that heard [it].

" **Let us therefore fear.**" An instance and example of God's severity against unbelievers is laid down and proposed unto our consideration in the preceding discourse. In this example of God's dealing with them of old, the Apostle declares that there is included a threatening of dealing with all others in the same manner, who shall fall into the same sin of unbelief with them. In this word "*fear,*" two things are intended; first, An apprehension of the holiness and greatness of God, with His severity against sin; second, A careful diligence in the use of means to avoid the evil threatened unto unbelief and disobedience.

Gospel threatenings respect *professed unbelievers*; they are called gospel inasmuch as they are proper to the gospel, and distinct from the threatenings of the law. The law knows no more of gospel threatenings than of gospel promises. The threatenings of the law lie against sinners for sins committed ; the threatenings of the gospel are against sinners for refusing the remedy provided and tendered unto them. Gospel threatenings have respect unto all those who are *unsound and temporary believers.*

And this duty is always incumbent on them to whom the dispensation of the gospel is committed, to declare these threatenings against all that may be found in this condition. For not only may they justly suppose that such there are, and always will be, in all churches, but also many do continually declare and evidence themselves to be in no better state. Gospel threatenings have respect unto *believers* themselves; their design is to work them from their unbelief and to confirm them in their faith. This *"fear"* includes, a serious consideration of the due debt of sin, and the necessary vindication of God's glory; also a consideration of the greatness, terror, and majesty of God; also a conviction and acknowledgment that in the justice and righteousness of God the punishments threatened might befall us; also an abhorrency of all sin, both with respect unto its nature and its end; also a sedulous watching against all sin, with a diligent use of the means appointed thereunto; also a constant watchfulness against all carnal confidence and security.

"**Lest a promise being left us of entering into His rest.**" There is then in the gospel a promise left unto believers of entering into His rest, that is, the rest of God. The "rest" here spoken of cannot be the rest of heaven and glory as some have affirmed, wholly misunderstanding the argument of the Apostle, which is the superiority of Christ over Moses, that is, the dispensation which is committed unto Christ, and that dispensation which was committed unto Moses. The design of the Apostle is to set out the excellency of the gospel with the worship of it, and the Church state whereinto we are now called by Christ Jesus, above all the privileges and advantages which the people of old were made partakers of under Moses. If this be not duly considered, no part of the epistle can be rightly understood. The rest here intended is that rest which believers have an entrance into by Jesus Christ in this world.

This rest consisteth of five things. 1. *In peace with God* in the free and full justification of the person of believers from all their sins by the blood of Christ. This is fully expressed in Acts xiii. **32, 33, 38, 39.** The whole of what we contend for is contained in these words. 2. In our *freedom from a servile bondage-frame of spirit* in the worship of God. 3. In our *deliverance from the yoke and bondage of Mosaical institutions.* 4. In that *gospel worship* whereunto we are called; this is the rest of liberty and freedom of spirit which believers have in obedience unto the gospel; also of strength and assistance granted unto the worshippers for the performance of their worship in an acceptable manner; and then the worship itself is not grievous but easy, and suited unto the principles of the new nature of the worshippers. 5. In its being *God's rest*, and by entering into it believers enter into the rest of God. It is called God's rest, because He resteth ultimately and absolutely, as to all the ends of His glory, in Christ, as exhibited in the gospel; that is, in Him in whom His "soul delighteth," and in whom "He is well pleased." Through Him, He rests in His love to believers. As of old, in the sacrifices, He "smelled a savour of rest;" so now in Christ He is expressly said to "rest in His love" towards Zion.

It is also called "*His rest*" because gospel worship, or worship according to the gospel, is that which He requireth unchangeably in this world; He will not make any additions unto that which is already appointed and instituted by Christ; nor is it liable to any alteration or change unto the consummation of all things. It is a matter of great and tremendous consequence to have the promises of God left and proposed unto us; they are "left us," in the sense of being made known to us in the dispensation of the word; and in a day, time, or season of patience being left unto us, wherein we may enter in.

The *whole love, goodness and grace* of God towards mankind, the infinite wisdom of the counsel of His will about their salvation, are contained and exhibited in the promise. Severe will be the issue of so much love and kindness despised, as is set before men in the gospel. The failing of men through their unbelief doth no way cause the promise of God to fail or cease. "Not as though the word of God (that is, the word of the promise) hath taken none effect." Whosoever, and how so ever many reject the promise, yet they do it to their own ruin; the promise shall have its effect in others, even in those whom God hath graciously ordained unto a participation in it.

Men by their unbelief may disappoint themselves of their expectation, but cannot rob God of His faithfulness. And therefore, when the gospel is preached unto any nation, city, or assembly, the glory and success of it doth not depend upon the wills of them to whom it is preached, neither is it frustrated by their unbelief. God hath blessed ends in granting the outward dispensation of the promises, even unto them by whom they are rejected. Hence the Apostle tells us, that those who preach the gospel are a sweet savour of Christ unto God, as well in them that perish as in them that are saved. Christ is glorified, and God in and by Him, in the dispensation of the gospel, whether men receive it or no.

"Lest any of you should seem to come short of it." Any one of you; the Apostle regarded them all so in general, as that he had a regard to each one of them in particular. To "*seem to come short*" means: Let there be no semblance or appearance of any such thing among you. The allusion in the expression "*to come short*" is to the people in the wilderness; most of them were heavy through unbelief, lagged in their progress, and were, as it were, left behind in the wilderness, where they perished, and came short of entering into the promised land. Observe, 1. That many to whom the promise of the gospel is proposed and preached do or may, through their own sins, come short of the enjoyment of the things promised. That sentence of our Saviour contains the lot and state of men under the dispensation of the gospel : "Many are called, but few are chosen." It is true "faith cometh by hearing," but bare hearing will denominate no man a true believer. Men would indeed probably esteem the gospel, if it would save them merely at the cost and pains of others preaching it. But God hath otherwise disposed of things ; their own faith and obedience are indispensably required thereunto.

2. Not only backsliding through unbelief, but all appearances of hesitation in profession in times of trial and difficulty ought to be carefully avoided. Not only a profession, but the beauty and glory of it, is required of us. These consist in personal holiness, righteousness, and upright universal obedience ; also in the due observance of all the commands, ordinances, and institutions of Christ in the gospel. The danger is great in any neglect of these things ; our corrupt nature is apt to compensate in the conscience the neglect of one duty by diligence in another; so you will see many diligent in the use of outward means who attend not unto personal holiness. This is the ruin of most hypocrites and false professors.

Let us be especially diligent to secure in our own persons, families, and whole conversation in the world, a diligent attendance unto all manner of holiness, in all faith, love, humility, patience, purity, self-denial, weanedness from the world, readiness to do good; and let these things be bright in us and shine in our lives, if we would not seem to come short. God hath no regard unto the observance of ordinances, where duties of holiness, righteousness, and love are neglected.

They who mix not the promises of the gospel with faith shall utterly come short of entering into the rest of God. And this the Apostle proceeds to demonstrate.

" **For unto us was the gospel preached as well as unto them.**" The gospel was preached unto them in the wilderness ; the promise made unto Abraham did contain the substance of the gospel. All the typical institutions of the law had no other end but to instruct the people in the meaning, nature and manner of the accomplishment of the promise. With the spiritual part of the promise made unto Abraham, there was annexed unto it a promise of the land of Canaan, the fulfilment of which was to be a pledge of the love, power, and faithfulness of God, in accomplishing the spiritual and invisible part of the promise, that is, the gospel, in sending the blessing and the blessed Seed to save and deliver from sin and death, and to give rest to the souls of them that do believe.

Observe, 1. It is a signal privilege to have the gospel preached unto us—to be "evangelized." 2. Barely to be evangelized—to have the gospel preached—is a privilege of dubious issue and event. If herein we fail, that which should have been for our good will be for our snare. 3. The gospel is no new doctrine, no new law ; it was preached unto the people of old. In the preaching of the gospel by the Lord Jesus Himself and His apostles, it was new in respect of the manner of its administration with sundry circumstances of light, evidence, and power, with which it was accompanied ; but as to the substance of it, the gospel is " that which was from the beginning." (1 John i. 1.) The promise of Christ was given from the foundation of the world. "The seed of the woman shall bruise the serpent's head ; " this is the sum and substance of the gospel. From all which it appears, that from first to last, the gospel is and ever was the only way of coming unto God, and to think of any other way or means for that end is both highly vain and exceedingly derogatory to the glory of God's wisdom, faithfulness and holiness.

" **But the word preached did not profit them, not being mixed with faith in them that heard it.**" The " word preached " is the " word of hearing ; " that is, the word is so managed by God that we may hear it, otherwise we could have no advantage by it. The " word of hearing," then, is the " promise preached," and as preached. But this did not profit, for we find that, notwithstanding the promise of entering into the rest of God— the land of Canaan—they entered not in. It was so far from benefiting them that it became their ruin. It is as if the Apostle said, " Consider what befell them, how they perished in the wilderness under the indignation of God, and you will see how far they had any advantage by the word which they heard. And such will be the issue with all that shall neglect the word in like manner."

The cause of their ruin was that the word was not " *mixed with faith in them that heard it.*" The sum of these words is, that spiritual truths, in order to be savingly believed, must be united with that faith which receives them, so that they become incorporated into the principle of that new nature whereby we live unto God. Observe, 1. God hath graciously ordered that the word of the gospel shall be preached unto men, whereon depends their welfare or ruin ; this the Scriptures testify everywhere.

2. The sole cause of the gospel being ineffectual unto salvation in and towards them to whom it is preached is in themselves and in their own unbelief. This the Apostle expressly asserts. The word preached did not profit, not being mixed with faith. God hath not appointed to save men whether they will or no ; nor is the word of the promise suited unto any such end or purpose. It is enough that in every way it is sufficient unto the end whereunto of God it is designed. If men believe it not, no wonder if they perish in their sins.

3. The great mystery of useful and profitable believing consists

in the mixing, or incorporating, of faith and truth in the souls or minds of believers.

The promise of the gospel is peculiar, divine, supernatural; and therefore for the receiving it God requireth in us, and bestoweth upon us, a peculiar, divine, supernatural habit, by which our minds may be enabled to receive it. This is "*faith*"—" not of ourselves, it is the gift of God." Now, "faith is the substance of things hoped for," not absolutely and physically, but morally and in respect of use. It brings the things into, makes them present with, and gives them a subsistence as to their use, efficacy and comfort in the soul. For instance, the death of Christ, or "Christ crucified," is proposed unto our faith in the gospel. The genuine, proper effect hereof is to destroy, mortify and crucify sin in us.

By faith we receive the " ingrafted word," and the effect of receiving that word is to cast out the filth and superfluity of evil within us, and to cast us into the mould, type, and image of the word. Hence the word of Christ is said to "dwell in us." Without this inhabitation of the word, it may have various effects upon us, but it comes to no abiding; it comes and departs like lightning, which rather amazeth than guideth. Constant fixing the mind by spiritual meditation on its proper object—the word of God—will be a principal means whereby faith mixeth it with itself. This faith sets *love* at work upon the objects proposed to be believed. There is in the gospel and its promises not only the truth to be considered, but also the goodness, excellency, desirableness of the things themselves which are comprised therein.

V. 3.   *For we which have believed do enter into rest, as He said, As I have sworn in My wrath, If they shall enter into My rest : although the works were finished from the foundation of the world.*

" For we which have believed do enter into rest." Into that rest, the promised rest. This rest is principally that spiritual rest of God which believers obtain an entrance into by Jesus Christ, in the faith and the worship of the gospel, as we have already shown. It is by faith we have an actual personal interest in this rest, with all the privileges wherewith it is attended ; but it is only an *entrance into rest*; look at what is past, what we are delivered and secured from, and it is a glorious rest. But look unto what is to come, and it is but a passage into a more glorious rest. So that we say that the state of believers now under the gospel is a state of blessed rest, it is God's rest and theirs ; this rest consisteth of peace with God, satisfaction and acquiescency with God, and means of communion with God. All these were lost by the entrance of sin; in the restoration of these, and that in a better and more secure way, doth this gospel rest consist. This spiritual inward rest in and with God is not inconsistent with outward, temporal trouble in the world. No outward thing, no possible opposition shall prevail to cast us out of that rest which we have obtained an entrance into, or impede our future entrance into eternal rest with God.

" As He said, As I have sworn in My wrath, If they shall enter into My rest." For proving that those who believe under the gospel do enter into rest, from these words of the Psalmist, " if they shall enter into My rest," it was incumbent on him to manifest that the rest intended in these words had respect unto the rest of the gospel, which was now preached, and entered into by all that believed. He proceeds to consider the various rests that are on various accounts, in the Scriptures, called the rest of God, and he concludes that after all other rests formerly enjoyed by the people of God were past, there yet remained a rest for them under the Messiah, which was the rest principally intended by David's prophetic words. This is the design of the ensuing discourse, which he introduces somewhat abruptly.

" Although the works were finished from the founda= tion of the world." In these words the Apostle begins his answer unto such objections as his former assertion, concerning the entrance of believers into God's rest under the gospel, seems to be liable unto. And this he does by showing that God rested from all His works which were finished from the foundation of the world, and therefore this cannot be the rest to which He refers as " My rest " in David's psalm, and concerning which rest He says, " there remaineth a rest." That rest then must be future.

V. 4.   *For He spake in a certain place of the seventh [day] on this wise, And God did rest the seventh day from all His works.*

The sum of what here is laid down is, that from the foundation of the world there was a work of God, and a rest ensuing thereon, and an entrance proposed unto men into that rest, and a day of rest given as a pledge thereof, which yet is not the rest intended by the Psalmist, as we shall see as we proceed.

V. 5.   *And in this [place] again, If they shall enter into My rest.*

So, then, there was another rest of God, besides that upon the creation of all, as is evident from this place, which he further confirms in the next verse.

V. 6.   *Seeing therefore it remaineth that some must enter therein, and they to whom it was first preached entered not in because of unbelief.*

The substance of this verse is that besides the rest of God from the foundation of the world, and the institution of the seventh day —Sabbath—as a pledge thereof, there was another rest for men to enter into, namely, the rest of God and His worship in the land of Canaan. This being proposed unto the people of old, they entered not into it, by reason of their unbelief.

V. 7. *Again, He limiteth a certain day, saying in David, To-day, after so long a time ; as it is said, To-day if ye will hear His voice, harden not your hearts.*

The Apostle's argument is this, that after the constitution of the sabbatical rest, and the proposition of the rest of Canaan to the people in the wilderness, God, besides them, hath limited, determined another day, which was neither of the former. This must needs, therefore, be " another day," and that can be no other but the day of the gospel. In this verse he lays great stress on the time of entering into the rest of the gospel—" To-day ; " whence he educeth the great mystery of a gospel rest. Observe from these words, 1. That in reading and hearing the Scripture we ought to hear God speaking in it and by it unto us. God spake " in David," and by David He speaks unto us. And this also concerns the word preached ; provided that those who preach it are sent of God ; that what is preached be according to the analogy of faith ; that it be drawn from the written word ; and that it be delivered in the name and authority of God. 2. The Holy Scripture is an inexhaustible treasury of spiritual mysteries and sacred truths, many of which lie deep and secret, and stand in need of diligent search and hard digging in their investigation and for their finding out. Let us endeavour in all inquirings into the word to mind and aim at the same ends which God hath in the granting of it unto us.

V. 8. *For if Jesus had given them rest, then would He not afterward have spoken of another day.*

Whatever Jesus—Joshua— might pretend or plead, it is evident he did not give them rest, that is, the rest which in all these things God aimed at ; this is clear when we consider that five hundred years after Joshua, God in David and by him proposeth another day of rest, and invites the people unto an entrance into it, after they were so long fully possessed of all that Joshua led them into. Therefore David directs them still to look out after the rest to come. Observe then, 1. There is no true rest for the souls of men but only in Jesus Christ by the gospel. 2. The gospel church state is one of spiritual rest in Christ.　3. It is a great mercy and privilege to have a day of rest given unto us.

V. 9.　*There remaineth therefore a rest to the people of God.*

The Apostle shows that the privilege of being the people of God, with the enjoyment of a day of rest, is now transferred from the old estate and the Canaan rest unto them that shall and do enter into this rest of God under the gospel.　Hence, instead of these Hebrews to whom he is writing in the first place losing the privilege of being the people of God through faith in Christ, he lets them know that they could no longer retain it without faith in Christ.　If they failed in this, they would no longer be the people of God.　Let us then observe, 1. That believers under the New Testament have lost nothing, no privilege that was enjoyed by them of old.　2. It is the people of God alone, who have a right unto all the privileges of the gospel, and who in a due manner can perform all the duties of it.　3. The people of God as such have work to do, and labour incumbent on them.　Rest and labour are correlates ; the one supposeth the other.　4. God hath graciously given His people an entrance into rest during their state of work and labour, to sweeten it unto them, and to enable them for it. 5. Believers may and do find assured rest in a due attendance unto and performance of the duties of the gospel.　This is that which the Apostle asserts and proves.　6. There is a weekly sacred day of rest appointed for believers under the gospel, as will appear from the next verse.

V. 10.　*For he that is entered into his rest, he also hath ceased from his own works, as God* [*did*] *from His.*

Expositors generally apply these words to the believer, and their entering into the rest of God.　I shall not contend with any, but will with all humility propose my own thoughts to the consideration of them who are wise and learned and godly.　I am not satisfied with above exposition.　Supposing believers to be here intended, what are the works they are here said to rest from ? to rest from them as God did from His ?　God so rested as to take the greatest delight in His works.　He so *rested from* His works as *to rest in them*.　The rest here spoken of cannot be heaven, for that utterly excludes the rest in and of the gospel which is the matter of which the Apostle is discoursing.　It appears to me that it is the rest of another that is spoken of, even the rest of Christ from His works, which is compared with the rest of God from His works in creation. This gives an account of the connection in the word " for." " There remaineth therefore a rest to the people of God, ' for ' Christ is entered into His rest."　The " works " from which Christ

" ceased " include all that He did and suffered from His incarnation to His resurrection, as the Mediator of the new covenant. Christ's rest consists in an entire cessation from all these works, and an entire satisfaction in them and their results. His entrance into this rest was upon His resurrection " on the morning of the first day of the week," when He arose from the dead, the foundation of the new creation being laid and perfected.

V. 11. *Let us labour therefore to enter into that rest, lest any man fall after the same example of unbelief.*

In verse 9 the Apostle useth the word "sabbatism" for rest ; " *there remaineth therefore a sabbatism to the people of God,*" by which he intended to express the rest of the gospel not absolutely, but with respect unto the pledge of it in the day of rest ; but here in this verse 11 the Apostle returns to exhort them to enter in to the whole rest of God in the gospel, and therefore resumes the word " rest," whereby he had before expressed the rest of God in general. He exhorts them here to labour—to diligently study—to endeavour to enter into that rest.

We may observe from this exhortation, 1. That great oppositions will and do arise against men in the work of entering into God's rest, that is, into gospel faith and obedience. But notwithstanding all these difficulties, the promise of God being mixed with faith will carry us safely through them all. 2. That as the utmost of our endeavour and labours are required to our obtaining an entrance into the rest of Christ, so it doth very well deserve that they should be laid out therein. Men are content to lay themselves out to the utmost, and to spend their strength for the " bread that perisheth," yea, " for that which is not bread." " This their way is their folly." But the rest of the gospel deserves our utmost diligence and endeavour. To convince men thereof is one of the chief ends of the preaching of the gospel, and so needs not to be here insisted on. 3. There is a present excellency in and a present reward attending gospel faith and obedience. They give us present entrance into the rest of Christ, and are the means of entering into the future eternal rest with God.

" Lest any fall after the same example of unbelief." This I take to be the meaning intended—" You have the gospel and the rest of Christ therein preached unto you ; some of you have already taken upon you the profession of the gospel, as they of old did, when they said, ' All that the Lord our God shall command, that will we do.' Your condition is now like theirs, and represented therein. Consider now how things fell out with them, and what was the event of their sin and God's dealing with them. They believed not, they made not good their engagement, they were stubborn and disobedient, they fell in the wilderness and perished, not entering into God's rest. If now you, or any amongst you, shall be found guilty of their sin, or the like answering unto it, do not think or hope that you shall avoid the like punishment. If you would not fall into it, or fall under it, labour by faith and obedience to enter into the rest of Christ." Observe from this, 1. That precedent judgments on others are monitory ordinances unto us. 2. It is better to have an example, than to be made an example of divine displeasure. 3. We ought to have no expectation of escaping vengeance under the guilt of those sins, which others in a like manner guilty of have not escaped. There is no more certain rule for us to judge of our own condition than the examples of God's dealings with others in the same condition ; for " with God there is no respect of persons."

Vs. 12, 13. *For the word of God [is] quick, and powerful, and sharper than any two-edged sword, piercing even to the dividing asunder of soul and spirit, and of the joints and marrow, and [is] a discerner of the thoughts and intents of the heart. Neither is there any creature that is not manifest in His sight : but all things [are] naked and opened unto the eyes of Him with whom we have to do.*

" For the word of God." Having exhorted them to perseverance, and to take heed that they neglect not the promise of entering into rest through unbelief, he presseth them to care, diligence and constancy in the performance of this duty. And this he doth from a consideration of the Person of Christ, as his manner is in all his arguings to bring all to that centre. I judge therefore that it is the eternal Word of God or the Person of Christ who is here spoken of.

"Quick and powerful, sharper than any two-edged sword, piercing even to the dividing asunder of soul and spirit, and of the joints and marrow, and is a discerner of the thoughts and intents of the heart." The attributes here ascribed unto the word do all of them properly belong unto the Person of Christ, and cannot firstly and directly be ascribed unto the gospel. It is said to be " *quick*," that is, living. Jesus Christ is the living One who " hath life in Himself ; " and He is the "Lord of life " unto others. This one property of Him with whom we have to do contains the two great motives unto obedience, namely, that He is able to support us in it and reward us eternally for it ; also He is able to avenge all disobedience.

" *And powerful.*" This power signifies actual power, power acted or exerted. This was necessary to be added to the property of life, to manifest that the Lord Christ, the Word of God, would effectually put forth His power in dealing with professors, according to their deportment; and herein we see that this power in Christ lies not idle, is not useless, but is continually exercising itself toward us as the matter doth require.

This word of God is " *sharper than a two-edged sword.*" This sword is often mentioned with respect unto the Lord Christ. " Out of His mouth went a sharp two-edged sword; " it is Christ who Himself makes His word powerful and sharp; He acts in it and by it. This power is described by its effects, " *piercing even to the dividing asunder of soul and spirit.*" The meaning of this and the following expressions is that the word of God doth pierce into the innermost recesses of our souls, and, as it were, the secret chambers of our minds and hearts. " *And of the joints and marrow* ; " using bodily parts as representing the most secret and hidden parts of the heart.

All this teacheth us that the Son of God has absolute power to judge of the rectitude and crookedness of the ways and walkings of the sons of men under a profession of religion, from the inward frames of their minds and hearts under all their outward duties and performances, either in perseverance or backsliding. " *And is a discerner of the thoughts and intents of the heart.*" The heart includes the soul and spirit before mentioned, the thoughts of which, with all its designs and purposes, are entirely known to Him with whom we have to do.

" **Neither is there any creature that is not manifest in His sight.**" Angels, men, devils, professors, persecutors, all men of all sorts, and all things concerning them, their inward frames of mind and heart, their affections and temptations, their secret actings and thoughts, all are continually under His view.

" **But all things are naked and opened unto the eyes of Him with whom we have to do.**" The allusion is probably to the bodies of sacrificed beasts, which were flayed, opened, and cut to pieces, and thus perfectly exposed to the view of the priest before being offered up. The general design of these words is evident. All things are *visible* " *unto the eyes of Him* " who knoweth and seeth all things exactly as they are, and with Him " *we have to do ;* " that is, " to whom we must give an account." And this answers the design of the Apostle in this place. For evidencing unto them the efficacy and omniscience of the word of God, trying all things and discerning all things, he minds them of their near concernment in these matters, in that he and they must all give up their final accounts unto and before Him who is so intimately acquainted with what they are, and with whatsoever they shall do in this world.

Observe, 1. It is the way of the Spirit of God to excite us unto special duties by proposing unto us and minding us of such properties of God as the consideration whereof may in an especial manner incline us unto them. They are here minded that the word of God is living and powerful, actually efficacious towards the end mentioned.

2. The life and power of Christ are continually exercised about the concernments of the souls of professors, and are always actually efficacious in and upon them. This power He putteth forth by His word and His Spirit; for the effects here ascribed unto the *essential* word are such as He produceth by the *preached* word, which is accompanied with and made effectual by the dispensation of the Spirit. Every impression made on the heart by the preached word is an effect of the power of Christ. This will teach us how to value and esteem the preaching of the word, as it is the great means whereby the Lord Christ exerciseth His mediatory power towards us on behalf of God, and effectual it will be unto the ends whereunto He designs it.

3. The power of Christ in His word is irresistible, as to whatever effects He doth design by it. Had the Lord Christ no other end to accomplish by His preached word but the conversion of the elect—which is its principal end—it might be conceived to fail towards the far greater number of them to whom it is preached. But it is with Him in His word as in His own Person. He was " set for the fall " as well as for " the rising of many in Israel." To some He was " for a sanctuary ; " to others He was " for a stone of stumbling and a rock of offence." And these things are all of them effectually accomplished towards them to whom He is preached. They are all of them either raised by Him unto God out of their state of sin and misery, and do take sanctuary in Him from sin and law, or they stumble at Him through their unbelief and perish. None can ever have Christ proposed unto them upon indifferent terms, so as to be left in the condition wherein they were before. Sometimes Christ designs by His word the hardening and blinding of wicked sinners, that they may be the more prepared for deserved destruction (see Isaiah vi. 9—11). Some reject and despise His word, and by that word so despised they are hardened in their sins ; others are convicted by the word, and yet resist and reject the word as to any saving work of conversion ; and others " hear the voice of the Son of God and live." It is then certainly of high concernment unto all men unto whom Christ comes in His word to consider diligently what is, or is like to be, the issue and consequence of it unto themselves.

4. Though men may close and hide things from themselves and others, yet they cannot exclude the power of Christ in His word from piercing unto them. By His word He discerns the thoughts and intents of their hearts ; His word shows them what they are inwardly, and then they either betake themselves wholly to their sins so as to free themselves from their convictions and fears, or they sincerely give themselves up to Him for relief. It is a great and difficult matter really and practically to convince professors of

the practical judging omnisciency of Jesus Christ, the Word of God. Nothing would be of more use unto them in the whole course of their walking before Him. And therefore the Apostle instructs them that the beginnings into declensions in a profession, or backsliding from Christ and the ways of the gospel, are secret, deep, and hardly discoverable, being open and naked only to the all-discerning eye of Christ. Also that the consideration of the omniscience of Christ, His all-searching and all-seeing eye, is an effectual means to preserve the soul from destructive entrances into backsliding from the gospel. And also the same consideration, duly improved, is a great relief and encouragement to them who are sincere and upright in their obedience. The Apostle encourages the meanest and weakest sincere believer who desireth to commend his conscience to the Lord Jesus in walking before Him; for a due and holy consideration at all times of the all-seeing eye of Jesus Christ is a great preservation against backslidings in profession.

V. 14. Seeing then that we have a great High Priest, that is passed into the heavens, Jesus the Son of God, let us hold fast [our] profession.

"Seeing then that we have a great High Priest." Believers have great encouragement unto and assistance in the constancy of their profession by and from the priesthood of Christ. He is our High Priest; "the High Priest of our profession;" the "High Priest over the house of God." He is a High Priest who pitieth and hath compassion upon us; this is part of His duty and office (chap. v. 2). From the habitation of His holiness He looks upon His suffering, labouring, tempted disciples, and is " afflicted in all their afflictions," and is full of compassion towards them. Not only doth He pity, but He gives us actual help and assistance in holding fast our profession.

He is a "*great High Priest.*" He is comparatively great with respect unto Aaron; the Apostle proves in this epistle how incomparably exalted above Aaron and his successors is "our High Priest." He is absolutely great, whereof the Apostle gives a double proof; He is "*passed into the heavens,*" and His name is "*Jesus the Son of God.*" He was received gloriously into the highest heaven; He sat down upon His throne on the " right hand of God." This God promised Him, and gave Him the actual possession of it when He " passed into the heavens." And this great High Priest is Jesus the Son of God."

Let us here observe, 1. Before the entrance of sin there was no need of the office of priesthood between God and man; 2. Sin being come into the world, there was no more worship to be performed immediately unto God; 3. In order that the worship of God might be restored again in the world, it was indispensably necessary that someone must interpose between sinners and the holy God.   This is the use, reason, and foundation of the office that was undertaken by the Son of God.

4. No creature could undertake the office of being a priest for .the Church of God, which now consisted all of sinners, as the very nature of the office itself, and the work which He was to perform who should undertake it, do declare ; for the office of a priest is to be a gracious interposition between God and sinners.   The priest must approach unto God representing the persons and worship of the Church unto Him, making them and it acceptable on his account.   Who was meet to be intrusted with this honour ?   What creature could undertake this office ?   The work of such a priest is utterly exclusive of the whole creation engaging therein ; for the first thing that he undertakes must be to make an atonement for sin and sinners—He must make reconciliation for the sins of the people in whose stead He appeareth before God.   Now it is Jesus the Son of God who undertakes to be this great High Priest.   It was necessary that " He should have somewhat to offer," being a real priest ; and so the Son of God became Jesus.   He took human nature—the seed of Abraham—into union with Himself, that He might have of His own to offer unto God.   This by its oneness with our nature, the nature that had sinned, being itself not touched with sin, was meet to be offered for us ; and by its union with His Person was meet and able to make atonement with God for us, and so " God redeemed the Church with His own blood " (Acts xx. 28).

V. 15.   *For we have not an High Priest which cannot be touched with the feeling of our infirmities ; but was in all points tempted like [as we are,] yet without sin.*

"**For we have not an High Priest which cannot be touched with the feeling of our infirmities.**"   Jesus the Son of God is an High Priest who can be *"touched with the feeling of our infirmities,"* and in this the Church of God hath a standing perpetual advantage, as He who is touched with the feeling of our infirmities is our High Priest—even Jesus the Son of God.   His nature was spotlessly innocent and pure, and there was an addition of all grace unto it, by virtue of its union with the Person of the Son of God, and the unction it had from the Spirit of God.   He took an experience of such sufferings in Himself as are the proper objects of compassion when they are in others.   Herein lies a great encouragement to make our addresses unto Him in all our straits and weaknesses, as we shall see in the next verse.

"**But was in all points tempted like as we are, yet without sin.**"   He was tempted—tried, exercised—for no more doth the word import.   Whatever is the moral evil in temptation is due to the depraved intention of the tempter, or from the weakness and sin of the tempted. In itself, it is but a trial which may have a good or bad effect. He was tempted like as we are, yet without sin. Sin may be considered as to its principle, and as to its effect. Men are tempted to sin by sin, to actual sin by habitual sin, to outward sin by indwelling sin. And this is the greatest source of sin in us who are sinners. The Apostle reminds us of the holiness and purity of Christ, that we may not imagine that He was liable unto any such temptations unto sin from within as we find ourselves liable unto, who are never free from guilt and defilement. Whatever temptation He was exposed unto or exercised withal, as He was with all and of all sorts that can come from without, they had none of them in the least degree any effect in or upon Him. He was absolutely in all things " without sin ; " He neither was tempted by sin, such was the holiness of His nature ; nor did His temptation produce sin, such was the perfection of His obedience.

V. 16. *Let us therefore come boldly unto the throne of grace, that we may obtain mercy, and find grace to help in time of need.*

"**Let us therefore come boldly unto the throne of grace.**" The Apostle would remove and have us delivered from, in our drawing near to the throne of grace through the interposition of our High Priest, a "*spirit of bondage unto fear,*" also from a *disbelief of acceptation*, arising from a sense of our unworthiness. To " come boldly " implies a freedom and liberty in speaking ; this liberty is internal and spiritual, and is opposed unto legal bondage and fear. It also implies a spiritual confidence of acceptance with God through the interposition of Jesus Christ. In another epistle the Apostle refers to this. He says : " In whom we have boldness and an access with confidence, through the faith that is in Him." The "*throne of grace,*" whereunto we are exhorted to " *come boldly,*" is, unto us, God as gracious in Christ, as exalted in a way of exercising mercy and peace towards them that through the Lord Jesus believe in Him and come unto Him.

"**That we may obtain mercy, and find grace to help in time of need.**" To receive " mercy " is to be made partakers of gracious help and support from the benignity and kindness of God in Christ when we are in straits and necessities, which spring from the same root as pardoning grace, and is therefore called " mercy." Mercy and grace to help in time of need ; that is, in its proper and seasonable time. Help that is fit and seasonable ; that is, on the part of God who gives it, of the persons who receive it, of the time wherein it is afforded, and of the end for which it is bestowed.

Observe, 1. That there is and will be a season, many a season, in the course of our profession and walking before God, wherein we do and shall stand in need of special aid and assistance. A time of affliction is such a season; also a time of persecution; also a time of temptation; also a time of spiritual desertion; also a time when we are called unto the performance of any great and signal duty; and the time of death will be such a season. 2. There is with God in Christ, God on His throne of grace, a spring of seasonable and suitable help for all times and occasions of difficulty. He is the "God of all grace," and a fountain of living waters is with Him for the refreshment of every weary and thirsty soul. 3. All help, succour, or spiritual assistance in our straits and difficulties proceed from mere mercy and grace, or the goodness, kindness, and benignity of God in Christ. 4. When we have, through Christ, obtained mercy and grace for our persons, we need not fear but that we shall have suitable and seasonable help for our duties. If we "obtain mercy" and "find grace," we shall have "help." 5. The way to obtain help from God is by a due gospel application of our souls for it to the throne of grace. 6. Great discouragements are used to interpose themselves in our minds and against our faith, when we stand in need of special help from God, and would make our application to Him for relief. We are therefore exhorted to "come boldly." 7. Faith's consideration of the interposition of Christ in our behalf as our High Priest is the only way to remove discouragements, and to give us boldness in our access unto God. 8. In all our approaches unto God, we are to consider Him as on a throne; and though it be "a throne of grace," yet it is still a throne; the consideration whereof should influence our minds with "reverence and godly fear" in all things wherein we have to do with Him.

CHAPTER FIVE

V. 1. *For every high priest taken from among men is ordained for men in things [pertaining] to God, that he may offer both gifts and sacrifices for sins.*

The office of a priest is to offer gifts and sacrifices for sins; priests and sacrifices are so related that you cannot separate them. These sacrifices are to make an atonement for sin; and Jesus Christ alone could offer a sacrifice that would make an atonement. This the Apostle designs to prove, and doth it accordingly in this and the ensuing chapters.

V. 2. *Who can have compassion on the ignorant, and on them that are out of the way; for that he himself also is compassed with infirmity.*

"**Who can have compassion on the ignorant, and on them that are out of the way.**" The qualification for being a high priest is that he is one who can bear with the weaknesses and sinful provocations of them that are ignorant, and wander out of the way, as also commiserate or pity them unto such a measure and degree as never to be wanting unto their help and assistance; such a person as one that is so wise and understanding in the state and condition of the poor, as duly to relieve them. This state of being " ignorant " and " out of the way," is in general the condition of all the people of God, and they are hereby encouraged to expect relief from the High Priest. The " ignorant " are such as through the inadvertency of their minds, or want of a due and diligent attendance unto the rule of their actions, do fall into sin, as well as those who do so through a mere ignorance of their duty. Those who wander " out of the way " are those who by the power of their temptations have been seduced and turned from the straight paths of holy obedience, and have wandered in some crooked paths of their own.

"**For that he himself also is compassed with infirmity.**" The high priest of old was prompted to compassion with the ignorant, and those out of the way, by a consideration of his own state—beset and compassed about on every hand with infirmity. This infirmity was natural and moral. Natural infirmity is that which is inseparable from human nature, and this our Lord Jesus Christ Himself was compassed withal; He was a " Man of sorrow and acquainted with grief." But there is also a moral infirmity consisting in an inclination to sin, and a weakness as to obedience. This is affirmed in the next verse, where we read, that "for this cause " the high priest had " to offer sacrifice for himself." He was subject to sin even as the rest of the people, and therefore peculiar sacrifices were appointed for the high priest to offer for himself and his own sin. This shows us that the things intended here by the Apostle belong peculiarly to the high priest according to the law. It was then natural infirmity alone whereof our High Priest, Jesus Christ, had full experience, that qualified the legal high priest with due compassion. His moral infirmity was not any advantage unto him, so as to help his compassion toward the people, which was, as all other graces, weakened thereby. Now the Lord Christ, being absolutely free from this kind of infirmity, doth in a most perfect manner perform all that is to be done on our behalf. Observe, 1. That our ignorance is both our calamity, our sin, and an occasion of many sins unto us. 2. That all sin is a wandering out of the way. 3. It is well for us and enough for us, that the Lord Christ was compassed about with the sinless infirmities of our nature.

V. 3. *And by reason hereof he ought, as for the people, so also for himself, to offer for sins.*

There was none who could offer sacrifices for the sins of the high priest ; therefore, he must do it for himself. He was to offer for himself in the same way and for the same reasons as he offered for the people, and this was necessary, for he was encompassed with infirmities and was obnoxious unto sin, and so stood in no less need of expiation and atonement than the people.

V 4. *And no man taketh this honour unto himself, but he that is called of God, as [was] Aaron.*

The foregoing verses declare the personal qualifications of a high priest, but these alone are not sufficient to invest anyone with that office ; for it is required that he be lawfully called thereunto. Aaron was called of God immediately, and in an extraordinary way. He was called by the command of God given to Moses, and entrusted to him for execution ; he was actually separated and consecrated unto the office of high priest, and this was accompanied by special sacrifices made by another for him; and all these things were necessary unto Aaron, because God, in his person, erected a new order of priesthood.

V. 5. *So also Christ glorified not Himself to be made an High Priest ; but He that said unto Him, Thou art My Son, to-day have I begotten Thee.*

As the high priest of old was called of God to his office, so in like manner was Christ also. Aaron did not take this honour upon himself, neither did the Lord Christ ; it was conferred upon Him by His Father, who said, " Thou art My Son, this day have I begotten Thee." Some say, that this implies that Christ did not enter upon His office of High Priest till after His resurrection; but this is destructive of all the instructive parts of the type, and overthrows the very design of the Apostle, which is to prove that Christ, in the offering which He made in the days of His flesh, did not glorify Himself to be made a Priest, but was made so by Him who said, " Thou art My Son, this day have I begotten-Thee." For the clearing of this, let us observe that it is not the priesthood of Christ, but His call thereunto, which the Apostle here asserts, by which he intends to show that it was God the Father from whom He received all His mediatory power, as King, Prophet and Priest to the Church.

V. 6. *As He saith also in another [place], Thou [art] a Priest for ever after the order of Melchisedec.*

This is another proof that He was called of God to the office of High Priest as was Aaron, that is, immediately of God, and in an extraordinary manner. The call of Christ had no need of *outward ceremony* to express it, yet it had a glory in it which no ceremony could express. It consisted of the words of God spoken immediately to Himself, and not to any others concerning Him ; only they are reported unto the Church in the two Psalms—(ii. and cx). These words, " Thou art My Son ; " and " Thou art a Priest for ever," are present, effective, constituting, authoritative words, and not merely declarative of what God would have done ; they also indicate God's infinite love and acquiescence in the Person of Christ as a High Priest.

V. 7. *Who in the days of His flesh, when He had offered up prayers and supplications, with strong crying and tears, unto Him that was able to save Him from death, and was heard in that He feared.*

" Who in the days of His flesh." By the word " flesh " is meant in this place human nature not yet glorified, with all its infirmities, wherein He was exposed unto hunger, thirst, weariness, sorrow, grief, fear, pain, wounding, death itself. By the " days of His flesh " is intended not so much the whole of His time on this world, from the cradle to the grave, as specially the close of those days, in His last suffering, where all His sorrows, trials and temptations came to a head ; the design of the Apostle being to show, that when He offered up His sacrifice He was encompassed with our infirmities, which hath an especial influence unto our faith and consolation.

"When He had offered up prayers and supplications." His offering up prayers and supplications, is part of His office as a Priest. These words, " prayer " and " supplication," agree in this, that they respect an especial kind of prayer, which is for the averting or turning away of impending evils, or such as are deserved and justly feared. All prayer may be referred unto two heads, either for that which is good, or for the keeping off and turning away that which is evil ; the latter sort only are here intended. So it is not the mere supplications of our blessed Saviour that are here intended, but as they accompanied and were a necessary adjunct of the offering up of Himself, His soul and body, a real propitiatory sacrifice unto God. And so in the type, when Aaron in the great sacrifice of expiation confessed over the head of the scapegoat " all the iniquities of the children of Israel," he did so, not without prayers for the expiation of their sins, and supplication for their deliverance from the curse of the law. Christ " *offered up prayers and supplications* " from the " lions' mouth," from " the horns of the unicorn ; " He was in earnest, and pressed to the utmost in the work that was before Him. From this we may learn how great a work it was to expiate sin ; it required not only death, and that a bloody death, but was accompanied by " prayers and supplications," that it might be effectual unto the end designed, and that He who suffered it might not be overborne in His undertaking.

"**With strong crying and tears.**" In prophecy, the supplications here intended are called His " roaring." " My God, My God, why hast Thou forsaken Me ? Why art Thou so far from helping Me, and from the words of My roaring ? " If we well consider this Psalm xxii., especially from vs. 9-21, we shall find that every word almost hath in it the spirit of roaring and a strong cry, however it were uttered. For it is not merely the outward noise, but the inward earnest intercession and engagement of heart and soul with the greatness and depth of the occasion of them, that is principally intended. In the story as related by the evangelists we read of those prayers which He offered to God during His passion, both in the garden and on the cross.

" And being in agony, He prayed more earnestly, and His sweat was as drops of blood falling on the earth." The inward frame is here declared, which our Apostle shadows out by the external expressions and signs of it in " strong cries and tears." He was wholly pressed by " an agony," that is, a strong and vehement conflict of mind in and about things dreadful and terrible. He prayed " more earnestly," with more vehement intension of mind, body and spirit ; not, as some have thought, with a greater degree of the actings of grace, but the highest degree of earnestness in the actings of His mind, body and soul ;—another token of that wonderful conflict wherein He was engaged, which no heart can conceive, nor tongue express. Then on the cross, it is plainly said, He " cried with a loud voice,"—with a great outcry, with a loud and strong cry. This was the manner of His prayers as a priest when He offered up Himself a sacrifice for sin. The other part of His prayers as a priest were offered with all calmness, quietness, sedateness, with all assurance and joyful glory as if He were already in heaven, as we may see from John xvii.

"**Unto Him that was able to save Him from death.**" Ability or power is either natural or moral. In God natural power is omnipotency ; moral power is absolute sovereignty. The Lord Christ had respect unto both of those : as to the first, He relied upon it for deliverance ; in the latter, as that unto which He submitted Himself. The former was the object of His faith, that God could support and deliver Him in and under His trial ; the latter was the object of His fear, as to the dreadful work which He had undertaken. Let us enquire, 1. What were the general causes of the state and condition wherein the Lord Christ is here described by the Apostle, and of the actings ascribed unto Him therein. He considered God as the supreme Rector and Judge of all, the Author and the Avenger of the law, who had the power of life and of death, the one to be destroyed and the other to be inflicted, according to the curse and sentence of the law. God represented Himself unto Him as armed and attended with infinite holiness, righteousness and severity, as one that could not pass by sin nor clear the guilty. He also considered death not naturally as a separation of body and soul, nor yet merely as a painful separation of them, such as was that death in particular He was to undergo; but He looked upon it as the curse of the law due to sin, inflicted by God as a just and righteous Judge. Hence in and under that law He Himself is said to be "made a curse." Some have thought that upon the confidence of the indissolubleness of His Person, and the actual assurance which they suppose He always had of the love of God, His sufferings could have no effect of fear, sorrow, or perplexity on His soul, but only what respected the natural enduring of pain and suffering to which He was exposed. But the Scripture gives us another account of these things. It informs us that " He began to be afraid and sore amazed;" that "His soul was heavy and sorrowful unto death;" that "He was in an agony," and afterwards cried out, "My God, My God, why hast Thou forsaken Me?" under a sense of divine desertion. There was indeed a mighty acting of love in God to the Person of His Son, and an ineffable complacency in His obedience, especially that which He exercised in suffering; but yet the curse and punishment which He underwent was the effect of vindictive justice. Whatever was due to us from the justice of God and the sentence of the law, that He underwent and suffered.

2. We are to enquire as to the effects of His sufferings in Himself, or His sufferings themselves. First, His desertion by His Father. He was under a suspension of the comfortable influences of His relation unto God; this relationship was the fountain of all His comforts and joys. "His soul was exceeding sorrowful, even unto death;" such expressions declare a sorrow that is absolutely inexpressible; and this sorrow was the effect of His penal desertion; for sorrow is that which is the life of the curse of the law. With this sorrow Christ was now filled, which put Him upon those strong cries and tears for relief. Second, He had an intimate sense of the wrath and displeasure of God against the sin that was imputed unto Him. All our sins were then caused, by an act of divine and supreme authority, " to meet on Him," or " The Lord laid on Him the iniquity of us all." In that great hour and wonderful transaction of divine wisdom, grace and righteousness, whereon the glory of God, the recovery of fallen man, with the

utter condemnation of Satan, depended, God was pleased for a while, as it were, to hold the scales of divine justice at a balance, that the turning of them might be more conspicuous, eminent, and glorious. In the one scale, as it were, there was the weight of the first sin and apostasy from God, with all the consequences of it, covered with the sentence and curse of the law,—a weight that all the angels in heaven could not stand under one moment. In the other was the holiness, obedience, righteousness, and penal sufferings of the Son of God,—all having weight and worth given them by the dignity of His Person. Infinite justice kept these things for a season, as it were, at a poise, until the Son of God, by His tears and prayers and supplications, prevailed upon a glorious success in the delivery of Himself and us.

3. Wherefore we may conclude that there was a limitation of the effects of Christ's sufferings in and upon Himself. They were such only as are consistent with absolute purity, holiness, and freedom from the least appearance of sin ; nor were they such as did in the least impeach the glorious union of His natures in the same Person ; nor such as took off from the dignity of His obedience and merit of His suffering, but were all necessary thereunto. As He underwent whatever is or can be grievous, afflictive and penal in the wrath of God, and sentence of the law executed, so these things wrought in Him sorrow, amazement, dread, anguish, with the like penal effects of the pains of hell ; from whence it was that He " offered up prayers and supplications, with strong cries and tears unto Him that was able to save from death," the event whereof is described in the last clause of the verse.

"**And was heard in that He feared.**" To be heard in Scripture signifies two things : to be accepted in our request, though the thing requested be not granted. Also to be answered in our request ; to be heard is to be delivered. In the first way there is no doubt but that the Father always heard the Son. (John xi. 42.) But our inquiry here is how far the Lord Christ was heard in the latter way. The prayers of Christ to His Father were conditional or absolute. He prayed conditionally when He said, " Father, if Thou wilt, remove this cup from Me." But the chief and principal supplications which He offered to Him that was able to save from death were absolute ; and in them He was absolutely heard and delivered. For upon the presentation of death to Him, as attended with the wrath and curse of God, He had deep and awful apprehensions of it ; and how unable the human nature was to undergo it, and prevail against it, unless mightily supported and carried through by the power of God. In this condition it was part of His obedience, it was His duty, to pray that He might be delivered from the prevalency of it, that He might not be cast in His trial, that He might not be confounded and condemned. This He hoped, trusted and believed, and therefore prayed absolutely for it. (Isa. l. 7-8.) And herein He was heard ; for so it is said, " *He was heard in that He feared.*" He was heard—delivered—from the things He feared. To deny that the soul of Christ was engaged in an ineffable conflict with the wrath of God in the curse of the law, and that His faith and trust in God were pressed and tried to the utmost by the opposition made unto them by fear, dread, and a terrible apprehension of divine displeasure due to sin, is to renounce the benefit of His passion, and turn the whole of it into a mere show, fit to be represented by pictures and images, or acted over in ludicrous scenes, as it is by the Papists.

Let us here observe, 1. The Lord Christ Himself had a time of infirmity in this world, which was followed by a time of glory. 2. The Lord Christ is now no more in a state of weakness and infirmity ; the days of His flesh are past and gone. 3. The Lord Christ, in His offering up Himself for us, laboured and travailed in soul to bring the work unto a good and holy issue. 4. The Lord Christ in the time of His offering and suffering, considering God, with whom He had to do, as the supreme Rector and Judge of all, casts Himself before Him with most fervent prayers for deliverance from the sentence of death and the curse of the law. 5. That in all the pressures that were on the Lord Christ, in all the distresses with which He had to conflict in His sufferings, His faith for deliverance and success was firm and unconquerable. This was the ground He stood upon in His prayers and supplications. 6. The success of our Lord Christ, in His trials, as our Head and Surety, is a pledge and assurance of success unto us in all our spiritual conflicts.

V. 8. *Though He were a Son, yet learned He obedience by the things which He suffered.*

He was " God's own Son," the " only begotten of the Father," who was Himself " in the form of God." That He should do the thing here spoken of is great and marvellous. " *He learned obedience.*" There is a *peculiar obedience* of Christ which is intended here; this was His obedience in dying, and in all things that tended immediately thereunto. " He became obedient unto death, even the death of the cross ; " for this commandment had He of His Father, that He should lay down His life, and therefore He did it in a way of obedience. He can only be said to learn obedience on the account of having *an experience* of it, in the exercise of it. He could have no experience of obedience but by suffering the things He was to undergo ; thus He learned obedience, and experienced in Himself the difficulty connected therewith, and how great an exercise of grace is required in it. This is the spring of His pity and compassion toward us ; and He is constantly ready to give us relief as the matter shall require. There was somewhat peculiar in that obedience which the Son of God is said to learn from His own sufferings, namely, what it is for a *sinless* Person to suffer for sinners—"the just for the unjust." This obedience was peculiar to Him, nor do we know, nor can we have an experience of the ways and paths of it.

Observe, 1. That infinite love prevailed with the Son of God to lay aside the privilege of His infinite dignity, that He might suffer for us and our redemption. He "took on Him the form of a servant;" and therein "made Himself of no reputation;" and He "became obedient unto death, even the death of the cross." The reason why He condescended unto this condition was that He might redeem and save the children which God gave unto Him, and this out of His own unspeakable love to them. Here we may lose ourselves in an holy admiration of this infinite love of Christ. 2. In all His sufferings, and notwithstanding them all, the Lord Christ was the " Son "—still the Son of God. " God spared not His own Son, but delivered Him up for us all "—that is, to suffering and death. He who suffered was the Son of God ; in all that He suffered, the union of His natures was never dissolved. 3. Sufferings undergone according to the will of God are highly instructive. Even Christ Himself learned obedience by the things which He suffered. 4. In all these things both as to suffering and learning thereby, we have a great example in our Lord Jesus Christ. 5. The love of God towards any, and the relation of any unto God, hinders not but that they may undergo great trials and sufferings.

V. 9. *And being made perfect, He became the Author of eternal salvation unto all them that obey Him.*

"And being made perfect." Christ was *"made perfect,"* consecrated, dedicated sacredly. It was the Father, who by His sovereign authority disposed, designed and separated the Lord Christ unto this office ; and Jesus Christ of His own will gave Himself up obediently unto the authority and will of His Father, and that out of love to and delight in the work itself. The external means of His being made perfect were in His own sufferings, especially in the offering of Himself. Nothing was now wanting unto the great end aimed at in all these things, which is expressed in the next place.

"He became the Author of eternal salvation." Christ is the Author of salvation, *meritoriously,* by His oblation and by His intercession. By His intercession He makes effectual to us what He purchased and procured by His oblation. He is the Author of salvation, *efficiently,* inasmuch as He doth by His Spirit, His grace, His glorious power, actually communicate salvation unto us. And this salvation is " eternal ; " it is endless, unchangeable and permanent.

" Unto them that obey Him." To all and everyone of them that obey Him; none who obey Him shall be excepted from an interest in this salvation, nor shall any other sort be admitted thereunto. To obey Him is the "obedience upon hearing." Hence it is faith in the first place which is here intended. The ensuing subjecting our souls unto Christ in the keeping of His commands is the "obedience of faith." Observe, 1. That all that befell the Lord Christ, all that He did and suffered, was necessary to this end, that He might be the Author of eternal salvation to believers.

2. The Lord Christ was consecrated Himself in and by the sacrifice He offered for us, and what He suffered in so doing. This belonged to the perfection of His office and of His offering. He had none to offer for Him but Himself; and He had nothing to offer but Himself.

3. The Lord Christ alone is the only principal cause of our salvation. There are many instrumental causes,—such as faith, the word, the ordinances of the gospel—but they are all in subordination unto Christ, who alone gives use and efficacy unto all others.

4. Salvation is confined to believers; and those who look for salvation by Christ must secure it unto themselves by faith and obedience. It is Christ alone who is the cause of our salvation; but He will save none but those who obey Him. He came to save sinners, but not such as choose to continue in their sins; though the gospel be full of grace, of mercy, of pardon, yet herein the sentence of it is peremptory and decretory. "He that believeth not shall be damned."

V. 10.   *Called of God an High Priest after the order of Melchisedec.*

The Apostle refers to the testimony produced (v. 6). In my judgment, the special word "called," as used here, denotes the denomination of Him who is called. "Because," saith the Apostle, "of the especial resemblance between what Melchisedec was and what Christ was to be, God called His priesthood Melchisedecian, whereon I must necessarily declare wherein that resemblance consists;" which he soon proceeds to do (chap. vii). The Lord Christ is called an "High Priest," because all the pre-eminences of the priesthood were in Him alone, and He really answered to what was typed out by the singular actings of the Aaronical high priest. Melchisedec became a priest, without ceremony, without sacrifice, without visible consecration, without the law of a "carnal commandment;" so also Christ by the immediate word of the Father, saying unto Him, "Thou art My Son, a priest for ever," or after the "power of an endless life."

V. 11.   *Of whom we have many things to say, and hard to be uttered, seeing ye are dull of hearing.*

That is, many things concerning Melchisedec, so far and wherein
he was a type of Christ ; the " *many things* " refers not so much to
the number of them only, but to the weight and importance of
them ; for they are things " hard to be uttered," for in their own
nature they are sublime and mysterious; not only so, but our
understandings of such things are so weak and imperfect.

" **Seeing ye are dull of hearing ;** " that is, slothful, slow,
dull. The natural dulness of our minds in receiving spiritual
things may be included in these words ; but it is our depraved
affections, casting us on a neglect of our duty, that is condemned.
Observe, 1. There is a glorious light and evidence in all divine
truths, but by reason of our darkness and weakness we are not
always able to comprehend them. 2. Many who receive the word
at first with readiness, do yet afterwards make but slow progress in
knowledge or grace. This the Apostle here chargeth upon these
Hebrews, which we must consider further afterwards. 3. It is
men's slothfulness in hearing which is the sole cause of their not
improving the means of grace, or not thriving under the dispensation of the word. The Apostle reproveth the want in general of
such an attendance unto the word as to be edified thereby, proceeding from corrupt affections and neglect of duty.

Vs. 12—14. *For when for the time ye ought to be teachers,*
ye have need that one teach you again which [be] the first
principles of the oracles of God ; and are become such as
have need of milk, and not of strong meat. For every one
that useth milk [is] unskilful in the word of righteousness ;
for he is a babe. But .strong meat belongeth to them that
are of full age, [even] those who by reason of use have their
senses exercised to discern both good and evil.

The Apostle complains of their slow progress, considering the
time and opportunities they had enjoyed. He sets before them two
sorts of hearers of the word, and gives a description of them by their
several qualities. Some are " *babes,*" and continue so; and some
are of " *full age* "—perfect. These " *babes* " are " *dull in hearing,*"
and " *unskilful in the word of righteousness.*" Those of " *full age,*"
spiritual adults, are such as have an understanding, so as to be
capable of instruction, and are said to have " *senses exercised to dis-*
cern both good and evil." " *Milk* " is suitable food for " *babes,*" and
" *strong meat* " for those of " *full age.*"

We need not fix upon any special length of time during
which they had many advantages ; it is enough that they one and
all had more time than they had well used or improved. It was
the sin of these Hebrews that they were not qualified to be the
teachers of others, considering the time they themselves had been

instructed. Instead of their being able to teach others, they had need that some one should teach them again "*which be the first principles of the oracles of God.*" The Apostle names some of these first principles in the beginning of the next chapter. These principles are such as, if they alone are known, received, believed, obeyed, provided their progress in knowledge be not obstructed by men's own negligence, prejudices, or lusts, they may attain the end of their faith and obedience in the salvation of their souls.

Through their neglect they had "*become such as have need of milk and not of strong meat.*" Milk is a kind of food easy of digestion, and is the common nourishment of babes and children and sick persons, not sufficing to maintain the health and strength of persons of full age and healthy constitution. In his epistle to the Corinthians, he tells us what he intends by "babes," even such as are "carnal," that is, such as by reason of their indulgence unto their carnal affections had kept their souls in a weak and distempered condition as to spiritual things. He says also, they had no need of "*strong meat.*" If the solid doctrines concerning the offices of Christ, especially His priesthood and sacrifice, are suited to the mind and affections, and if food and spiritual nourishment is found in them, it is a good evidence of progress in the knowledge of Christ and the gospel. But if such things have neither taste nor relish in them, if they are not readily digested nor benefit found in them, it is proof of weakness and feebleness.

These "babes" are said to be "*unskilful in the word of righteousness;*" they had some knowledge of it, but were not able wisely to manage and improve it unto its proper end. This "word of righteousness" is none other but the gospel, in which is "revealed the righteousness of God." These Hebrews were not utterly ignorant of the gospel, for they owned and made profession of it; but they had not attained unto a clear and distinct understanding of the truths of the gospel, so as to be able to improve them to their proper ends, hence they are called "*babes,*" who, though enjoying the dispensation of the word, or having done so for some time, yet through their own sloth and negligence have made little or no proficiency in spiritual knowledge.

God requires of those who live under the dispensation of the gospel, that they should be skilful in the word of righteousness. To be skilful is to have a spiritual sense, taste, or relish, of the goodness, sweetness, useful excellency of the truths of the gospel, endearing our hearts to God, and causing us to adhere unto Him with delight and constancy. This experience consisteth in a *mixture of the promises with faith:* also in a spiritual sense of the excellency of the things believed, wherewith the affections are touched and filled; also in experiments of the power of the word as a word of righteousness. There is in this a sense of the power of the word in giving peace with God. This is the most difficult thing in the world to be impressed on the mind of a man really convinced of the guilt of sin. This is to have an experiment of the word, when we find our souls satisfied and fortified by the authority of it, against all oppositions, that through Christ we are accepted of God and are at peace with Him. This experience of the word satisfies the heart to choose spiritual, invisible, and eternal things, before those that are present, and offers us the security of their immediate enjoyment.

"**But strong meat belongeth to them that are of full age, [even] those who by reason of use have their senses exercised to discern both good and evil.**" Those of "*full age*" are here opposed to those that are "babes." Those of "full age" have their understandings enlarged and their minds settled in the knowledge of Christ and the mysteries of the gospel. These are "spiritual men;" an equal measure is not designed unto all, for to "every one of us grace is given, according to the measure of the gift of Christ." Each one hath his distinct size, stature or age, unto which he is to arrive. So each one may grow up into a "perfect man," though one be taller than another. Those of "full age" are such as, being instructed in the doctrine of the gospel and using diligence in attending thereunto, have made a good progress according to their means and capacities in the knowledge of Christ and His will.

"*Strong meat*" belongs to these; that is, it is to be provided for them and proposed unto them, and that because they have "their senses exercised to discern both good and evil." This is to have our understanding and mind, through constant, sedulous study, meditation and prayer, hearing of the word, and the like means of the increase of grace and knowledge, to become ready, fit, and able to receive spiritual truths and to turn them into nourishment for our souls. By such exercise those of "full age" will be able to judge what is "good," and so to receive it for the nourishment of their souls; and what is *evil*, and so to reject it.

"*By reason of use*" means a fixed habit, and this in respect of all the ways and means that are appointed for our increase in the gospel. Let us then observe, 1. That the word of the gospel, in the dispensation of it, is food provided for the souls of men. No judgment is to be feared as a deprivation of the dispensation of the word. No judgment like famine, and no famine like that of the word. The word is to be esteemed, valued, and sought after as our "*daily food*." Negligence and carelessness about the food of our souls is too great an evidence that there is no principle of life within us. 2. Whereas the word is food, it is evident that it will not profit our souls unless it be eaten and digested. 3. It is an evidence of a thriving and healthy state of soul to have an appetite for the deepest mysteries of the gospel or most solid doctrines of truth, and to be able profitably to digest them. 4. The assiduous exercise of our minds about spiritual things in a *spiritual manner*, is the only means to make us profit in hearing the word. When our spiritual senses are exercised by reason of constant use, they are in a readiness to receive, embrace, and improve what is tendered unto them. Without this we shall be dull and slow in hearing— the vice here so severely reproved. 5. The spiritual sense of believers, well exercised in the word, is the best and most undeceiving help in judging of what is good or evil, true or false, that is proposed unto them.

CHAPTER SIX

V. 1. *Therefore leaving the principles of the doctrine of Christ, let us go on unto perfection.*

"**Therefore leaving.**" The signification of the word "leaving" is to be limited unto the present occasion ; for consider the things here spoken of absolutely, and they are never to be left either by teachers or hearers. There is a necessity that teachers should often insist on the rudiments or first principles of religion, and this course we find the Apostle steered in his epistles. Nor are any hearers so to leave these principles as to forget them, or not duly to make use of them.

"**The principles of the doctrine of Christ.**" The doctrine —word—of Christ is no more but the doctrine of the gospel as preached and taught. The principles of the gospel are those beginnings which men usually were first instructed in, and which from their own nature it was necessary that so they should be. What these doctrines are, the Apostle immediately declares in the end of this verse and in the next. He declares that for the present he would omit and pass by these, so that he in teaching, and they in learning, might go on "unto perfection." He says—

"**Let us go on unto perfection.**" That is, unto such a knowledge of the mysterious and sublime doctrines of the gospel as those who were completely initiated and thoroughly instructed were partakers of. This "perfection" is *comparative*, and not absolute. The Apostle denies absolute perfection in himself. (Phil. iii. 12.) By "perfection" is intended such a degree and measure as God is pleased to communicate to believers in the ordinary use of means ; it is a clear perception of the mysteries of the gospel, especially of those which concern the Person and offices of Christ, and particularly His priesthood. "Let us go on;" the word is emphatical; let us be carried on with the full bent of our minds and affections, with the utmost endeavour of our souls.

Observe, 1. It is the duty of ministers of the gospel to take care not only that the doctrine they preach be true, but also that it be seasonable to the state and condition of their hearers. 2. Some important doctrines of truth may, in the preaching of the gospel, be omitted for a season, but none ever must be forgotten or neglected. 3. It is a necessary duty of the dispensers of the gospel to excite their hearers by all pressing considerations to make a progress in the knowledge of the truth ; because their hearers do greatly need the exercise of it, they are apt to be slothful and weary ; also because the advantage which professors have by a progress in the knowledge of spiritual things makes it a necessary duty to stir them up and lead them on therein. 4. The case of that people is deplorable and dangerous whose teachers are not able to carry them on in the knowledge of the mysteries of the gospel. The key of knowledge may be taken away by ignorance as well as by malice. 5. In our progress towards an increase in knowledge, we ought to go on with diligence, and the full bent of our wills and affections. This exercise includes diligence in the use of the best means for the end in view, also the diligent practice of what we know.

Vs. 1, 2. *Not laying again the foundation of repentance from dead works, and of faith toward God, of the doctrine of baptisms, and of laying on of hands, and of resurrection of the dead, and of eternal judgment.*

"**Not laying again the foundation.**" The Apostle knew they had been instructed in those truths which are the foundation of a true profession of the gospel, and so he says he will not at this time go over them again. He then proceeds to declare in particular some of those doctrinal principles which he had in general referred to, and which he will not now insist upon.

"**Repentance from dead works.**" This expression, "dead works," is peculiar to the Apostle and to this epistle (see ix. 14). Elsewhere he speaks of men being "dead in trespasses and sins." What he there ascribes to their persons he here ascribes to their works. The sins of unregenerate persons are called "dead works;" in respect of their *nature*, they proceed from a state of spiritual death ; and in respect of their *end*, they are dead because deadly ; they procure death, and end in death. That which is required, and which they were taught with respect unto these "dead works," is repentance.

Repentance is the first thing required of them who take upon them the profession of the gospel ; without this, whatever is attempted or attained to is only a dishonour to Christ and a disappointment unto men. This is the method of preaching, confirmed by the command and example of Christ Himself; "Repent and believe the gospel." And almost all the sermons that we find, not only of John the Baptist in a way of preparation for the declaration of the gospel, but of the apostles also in pressing the actual reception of it on the Jews and Gentiles, have this as their first principle, namely, the necessity of repentance. Hence, in the preaching of the gospel, it is said, "God commandeth all men everywhere to repent."

It is therefore evident that this was the first doctrinal principle, as to their own duty, which was pressed on and fixed in the minds of men on their first instruction in the gospel. The *supreme original* cause of repentance is the goodwill, grace, and bounty of God. It is *immediately collated* on the souls of men by Jesus Christ as a fruit of His death; and the *nature* of it is expressed in the conversion of the Gentiles—it is "unto life." (Acts xi. 18.) Repentance is a change of mind concerning "dead works," everything that hath the nature of sin is now seen to be evil, evil in itself, evil to the sinner, evil in its present effects and consequences. Repentance respects the will and affections; the change of the will, or taking away of the will of sinning, is the principal part of repentance; it is a repentance *from* dead works, that is, in the relinquishment of them.

There is no interest in Christ or Christian religion to be obtained without "repentance from dead works;" the Lord Jesus came not only to *save* men from their sins, but to *turn* them from their sins, —to turn them from their sins that they may be saved from them. That any person living in sin without repentance should have an interest in Christ is inconsistent with the glory of God and the honour of Jesus Christ.

"**And of faith toward God.**" Repentance is coupled with faith, they can never be severed; where the one is, there is the other, and where either is not there is neither, whatever be pretended. The whole is expressed by "Repent ye, and believe the gospel." Hence you read that Paul testified both to Jews and Greeks "repentance toward God, and faith toward our Lord Jesus Christ." Faith in God, as to the accomplishing of the great promise, in sending His Son Jesus Christ to save us from our sins, is the great fundamental principle of our interest in and profession of the gospel. The promise of sending Jesus Christ was the *first express engagement that God ever made of His faithfulness and veracity unto any creatures.* Hence this was the first and immediate object of faith in man after the fall. The first thing proposed to man was to believe in God, with respect unto His faithfulness in the future accomplishment of this promise; and faith concerning its actual accomplishment is the first thing required of us. This is the *greatest promise* that God ever gave to the children of men, and therefore faith in Him with respect hereunto is both necessary unto us, and tends greatly to His glory.

The third principle of the doctrine of Christ, according to the order and sense of the words, is the **"resurrection from the dead."** The doctrine of the resurrection is a *foundation principle* of the gospel, the faith whereof is indispensably necessary unto the obedience and consolation of all who profess it. It is *most clearly, evidently and fully* taught and declared in the Scriptures. It hath the most solemn confirmation and pledge in the resurrection of Christ from the dead. It hath a peculiar influence unto obedience under the gospel, for it is an animating principle of gospel obedience, because we are assured by it that nothing we do therein shall be lost. "God is not unrighteous to forget our work and labour of love;" this teaches us that such work and labour shall not only be *remembered* but *rewarded*. It is such a reward as is absolutely a free gift, a gift of grace.

"And of eternal judgment." This is the fourth foundation principle. It is the immediate consequent of the resurrection from the dead. All men, good and bad, must stand in their lot at the general judgment. "We shall all stand before the judgment-seat of Christ." "Eternal" respects not the duration of the judgment, but its end and effect. "God hath appointed a day wherein He will judge the world in righteousness," and this day is commonly called "the day of judgment." God hath not only not revealed when that day shall be, but He hath decreed not to reveal it. Jesus Christ is the Judge; the persons to be judged are, 1. Fallen angels. 2. All men universally; in especial, all the *godly*, all such as have believed and obeyed the gospel, shall be judged (Luke xxi. 36; Rom. xiv. 12; 2 Tim. iv. 8) (whether all their sins shall be then called over and made known unto others, seeing they are known unto Him who is more in Himself and unto us than all the world besides, I question); and all the *ungodly* and impenitent sinners. (2 Peter ii. 9; Jude 15.)

The *rule* whereby all men shall be judged is the law of their obedience made known unto them. As, 1. The Gentiles before the coming of Christ shall be judged by the *law of nature*, which all of them openly transgressed. (Rom. ii. 12-14.) 2. The Jews of the same time by the *law*, and the light into redemption from sin super-added thereunto, that is, by the rule, doctrine, precepts, promises of the law and the prophets. 3. By the *gospel* unto all men unto whom it hath been offered or preached. (Rom. ii. 16.) The rule of judgment at the last day neither is nor shall be any other but what is preached every day in the dispensation of the gospel. In the word of the gospel is the eternal condition of all the sons of men positively determined and declared. These then are the fundamental principles of the Christian religion, which the Apostle calls in the text, *"the doctrine of baptisms, and of laying on of hands.*" That is, this is a summary of the doctrine wherein they were to be instructed who were to be baptized, and to have imposition of hands.

"**The doctrine of baptisms.**" There is no little difficulty by the word "baptisms" being in the plural. The most general interpretation of the words and meaning of the Apostle is, that though baptism is never to be repeated on the same subject, yet because those who are baptized are many, every one of them being made partakers of the same baptism in special, that of them all is called "baptisms," or the baptism of the many. Some have thought the reference is to the various baptisms, such as baptism of external purification, baptism of the Spirit, baptism of affliction, even unto blood; and this hath in it much probability, and which next unto what I have fixed on I should embrace. I adhere to my interpretation, because unto baptisms is added,

"**And of laying on of hands.**" Some have thought that the rite in the Church which is called "Confirmation" is intended, but as the whole business of confirmation is of a much later date, it cannot be that rite to which the Apostle refers. It must have respect to something that was then in common use. In Scripture mention is made of a fourfold imposition of hands by the Lord Christ and His apostles. 1. In the way of *authoritative benediction*; this was peculiar to the Lord Himself. 2. In healing diseases. 3. In setting apart of persons to the office and work of the ministry. 4. It was used by the apostles in the collation of the supernatural gifts of the Holy Ghost unto them that were baptized. This is that which is most probably intended by the Apostle.

V. 3. *And this will we do, if God permit.*

That is, we will "go on to perfection," I in teaching and you in learning. I will for the time present leave the foundation principles of the gospel, and I will proceed unto the mysteries of the gospel, especially those which concern the priesthood of Christ, and thereby raise up the building of your faith and profession upon the foundation that hath already been laid, whereby, through the grace of God, you may be carried on to perfection, and become skilful in the word of righteousness. From this determination of the Apostle, we may learn that no discouragements should deter the ministers of the gospel from proceeding in the declaration of the mysteries of Christ. Among the various discouragements they meet, the least is not what ariseth from the dulness of them that hear. There is nothing more irksome and grievous unto faithful preachers than the incapacity of their hearers to receive gospel mysteries, through their own negligence and sloth.

"**If God permit.**" If He in whose hand are my life and breath and all my ways, whose I am and whom I serve, and to whose disposal I willingly submit myself in all things, see good and be pleased to continue my life, opportunity, His assistance and all other things necessary to the work, I will proceed with my design and purpose to acquaint you with and instruct you in the great mysteries of the priesthood and sacrifice of Christ. There is indeed a supposition in these words of the continuance of God's gracious assistance and especial presence with him, without which he frequently declared that he could neither undertake nor accomplish anything that lay before him.

Vs. 4—6. *For [it is] impossible for those who were once enlightened, and have tasted of the heavenly gift, and were made partakers of the Holy Ghost, and have tasted the good word of God, and the powers of the world to come, if they shall fall away, to renew them again unto repentance; seeing they crucify to themselves the Son of God afresh, and put [Him] to an open shame.*

The Apostle had told them to whom he is writing that they were slow as to making progress in knowledge and in a suitable practice; he now lets them know the danger that there was in continuing in that slothful condition. That they might be acquainted with their danger, and stirred up to avoid it, he gives them an account of those who, after a profession of the gospel, beginning with a non-proficiency in it, do end in apostacy from it. The *first* thing in this description is that they **"were once enlightened."** They were "illuminated" by the instruction they had received in the doctrine of the gospel, and the impression thereby made on their minds by the Holy Ghost, for this is a common work of His, and is here so reckoned. The Apostle would have us know that it is a great mercy, a great privilege, to be enlightened with the doctrine of the gospel by the effectual working of the Holy Ghost; also, that it is such a privilege as may be lost, and end in the aggravation of sin, and the condemnation of those who were made partakers of it; also, that where there is a total neglect of the due improvement of this privilege and mercy, the condition of such persons is hazardous, as inclining towards apostacy. Let us learn from this, that there is a saving, sanctifying light and knowledge which this spiritual illumination riseth not unto, for though it transiently affects the mind with some glances of the beauty and glory and excellency of spiritual things, yet it doth not give that direct, steady, intuitive insight into them which is obtained by grace. Neither doth it renew, change or transform the soul into a conformity unto the things known by planting of them in the will and affections, as a gracious saving light doth.

The *second* thing asserted is that they have "**tasted the heavenly gift.**" So far as I can observe, "the gift" with respect unto God, as denoting the thing given, is nowhere used but to signify the Holy Ghost; and if this be so, the sense in this place is determined. The Holy Spirit is signally the gift of God under the New Testament. He is said to be "heavenly," or from heaven. An objection may be made to this interpretation, as the Holy Ghost is expressly mentioned in the next clause. But it is ordinary to have the same thing twice expressed in various words, to quicken the sense of them ; and then the following clause may be exegetical of this, declaring more fully and plainly what is here intended. It was the Holy Ghost who removed all the carnal worship and ordinances of Moses, and that by the full revelation of the accomplishment of all that was signified by them, and appoints the new, holy, spiritual worship of the gospel, that was to succeed in their room. Thus the Apostle warns these Hebrews that they "turn not away from Him that speaketh from heaven" (chap. xii. 25), that is, from Jesus Christ speaking in the dispensation of the gospel by the "Holy Ghost sent from heaven."

Let us enquire what it is to "taste" this heavenly gift. The word "taste" is used metaphorically. We taste things, and then either receive or refuse them, as we find occasion. That then which is ascribed to these persons is, that they had an experience of the power of the Holy Ghost, in the dispensation of the gospel and the institution of spiritual worship by it, a privilege which all men were not made partakers of. Observe that there is a goodness and an excellency in this heavenly gift, which may be tasted or experienced in some measure by such as never receive them in their life, power, and efficacy. They may taste of the word in its *truth*, not in its *power ;* also of the *outward* order of gospel worship, not its *inward* beauty ; also of the *gifts* of the Church, not its *graces*. Also observe, that a rejection of the gospel, its truth and worship, after some experience had of their worth and excellency, is a high aggravation of sin, and a certain presage of destruction.

The *third* thing said about these persons is added in these words, "**And were made partakers of the Holy Ghost.**" This is placed in the middle of the privileges enumerated, two preceding it, and two following after, as that which is the root and animating principle of them all. Observe, that the Holy Ghost is present with many as unto powerful operations, with whom He is not present as to gracious inhabitation ; many are made partakers of Him in spiritual gifts, who are never made partakers of Him in His saving graces.

It is added *fourthly*, "**And have tasted the good word of God.**" Observe, there is a goodness and excellency in the word of God, able to attract and affect the minds of men, who yet never arrive at sincere obedience unto it. Also that there is an especial

goodness in the word of the promise concerning Jesus Christ, and
the declaration of its accomplishment.

Lastly, it is added, " **And the powers of the world to come.**"
These powers were the gifts whereby those signs, wonders, and
mighty works were then wrought by the Holy Ghost; they had
been wrought either in or by these men, or by others in their sight,
whereby they had an experience of the glorious and powerful
working of the Holy Ghost in the confirmation of the gospel.
Yea, I judge that they in their own persons were partakers of these
powers, which was the highest possible aggravation of their apostacy, and that which peculiarly rendered their recovery impossible.

We may now see what it is the Apostle here intendeth when he
says, " **If they shall fall away.**" 1. It is not a falling into
this or that *actual sin,* be it of what nature it may. 2. It is not a
falling upon *temptation or surprisal,* for this falling away is pre-
meditated, and is of deliberation and choice. 3. It is not a falling
by a relinquishment or renunciation of some, though very material,
principles of Christian religion by error or seduction. But it is a
total renunciation of all the constituent principles and doctrines of
Christianity. Such was the sin of them who forsook the gospel
and returned to Judaism; this was accompanied by the open and
public renunciation of the gospel. This is the " falling away,"—a
voluntary resolved relinquishment of and apostasy from the gospel,
the faith, rule, and obedience thereof, which cannot be done without casting the highest reproach and contumely upon the Person of
Christ Himself.

" **To renew them again unto repentance.**" Upon their
profession of repentance toward God and faith in our Lord Jesus
Christ, they received the baptismal pledge of an inward renovation,
though really they were not partakers thereof. This state was
their renovation, and from this they fell. It is impossible to renew
them again, that is, to bring them again into this state of profession
by a second renovation and a second baptism.

" **Seeing they crucify to themselves the Son of God
afresh, and put Him to an open shame.**" They do it not
really, they cannot do so; but they do it to themselves morally.
By their apostasy they showed that they approved of the Jews in
crucifying Him as a malefactor. After having professed to have
had some knowledge and experience of the ways of Jesus Christ,
they now openly profess that upon trial of them they find nothing
in them for which they should be desired; now no man living can
attempt a higher dishonour against Jesus Christ than this. The
sin of those who forsake Christ and the gospel, after their conviction
of its truth and profession of it, is on many accounts far greater
than that of those who actually crucified Him.

Vs. 7, 8.   *For the earth, which drinketh in the rain that*

cometh oft upon it, and bringeth forth herbs meet for them
by whom it is dressed, receiveth blessing from God : but that
which beareth thorns and briers [is] rejected, and [is] nigh
unto cursing ; whose end [is] to be burned.

Observe, 1. The minds of all men by nature are universally and
equally barren with respect unto fruits of righteousness and holiness, meet for and acceptable unto God.   2. The dispensation of
the gospel unto men is an effect of the sovereign power and
pleasure of God, as much so as the giving of rain unto the earth.
3. God ordereth things in His sovereign unsearchable providence
so, that the gospel shall be sent unto what places and at what times
seem good unto Himself, even as He orders the rain to fall on one
place and not on another.   4. It is the duty of those unto whom
is committed the dispensation of the word of God to be diligent,
watchful, instant in their work, that their doctrine may, as it were,
continually drop and distil upon their hearers.   5. Attendance
unto the word preached, hearing of it with some diligence, and
giving it some kind of reception, makes no great difference among
men ; for this is common to those who never become fruitful.
6. God is pleased to exercise much patience towards those to whom
He once grants the mercy and privilege of His word.   7. Where
God grants the means, there He expects fruit.   8. Duties of gospel
obedience are fruits meet for God ; they are things that have a
proper and special tendency unto His glory.   9. Wherever there
are any sincere fruits of faith and obedience found in the hearts
and lives of professors, God graciously accepteth and blesseth
them.   10. Whilst the gospel is preached unto men, they are
under their great trial for eternity.   The application that is made
unto them is for an experiment as to how they will prove.   If they
acquit themselves in faith and obedience, they receive the blessing
of eternal life from God.   If they prove barren and unprofitable,
they are rejected of God, and cursed by Him.   11. Barrenness
under the dispensation of the gospel is always accompanied by an
increase of sin.   The utmost aim and work of the natural conscience and of the law is but to restrain sin ; they set a dam, as it
were, before the streams of sin ; but the gospel by converting the
sinner dries up the spring.   Now if this be rejected and despised,
what remains to set any bounds unto the lusts of men ?   *There are*
no sinners like barren Christians.   12. Ordinarily God proceeds to
the rejection and destruction of barren professors by degrees,
although they are seldom sensible of it until they fall irrecoverably
into ruin.

V. 9.   *But, beloved, we are persuaded better things of you,*
and things that accompany salvation, though we thus speak.

" **But, beloved,**"—notwithstanding this severe admonition, which I have upon the consideration of all circumstances been forced to use, yet my heart stands no otherwise affected toward you but as towards my countrymen, brethren and saints of God.

"**We are persuaded better things of you, and things that accompany salvation.**" His persuasion, being built upon a supposition that a good work was begun in them, was an act of faith built on the promises of God and the unchangeableness of His covenant. From this we may learn that we may, as occasions require, publicly testify that good persuasion which we have concerning the spiritual condition of others, and that unto themselves. The "better things" are these : they were not destitute of all saving grace and fruits, and therefore they were not liable to be destroyed.

"*And things that accompany salvation.*" There are, according to the tenor of the covenant of grace, such things bestowed on some persons as salvation doth infallibly accompany and ensue upon. For instance, there is a saving faith, which is the effect of God's immutable purpose of election. If that cannot be changed, then this faith cannot utterly fail and be lost.

V. 10. *For God [is] not unrighteous to forget your work and labour of love, which ye have showed toward His name, in that ye have ministered to the saints, and do minister.*

"**God is not unrighteous to forget your work.**" The work here intended is the "work of faith,"—the whole work of obedience to God, whereof faith is the principle, and that which moves us thereunto. Religion was their business, and gospel obedience their daily work. Observe, 1. That faith, if it be a living faith, will be a working faith. 2. We ought to look upon obedience as our work, which will admit of neither sloth nor negligence.

"**And labour of love.**" Love is the second great duty of the life of God which is brought to light by the gospel. Faith gives glory to God on high ; love brings peace on the earth; and there is no love in the whole world but what is derived from the gospel. Love is a fruit of the Spirit of Holiness, and is as much the gift of God as faith is. It is the effect of faith, for " faith worketh by love ; " believers are knit together by it, it is the cement whereby the whole mystical body of Christ is " fitly joined together and compacted." The mutual love among believers springs from and is animated by their mutual interest in Christ. This love acts by valuation, esteem and delight. The Psalmist says, " all his delight was in the saints, and in the excellent of the earth." John says, " we ought to lay down our lives for the brethren."

This love acts by all means in all ways and duties whereby the eternal, spiritual and temporal good of others may be promoted. Jesus Christ declares this love to be the great evidence unto the world of the truth and power of the gospel, as also of His own being sent of God. The great evidence of our being the disciples of Christ depends on our mutual love, in which consists the communion of saints. Without this love we are of *no use* in the Church of God; indeed, if we live not in the exercise of it, we have no grace in truth, nor any real interest in the gospel. This love hath a labour to undergo—your "labour of love."

A *lazy love* like that described by the Apostle James (chap. ii. 15, 16), and with which most men satisfy themselves, is no evidence of *saving faith*. Love meets with great opposition, hence the labour. It is opposed by *self-love*, which makes a man's own self his own centre, the beginning and end of all he doth ; also by *evil surmises*—these often require no small labour to cast out, so that we may give ourselves up to that love which " beareth all things, believeth all things, hopeth all things, endureth all things ; " also by *distrust of God's promises*—men are afraid that if they should enlarge themselves in a way of bounty towards others they may in time be brought to want themselves ; for where the objects of this exercise of love are multiplied, weariness is apt to befall us. From these and the like considerations, the Apostle here mentions the industrious " labour of love " that was in these Hebrews, as an evidence of their saving faith and sincerity.

" **Which ye have shewed towards His name.**" James saith, " Show me thy faith by thy works." To show the labour of love is so to labour in the duties of it, that the love shall be evident. " Let your light so shine before men, that they may see your good works, and glorify your Father which is in heaven." " In His name," may be read " towards His name,"—this makes it more emphatical. The words ensuing declare that the *saints* were the immediate object of this love ; wherefore, it is a love unto the saints on the account of the name of God that is intended. It is a due regard unto the name of God that gives life, spirituality, and acceptance unto all the duties of love which we perform towards others.

" **In that ye have ministered to the saints and do minister.**" All believers are " saints ; " they are the " called " and the " sanctified in Christ Jesus." Every believer is sanctified, and every one who is not sanctified is no true believer, so that " believers " and " saints " are the same. These saints here referred to are supposed to be in such an outward condition as to stand in need of being administered unto ; they were in some kind of want or distress. It may be said that if the Church in general is principally composed of the poor, how can they exercise the labour of love in administering to the wants of others? I fear we do not sufficiently understand what was the frame and spirit of these early believers.

The Apostle tells us concerning the church in Macedonia, when they were under trials, afflictions, persecutions, " their deep poverty abounded unto the riches of their liberality." The contribution of outward things is but one way of ministration unto the saints; there are spiritual aids and assistances in visiting, exhorting, comforting, that belong to the "labour of love."

Observe, 1. That it is the will and pleasure of God, that many of His saints be in a condition in this world wherein they stand in need of being ministered unto. 2. The great trial of our love consists in our regard unto the saints that are in distress. 3. It is the glory and honour of a church, the principal evidence of its spiritual life, when it is diligent and abounds in those duties of faith and love which are attended with the greatest difficulties.

Now, " *God is not unrighteous to forget the work of faith and the labour of love.*" By the righteousness of God is to be understood His fidelity in keeping and accomplishing His promises. He who is righteous will not forget. Observe, 1. Our perseverance in faith and obedience, though it requires our duty and constancy therein, yet depends not on them absolutely, but on the righteousness of God in His promises. 2. Nothing shall be lost that is done for God, or in obedience unto Him. He is not unjust to forget our labour of love. 3. The certainty of our future reward, depending on the righteousness of God, is a great encouragement unto present obedience.

V. 11. *And we desire that every one of you do show the same diligence to the full assurance of hope unto the end.*

" **And we desire.**" Zeal for the glory of God, real compassion for the souls of men, and an especial conscientious regard unto our duty and office, kindle and supply fuel unto those fervent desires for the good of our people.

" **That every one of you.**" He had such a care of the whole flock, as to be solicitous for the good of each individual among them.

" **Do show the same diligence.**" Continue in the performance of these duties, so as to give the same evidence of your state and condition as formerly. Our profession will not be preserved, nor the work of faith and love carried on unto the glory of God and our own salvation, without a constant studious diligence in the preservation of the one, and the exercise of the other. This shows us that ministerial exhortation unto duty is needful, even unto them who are sincere in the practice of it, that they may abide and continue therein.

" **To the full assurance of hope.**" Faith hath respect unto the promise; hope to the thing promised; hope is the fruit of faith, it being the proper acting of the soul towards things believed as good, absent and certain. Where faith begets no hope, it is to be feared the faith is not genuine; where hope exceeds the evidence or assurance of faith, it is but presumption. In the due exercise of hope they would be relieved and supported in the midst of all their troubles, and enabled to rejoice and glory in them. The full assurance of hope is an especial degree of it in its own improvement. Diligence promotes a full assurance of hope, because, 1. God hath appointed it as the way and means by which we shall come to assurance. 2. It hath a proper and natural tendency to this end, for by diligence hope is increased in us. 3. By our diligent attendance unto our duties of faith and love, every sin will be prevented, whereby our hope would be weakened or impaired.

" Unto the end." There is no time or season when we may be discharged from the work of faith and labour of love; no condition to be attained in this life, wherein this diligence will not be necessary. We must attend unto it until we are absolutely discharged from the whole warfare. Observe, that we are not only to have " hope," but we are to labour for the "assurance of hope." It is one of the best evidences that any grace is true and saving when we labour to grow and thrive in it; also that hope, being improved by the due exercise of faith and love, will grow up into such an assurance of rest, life, immortality and glory, as shall outweigh all the troubles and persecutions that in this world may befall us on the account of our profession.

V. 12. *That ye be not slothful, but followers of them who through faith and patience inherit the promises.*

"That ye be not slothful." In chap. v. 11 the Apostle had warned them not to be dull—slothful in hearing; here he warns them against being dull—slothful in works. Spiritual slothfulness is ruinous of any profession, though otherwise never so hopeful; it is the habitual indisposition and unreadiness of the mind to the entire principle of our spiritual welfare. The principal cause of slothfulness is unbelief, as faith is the principal cause of diligence and watchfulness.

"But followers of them who through faith and patience." The persons referred to in the word " them " are the patriarchs of the Old Testament, and more especially Abraham, the " father of the faithful." By inheriting the promises is meant a real participation in the grace and mercy proposed in them, with eternal glory. This they all received, being saved by faith even as we. The way they took to inherit the promises was "through faith and patience." This faith was with respect to the covenant and promise of grace in Christ Jesus. The benefits of the mediation of Jesus Christ, who had not yet come in the flesh, were made present and effectual unto them by the promise. The word "patience" is elsewhere translated "longsuffering." The way of God's heroes, the patriarchs of the Church and people, unto their rest and glory, was by faith, patience, longsuffering, humility, enduring persecution, self-denial, and the spiritual virtues so despised by the world.

"**Inherit the promises.**" How come we to inherit the promises ? By being heirs unto it; heirs by God's gratuitous adoption (see Rom. viii. 15, 17). Observe, 1. All believers have a right unto an inheritance, which is secured to them by the promise, covenant and oath of God. The *value* of this inheritance is inexpressible ; it is a " kingdom ; " it is " salvation ; " it is the "grace of life ; " it is " eternal life;" it is God Himself who hath promised to be our reward (Rom. viii. 17). 2. The providing of examples for us in the Scriptures, which we ought to imitate and follow, is an effectual way of teaching, and a great fruit of the care and kindness of God towards us. 3. There is in these examples made known to us what disturbances may befall us in our course of obedience. I confess great wisdom and caution are necessary in the consideration of the sins and falls of the saints under the Old Testament ; we know not their circumstances, their light, their grace, their temptations, their repentance, nor what was the indulgence of God towards sinners before the fulness of the dispensation of grace came by Jesus Christ. 4. The certain end of a course of holy obedience is in them proposed unto us. If we follow them in their work, we shall not fail to partake with them in their reward.

Vs. 13—16. *For when God made promise to Abraham, because He could swear by no greater, He sware by Himself, saying, Surely blessing I will bless thee, and multiplying I will multiply thee. And so, after he had patiently endured, he obtained the promise. For men verily swear by the greater ; and an oath for confirmation* [*is*] *to them an end of all strife.*

"**For when God made promise to Abraham.**" The person to whom the promise was made was Abraham. Now on many accounts it was meet that he should be proposed as an example. Naturally he was the head of their families ; it was he who, as it were, got them their inheritance, for the *promise* now accomplished was first signally given to him, and therein the gospel was declared, in the faith whereof they are now exhorted to persevere. And then the promise was not given to him merely on his own account, but he was singled out to be a pattern and example for all believers. It was God who made promise to Abraham.

"**Because He could swear by no greater, He sware by Himself.**" He gave His promise in the way of an oath, yet the oath and the promise are to be considered separately. The nature of this oath of God consists in an express engagement of those holy properties whereby He is known to be God unto the accomplishment of what He promiseth or threateneth. God sware by Himself, because there was none greater whereby He might swear. We shall see the end and use of this oath when we come to consider v. 17.

"**Saying, Surely blessing I will bless thee, and multi= plying I will multiply thee.**" By Myself have I sworn— surely, undoubtedly, "*Blessing I will bless thee,*" I will do so without fail, I will do so greatly without measure, and eternally without end. By the redoubling of the word, God would impress our minds with the sincerity of His intentions, and the stability of His purposes. This promise may be considered as personal unto Abraham, also as it regards all the elect of God, and their interest in it, of whom he was the representative. There is that which was carnal, temporal, and typical in the promise; and there was also that which is spiritual and eternal, typed out by those other things.

As to the carnal things, God increased him in wealth and riches and power until he was esteemed as a " mighty prince." (Gen. xxiii. 6.) And this in the blessing was a type and pledge of that full administration of grace and spiritual things which was princi- pally intended. Also he was blessed in his posterity,—they were to be as the " stars in heaven," or as the " sand on the seashore," innumerable, and their success and prosperity was to be such " that they should possess the gates of their enemies." In all these things they were typical of the more numerous subjects of the kingdom of Christ, and of His spiritual conquest for them and in them of all their spiritual adversaries.

The peculiar interest of Abraham in this promise as to spiritual things may also be considered, especially that the Lord Christ should come of his seed according to the flesh, and being the first to embrace this promise, he became the spiritual father of all that do believe. Wherever the promise of God is absolutely engaged, it will break through all difficulties and oppositions unto a perfect accomplishment.

"**And so, after he had patiently endured, he obtained the promise.**" Observe, 1. That Abraham was exposed to trials and temptations about the truth and accomplishment of this promise; he " patiently endured." 2. That he was not discom- posed or exasperated by them so as to wax weary, or to fall off from a dependence on God; " against hope he believed in hope." 3. That he abode a long time in this state and condition, waiting on God and trusting in His power. It is not a thing quickly tried whether a man will " patiently endure."

" *He obtained the promise.*" Some have thought this refers to the birth of Isaac, but as the promise which the Apostle hath respect unto was made when Isaac was upwards of twenty years old, it cannot be his birth that is the thing promised. That which

the Apostle intends is the actual exhibition of the promised Seed.
Abraham's obtaining the promise was his enjoyment of the mercy,
benefit, and privilege of it, in every state and condition, whereof in
that state and condition he was capable.   Spiritually he was
justified in his own person, and therein enjoyed all the mercy and
grace which by the promised Seed, when actually exhibited, we can
be made partakers of.   Whatever difficulty and opposition may lie
in the way, patient endurance in faith and obedience will infallibly
bring us into the full enjoyment of the promise.   Faith gives such
an interest unto believers in all the promises of God, as that they
obtain even those promises—that is, the benefit and comfort of
them—whose actual accomplishment in this world they do not
behold.

" For men verily swear by the greater, and an oath for
confirmation is to them an end of all strife."   Observe,
1. That there is, as we are in a state of nature, a strife and difference
between God and us.   2. That the promises of God are gracious
proposals of the only way and means for the ending of that strife.
3. That the oath of God, interposed for the confirmation of these
promises, is every way sufficient to secure believers against all
temptations and objections, in all trials and straits about peace
with God through Jesus Christ.   4. That the custom of using
oaths, swearing, cursing, &c., in common communication is not only
an open transgression of the third commandment, but it is a
practical renunciation of the authority of Jesus Christ, who hath
expressly interdicted it.   5. That swearing by the name of God in
truth, righteousness, and judgment is an ordinance of God for the
end of strife amongst men; perjury is justly reckoned among the
worst of sins, and is that which reflects the greatest dishonour on
God, and tendeth to the ruin of human society.

Vs. 17—20.   *Wherein God, willing more abundantly to
show unto the heirs of promise the immutability of His
counsel, confirmed [it] by an oath : that by two immutable
things, in which [it was] impossible for God to lie, we might
have a strong consolation, who have fled for refuge to lay
hold upon the hope set before us : which [hope] we have as
an anchor of the soul, both sure and stedfast, and which
entereth into that within the veil; whither the Forerunner is
for us entered, [even] Jesus, made an High Priest for ever,
after the order of Melchisedec.*

"Wherein God willing."   The words direct unto the introduction of the end of God's oath, expressed in the words following,
" In this matter God sware by Himself, that thereby the heirs of
promise might not only be settled in faith, but moreover receive

strong consolation." God willed to do this; not only was it according to His inclination and disposition to do so, but it was a determinate act and purpose which He willed. The sovereign will of God is the sole cause and spring of all the mercy, grace, and consolation of which believers are made partakers in this world. God wills the grace and the consolation, and it is so.

" **More abundantly to show unto the heirs of promise the immutability of His counsel.**" The "*counsel*" of God is the eternal purpose of His will : in this particular place it was His holy, wise purpose to give His Son to be of the seed of Abraham, for the salvation of the heirs of promise. This is the counsel which contained all the mercy and the grace of the promise, with the securing of them unto believers. Of this counsel it is affirmed that it is immutable—not subject to any change. God takes the whole absolutely on Himself, both as to the ordering and disposing of all things and means unto the end intended. Such was the counsel of God concerning the sending His Son to be of the seed of Abraham, and the blessing that should ensue thereon. This "*immutability of His counsel*" He was willing to "*show unto the heirs of promise.*" All the gracious actings of God toward us are the execution of His holy, immutable purpose; and all the promises are the declarations of those purposes. God's essential veracity is engaged in His promises, and this declareth the nature of unbelief, "*He that believeth not God hath made Him a liar.*"

God was willing to give a peculiar evidence of the immutability of His counsel; He would do so "*more abundantly;*" the promise of God is sufficient to give us security; yet, because something further might be useful, He would add a further confirmation to His word; this He did from a superabounding love and care; He confirmed His promise by an oath. He showed this immutability of His counsel to the "*heirs of promise;*" to all believers under the Old and New Testament. Believers are called heirs of promise with respect unto the promise itself, and with respect unto the thing promised. The "*heirs of promise*" are "*heirs of God,*" that is, of the whole inheritance that He has promised His children.

" **Confirmed it by an oath.**" He interposed Himself with an oath, and thus gives security to faith. He mediated by an oath; He interposed Himself between the promise and the faith of believers; and swearing by Himself, He takes it on His life, holiness, being, truth, to make the promise good. Observe, 1. That the purpose of God for the saving the elect by Jesus Christ is an act of infinite wisdom as well as of sovereign grace. 2. That the life and assurance of our present comfort and future glory depend on the immutability of the counsel of God. 3. That the purpose of God concerning the salvation of the elect by Jesus Christ became immutable from hence, that the determination of His will was accompanied by infinite wisdom. 4. That infinite goodness, as acting itself in Christ, was not satisfied in providing and preparing good things for believers, but it would also show and declare itself unto them, for their present consolation. 5. That it is not all mankind universally, but a certain number of persons, under certain qualifications, to whom God designs to manifest the immutability of His counsel, and to communicate the effects thereof. It is only the " *heirs of promise* " whom God intendeth. 6. That God alone knows the due measure of divine condescension, or what becomes the divine nature therein. Who could have once apprehended, who durst have done so, that the holy God should swear by Himself, to confirm His word and truth unto such worthless creatures as we are ? 7. That so unspeakable is the weakness of our faith that we stand in need of unconceivable condescension for its confirmation. Who would not think that the declaration of the immutability of His counsel by way of promise was every way sufficient ? But God knew that we stood in need of yet more; not that there was want of sufficient evidence in His promise, but such a want of stability in us as stood in need of a superabundant confirmation, as we shall see in the next verse.

"**That by two immutable things, in which it was impossible for God to lie.**" The " *two immutable things* " are the promise and the oath of God. Both of these are *equally immutable*. The promise is not confirmed by the oath because it was weak, and therefore needed the oath to strengthen it. We must carry along with us the infinite and inconceivable condescension of God in this matter. " *In which it was impossible for God to lie* "— that is, to deceive. The highest security among men consists in a promise confirmed by an oath ; God uses these in our case, and therefore it is impossible that He should lie. The special design in this was that,

"**We might have strong consolation, who have fled for refuge to lay hold upon the hope set before us.**" Strong consolation is that which prevails against opposition. There are comforts to be taken, or often are taken, from earthly things, but they are weak, languid, and such as fade and die upon the first appearance of a vigorous opposition, but this " strong consolation " will prevail against all creature oppositions whatever. The people unto whom God designs this strong consolation are those who " *have fled for refuge to lay hold upon the hope set before them.*" In the judgment of many there is an allusion here to the manslayer fleeing to the " city of refuge." These words convey an apprehension of danger, and speed and diligence in an endeavour to reach a place of safety.

In our case they flee to. " *lay hold of the hope.*" The promise being proposed unto us, is the cause and object of our faith, on the account of the faithfulness of God therein ; faith brings hope, whose object is the same promise, or the good things thereof.

Hence it is called, " *the hope;*" without it we could have none, there being neither cause nor object for it. And this hope is "*set before us*," or proposed unto us, which it is in the declaration of the promise of the gospel. Therein it is proposed to us as the object of our faith and hope, and as the means of the strong consolation which God is so abundantly willing that we should receive. And we "*lay hold*" of this hope ; that is, we hold fast what we lay hold on, with all our might and power.

There will be many endeavours to strike off the hand of faith from laying hold on the promise ; and many more to loosen its hold when it hath taken it ; but it is in the nature of faith, and it is a part of our duty, strongly to lay hold upon, and firmly to retain the promise when we have reached unto it. Observe, 1. That a sense of danger and ruin from sin is the first thing which occasions a soul to look out after Christ in the promise. 2. A full conviction of sin is a great and shaking surprisal unto a guilty soul. 3. The revelation, or discovery of the promise, or of Christ in the promise, is that alone which directs convinced sinners unto their proper course and way. 4. Where there is the least of saving faith, upon the first discovery of Christ in the promise, it will stir up the whole soul to make out towards Him. In going to Christ upon His invitation and call, in laying hold upon Him in the promise, consists the nature, life, and being of the duty, obedience, and grace of that faith which is in the heirs of promise. 5. It is the duty and wisdom of all those unto whom Christ in the promise is once discovered, by any gospel means or ordinance set before them, to admit of no delay of a thorough closing with Him. 6. There is a spiritual strength and vigour required unto the securing of our interest in the promise,—we are to lay fast and firm hold upon it. 7. The promise is an assured refuge unto all sin-distressed souls who betake themselves thereunto. 8. Where any soul convinced of sin doth betake himself unto the promise for relief, God is abundantly willing that he should receive strong consolation.

" **Which hope we have as an anchor of the soul, both sure and stedfast.**" This hope is that grace whereon our assurance, or that full persuasion of faith which gives confidence, and glory doth depend. This hope is a firm trust in God for the enjoyment of those good things contained in the promise, at the appointed season, raising in the soul an earnest desire after them, and an expectation of them. This hope springs from faith ; its very nature and essence consists of *trust in God*. This hope is compared to an " anchor." Anchors are of use in storms and tempests, also when the ship is in harbour to keep it steady in some particular position. Our souls are exposed to storms—a stress of spiritual dangers, persecutions, afflictions, temptations, fears, sins, death, &c. And these dangers sometimes come with violence, and in their own nature they tend to our ruin and destruction. The Apostle gives us a description of these storms, with the use of this " anchor " in them, and the success thereof in the safety of the souls of believers. (Rom. viii. 33—38, etc.)

The ordinary occasions of this life, and our duties towards God and man therein, are like unto the tradings of ships in their harbour, and therein a good and sure anchor is necessary, the neglect of the use of which has proved ruinous unto many. This anchor—hope—is " sure ;" it will not fail, it may be safely trusted in ; and it is " *stedfast;* " no violence of winds or storms can either break it or move it from its hold. Hope proceeding from, and built on faith, is infallible, and will not deceive. It is firm and invincible, against all oppositions ; not indeed from itself, but from the ground which it fixeth upon, namely Christ in the promise, as the next words declare.

" **And which entereth into that within the veil.**" Notice —an anchor is cast downwards, and fixeth itself in the bottom of the sea ; but hope ascends upwards, and fixeth itself in heaven, or in that which is therein. " *Within the veil,*" is within and above the visible heavens, the place of God's glorious residence, the holy tabernacle not made with hands, where the Lord Christ continueth to administer for His Church, and this hope " *entereth into.*" The heavens are as a veil unto the sense and reason of men, there their sight and thoughts are bounded, they can neither discern nor judge of anything that is above or within the veil. But faith, with hope, pierceth through the veil ; no created thing can keep them at a distance from God Himself. That which hope fixeth on is, the Father as the Author, the Lord Christ as the purchaser, and the covenant as the conveyance of all grace ; all of which things were typically represented by the things within the veil of old.

Observe, 1. That all true believers are exposed to storms and tempests ; this makes anchors so necessary for them. 2. These storms would prove ruinous unto the souls of believers, were they not indefeasibly interested by faith and hope in the promise of the gospel. 3. No distance of place, no interposition of difficulties, can hinder the hope of believers from entering into the presence of and fixing itself on God in Christ. 4. The strength and assurance of the faith and hope of a believer is invisible unto the world. 5. Hope, firmly fixed on God in Christ by the promise, will hold steady and preserve the soul in all the storms and trials that may befall it. 6. It is our wisdom at all times, but especially in times of trial, to be sure that our anchor has a good holdfast in heaven.

" **Whither the Forerunner is for us entered, even Jesus, made an High Priest for ever after the order of Melchisedec.**" The Apostle aims to give new assurance unto the efficacy and prevalency of hope fixed on the promise, as it enters within the veil ; namely, because Christ, our High Priest, is there. He calls Him here by His name " Jesus," that is, Saviour ; He had this name given Him by God Himself, with respect unto the work which He was to do. And He is Jesus still, " able to save them to the uttermost that come unto God by Him." This " same Jesus " is our Saviour in every state and condition ; the same on the cross, and the same at the right hand of the Majesty on high. The Apostle describes Him here as a " *Forerunner for us.*" Great mysterious truths of Scripture may often be comprised in one word ; in this place alone is this title given to the Lord Jesus, and so it may be said of the name " Surety," which the Apostle makes use of in the next chapter (v. 22). He is called " *the Forerunner ;* " because of the greatness of the matter He had in hand, not manageable by any other. When He entered heaven, He did it not merely for Himself, but to go before, to lead and conduct the whole Church unto the same glory. He is a Forerunner " *for us ;* "—for all believers in all ages, times, and places.

As a Forerunner He " *entered within the veil,*" that is, into heaven itself, into the presence of God. In connection with this it should be remembered what *He hath already done for us,* that He hath completely finished the work He had to do upon the earth, and that God gave His blessed approbation of all that He had done. We also should remember what *He hath yet to do for us.* He entered as a Priest into heaven, where He continues as our Forerunner in the exercise of that office, as the Apostle declares, " *made an High Priest for ever after the order of Melchisedec :* " whereof we must treat in the next chapter.

Observe, 1. That the Lord Jesus, having thus entered heaven as our Forerunner, gives us manifold security of our entrance hither in the appointed time. He passed through all the storms and trials, temptations, persecutions, and death itself, that we are exposed to, and yet is landed safe in eternal glory. His anchor was trust and hope in all His storms, and it was tried to the utmost, yet it preserved Him in them all. He is now *where our hope is fixed,* within the veil, where He takes care of it and will preserve it unto the end. 2. If Christ be entered as our Forerunner, it is our duty to be following Him with all the speed we can. It is required of us that we be willing to follow Him in *the way* He went, as well as unto the place He went. He went the way of *obedience* (Heb. v. 8, 9). He walked the path of *suffering* (Heb. xii. 2). Holiness and the cross are the two essential parts of the way whereby our forerunner entered into glory. Let us take heed that we burden not ourselves with anything that will retard us. 3. What will not He do for us, who in the height of His glory is not ashamed to be esteemed our Forerunner ? What love, what grace, what mercy may we not expect from Him? 4. When our hope and trust enter within the veil, it is Christ as our Forerunner that in a peculiar manner they are to fix and fasten themselves upon.

CHAPTER SEVEN

Vs. 1—3. *For this Melchisedec, king of Salem, priest of the most high God, who met Abraham returning from the slaughter of the kings, and blessed him; to whom also Abraham gave a tenth part of all; first being by interpretation King of righteousness, and after that also King of Salem, which is, King of peace; without father, without mother, without descent, having neither beginning of days, nor end of life; but made like unto the Son of God; abideth a priest continually.*

"**For this Melchisedec.**" He was a mere man, and no more, for " Every high priest " was to be " taken from among men ; " so that the Son of God Himself could not have been a priest had He not assumed our nature. He—Melchisedec—came not to his office by the right of primogeniture (which includes a genealogy) or any other successive way, but was raised up and immediately called of God thereunto, for in that respect Christ is said to be a Priest after his order ; neither did he have any successor on the earth, nor could have, for there was no law to constitute an order of succession, and he was a priest only after an extraordinary call.

"**King of Salem.**" His being a king made his typical ministry the more eminent and conspicuous ; and by his wealth and possessions as a king, he was enabled unto the solemn and costly discharge of his office of priesthood in sacrifices and other solemnities. Observe that the Lord Christ as King of His Church is plentifully stored with all spiritual provisions for the relief, support-ment, and refreshment of all believers, in and under their duties, and will give it out to them as their occasions do require. For as Melchisedec represented the Lord Christ in what he did, so Abraham in his battle and victory was a type of all believers in their warfare and conflict with all their spiritual adversaries. Wherefore, as he and all his were refreshed by the kingly bounty of Melchisedec,. so shall believers be from the munificence and unsearchable riches of Christ. " *King of Salem.*" There have been many inquiries and opinions as to where this Salem was. As Jerusalem was designed to be the place where the Lord Christ was to begin and exercise His priestly office, it may well be supposed that there His illustrious type was to appear and be manifested.

"**Priest of the most high God.**" In this general assertion that he was a priest, we may learn that he was *truly and really a man*, and not an angel, or, as some have thought, an appearance of the Son of God, for "every high priest is taken from among men ; "

also that he had an extraordinary call to this office, for he falleth under that rule of the Apostle, "No man taketh this honour unto himself, unless he be called of God" (chap. v. 4). "Most high" is descriptive of the majesty, power, and authority of God over all.

"**Who met Abraham returning from the slaughter of the kings.**" Abraham having slain the kings and overthrown their armies, is returning with great glory and honour, when Melchisedec, knowing the state of things, comes out to meet him.

"**And blessed him, to whom also Abraham gave a tenth part of all.**" This blessing included *prayer* for Abraham, and *thanksgiving* on his account unto God. In virtue of his office as a priest, he blessed. Melchisedec was a type of Christ, and represented Him in what he did. And Abraham in all these things represented his posterity according to the faith. As a priest, Melchisedec received tithes from Abraham. Observe, that whatever we receive signally from God in a way of mercy, we ought to return a portion of it unto Him in a way of duty. A bountiful part of our enjoyments is to be separated unto the use and service of the worship of God, particularly unto the comfortable and honourable support of them that labour in the ministry.

"**First, being by interpretation King of righteousness, and after that King of Salem, that is, King of peace.**" That is typically, he was king of righteousness, and king of peace ; to be the king of righteousness and peace is to be the dispenser of righteousness and peace to others. Thus it was with Melchisedec as a type of Jesus Christ.

"**Without father, without mother, without descent, having neither beginning of days nor end of life, but made like unto the Son of God.**" Melchisedec was without genealogy, in that the Spirit of God, who so faithfully recorded the genealogies of other patriarchs and types of Christ, speaks nothing unto the purpose concerning him. We have no more to do with him, to learn from him, nor are concerned in him, but only as he is described in Scripture, and there is no mention there of his birth or death. All this that he might be the more signal representative of the Lord Christ in His priesthood. The Aaronic priesthood depended solely on their genealogy; but the priesthood of Christ was to depend on no such descent, "for it is evident that our Lord sprang of Judah, whereof Moses spake nothing concerning priesthood."—It was therefore necessary that he should be represented by a priest without genealogy, seeing that, as unto His office, He Himself was to have none. We must enquire wherein Melchisedec was a type of Christ, that is, how "he was made like unto the Son of God," or rather enquire as to those especial excellencies in Christ which were typified in Melchisedec.

Jesus Christ is "first, the King of Righteousness, and then the King of Peace ; " He is really and truly "the Priest of the most high God ; " He blesseth all the faithful, as Abraham, the father of the faithful, was blessed by Melchisedec ; He receiveth all the homage of His people, and all their grateful acknowledgments of the love and favour of God in their deliverance from all their enemies, as Melchisedec received the tenth of the spoils from Abraham ; He was really without progenitors or predecessors unto His office ; neither would I exclude a mystical sense from the intention in this place, for He was without a father as to His human nature, and without a mother as to His divine ; He was a Priest without genealogy, or derivation of His pedigree from the loins of Aaron, or any other that ever was a priest, and, moreover, was of a generation that none can declare ; He had in His divine Person, as the High Priest of the Church, neither beginning of days nor end of life, for the death which He underwent in the discharge of His office, being not the death of His whole Person, but of His human nature only, no interruption of His endless office did ensue thereon ; He was really the Son of God, as Melchisedec was like the Son of God ; He alone abideth a priest for ever, therefore hath no more a vicar, or substitute, in His office, or any deriving a real priesthood from Him, than had Melchisedec, whereof we shall speak afterwards.

V. 4. *Now consider how great this man* [*was*], *unto whom even the patriarch Abraham gave the tenth of the spoils.*

" **Now consider how great this man was.**" The Apostle doth four times in this epistle call upon the Hebrews to " consider" the things proposed to them, and that not unduly (chap. iii. 1 ; x. 24 ; xii. 3) ; and in this place. The word here means "diligently to behold or look into ; " from this exhortation we may learn that it will be fruitless and to no advantage to propose or declare the most solemn truths of the gospel, if those unto whom they are proposed do not diligently inquire into them, by study, meditation and prayer, with the careful use of all other means appointed for the search and investigation of the truth. Without these things in the hearers, ministers lose all their labour in the declaration of the most important mysteries of the gospel. The greatness of Melchisedec, here proposed unto earnest consideration, is that which he had in representing Jesus Christ, and his nearness unto God on that account ; and it were well that we all were really convinced that all true greatness consists in the favour of God, and our nearness unto Him, on account of our relation unto Jesus Christ.

"**Unto whom even the patriarch Abraham gave the tenth of the spoils.**" The proof of the greatness of Melchisedec here given is threefold. 1. In the nomination of the person that was subject unto him—Abraham ; he was the stock and root of the whole people, their common father, in whom they were first separated from the other nations to be a people of themselves. It was he who first received the promise and the covenant, with the token of it; therefore, the Hebrews esteemed Abraham next unto God Himself. 2. In the fact that Abraham was a patriarch, that is, a father who is a prince and ruler in his family. Those who succeeded Abraham are called "patriarchs;" but he, being the first of all these, is accounted the principal, and hath the pre-eminence over all the rest. If anyone were greater than Abraham in his own time, it must be acknowledged that it was upon the account of some privilege that was above all that ever that whole nation as descendants of Abraham were made partakers of. But that this was so the Apostle proves by the instance ensuing, namely, that Abraham gave to Melchisedec. 3. Abraham "gave the tenth of the spoils," not arbitrarily but in the way of a necessary duty; not as an honorary respect, but as a religious office. He gave "the tenth," delivering it up to the use and disposal of the priest of the most high God. He gave the tenth of the spoils, a portion taken out of the whole, and representing the whole. What further concerns the greatness of Melchisedec the Apostle declares in the ensuing verses, where it will fall under consideration. The sole reason that can be given for the greatness of Melchisedec is, that God raised him up, and disposed of him into that condition of His own good pleasure.

V. 5. *And verily they that are of the sons of Levi, who receive the office of the priesthood, have a commandment to take tithes of the people according to the law, that is, of their brethren, though they come out of the loins of Abraham.*

"**And verily they that are of the sons of Levi, who receive the office of the priesthood.**" The continuation of the argument, with further proof, is intended. All the Levites received tithes, but the Apostle refers to those Levites who received tithes as priests; the privilege of priesthood was granted only to one family among the Levites, even the family of Aaron; these are the sons of Levi whom the Apostle instructeth; and this order of His sovereign pleasure God required of them all to submit unto and acquiesce in.

"**Have a commandment to take tithes of the people according to the law.**" The command which obliged the people to pay tithes, obliged the "sons of Levi" to receive them. Those who on slight pretences do forego what is due to them with respect unto their office will on as slight pretences, when occasion serves, neglect what is due from them in their office. The priests of old neglected their wages, that they might have countenance in the neglect of their work. We take it for granted that the way of maintenance is changed as to the ministers of holy things under the New Testament. What was *legally* due to the priests, is now referred unto the voluntary *contributions* of them that have the benefit and advantage of the labours of the ministers of Christ. He hath "ordained that those who preach the gospel shall live of the gospel;" it is His command that those unto whom they dispense spiritual things shall supply them with temporal things.

"**That is, of their brethren, though they came out of the loins of Abraham.**" The whole people being equally interested in all the privileges of Abraham, or the Church of believers, it is manifest how great was the honour and pre-eminence of the priests, in that they took tithes from them all. If God will have some of the sons of Abraham to pay tithes, and some to receive them, is there any ground of complaint? Unto him that hath the most eminent gifts, God hath given of His own, and not of ours; He hath taken nothing from us with which to endow others, but supplied them out of His own stores. It is the prerogative of God to set up one and to put down another; He calleth whom He will to fill the office of the ministry, and there is no greater usurpation therein than the constitution of ministers by the laws, rules, and authority of men. For any to set up such in office as He hath not gifted for it, nor called unto it, is to sit in the temple of God, and to show themselves to be God.

V. 6. *But he whose descent is not counted from them received tithes of Abraham, and blessed him that had the promises.*

"**But he whose descent is not counted from them.**" Melchisedec was without descent—without genealogy, as we have seen. He could not be descended from the "sons of Levi," for in his days Levi was yet in the loins of Abraham. The Apostle is about to show by what *right* and title Melchisedec received tithes. There are but two ways by which men could have such a title, either by the law, and this way was confined to the sons of Levi; or by some special grant or privilege either before or above the law, and it was in this way Melchisedec had the right to receive tithes.

"**Received tithes of Abraham, and blessed him that had the promises.**" The Levitical priests received tithes of "*their brethren*," which was an evidence of their dignity by God's appointment; but Melchisedec received them of Abraham himself, which evidently declares the superiority of Melchisedec over the sons of Levi, and over Abraham himself. It is plain from the gospel that all the Jews looked on this as their great privilege and advantage that they were the sons of Abraham, whom they considered on all accounts the greatest and most honourable person that ever was in this world. Now, although there was much in this, yet when they began to abuse it, and trust in it, it was necessary that their confidence should be abated and taken down. But so difficult a matter was this to effect that the Apostle had to use every argument that had a real force and evidence in it; as it is plain that they were utterly ignorant in the instructive part of this story of Melchisedec.

That it may appear yet further how great Abraham was, the Apostle declares that it was he who "*had the promises.*" Hereby Abraham became " the father of the faithful," " the heir of the world," and the " friend of God ; " so that it exceedingly illustrates the greatness of Melchisedec, in that this Abraham paid tithes unto him. Others had received the promise before Abraham, yet in sundry things Abraham is preferred before them all : 1. He had the promise more plainly and clearly given unto him than any of his predecessors in the faith. 2. The promise was confirmed unto him by an *oath*, which it had not been unto any before. 3. The *promised Seed* was in it particularly confined to his posterity. 4. His receiving of the promise was that which was the foundation of the Church in his posterity, which he had peculiarly to deal withal. Abraham was blessed by Melchisedec, and by this blessing He was confirmed in his faith in God.

V. 7.　*And without all contradiction the less is blessed of the better.*

Observe, it is a great mercy and privilege when God will make use of any in the blessing of others with spiritual mercies. It is God alone who can originally and efficiently do so, who can actually and infallibly bless anyone. But yet He maketh use of others in various degrees of usefulness for their communication. Ministers bless the Church in the dispensation and preaching of the word unto the conversion and edification of the souls of men. So the Apostle speaks: " Unto you first God, having raised up His Son Jesus, sent Him to bless you, in turning away every one of you from his iniquities." This sending of Christ after His resurrection was the sending of Him in the ministry of the apostles and others. And the end thereof is to bless them unto whom He is preached. It is well if Christians do rightly consider what their duty is unto them who are appointed as a means of communicating spiritual blessings unto them.

V. 8.　*And here men that die receive tithes ; but there he* [*receiveth them*], *of whom it is witnessed that he liveth.*

" **And here** " is put in contrast with " **but there.**" " *Here*" is in respect of the case of the Levitical priesthood, and "*there*" respects the case of Melchisedec.

" **Men that die receive tithes, but there he receiveth them, of whom it is witnessed that he liveth.** " The foundation of the comparison is in this : they both received tithes, one "*here*," the other "*there*." The opposition and difference between them lies in this : the Levitical priests were "*men that die*," but it is witnessed that Melchisedec "*liveth*." 1. He had "neither beginning of days nor end of life " recorded in the Scripture ; it is thereby witnessed that, not absolutely but as to this typical consideration, "*he liveth*."

2. He did actually *continue his office* unto the end of that dispensation of God and His worship in which he was employed, and this witnesseth the perpetuity of his life in opposition to the Levitical priests. There was a time limit to the priesthood in the family of Aaron, and during that time one priest died and another succeeded him. But during the whole dispensation of things with respect unto Melchisedec, he continued in his own person to execute his office from first to last without being subject to death.

3. He is said to "*live*" because his office *continueth for ever*, and yet no mere mortal man succeeded him therein. 4. In the whole matter he is considered not absolutely and personally but *typically*, as representing someone else ; and what is represented in the type, but is really subjectively and properly found only in the antitype, may be affirmed of the type as such.

The life of the Church depends on the everlasting life of Jesus Christ. It is said of Melchisedec as a type of Him, that "*he liveth*." Christ doth so, and that for ever, and hereon, under the failings, infirmities, and death of all other administrators, doth depend the life, preservation, continuance, and salvation of the Church. But this must be spoken to particularly when we come to v. 25.

Vs. 9, 10. *And, as I may so say, Levi also, who receiveth tithes, paid tithes in Abraham. For he was yet in the loins of his father when Melchisedec met him.*

"**And as I may so say.**" The words are as if that which is expressed were *actually* so, namely, that Levi himself paid tithes, whereas it was only so *virtually*.

"**Levi also.**" He intendeth not the person of Levi absolutely, but his posterity, or the whole tribe proceeding from him. Levi is the same with the sons of Levi, who received the priesthood in the days of Aaron, the great-grandchild of Levi.

"**Who receiveth tithes, paid tithes in Abraham.**" When Abraham gave tithes to Melchisedec he did not in his own name only, but in the name of himself and his posterity. And this, upon the principles laid down, proves the pre-eminence of the priesthood of Melchisedec above that of the house and family of Levi. All the difficulty in the argument now is to prove the assertion that Levi did pay tithes in Abraham. This the Apostle proceeds to prove.

"**For he was yet in the loins of his father when**

Melchisedec met him.'' The force of this depends on this: that children, the whole posterity of anyone, are in his loins before they are born ; they can have no existence but with relation to their progenitors, even the remotest of them. It is not merely Levi being in the loins of Abraham with respect unto natural generation that he is said to be tithed in him; but his being in him with respect unto the covenant which Abraham entered into with God in the name of his whole posterity.

V. 11. *If therefore perfection were by the Levitical priesthood (for under it the people received the law), what further need [was there] that another priest should rise after the order of Melchisedec, and not be called after the order of Aaron ?*

" If therefore perfection were by the Levitical priest= hood." His reasoning is built upon a supposition that the Hebrews could not deny that " perfection " is the end aimed at in the priesthood of the Church. That priesthood which perfects the people in order unto their acceptance with God and future enjoyment of Him, their present righteousness and their future blessedness, is that which the Church stands in need of, and cannot rest till it comes unto. That priesthood which doth not do so, whatever use it may be for a season, yet it cannot be perpetual to the exclusion of another. The Hebrews knew that they could not be made perfect in any other way than by priesthood; they knew that all the ways appointed by the law to make atonement for sin, to attain righteousness and acceptance with God, depended on the priesthood and the services of it, in the sacrifices and other parts of divine worship. If therefore the Apostle proves that *"perfection"* could not be attained by the Levitical priesthood, it necessarily follows that there must be some more excellent priesthood remaining, as yet to be introduced.

The Hebrews would grant that the Levitical priesthood never rose to a higher pitch of glory than in the days of David and Solomon. Yet the Apostle says that " perfection " was not then attainable ; this he proves by the testimony of David himself, who prophesied that there was to be " another priest after the order of Melchisedec." If perfection was that which God designed by priesthood, and if it were attained to in David's day, to what end should another priest be promised to be raised up ? The Levitical priests could not by their utmost efficacy bring the Church into that state of perfection which God had designed for it in this world, and without which the glory of His grace had not been demonstrated. The chief thing now before us is to enquire what this state of perfection is. The things that belong to it are of two sorts, 1. Such as belong unto the souls and consciences of believers

—that is, of the Church ; and, 2. Such as belong to the worship of God itself.

As unto the first, there are seven things concurring unto the constitution of this state of perfection : 1. Righteousness. 2. Peace. 3. Light or knowledge. 4. Liberty with boldness. 5. A clear prospect into a future state of blessedness. 6. Joy. 7. Confidence and glorying in the Lord. As to the second there is, 1. The worship being spiritual. 2. Easy, as absolutely suitable unto the principles of the new creature. 3. In its being instructive. 4. From its relation to Christ as the High Priest. 5. From the entrance we have therein into the holy place. This is that " kingdom of God" which " is not meat and drink, but righteousness, and peace, and joy in the Holy Ghost."

It may be said that some of these things were enjoyed under the Levitical priesthood. The Apostle does not deny that it was so, yea, he proves at large that it was so (see c. xi.), only he denies that they had it by virtue of the Levitical priesthood. What they enjoyed of this kind was in virtue of " *another priesthood*," which was therefore to be introduced, and *the other*, which could not effect it, was to be removed. God had designed the whole dispensation of the law under the priesthood to this very end, that it should give the people *neither rest nor liberty*, but press and urge them to be looking after their full relief in the promised Seed. Here could be no perfection, for there was no rest.

" **For under it the people received the law.**" He proceeds to bring the law itself under the same censure of disability and insufficiency. It was " under" the Levitical priesthood that the people received the law. In vs. 18, 19, the Apostle concludes of the law, as of the priesthood here, that " it made nothing perfect."

" **What further need was there that another priest should arise after the order of Melchisedec, and not be called after the order of Aaron?** " By " *another priest*" he means one who was of another stock or order, one not of the tribe of Levi, nor of the order of Aaron, who was to arise and execute the office of a priest in compliance with the call and appointment of God. Though " another priest "—Christ—should *arise* after the order of Melchisedec, yet He was not *called* after that order, nor after the order of Aaron. The call of Christ unto His office, and that of Melchisedec, are nowhere compared. The call here spoken of denotes an external call to office, not an internal call. The real call of Christ unto His office, by Him who said unto Him, " Thou art My Son, this day have I begotten Thee," was such as the call of Melchisedec could not represent.

V. 12. *For the priesthood being changed, there is made of necessity a change also of the law.*

In this verse the Apostle evidently declares what he intended by "the law" in that foregoing, which "the people received under the Levitical priesthood." It was the whole "law of commandments contained in ordinances," or the whole law of Moses, so far as it was the rule of worship and obedience unto the Church ; for that law it is that followeth the fates of the priesthood. It appears, that in the preaching of the gospel, what most provoked the Jews was, that there was thereby inferred a cessation of and a taking away of the Mosaical institutions. They fell on Stephen under pretence that he had said, that "Jesus of Nazareth should change the customs which Moses delivered." This provoked their rage against the Apostle also. Yea, many of those who were converted to the faith of the gospel, yet continued obstinate in this persuasion, that the law of Moses was yet to continue in force (see Acts xxi. 20).

"**For the priesthood being changed.**" The office of priesthood might be transferred from one person to another, from one family to another, and yet the priesthood as to the kind and nature of it remain the same. This the Apostle mentions (vs. 13 and 14) as a part of his argument, to prove that the priesthood itself is changed ; the proof is this, that Moses in the institution of the priesthood made no mention of the tribe of Judah, and therefore, if the priesthood be transferred to that tribe, it must be of another kind than that before instituted. But the change is yet more than transferring the priesthood from one tribe to another, for the change in the priesthood is the same as that in the law. Now in v. 18 we are told that the change of the law was a "disannulling" or abolishing ; such therefore must be change in the priesthood. The Apostle proves that the priesthood was changed—abolished ; it was impossible that the priesthood of Levi could continue after that was brought in which is after the order of Melchisedec, for, 1. He —the new Priest—was to be of another tribe, as the Apostle immediately shows. 2. Because His priesthood was to be of another kind than that of Levi, which is demonstrated at large in the three ensuing chapters. 3. Because the priesthood of Aaron could never accomplish and effect the true and proper ends of priesthood, which the Church stood in need of, and without which it could not be made perfect.

"**There is made of necessity a change also of the law.**" God made the change ; it was necessary upon the removal of the priesthood to change the law. The whole administration of the law was confined to the Aaronical priesthood, so that without it no one could sacrifice to God, nor any ordinance of divine worship be observed ; the priesthood being taken away, the law itself, of necessity and unavoidably, ceaseth and becometh useless. So is the "law of commandments contained in ordinances taken out of the way," being "nailed unto the cross of Christ," where He left it completely accomplished. Observe, 1. How it is a fruit of the manifold wisdom of God, that it was a great mercy to give the law, and a greater to take it away. 2. If under the law the whole worship of God did depend so on the priesthood, that that failing or being taken away, the whole worship of itself was to cease, as being no more acceptable before God ; how much more is all worship under the New Testament rejected by Him, if there be not a due regard therein unto the Lord Christ, as the only High Priest of the Church, and to the efficacy of His discharge of that office !

V. 13.   *For He of whom these things are spoken pertaineth to another tribe, of which no man gave attendance at the altar.*

"**For He of whom these things are spoken.**"   All "*these things*" that have been spoken concerning Melchisedec and his priesthood, with all things that do naturally follow and ensue there-on.   All "*these things*" do belong perfectly and ultimately unto Christ alone, whom they did represent and make way for.

"**Pertaineth to another tribe.**"   The priesthood was granted, confined, and confirmed unto the tribe of Levi, and unto the family of Aaron, one of that tribe.   And it was so confined that all the other tribes were for ever excluded from any interest therein.   But unto one of these tribes so excluded from an interest in the legal priesthood did He belong of whom " these things " are spoken.

"**Of which no man gave attendance at the altar.**"   He thus describes in general that other tribe, whereof He was of whom " these things are spoken."   No man in this other tribe had a right to give "attendance " at the altar ; none of them ever did or might draw near, nor minister at the altar in any sacred services whatever.

V. 14.   *For [it is] evident that our Lord sprang out of Judah ; of which tribe Moses spake nothing concerning priesthood.*

Nothing was more plainly promised under the Old Testament, nor more firmly believed by the Church, than that the Messiah was to be of the tribe of Judah and of the family of David.   The promise was solemnly confined to Judah, and frequently reiterated unto David.   Whoever therefore acknowledged our Lord Jesus Christ to be the Messiah—as all the Hebrews did unto whom the Apostle wrote, though the most of them adhered to the law and its ceremonies—they must and did grant that He sprang out of Judah.

"**Of which tribe Moses spake nothing concerning priesthood.**"   The silence of Moses in this matter the Apostle takes to be a sufficient argument to prove that the *legal priesthood* did not belong, nor could be transferred, to the tribe of Judah.

Vs. 15—17.　*And it is yet far more evident: for that after the similitude of Melchisedec there ariseth another Priest, who is made, not after the law of a carnal commandment, but after the power of an endless life.　For He testifieth, Thou [art] a Priest for ever, after the order of Melchisedec.*

"**And it is yet far more evident.**" There is more immediate force in this consideration, to prove the cessation of the Levitical priesthood, that "another Priest was to arise after the order of Melchisedec," than was merely in this, that our Lord sprang of the tribe of Judah. The design of the Apostle is to prove that now, utterly unexpectedly unto the Church, after so long a season, their whole worship, though instituted by God Himself, was to be removed, to be used no more, but that another system of ordinances and institutions, absolutely new, was to be introduced. And upon the compliance of the Hebrews with this doctrine, or the rejection of it, depended their eternal salvation or destruction. It was therefore necessary that the Apostle should proceed distinctly and gradually, omitting no argument that was of force and pleadable in this cause, not failing to remark on them in an especial manner, which contained special evidence and demonstrative force in them, as he doth in this instance. From this observe, 1. That present truths are earnestly to be pleaded and contended for. 2. That important truths should be strongly confirmed. 3. In the confirmation of the truth, we may use every help that is true and seasonable, though some of them may be more effectual unto our end than others.

"**For that after the similitude of Melchisedec there ariseth another priest.**" "Another priest," in this case a stranger, one that is not of the house or family of Aaron ; "Aaron and his sons, they shall wait on the priest's office, and the stranger that cometh nigh (that is, to discharge any sacerdotal duty) shall be put to death." We have a solemn instance of the severity of God with respect unto this law in the punishment of Korah for the transgression of it, though he was of the tribe of Levi. When "another Priest arose," the former priesthood was abolished. The arising of Christ in His office as a High Priest put an end to all things that went before in connection with the priesthood.

"**Who is made not after the law of a carnal commandment.**" The Apostle means the law of the Levitical priesthood, or the way and manner by which the Aaronic priests were first called and vested with their office. The whole law of worship among the Jews is called "the law of commandments in ordinances ;" commands were so multiplied, that the whole law was denominated from them ; and it was said to be "*a yoke hardly to* *be borne."* They are called "carnal," because of the sacrifices which reached no further than purifying the flesh, also because the priesthood was confined unto the carnal seed and posterity of Aaron ; and they were all carnal in opposition unto the dispensation of the Spirit under the gospel and the institutions thereof.

" But after the power of an endless life." Some have thought that this refers to entering upon priesthood after His resurrection ; but such an exposition diverts from the truth, for Christ was installed into the priesthood before His resurrection, or He did not offer Himself as a sacrifice unto God in His death and blood-shedding. And to suppose that Christ performed the *principal act* of His sacerdotal office before He was installed as a priest, is contradictory to Scripture and reason itself. " The power of the endless life " was the power of Him who is " the Life,"—the power of the Son of God. His life was an " endless life." Although He truly and really died in His human nature, He was still alive in His indissoluble Person. His soul and body were inseparably united in His Person unto the Son of God.

" For He testifieth, Thou art a Priest for ever after the order of Melchisedec." That is to say, the Holy Ghost doth so testify by David in Psa. cx. He testifies, " Thou art a Priest," although a stranger from the Aaronical line. He was made a *" Priest for ever "* by Him who said, *" Thou art a Priest ; "* this was the "power of an endless life." He is a " Priest for ever " in respect of His Person,—endued with "endless life ; " in respect of the execution of His office unto the final end of it—" He liveth for ever to make intercession ; " and in respect of the effect of His office, which is to "save unto the utmost all them that come unto God by Him." Observe, 1. The eternal continuance of Christ's Person gives eternal continuance and efficacy to His priesthood. His endless life is the foundation of His endless priesthood. Whilst He lives we want not a Priest, and therefore, " because He lives we shall live also." 2. To make new priests in the Church is virtually to renounce the faith of His living for ever as our Priest, or to suppose that He is not sufficient for His office. 3. The alteration that God made in the Church by the introduction of the priesthood of Christ was progressive towards its perfection. To return therefore unto or to look after legal ceremonies in the worship of God is to go back unto poor " beggarly elements " and " rudiments of the world."

Vs. 18, 19. *For there is verily a disannulling of the commandment going before, for the weakness and unprofitableness thereof. For the law made nothing perfect ; but the bringing in of a better hope [did] : by the which we draw nigh unto God.*

"For there is verily a disannulling of the command=ment going before." " The commandment " in v. 18 is of as wide signification as " the law " in v. 19 ; it includes the whole system of the Mosaical institutions. The law as a command is opposed unto the gospel as a promise of righteousness by Jesus Christ. Nor is it the *whole ceremonial law only* that is intended by " the commandment " here, but the *moral law* also, so far as it was compacted with the other into one body of precepts for the same end. The commandment is described as " going before,"—that is, before the gospel as now preached and dispensed. " *The command-ment going before* " is the law whereby the worship of God and obedience unto Him were regulated before the coming of Christ and the introduction of the gospel. It is affirmed that " there is verily a disannulling " of the commandment—or law. The law was *established* by Christ and the gospel as unto its end, use, and scope; it was *disannulled* as unto its obligatory power unto the observance of its commands.

We must enquire how this law was annulled. 1. It was done by Christ Himself, in His own Person. An answer is made ready unto all its demands, namely, that they are fulfilled, and as unto what was significative in its duties, it is all really exhibited, so that on no account can it any more oblige or command the conscience of men. 2. It was annulled declaratively, or the will of God as to its abrogation was made known by the preaching of the gospel; by the institution of new ordinances of worship; by the determination made by the Holy Ghost, the substance of which was that the gospel as preached unto the Gentiles was not a way or means of bringing them unto Judaism, but of bringing them into a new Church state, by an interest in the promise and covenant of Abraham, given and made four hundred and thirty years before the giving of the law ; and lastly by the total irrevocable destruction of the city and the temple with all the instruments and vessels of its worship, especially of its priesthood and all that belonged thereunto.

" For the weakness and unprofitableness thereof." The whole law is charged by the Apostle with " weakness and un-profitableness," both of which make a law fit to be disannulled. There is a difficulty here, for this law was given by God Himself. In itself, no reflection can be made upon it, because it was an effect of the wisdom, holiness, and truth of God. Its weakness and unprofitableness are seen in this ; that it was given unto sinners who were guilty and defiled before it was given, being so by nature. Now they needed two things : 1. Sanctification by an inherent holiness and purity, with a complete righteousness from thence. This the moral law was at first the rule and measure of. It could never take away the defilement of sin from the soul, but it could have prevented such defilement. But as it was given to sinners, it became weak and unprofitable unto their sanctification.

2. Sinners do stand in need of an expiation for sin, for being actually guilty already, it is to no purpose to think of a righteousness for the future unless their present guilt be first expiated. Hereof there is not the least intimation in the *moral* law. This therefore was to be expected from the *ceremonial* law, and the various ways of atonement therein provided ; but this of themselves they could not effect. They did indeed prefigure what could do so, but of themselves they were insufficient unto any such end. For, says the Apostle, "it is not possible that the blood of bulls and goats could take away sin." The Apostle then pronounces the law weak and unprofitable, seeing that the people must be sanctified, and an atonement for their sin actually made, neither of which things it could reach unto. Observe that it is vain for any man to look for that from the law, now it is abolished, which it could not effect in its best estate : and what that is the Apostle declares in the next verse.

"**For the law made nothing perfect.**" It made none of the things of which the Apostle treats perfect. It did not make the Church-state perfect ; it did not make the worship of God perfect ; it did not perfect the promises given unto Abraham in their accomplishment ; it did not make a perfect covenant between God and man ; it had a shadow, an obscure representation, of all these things, but it "made nothing perfect."

"**But the bringing in of a better hope did.**" This neither was nor could be anything but Christ Himself and His priesthood ; "by one offering He hath perfected them for ever that are sanctified." "Hope" is used here to signify the thing hoped for. Christ and His coming into the world was the hope of all believers, the great thing they desired, longed, hoped for. Observe, 1. That believers of old who lived *under* the law, did not live *upon* the law, but upon the hope of Christ, or rather *upon Christ hoped for*. 2. The Lord Christ, by His priesthood and sacrifice, makes perfect the Church, and all things belonging thereunto (Col. ii. 10).

"**By which we draw near to God.**" Under the Levitical priesthood the priests alone in their sacrifices did draw nigh to God. The same now is done by all believers, under the sacerdotal ministration of Jesus Christ. They all of them now draw nigh to God. All believers being made a royal priesthood, every one of them hath an equal right and privilege by Christ of drawing nigh unto God. By sin we are "far off" from the love and favour of God, from the knowledge of Him and obedience unto Him. Our "drawing nigh" unto God denotes our delivery and recovery from this estate. So it is expressed in the place, "But now in Christ Jesus, ye who sometimes were far off are made nigh by the blood of Christ." In this "drawing nigh unto God" there must be a removal of those things that kept us at a distance from Him. What was upon us from God that kept us at a distance was, 1. His wrath and curse for our sin and apostacy. 2. Guilt within us, with its consequences of fear, shame, and alienation from God. How these were removed by the " bringing in of a better hope " the Apostle declares in this epistle, as we shall see, God willing, in our progress.

Observe, 1. Out of Christ, or without Him, all mankind are at an inconceivable distance from God. And a distance it is of the very worst sort, even that which is the effect of mutual enmity. 2. It is an effect of infinite condescension and grace that God should appoint a way of recovery for those who had wilfully cast themselves into this woful distance from Him. He chose to act like Himself in infinite grace and wisdom, to bring us *yet nearer unto Him* than ever we could have approached by the law of our creation. 3. All our approximation unto God in any kind, all our approaches unto Him in holy worship, is by Him alone who was the blessed hope of the saints under the Old Testament, and is the life of them under the New.

Vs. 20—22. *And inasmuch as not without an oath* [*He was made Priest*]; (*for those priests were made without an oath ; but this with an oath by Him that said unto Him, Thou* [*art*] *a Priest for ever after the order of Melchisedec;*) *By so much was Jesus made a surety of a better testament.*

" **And inasmuch as not without an oath He was made Priest.**" Nothing was wanting on the part of God that might give eminency, stability, glory, and efficacy unto the priesthood of Christ ; " *Not without an oath.*" This was due unto the glory of His Person ; He was in everything He undertook to be preferred and exalted above all others, and therefore He was made a Priest not without an oath. God also saw that this was needful to encourage and secure the faith of the Church. Upon the introduction of the priesthood of Christ, God really and actually proposeth and exhibiteth unto the Church all that they were to trust unto, all that He would do, or was in any way needful to be done, for their peace and salvation. Thus all and the whole of Scripture, and all contained therein, direct us unto our ultimate hope and rest in Christ alone.

" **For those priests were made without an oath.**" The dedication of the Aaronic priesthood consisted in, 1. A call from God. 2. In the peculiar garments and mystical ornaments wherein they were to administer their office, and their unction with the holy anointing oil. 3. In the sacrifices wherewith they were consecrated and actually set apart unto that office whereunto they were called. They did not "take this honour unto themselves," but were called of God.

" **But this with an oath by Him that said unto Him,**

Thou art a Priest for ever after the order of Melchisedec."
The call of Jesus Christ to the office of Priest was confirmed and
ratified by an oath. The *form* of the oath is in these words, " The
Lord sware, and will not repent ; " and the *matter* of the oath, or
the thing sworn, is " Thou art a Priest for ever." The Person
swearing is God the Father, who speaks unto the Son in Ps. cx.,
" The LORD said unto my Lord." The time when the Father
swore unto the Son belongs entirely to those federal transactions
between the Father and the Son, which were the original of the
priesthood of Christ. The peculiar revelation and declaration of
this oath was when He gave it in the psalm by David. Some
have supposed that this oath was made to Christ on His ascension
into heaven ; but this is to suppose that the principal discharge of
the priesthood of Christ, in His sacrifice, was antecedent unto this
oath, which utterly enervates the argument of the Apostle.

It must necessarily be that this oath of God was before His
actual entrance upon or discharge of any solemn duty of His office.
He was not only made a Priest by an oath, but He was made a
Priest " for ever." This adds unto the unchangeableness of His
office, that He Himself in His own Person was to bear, exercise,
and discharge it without substitute or successor. Observe then,
1. That our High Priest was peculiarly designed unto and initiated
into His office by the oath of God, which none other ever was.
2. That the Person of the High Priest is hereby so absolutely determined as that the Church may continually draw nigh unto God in
the full assurance of faith. 3. That this priesthood is liable to no
alteration, succession, or substitution. 4. That from hence ariseth
the principal advantage of the New Testament above the Old, as is
declared in the next verse.

**"By so much was Jesus made a Surety of a better
testament."** " By so much was Jesus made," that is to say, His
being made a Priest by an oath made Him meet to be the " Surety
of a better testament." Also that the testament whereof He was
Surety must needs be better than the other. The priesthood of
Christ gives dignity unto the new testament, and the new testament
sets before us declaratively the dignity of the priesthood of Christ.
For the first time now doth the Apostle mention the name of Him
who, as the High Priest, was to be the Surety. It is Jesus who in
all these things is intended, in whose Person " God redeemed the
Church with His own blood." " *He was made a Surety*"—the whole
undertaking of Christ, and the whole efficacy of the discharge of
His office, depend on the appointment of God, even the Father.
He was not a Surety unto us for God, but was so for us unto God.
God swears by Himself, not by a surety ; if God would give any
other surety beside Himself, it must be someone greater than He ;
but this is in every way impossible. We alone are they who stood
in need of a surety, for without such a surety the covenant could

not be firm and inviolable on our part. " Jesus was made a Surety " according to the singular and absolute promise of God, and this appointment to this office was confirmed, ratified, and made irrevocable by His death, as the Apostle insists at large (c. ix. 15—20).

Jesus became "the Surety" by His voluntarily undertaking, out of His rich grace and love, to do, answer and perform all that is required on our part, that we may enjoy the benefits of the covenant, the grace and glory proposed, prepared and promised in it, in the way determined on by divine wisdom. He undertook to answer, as the Surety of the covenant, for all the sins of all those who are to be, and are made partakers of the benefits of it; that is, to undergo the punishment due unto their sins, to make an atonement for them, by offering Himself as a propitiatory sacrifice, redeeming them by the price of His blood from their state of misery and bondage under the law and the curse of it.

He also undertook that those who were to be taken into this covenant should receive grace, enabling them to comply with the terms of it, fulfil its conditions, and yield the obedience therein required by God. Here we might stay a while to contemplate the glory of divine wisdom and grace in providing this Surety of the covenant, and to adore the infinite love and condescension of Him who undertook the discharge of this office for us ; but we must proceed, only observing that the Lord Christ's undertaking to be our Surety gives the highest obligation unto all duties of obedience according to the covenant.

Vs. 23—25. *And they truly were many priests, because they were not suffered to continue by reason of death : but this* [man] *because He continueth ever, hath an unchangeable priesthood. Wherefore He is able to save them to the uttermost that come unto God by Him, seeing He ever liveth to make intercession for them.*

" **And they truly were many priests.** " By the appointment of God there were many priests ; it is the high priest only— Aaron and his successors—of whom the Apostle speaks, and it is with respect unto their succession one to another that he affirms they were " many."

" **Because they were not suffered to continue by reason of death.** " God, in order to show the people of Israel the nature of the priesthood, and to manifest that the everlasting Priest was yet to come, commanded Aaron to die in the sight of all the congregation. There is such a necessity for the continual administration of the sacerdotal office in behalf of the Church, that the interruption of it by the death of the priests was an argument of the weakness of the priesthood.

"**But this [man] because He continueth ever, hath an unchangeable priesthood.**" The sole reason here insisted on by the Apostle, why the Levitical priests were many, is because they were forbidden by death to continue. It is sufficient therefore to prove the perpetuity of the priesthood of Christ, that He "continueth ever," therefore His administration of it is perpetual and uninterrupted. From the first moment of His being a Priest He abode so always, without interruption or intermission. It follows then that He hath an "unchangeable priesthood," a priesthood that doth not pass from one to another.

Observe, 1. The perpetuity of the priesthood of Christ depends on His own perpetual life. 2. The perpetuity of His priesthood, as unchangeably exercised in His own Person, is a principal part of the glory of that office. 3. The addition of sacrificing priests, as vicars of or substitutes unto Christ in the discharge of His office, destroys His priesthood as to its principal eminency above that of the Levitical priesthood.

"**Wherefore He is able to save them to the uttermost.**" The Apostle now applies all that he hath said concerning the excellency of the priesthood of Christ unto the encouragement of the faith and hope of them that endeavour to go to God by Him. That which is said to be in this Priest is power and ability; and ability not of nature, but of office is intended. The Apostle presses His ability not *absolutely*, but as the *High Priest of His Church*. The offices of King, Prophet, and Priest, as united in Christ, did perfectly answer all that belongs to the redemption, sanctification, protection, and salvation of the Church. " He is able to save ; " a salvation supernatural, spiritual, eternal, is intended by this word " save." To *save from* sin, with all its consequent misery in the curse of the law and the wrath to come ; and to *save to* an estate of present grace and right unto future blessedness, with the enjoyment of it in the appointed time. This salvation is called "great" and "eternal." It is good to secure this first ground of evangelical faith, that the Lord Christ, as vested with His offices, is "*able to save*" us. He is able to save to the "*uttermost.*" This may respect the perfection of His work, or its duration. He is able to save completely as to all parts, fully as to all causes, and for ever in duration.

"**That come unto God by Him.**" To come to God is to believe. Believing is a coming unto God ; unbelief is a refusal to come unto Him. " Ye will not come unto Me, that ye might have life." Our access unto God in worship, is coming unto Him, " drawing nigh unto God." We come unto God " by Him ; " as a High Priest, as it is at large explained by the Apostle (chap. x. 19—22). To come " by Him " is to come in obedience to His authority ; with faith in His Person and mediation.

"**Seeing He ever liveth to make intercession for them.**" It is a matter of strong consolation to the Church, that Christ liveth in heaven for us. He lives for ever to send the Holy Spirit to the Church ; hereon depends all saving light to understand the word of God, all habitual grace, all supplies of actual grace, all spiritual gifts, and all comfort and consolation. He ever liveth to " make intercession." This intercession was typed under the Old Testament by the *living fire* that was continually burning on the altar ; by the *daily sacrifice*, morning and evening, for the people; and by the *incense* that was burned in the sanctuary. The actual intercession of Christ in heaven is a fundamental article of our faith, and a principal foundation of the consolation of the Church. This intercession of Christ is no other but such as may become Him who sits at the right hand of the Majesty on high. In John xvii., He gives us the best estimate and representation of His present intercession that we are able to comprehend.

It must be granted that there is *no use for words* in the immediate presence of God ; here we need words for many reasons, but in the glorious presence of God we shall not need words in order to express ourselves to Him in prayer or praise. The virtue and efficacy of the intercession of Christ flows from His one sacrifice of Himself. The safest conception that we can form of His intercession is His continual appearance for us in the presence of God, where by virtue of His office as a " High Priest over the house of God " He doth ever represent the efficacy of His oblation, accompanied by tender care, love, and desires for the welfare, supply, deliverance, and salvation of the Church.

Three things concur hereunto : 1. The presentation of His Person before the throne of God on our behalf. This renders it sacerdotal ; His appearance *in Person* for us is required thereunto. 2. The representation of His death, oblation, and sacrifice for us, which gives life, power, and efficacy unto His intercession. He appears " in the midst of the throne as a Lamb that had been slain." Both these are required to make His intercession sacerdotal. But, 3. There is moreover a putting up, a requesting, and offering unto God of His desires and will for the Church, attended with care, love, and compassion, without which He could not be said to make intercession.

Observe then, 1. That in His intercession He hath respect unto *every individual believer*, and all their special occasions ; " if any man sin, we have an Advocate." 2. That His intercession hath respect unto the application of all the fruits, effects, and benefits of His whole mediation unto the Church, whereby the continual application of all the benefits of His death, and all the effects of the promises of the covenant, shall be communicated unto us, unto His praise and glory. But what belongs to the manner of the transaction of these things in heaven I know not.

3. So great and glorious is the work of saving believers unto the utmost, that it is necessary that the Lord Christ should lead a

mediatory life in heaven for the perfecting and accomplishing of
it. The sure foundation of our salvation is laid in His death and
resurrection. The security of it rests upon the unchangeable love,
care, and power of Jesus Christ, gloriously to accomplish the work
which He had undertaken, for had He left it when He left the earth,
it had never been finished, for great was that great part of the work
which yet remained to be perfected.

4. Neither could the *remainder of the work* be committed unto
any other hand. Who can express the opposition that continues to
be made unto this work of completing the salvation of believers ?
What power is able to conflict and conquer the remaining strength
of sin, the opposition of Satan and the world ? God alone knows
how great is the work of saving sinners to the utmost ; He alone
knows how it may be perfected unto His own glory. He saw that
the continual intercession of Christ was needful and expedient unto
the salvation of the Church and His own glory. The good Lord
help me to believe and adore the mystery of it.

V. 26. *For such an High Priest became us, [who is] holy,
harmless, undefiled, separate from sinners, and made higher
than the heavens.*

" **For such an High Priest became us.**" Respect may be
had here to the wisdom of God, also to our state and condition ;
such an High Priest was meet for God to give, and such an High
Priest it was needful that we should have. We stand in need of just
such an High Priest who could, 1. Make atonement for our sins ;
2. Purge our consciences from dead works, or sanctify us throughout by blood ; 3. Procure assistance with God for us ; 4. Administer
supplies of the Spirit of grace unto us, to enable us to live unto
God in all duties of faith, worship, and obedience ; 5. Give us
assistance and consolation in our trials, temptations, and sufferings,
with pity and compassion ; 6. Preserve us by power from all
ruining sins and dangers ; 7. Be in a continual readiness to
receive us in all our addresses to Him ; 8. Bestow upon us the
reward of eternal life. Unless we have a High Priest that can do
all these things for us, we cannot be " saved to the uttermost."
Such an High Priest we stood in need of, and such an one it became
the wisdom and grace of God to give unto us.

" **[Who is] holy, harmless, undefiled, separate from
sinners.**" " Holy ; " by this word is intended the holy purity of
the nature of Christ. Hence, as He was conceived in the womb,
and came forth from the womb, He was that " Holy Thing " of
God. *Unholy sinners* do stand in need of a *holy Priest* and a *holy
sacrifice*. What we have not in ourselves we must have in Him, or
we shall not be accepted with the holy God, who is of purer eyes
than to behold iniquity. " Harmless ; " without evil, free from all

guile, fraud, or sin ; as Peter saith, " Who did no sin, neither was
guile found in His mouth." " Holy " is with respect unto His
nature ; "harmless " respects His life. " Undefiled." " Harmless " signifies, He did no evil ; " undefiled," that He contracted
none from any source whatever ; there was not any blemish to be
found in Him. "Separate from sinners," namely, in sin, in its
nature, causes and effects. Whatever of that sort He underwent
was upon our account, and not upon His own. He was in every
way, in the perfect holiness of His life and nature, distinguished
from all sinners, not only from the greatest, but from those who
were the most holy.

"**And made higher than the heavens.**" He was for a
season " made lower than the angels," for the discharge of the
principal part of His priestly office, namely, the offering Himself
for a sacrifice unto God. But He could not discharge the whole of
His priesthood till He was made higher than the heavens ; for He
was to live for ever to make intercession. He is no longer on the
earth, but exalted to a throne of majesty above the heavens. So it
is said, " He passed into the heavens " when He went into the
presence of God ; also " the heaven must receive Him till the restitution of all things." He is in a state of glory at the right hand
of the Majesty on high ; He is therefore higher than the sacred
inhabitants of those heavenly places. Observe, 1. If " such an
High Priest became us," then all persons, Christ alone excepted,
are absolutely excluded from all interest in the priesthood. 2. If
we consider aright what it is that we stand in need of, and what
God hath provided for us, that we may be brought unto Him in His
glory, we shall find it our wisdom to forego all other expectations,
and to betake ourselves to Christ alone.

V. 27. *Who needeth not daily, as those high priests, to
offer up sacrifice, first for his own sins, and then for the
people's : for this He did once, when He offered up Himself.*

"**He needeth not daily.**" It is not necessary for Him to do
as they did. It was necessary for them to sacrifice daily, for God
had appointed it, and by the constant daily sacrificing taught the
Church the utter incapacity of that priesthood to effect the work
committed unto them *at once*, whereon they were to multiply their
sacrifices. The nature of those sacrifices made their repetition
necessary ; they never attained the end of expiating sin, but only
represented that which could do so ; and then the state of the
priests themselves—sinners—rendered it necessary to repeat the
sacrifices day after day. From all such considerations our High
Priest was absolutely exempted, 1. On the ground of His Person,
holy, harmless, undefiled, and separate from sinners. 2. On the
ground of His offering, which, being *at once* perfectly expiatory of

the sins of the people, needed not to be repeated. And on these grounds God appointed that He should offer Himself only " *once for all*."

"**As those high priests.**" There is a threefold difference intimated between our High Priest and the Aaronic priests : 1. In the frequency of their offerings—they were to offer " daily," whereas He offered " *once*." 2. They offered sacrifices appointed by the law, which were of brute creatures only, whence their insufficiency and frequent repetitions (c. x. 1—3), whereas He offered up Himself. 3. They offered for their own sins, but He had none of His own to offer for.

"**To offer up sacrifice, first for his own sins, and then for the people's.**" This includes all sacrifices, and in particular the great anniversary sacrifice on the day of atonement, when the high priest offered up "*first*" a sin offering for himself and his house, and "*then*" for the people, both on the same day. He did this for " his own sins," for he was really a sinner, as the rest of the people ; also that upon the expiation of his own sins in the first place, he might be the more meet to represent Him that had no sin, and therefore he was not to offer for himself in the offering he made for the people, that is, for the sins of the whole congregation of Israel.

"**For this He did once when He offered up Himself.**" He did offer Himself once for the sins of the people. For Himself He did not offer. He did this " *once only* ; " this is directly opposed to the frequency of the legal sacrifices, which were repeated " *daily*." Observe, 1. That no sinful man was meet to offer the great expiatory sacrifice for the Church ; much less is any sinful man fit to offer Christ Himself. For a poor, sinful worm of the earth to interpose himself between God and Christ, and offer the one in sacrifice to the other, what an issue it is of pride and folly ! 2. No sacrifice could bring us unto God, and save the Church to the uttermost, but that wherein the Son of God Himself was both Priest and offering. Such a High Priest became us, who offered Himself. We may consider this as one of the greatest effects of divine wisdom and grace.

V. 28. *For the law maketh men high priests which have infirmity ; but the word of the oath, which was since the law, maketh the Son, who is consecrated for evermore.*

"**For the law maketh men high priests.**" He grants unto the Hebrews that the high priests were called and appointed by God unto their office, but he contends that it was designed by God that there should come a time when they would be removed, and a Priest of another order introduced in their room. This he proves by very cogent arguments, as, 1. Before the erection of the Levitical priesthood, there was another priest of the most high God, who was far more excellent than those priests, yea, than Abraham himself. 2. Because after giving the law, and the setting up of the Levitical priesthood, God promises to raise up another Priest in another kind, after another order, after the manner of him who was called into that office long before the giving of the law. 3. That this promised Priest could not be of the same stock, nature, or order as the Levitical priests, but one that was not only distinct from them, but really inconsistent with them. 4. Because under the Levitical priesthood there was no perfection ; there were so many defects and weaknesses as rendered them wholly unable to attain so great an end. On the other hand, he proveth that by this one single High Priest now introduced, and His one sacrifice offered once for all, the blessed end of perfection was completely accomplished. God appointed those priests in and by the law, but this High Priest was consecrated by " *the word of the oath.*"

"**Which have infirmity.**" They were men, mere men, nothing more. In opposition hereunto, the "word of the oath " made the Son an High Priest, that Son who is Lord over the whole house. The priests had " infirmity"—subject to infirmities—moral and natural. They had sins to make atonement for, and the issue of their natural weakness was death itself.

" **But the word of the oath, which was since the law, maketh the Son, who is consecrated for evermore.**" That which the Apostle intends by His being consecrated for evermore is His absolute freedom from the infirmities the Levitical priests were the subjects of. He had no sins to offer for, and He abideth for ever. Being exalted to heaven, He is freed from those infirmities which were necessary unto Him that He might be a sacrifice. Observe, 1. There never was nor ever can be any more than two sorts of priests in the Church, the one made by the law, the other by the oath of God. 2. As the bringing in of the priesthood of Christ after the law, and the priesthood constituted thereby, did abrogate and disannul it, so the bringing in of another priesthood after His will abrogate and disannul that also. Therefore, 3. Plurality of priests under the gospel overthrows the whole argument of the Apostle in this place ; and if we have yet priests that have infirmities, they are made by the law and not by the gospel. 4. The great foundation of our faith, and the hinge whereon all our consolation depends, is this, that our High Priest is the Son of God. 5. The everlasting continuance of the Lord Christ in His office is secured by the oath of God.

CHAPTER EIGHT

V. 1. *Now of the things which we have spoken [this is]
the sum: We have such an High Priest, who is set on the
right hand of the throne of the Majesty in the heavens.*

There are two general parts of this chapter; the first part contained in the first five verses, in which we have three instances of
the excellency of Christ in His priesthood. 1. In His exaltation
and the place of His present residence (v. 1). 2. In the sanctuary
whereof He is a Minister, and the tabernacle wherein He doth at
present administer (v. 2). 3. In the sacrifice He had to offer, or
which He offered, before His entrance into that sanctuary (v. 3);
which the Apostle illustrates by two special considerations (vs. 4—5).
The latter part, from v. 6 to end of the chapter, contains a further
confirmation thereof by the consideration of the two covenants,
the old and the new. Unto the old was the whole of the Levitical
priesthood confined; of the latter, Christ as our High Priest was
the Mediator and Surety.

**" Now of the things which we have spoken this is the
sum: We have such an High Priest."** The most important
thing that we have stated, and the summing up of all we have
stated, is that, *" We have such an High Priest."* The words, " We
have," denote our relationship to this High Priest. The Apostle
often calls attention to this: " Such an High Priest became us "
(chap. vii. 26). "We have not an High Priest that cannot be
touched" (chap. iv. 15). " The High Priest of our profession "
(chap. iii. 1). And here, "We have such an High Priest." The
Apostle seems to design herein the dignity of the Christian
Church; the Hebrews were apt to despise the Christians as those
who had no such visible high priest as they had; but on behalf of
the Christian Church the Apostle pleads their relation unto an
invisible, spiritual High Priest, exalted in glory and dignity far
above all that they could enjoy by virtue of a carnal commandment.
We are also taught that whatever be the glory and dignity of this
High Priest, that without an interest in Him, an especial relation
unto Him, unless *" we have such an High Priest,"* we are not concerned therein. None can come unto the Father but by Him,
through whom we have boldness of access unto and acceptance
with God. Without a daily improvement by faith of the office of
Christ unto these ends, we cannot be said to have an High
Priest. The Apostle says, *" We have such an High Priest;"* that is, such
an one as hath that dignity and those excellencies which he ascribeth
unto Him.

" Who is set on the right hand of the Majesty in the

heavens." This is repeated three times in the epistle. In the first place, the glory of His kingly power is intended by His sitting at the right hand of the Majesty (chap. i. 3) ; in the last (chap. xii. 2) His exaltation and glory, as they ensued on His sufferings ; and in this place the declaration of His glory in His priestly office. The immutable stability of His state and condition is intended by His "sitting." His dignity consists in the place where He is sitting—"*At the right hand of the Majesty in the heavens.*" Higher expression cannot be used to lead us into a holy adoration of the invisible and tremendous glory which is intended.

The principal glory of the priestly office of Christ depends on the glorious exaltation of His Person. This glory was given Him by God ; and be it observed, that it was not absolutely infinite and essentially divine glory. This cannot be communicated unto any. A creature, as was the human nature of Christ, cannot be made God, by an essential communication of divine properties unto it. Wherefore, they speak dangerously who assert a real communication of the properties of the one nature of Christ unto the other, so as that the human nature of Christ shall be omnipresent, omnipotent, and omniscient ; neither doth the union of the two natures in the Person of Christ require any more the transfusion of the divine properties into the human, than those of the human into the divine. Whatever belongs unto Christ with respect unto either nature, belongs unto the Person of Christ ; and therein He is all that He is in either nature, and in both hath done and doth what in either of them He hath done and doth, they yet continuing distinct in their essential properties.

This exaltation of the Person of Christ gives glory unto His office, as the Apostle here declares. It is the Person of Christ which is vested with the office of priesthood, or God could not have "redeemed the Church with His own blood." This is a manifest pledge and evidence of the absolute perfection of His oblation, and that "by one offering He hath for ever perfected them that are sanctified."

V. 2. *A Minister of the sanctuary, and of the true tabernacle, which the Lord pitched, and not man.*

" A Minister of the sanctuary, and of the true tabernacle." The high priest is here said to be a minister—a public minister of the Church. The Lord Christ, in the height of His glory, condescends to discharge the office of a public Minister in the behalf of the Church. He is a "*Minister of the sanctuary;*" this is nothing but heaven itself, the place of God's glorious presence, the temple of the living God, where the worship of the Church is presented, and all its affairs transacted. Heaven is called the "sanctuary" because there doth really and truly dwell all that was typically represented in the sanctuary below. And therein doth the Lord Christ discharge His priestly office for the good of the Church.

He is also a "*Minister of the true tabernacle.*" What this tabernacle is here intended deserves our diligent enquiry. Some have thought that the universal spiritual catholic Church is intended, for herein doth God dwell and walk amongst men. It is undoubtedly in behalf of this tabernacle that He ministers in the holy place, and all the benefits of His ministration do redound hereunto. But this doth not suffice to have the Lord Christ called the Minister of this tabernacle. I understand that by the "true tabernacle" the human nature of the Lord Christ Himself is intended. For hereof the old tabernacle was a type, and in opposition to the type He is called the *true* tabernacle. When He became incarnate, it is said, "He fixed His tabernacle—dwelt among us;" He, so to speak, fixed His tent among men. Then He Himself called His *own body* His temple, and this He did because His own body was that true, substantial temple and tabernacle whereof He was the Minister. That therefore wherein God dwells really and substantially, and on account whereof He is our God in the covenant of grace, that, and no other, is the true tabernacle. This is in Christ alone, for "in Him dwelleth all the fulness of the Godhead bodily." Jesus Christ was the body and substance of all the types—of priests, sacrifice, tabernacle, altar, and what belonged thereunto.

"**Which the Lord pitched, and not man.**" The preparation of the human nature or body of Christ is here intended; "a body hast Thou prepared Me;" and this body was to be taken down and folded up for a season, and afterwards to be erected again, without the breaking or loss of any part of it. Although the old tabernacle was pitched at the command of God, yet the ministry of men was used in the preparation, framing, and erecting of it. But the pitching of the true tabernacle was the work of God alone, without any service or ministry of men. In this then the Apostle hath an especial respect unto the incarnation of Christ, without the concurrence of man in natural generation.

V. 3. *For every high priest is ordained to offer gifts and sacrifices: wherefore [it is] of necessity that this man have somewhat also to offer.*

"**For every high priest is ordained to offer gifts and sacrifices.**" Every high priest was made, ordained, appointed by the law, and the principal end of their appointment was that they should offer gifts and sacrifices. None but the priests were to offer; the people might bring their offerings unto God, but they could not offer them on the altar. There is no approach unto God without continual respect unto sacrifice and atonement. Men do but dream of the pardon of sin or acceptance with God without atonement.

"**Wherefore it is of necessity that this man have somewhat also to offer.**" "This man" is Jesus, the Son of God, the High Priest of the New Testament. There was an absolute necessity, that in order to His being a High Priest, He must have somewhat to offer, for without this He could not discharge the office of priesthood. What He had to offer we are expressly told further on, "He offered Himself." As God designed unto the Lord Christ the work which He had to do, so He provided for Him and furnished Him with what was necessary thereunto. A body did God prepare for Him, as is declared at large (chap. x. 1—8).

V. 4. *For if He were on earth He should not be a priest, seeing that there are priests that offer gifts according to the law.*

The sense of the Apostle's reasoning in this place is, The priests of the order of Aaron continued by divine appointment their administration of holy things, or were to do so, until all was accomplished that was signified thereby. This was not done till the ascension of Christ into heaven, for the first tabernacle was to stand until the way was made open into the holiest of all, as we shall see presently. Now, the Lord Christ was not a Priest after their order, nor could He offer the sacrifices appointed by the law. Hence it is evident that He could not have been a Priest had He been to continue on the earth, for then their priesthood, with which His was inconsistent, could never have had an end.

V. 5. *Who serve unto the example and shadow of heavenly things, as Moses was admonished of God when he was about to make the tabernacle : for, See, saith He, [that] thou make all things according to the pattern showed to thee in the mount.*

"**Who serve unto the example and shadow of heavenly things.**" The persons spoken of are the "priests who offer gifts;" particularly in respect to the high priests "*who serve*," &c. Their service includes all they had to do in the worship of God, and this service was an example—a representation—and shadow of "*heavenly things ;*" the things included in these words are none other than what God showed to Moses in the mount.

"**As Moses was admonished of God.**" Moses had an *immediate word*, command or oracle from God to the purpose intended ; accompanied by a warning to use *great caution* about what was enjoined him, that there might be no miscarriage or mistake.

"**When he was about to make the tabernacle.**" He
was actually about to start on the making of the tabernacle, when
the warning was given him ; this made the warning so seasonable ;
it was given him on the entrance upon his work, that it might
make an effectual impression upon his mind.   And it is our duty,
upon an entrance upon any work we are called unto, to charge our
consciences with a divine admonition.   What immediate revelation
was to Moses, that the written word is to us.   " To make the
tabernacle," includes the beginning as well as the end of the work
which Moses was to perfect.

**For see, saith He, that thou make all things according
to the pattern showed thee in the mount.**"   In general, it is
certain that God intended to declare hereby that the tabernacle
Moses was to erect, and the worship thereof, was not, either in the
whole or in any part of it, a matter of his own invention or contrivance ; but an exact representation of that which God had
showed unto him.   The sense of these words, " *all things according
to the pattern showed thee,*" must be determined from the Apostle
himself.   And is evident,

1. That these " heavenly things " unto whose resemblance the
legal priests did minister, and the " pattern showed unto Moses in
the mount," were the same.   Hereon depends the whole force of
his proof from this testimony.   2. These " heavenly things," he
expressly tells us, were those which were consecrated, dedicated
unto God, and purified by the sacrifice of the blood of Christ
(chap. ix. 23).   3. That Christ by His sacrifice did dedicate both
Himself, the whole Church and its worship unto God.   4. That
God did spiritually and mystically represent unto Moses the incarnation of Christ and His mediation, with the Church of the
elect which was to be gathered thereby, and its spiritual worship.
And moreover, He let him know how the tabernacle and all that
belonged to it did represent Christ and His Church.   For the
tabernacle that Moses made was a sign and figure of the body of Christ.

These are the " *heavenly things,*" and it is most agreeable unto
the wisdom of God, that before the building of the tabernacle
below, God did show unto Moses what was to be represented
thereby, and what He would introduce when that was taken away.
He first showed the " true tabernacle," then appointed a figure of
it, which was to abide and serve the worship of the Church, until
that true one was to be introduced, when this one was to be taken
down and removed out of the way.

V. 6.   *But now hath He obtained a more excellent ministry,
by how much also He is the Mediator of a better covenant,
which was established upon better promises.*

In this verse beginneth the second part of the chapter, concern-

ing the difference between the two covenants, the old and the new,
with the pre-eminence of the latter above the former, and of the
ministry of Christ above the high priests on that account.

"**But now He hath obtained a more excellent ministry.**"
The reference is to the present time—at this time—which is the
season appointed by God for the introduction of the new covenant
and ministry.　The Lord Christ was a "Minister in holy things;"
He had a ministry, a service committed unto Him.　This does not
denote that He ministered in some things only, but rather that His
standing office was that of a Minister.　Included in this is,
subordination to God; with respect unto the Church, His office is
supreme, accompanied with sovereign power and authority; He is
"Lord over His own house."　But He holds His office in subordination to God, being "faithful unto Him that appointed Him."
The Lord Christ "obtained" this office according to the eternal
counsel and purpose of God, and by the actual call of God to it;
whereunto many things did concur, especially His unction with the
Spirit above measure, for the whole discharge of His whole office.
His ministry was "*more excellent;*" the ministry of the Levitical
priesthood was good and useful in its time and season, but this of
our Lord Christ so differed from it as to be better than it, and more
excellent.

"**By how much also He is the Mediator of a better
covenant.**"　The excellency of His ministry above the Levitical
priests bears proportion with the excellency of the covenant whereof
He is the Mediator above the old covenant wherein they
administered; whereof afterwards.　The office here assigned unto
Him is that of a "Mediator," one that interposed between God and
man, for the doing of all those things whereby a covenant might
be established between them and made effectual.　He is called the
"Mediator" of the covenant in the same sense that He is called
the "Surety" (c. vii. 22).　He is in the new covenant the Mediator,
Surety, Priest, Sacrifice, all in one Person.　The ignorance and
want of a due consideration hereof are great evidences of the
degeneracy of the Christian religion.　Whereas this is the first
general notion of the office of Christ, that which compriseth the
whole ministry committed unto Him, and containeth in itself the
especial offices of King, Priest, and Prophet, whereby He dischargeth His mediation, some things must be observed.

1. That unto the office of a mediator it is required that there
be different persons concerned in the covenant, and that by their
own wills.　"A mediator is not of one, but God is one," that is, if
there were none but God concerned in the matter, as it is in an
absolute promise, there would be no need of, no place for, a
mediator, such a mediator as Christ is.　Wherefore our consent in
and unto the covenant is required in the very notion of a mediator.
2. That the persons entering into covenant be in such a state and

condition as that it is no way convenient or morally possible that they should *treat immediately* with each other as to the ends of the covenant, for if they are so, a mediator to go between is altogether needless.   3. That he who is the mediator be accepted, trusted, and rested in on both sides, or the parties entering into covenant. An absolute trust must be reposed in him, so that each party may be everlastingly obliged in what he undertaketh on their behalf; those who admit not of his terms can have no benefit from nor interest in the covenant.   4. A mediator must be a middle person between both parties entering into covenant; and if they be of different natures, a perfect, complete mediator ought to partake of each of their natures in his own person.   The necessity of this, and the glorious wisdom of God in it, hath been already shown.   5. A mediator must be one who voluntarily and of his own accord undertaketh the work of mediator.   This is required of those who will effectually mediate between those who are at variance, to bring them to an agreement.   6. It was required of this Mediator that He should remove and take out of the way whatever kept the covenanters at a distance, or was a cause of enmity between them. Had there been no enmity, there would have been no need for a Mediator.   But the design of the covenant was to make reconciliation and peace, and hereon depended the necessity of satisfaction, redemption, and the making of atonement by sacrifice.   Wherefore none could undertake to be the Mediator of this covenant but He that was able to satisfy the justice of God, glorify His government, and fulfil His law.   It was also required of this Mediator that He should procure and purchase, in a way suited unto the glory of God, the actual communication of all the good things prepared and proposed in this covenant, that is, grace and glory, with all that belong unto them, for them and on whose behalf He is the Surety.   7. This Mediator must give assurance to and undertake for, the parties mutually concerned as to the accomplishment of the terms of the covenant.   This He does on the part of God towards men, that they shall have peace and acceptance with Him, in the sure accomplishment of all the promises of the covenant.   This He doth in the doctrine of the gospel and in the institution of the ordinances of evangelical worship.   On our part He undertakes unto God for our acceptance of the terms of the covenant, and our accomplishment of them by His enabling us thereunto.   The provision of this Mediator between God and us was an effect of infinite wisdom and grace, yea, it was the greatest and most glorious external effect of them that ever they did produce, or ever will do in this world.

To proceed with the text: this covenant whereof the Lord Christ is the Mediator is said to be a "*better covenant.*"   Wherefore it is supposed that there was another covenant of which He was not the Mediator.   This other covenant—called in this chapter the "old covenant"—is none other but that which God made with the children of Israel on Mount Sinai. So it is expressly affirmed (v. 9), "The covenant which I made with your fathers in the day when I took them by the hand to lead them out of Egypt." This was the covenant which had all the institutions of worship annexed unto it (c. ix. 1—3), whereof we must treat in its place. With respect hereunto it is that the Lord Christ is said to be the "Mediator of a better covenant." This better covenant, of which Christ is the Mediator, is no other in general but what we call the "*covenant of grace.*" This is in opposition to that of "*works;*" and these two, grace and works, do divide the ways of our relation to God, being diametrically opposite, and every way inconsistent. Of this covenant the Lord Christ was the Mediator from the foundation of the world, from the giving of the first promise.

"**Which was established upon better promises.**" By the word *established* the Apostle intends the *legal establishment* of the new covenant with all its ordinances of worship. Hereupon the other covenant was disannulled and removed, and not only the covenant itself but all that system of sacred worship whereby it was administered. When the new covenant was given out only in a way of *promise,* it did not introduce a worship and privileges expressive of it ; but when it was established all the worship of the Church was to be conformed to it. Every covenant between God and man must be founded on and resolved into promises ; God calls an absolute promise founded on absolute decree His covenant (Gen. ix. 11). The being and essence of a covenant lies in the promise ; hence they are called the "covenants of promise" (Eph. ii. 12). The want of due consideration of this hath perverted the minds of many to suppose an ability in ourselves of yielding obedience to the precepts of the covenant, without grace antecedently received enabling us thereunto, which overthrows the nature of the new covenant.

Then again, we are all actually guilty of sin with whom this covenant is made ; wherefore, unless there be a promise given of the pardon of sin, it is to no purpose to propose any new covenant unto us. For the "wages of sin is death," and we having sinned must die unless our sins be pardoned ; this therefore must be proposed unto us as the foundation of the covenant, or it will be of none effect. In this covenant of grace all things are founded in promises of present mercy and continual supplies of grace, as well as of future blessedness. There are certain differences between these covenants which may be reduced into the following heads.

1. As to time. The old covenant was made when God brought Israel out of Egypt; the new, "in the latter days" (c. i. 1, 2), "in the dispensation of the fulness of times" (Eph. i. 10). 2. As to place of their promulgation. The old was declared on Mount Sinai, the new on Mount Zion. 3. As to the manner of

their promulgation. The old was accompanied by terror and dread, a spirit of fear and bondage; but the new was declared by the Son of God in His own Person. "He spake from heaven," as the Apostle observes, in opposition unto the giving of the law "on the earth" (c. xii. 25). 4. As to their mediators. The mediator of the first covenant was Moses; "it was ordained by angels in the hand of a mediator." But the Mediator of the new covenant is the Son of God—the Man Christ Jesus. 5. As to their subject-matter. The old covenant in the preceptive part of it renewed the commands of the covenant of works; sin it forbade on the pain of death. But in the new covenant, the first thing proposed is the accomplishment and establishment of the covenant of works, in the sufferings and death of the Mediator. 6. As to the manner of their dedication and sanction. In the old covenant this was by the sacrifice of beasts, whose blood was sprinkled on all the people. But the new covenant was solemnly dedicated by the sacrifice and blood of Christ Himself. By His death He purchased all good things for His Church; and as a testator bequeathed them unto it. 7. As to the priests who were to officiate before God in behalf of the people. In the old covenant, Aaron and his posterity alone were to discharge that office; in the new, the Son of God alone is Himself the only Priest of the Church. 8. As to their sacrifices, whereon the peace and reconciliation with God which is tendered in them doth depend. This must be spoken to in the ensuing chapter, if God permit. 9. As to the way and manner of their solemn writing and enrolment. The old covenant, as to the principal part of it, was "engraven in tables of stone;" but the new in the "fleshy tables of the hearts" of them that do believe. 10. As to their ends. The principal end of the old covenant was to discover sin, to condemn it, and to set bounds unto it. This it did by conviction, by condemning the sinner, by the judgments and punishments wherewith on all occasions it was accompanied. The end of the new is to declare the love, grace, and mercy of God, and therewith to give repentance, remission of sin, and life eternal. 11. As to their effects. The old covenant being the "ministration of death and condemnation," it brought the minds and spirits of them that were under it into servitude and bondage; whereas spiritual liberty is the immediate effect of the new. There is no one thing wherein the Spirit of God doth more frequently give us an account of the difference between these two covenants than in this, of the liberty of the one and the bondage of the other. This liberty is granted principally by the communication of the Spirit of the Son as a Spirit of adoption, giving the freedom, boldness, and liberty of children, which liberty is obtained by the opening of the way into the holiest, and the entrance we have thereby with boldness unto the throne of grace. 12. As to the dispensation and gift of the Holy Ghost. It is certain that God did grant the Holy

Spirit under the old covenant, but it is no less certain that there always was a promise of His more signal pouring out upon the establishment of the new covenant. 13. As to the declaration in them of the kingdom of God. Augustine saith the very name, kingdom of heaven, "is peculiar unto the new testament." His kingdom under the old covenant had such a relation to secular things, especially with respect unto the land of Canaan, that it had the appearance of a kingdom of this world. But now in the gospel —under the new covenant—it is well known that the kingdom of God is internal, spiritual, and heavenly, unto the unspeakable consolation of believers. 14. As to substance and end. The old covenant was typical, shadowy, and removable. The new is substantial, permanent, as containing the body, which is Christ. 15. As to the extent of their administration according to the will of God. The old was confined unto the posterity of Abraham according to the flesh, with some few proselytes that were joined unto them, excluding all others. But the new is extended to all nations under heaven, none being excluded on the account of tongue, language, family, nation, or place of habitation. 16. As to their efficacy. The old covenant made nothing perfect; it could effect none of the things it did represent, nor introduce that perfect and complete state which God designed for His Church, as revealed in and secured by the new. 17, and lastly, as to their duration; the one was to be removed, and the other to abide for ever. Let us observe from these things, That the state of the gospel, or of the Church under the New Testament, being accompanied by the highest privileges and advantages that it is capable of in this world, there is a great obligation on all believers unto holiness and fruitfulness in obedience, unto the glory of God; and the heinousness of their sin, by whom this covenant is neglected or despised, is abundantly manifested (see c. ii. 2, 3, and x. 28, 29).

V. 7. *For if that first [covenant] had been faultless, then should no place have been sought for the second.*

The first covenant was, as we have seen, that made with the fathers at Sinai, with all the ordinances of worship belonging thereunto. There was no fault in this covenant itself; but it was insufficient to the perfection and salvation of the Church. What the Apostle designs to prove is, that the first covenant was of that constitution that it could not accomplish the perfect administration of the grace of God unto the Church, nor was it ever designed unto that end. The promise of a new covenant doth unavoidably prove the insufficiency of the former, at least unto the ends for which the new is promised. And we may here observe, that whatever God had done before for the Church, yet He ceased not in His wisdom and grace until He had made it partaker of the best and

most blessed condition whereof in this world it is capable. It was
God who found out a place for this better covenant.

V. 8. *For finding fault with them, He saith, Behold, the
days come, saith the Lord, when I will make a new covenant
with the house of Israel and with the house of Judah.*

"**For finding fault with them, He saith.**" It was not
God's complaint of the people that was any *cause* of the new
covenant being brought in, but it is true that God did actually
complain of the people that they "brake His covenant," and
therefore "He regarded them not;" and so God gives this new
covenant with a complaint against the people, that it might be
known to be an effect of free and sovereign grace. He who complains of the people for breaking the old covenant, promiseth to
make the new. It is God who saith, "*He saith;*" all other
foundations of faith are mere delusions; "thus saith the Lord"
gives rest and peace.

"**Behold, the days come when I will make a new
covenant.**" When God placeth a note of observation as He doth
by this word "Behold," we should carefully fix our faith and consideration; God sets not any of His marks in vain. "*Behold, the
days come;*" the near approach of these days was hereby intended;
not only so, but the certainty of the thing itself was fixed in their
minds. The subject-matter of the thing promised is a "covenant."
The word "testament" is better than covenant. A covenant,
strictly speaking, ought to proceed on equal terms, and a pro-
portionate consideration of things on either side; but the covenant
of God is founded on grace, and consists essentially in a free,
undeserved promise. This covenant is ratified and confirmed by
the death of Him that makes it; and the word "testament" properly
belongs to this; it was confirmed by the death of the Testator and
by the blood of a sacrifice, whereof we must treat at large afterwards,
if God will. He that maketh this covenant bequeatheth His goods
unto others by way of legacy; wherefore our Saviour calls this
covenant "the new testament in My blood." The first covenant is
called the "old testament;" it was so called because it was confirmed by the death of the sacrifices that were slain and offered at
its solemn establishment; also because it typically signified the
death and legacy of the great Testator.

"**With the house of Israel and with the house of
Judah.**" This is to be considered first as the whole and entire
posterity of Abraham; and second, as they were typical and
mystically significant of the whole Church of God. In the first
sense, because He in whom and through whom alone it was to be
established and made effectual was to be brought forth among them
of the seed of Abraham; also because, in the outward dispensation

of it, the terms and grace of it were in the counsel of God first to
be tendered unto them, and also because by them, by the ministry
of men of their posterity, it was to be carried unto all nations,
which was done by the apostles and other disciples of our Lord
Jesus Christ. In the second sense, the whole Church of elect
believers is intended under these denominations, being typified by
them. These are they alone, being one made of twain—namely,
Jews and Gentiles—with whom the covenant is really made and
established, and unto whom the grace of it is actually communicated.

V. 9. *Not according to the covenant that I made with
their fathers in the day when I took them by the hand to lead
them out of the land of Egypt; because they continued not
in My covenant, and I regarded them not, saith the Lord.*

" **Not according to the covenant that I made with their
fathers.**" It is here intimated that God made a covenant, that
the people brake it, and God disannulled it. It may be He did so
to distinguish their alterable covenant from that which was to be
unalterable. There were no evidences about this old covenant of
eternal duration ; nothing hath this but what is founded in the
blood of Christ. This former covenant was made " *with their
fathers,*" of whom these people always boasted ; they desired no
more but only what might descend unto them in the right of these
fathers. But God by His new covenant lets them know that He
had more grace and mercy to communicate unto His Church than
ever their fathers were made partakers of ; He also gave them
warning to take heed how they behaved themselves under the
tender of this new and greater mercy. The fathers here intended
were those with whom God made the covenant at Sinai ; and the
Apostle hath shown at large in the third chapter how they brake
and rejected this covenant through their unbelief and disobedience,
so perishing in the wilderness. A great warning was this unto
those who should live when God would enter into the new covenant
with His Church, lest they should perish after the same example.
But this warning was not effectual unto them, for the greatest
part of them rejected this new covenant, as their fathers did the old,
and perished in the indignation of God.

" **In the day when I took them by the hand to lead
them out of the land of Egypt.**" " In the day " is that great
and eminent season so famous throughout all their generations.
" When I took them by the hand," firmly laid hold of them with
the design of helping and delivering them. In this we may see
the woful, helpless condition that they were in when in Egypt. So
He speaks, " I taught them to go, taking them by their arms "
(Hos. xi. 3). He that can read the story of their deliverance with

any understanding will easily discern what pains God was at with that people to teach them to go when He thus took them by the hand. This also expresseth the infinite condescension of God towards this people in that condition, that He would bow down and take them by the hand.

These words, "*took them by the hand*," compriseth all the grace, mercy, and patience which God exercised towards that people, while He wrought out their deliverance by lifting up His hand against their adversaries. It was a great day when God so magnified His name and power in the sight of all the world. And therefore did God engrave the memorial of it on tables of stone: "I am the Lord thy God, which brought thee out of the land of Egypt, out of the house of bondage."

"**Because they continued not in My covenant, and I regarded them not, saith the Lord.**" Their not continuing in His covenant could be no reason why He made a new covenant. It is mentioned only to illustrate the grace of God, that He would make this new covenant, notwithstanding the sin of those who brake the former; as also the excellency of the covenant itself, whereby those who are taken into it shall be preserved from breaking it by the grace which it doth administer. Nothing but effectual grace will secure our covenant obedience one moment, and therefore in the new covenant this grace is promised in a peculiar manner, as we shall see in the next verse.

"*And I regarded them not, saith the Lord.*" It is as though He said, "I exercised the right, power, and authority of a husband towards them ; I dealt with them as a husband with a wife that breaketh covenant ; " that is, saith the Apostle, I regarded them not with the love, tenderness, and affection of a husband. We are concerned in all these things ; for although the covenant of grace be stable and effectual unto all who are really partakers of it, yet as unto the external administration of it, and our entering into it by a visible profession, it may be broken unto the temporal and eternal ruin of persons and whole churches. Take heed of the golden calf.

V. 10.   *For this is the covenant that I will make with the house of Israel after those days, saith the Lord ; I will put My laws into their mind, and write them in their hearts ; and I will be to them a God, and they shall be to Me a people.*

"**For this is the covenant that I will make with the house of Israel after those days, saith the Lord.**" This covenant, as reduced into the form of a testament, confirmed by the blood of Christ, doth not depend upon any condition or qualification in our persons, but on a free grant and donation of God, and so with all the good things prepared in it. The Author of this covenant is God Himself, " *I will make*." The abolishing of the old with the introduction of the new is an act of the mere sovereign wisdom, grace, and authority of God. This covenant is made with the house of Israel, " so that all Israel might be saved," by which the Church of the elect is principally intended.

" *After those days* " seems to me to comprise the whole time allotted unto the economy of the dispensation of the old covenant. That is, after their expiration, when they were coming to an end, whereby the first covenant waxed old and decayed, that then God would make this new covenant. As it was with the old covenant, so was it with the new. It was gradually made and established, and there are six degrees observable in it.

1. By the ministry of John the Baptist; hence his ministry is called "the beginning of the gospel." His ministry was designed to prepare the people, and to cause them to look out for the accomplishment of this promise of making a new covenant (Mal. iv. 4—6). 2. By the coming in the flesh and personal ministry of our Lord Jesus Christ Himself. The dispensation of the old covenant did yet continue, for He Himself was " made of a woman, made under the law." But His coming in the flesh laid an axe unto the root of that whole dispensation ; hence, upon His nativity, this covenant was proclaimed from heaven as that which was immediately to take place (Luke ii. 13, 14). 3. By the solemn confirmation of the covenant in and by His death, for herein He offered that sacrifice to God, whereby it was established. 4. By the complement of its making and establishment in His resurrection from the dead. This was the perfect end of the law. And this end had two parts : first, the perfect fulfilling of the righteousness which it required ; this was done in the obedience of Christ, the Surety of the new covenant, in the stead of them with whom the covenant was made. And second, that the curse of the law should be undergone. Until this was done, the law could not quit its claim upon poor sinners. And as this curse was undergone in the sufferings of Christ, so it was absolutely discharged in His resurrection. For the pains of death being loosed, and He delivered from the state of the dead, the sanction of the law was declared to be void, and its curse answered. Hereby did the old covenant so expire, that the worship that belonged unto it was only for a while continued, in the patience and forbearance of God toward that people. 5. By the first solemn promulgation of this new covenant on the day of Pentecost, seven weeks after the resurrection of Christ. Then was the Church absolved from any duty with respect unto the old covenant and the worship of it. 6. By the solemn promulgation by the apostles under the infallible conduct of the Holy Ghost, that the continuance of the obligatory force of the old covenant was passed away for ever.

"**I will put My laws into their mind, and write them in their hearts.**" The mind is the most secret, inward part or power of the soul. The excellency of covenant obedience consisteth not in the conformity of our outward actions to the law, although that be required therein; but it principally lieth in the inward parts, where God searcheth for and regardeth truth in sincerity (Psa. li. 6). This in the New Testament is called the "renewing of our minds" (Rom. xii. 2; Eph. iv. 23); also the "opening of the eyes of our understanding" (Eph. i. 17, 18).

The law of God in the mind is the saving knowledge of the mind and will of God, communicated unto it, and implanted in it. This is given, "*I will put.*" Here we may see the *freedom* of the grace promised, it is a mere gift or grant; also the *efficacy* of the grace promised; that which is given of God unto any is received by them, otherwise it is no gift. This the Apostle states emphatically, "I will put;" that is to say, This is that which I am doing in this covenant, namely, freely giving that grace whereby My laws shall be implanted on the minds of men. By the words "*My laws,*" we are to understand any way or revelation soever, whereby God makes known Himself and His will unto us, requiring our obedience therein. The promise is to put these laws into the mind, and to "write them in the heart." The heart, as distinguished from the mind, compriseth the will and affections, and these are compared unto the tables whereon the letter of the law was engraven. This work of grace is described as "taking out the heart of stone," and as "giving an heart of flesh;" wherefore in this promise the whole of our sanctification, in its beginning and progress, is comprised.

"**And I will be to them a God, and they shall be to Me a people.**" This is indeed a distinct promise by itself, summarily comprising all the blessings and privileges of the covenant. God could not enter into a new covenant with sinful, fallen man to be a "God to them" and they a "peculiar people" unto Him, immediately in their own persons. So He provided, in the first place, that there should be a Mediator of this new covenant, with whom alone He would treat, for there were many things necessary unto it that could in no otherwise be enacted and accomplished. Wherefore this covenant was made with Jesus Christ, the Surety and the undertaker of it. In the first covenant God committed at once unto man all that grace which was necessary to enable him unto the obedience of it. But all was lost that was committed to our keeping, so as that nothing at all was left to give us the least relief as unto any new endeavours. Wherefore God will now secure all the good things of this covenant, both as to grace and glory, in a third hand, in the hand of a Mediator. Hereon the promises are made to Him, and the fulness of grace is laid up in Him. As the Mediator God became His God, and He became the Servant of

God in a peculiar manner. God being in this covenant a God and Father unto Christ, He became in virtue thereof to be our God and Father; and we became "His heirs, joint heirs with Christ."

This is the *foundation* of the covenant relationship here declared. As to the *nature* of this covenant, whatever God is in Himself, whatever these properties of His nature extend to, in it all God hath promised to be our God. If He be our God, which He promiseth, then He will be an all-sufficient *preserver*, and an all-sufficient *rewarder*. We may observe, 1. As nothing less than God becoming our God could relieve, help, and save us, so nothing more can be required thereunto. 2. The efficacy, security, and glory of this covenant depend originally on the nature of God, immediately and actually on the mediation of Christ. 3. It is from the engagement of the properties of the divine nature, that this covenant " is ordered in all things and sure." Infinite wisdom hath provided it, and infinite power will make it effectual. 4. As the grace of this covenant is inexpressible, so are the obligations it puts upon us unto obedience. 5. That God doth as well undertake for our being His people, as He doth for His being our God. The promises contained in this verse do principally aim at that end, namely, the making of us a people unto Him. 6. That those with whom God makes a covenant are His, in a peculiar manner. And the profession hereof is that which the world principally maligneth, and ever did so from the beginning.

V. 11. *And they shall not teach every man his neighbour, and every man his brother, saying, Know the Lord: for all shall know Me, from the least to the greatest.*

"**And they shall not teach every man his neighbour, and every man his brother, saying, Know the Lord.**" The whole knowledge of God, prescribed in His law, is here intended. The teaching of this knowledge is not denied absolutely, but as unto a certain way and manner of teaching, which was in use and necessary under the old covenant. There was a knowledge of God under the Old Testament hidden under types, wrapped up in veils, expressed only in parables and dark sayings. It was the mind of God that the clear perception and full revelation of this knowledge should lie hid, till the Son came from His bosom to declare Him, to make Him known, and to " bring life and immortality to light." This secret, hidden knowledge of God principally concerned the incarnation of Christ, His mediation and suffering for sin, with the call of the Gentiles. These, and such like mysteries of the gospel, they that were under the old covenant could never attain the comprehension of. But yet they stirred up one another diligently to inquire into them, saying one to another, " Know the Lord." But it was little they could attain unto.

Now this kind of teaching under the new covenant is to cease, as being rendered useless by the full, clear revelation and manifestation of these hidden mysteries, made in the gospel. The knowledge of God shall under the new covenant be made plain to all believers. But this knowledge of the Lord must not be considered only objectively and doctrinally, but subjectively, for the renewing of the mind in the saving knowledge of God. This neither is nor can be communicated unto any by external teaching alone, in respect whereunto it may be said comparatively to be laid aside. The teaching of others, which is the duty of every man according to his ability and opportunity, in the knowledge of God, is not here either prohibited or superseded ; but only it is foretold that, as to a certain manner of teaching, it should cease.

"For all shall know Me, from the least to the greatest." None, upon the account of their difference from others on the one hand or the other, are excepted or excluded from the grace of this promise ; they shall all not only be taught to know, but they all shall actually know the Lord ; that is, the whole Church shall be taught of God, and shall so learn as to come unto Him by saving faith in Christ. There may be a great variety of degrees of abilities—natural, acquired, spiritual—among them, but it is promised that they each and all shall know the Lord. Persons destitute of this saving knowledge of God are utter strangers unto the covenant of grace, for this is a principal promise and effect of it.

V. 12. *For I will be merciful to their unrighteousness, and their sins and their iniquities will I remember no more.*

The word *"their"* is three times repeated ; only those with whom God makes this covenant are included. Some speak of a universal conditional covenant made with all mankind. If there be any such thing, it is not here intended, for they are all actually pardoned with whom this covenant is made. Some say that the condition of this grace of pardoned sin is that "men repent, believe, turn to God, and yield obedience unto the gospel." If so, then must they do all these things before they receive the remission of sins ? You say, " Yes ! " Then must they do them whilst they are under the law and the curse of it, for so are all men whose sins are not pardoned. This is to make obedience unto the law, and that performed whilst men are under the curse of it, to be the condition of gospel mercy ; which is to overthrow both law and gospel.

But then on the other hand it will follow, they say, " that men are pardoned before they do believe, which is expressly contrary to Scripture." I answer, that the communication and gift of faith is an effect of the same grace whereby our sins are pardoned, and they are both bestowed upon us by virtue of this new covenant.

Faith is not required unto the *procuring* of the pardon of our sins, but unto the *receiving* of pardon.

The subject-matter of this promise is the pardon of sin ; sin is spoken of with respect unto its guilt especially ; guilt is the desert of punishment, or the obligation of the sinner unto punishment according to the sentence of the law ; pardon is the dissolution of that obligation. Three words are used in this text concerning sin, " unrighteousness," " sin," " iniquity." Unrighteousness is in respect of sin as unto God ; it is an unequal and unrighteous thing that man should sin against God, his sovereign ruler and benefactor. Sin is properly a missing of, an erring from, that end and scope which it is our duty to aim at. Iniquity is lawlessness, a voluntary unconformity unto the law. As all sorts of particular sins are included in these multiplied names of sin, so the general nature of sin in all its causes and effects is declared and represented by them.

And we may learn from these words, " *I will be merciful to their unrighteousness*," &c., that there are grace and mercy in the new covenant provided for all sorts of sins, and all aggravations of them, if they be received in a due manner. Pardon is the thing intended in both of these expressions, " *I will be merciful*," and " *I will remember no more*." In this word " *merciful* " there is a respect unto the propitiation for sin made by the Mediator of the covenant ; without this there can be no remission, nor is any ever promised ; also unto the dissolution of the obligation of the law binding over the guilty sinner to punishment. These are the essentials of evangelical pardon, and respect is had in these words unto both of them.

V. 13. *In that He saith, A new [covenant], He hath made the first old. Now that which decayeth and waxeth old [is] ready to vanish away.*

The Apostle calls attention to this, that God calls this promised covenant, not another, or a second, but signally calls it " *a new covenant*." He infers from this, " *He hath made the first old*." It was God who gradually, by His providence, did break in upon and weaken the administration of the old covenant ; it received a total interruption during the seventy years of the Babylonish captivity ; then, upon the return of the people, neither the temple nor its worship were ever restored unto their pristine glory and beauty. God told them by Haggai how His coming amongst them would put an utter end unto all the administrations of that dispensation, and from that time forward it is easy to trace the whole process of decline and decay. And so the Apostle declares, that it was then when he wrote ready to vanish away, or near unto disappearance. All the glorious institutions of the law were, at best, but as stars in the firmament of the Church, and therefore were all to disappear at the rising of the Sun of Righteousness.

CHAPTER NINE

V. 1. *Then verily the first [covenant] had also ordinances of divine service, and a worldly sanctuary.*

The Apostle hath respect unto the time when the covenant was first made ; then it had these things annexed unto it, which were the privileges and the glory of it. It had *"ordinances of divine service ; "* these were appointments of God which He had right to prescribe ; whence their observation on the part of the Church was just and equal. That these ordinances of divine worship might be duly observed and rightly performed, there was a place appointed by God for their solemnization; it is called *" a worldly sanctuary."* He refers to the tabernacle of witness, erected in the wilderness in two parts, the holy and the most holy, with the utensils of them. This tabernacle was a visible pledge of the presence of God among the people, owning, blessing, and protecting them ; it was also the pledge and means of God's residence amongst them, and it was the fixed seat of divine worship, wherein the truth and purity of it were to be preserved.

It was also a continual representation of the incarnation of the Son of God, a type of His coming in the flesh to dwell among them, and by the one sacrifice of Himself to make reconciliation with God, and atonement for sins. It is called a " worldly sanctuary," because the place of it was on this world ; also because the materials of which it was made, though as durable as anything that could be procured, were fading and perishing things, as are all the things of this world ; also because all its services, sacrifices, &c., in themselves, separated from their typical use, were all worldly, and their efficacy extended only to worldly things, as the Apostle proves in this chapter. It is called worldly in opposition to that which is heavenly; all things in the ministration of the new covenant are heavenly ; its Priest, its sacrifice, its tabernacle, its altar, as we shall see in the process of the Apostle's discourse, are all heavenly.

V. 2. *For there was a tabernacle made ; the first, wherein [was] the candlestick, and the table, and the shewbread ; which is called the Sanctuary.*

" For there was a tabernacle made ; " the common name for the whole fabric. It was made ; this signifies more than its mere building. This one word includes the provision of materials made by the people, the workings of those materials by Bezaleel ; the erection of the whole by the direction of Moses, and the adorning of it unto its particular use.

" **The first, wherein was the candlestick, and the table, and the shewbread.**" The candlestick was placed on the south side of the tabernacle, near the veil that covered the most holy place; over against it on the north side was the table of shewbread; and in the midst, at the very entrance of the most holy place, was the altar of incense. This candlestick was all of beaten gold, of one piece, without any joints or screws, which is not without its mystery; pure oil olive was to be provided by the way of offering from the people, and it was the office of the high priest to " order it," that is, to dress its lamps every morning and every evening, supplying them with fresh oil, and removing whatsoever might be offensive. On the other side of the sanctuary was the table and the shewbread; this bread was renewed every Sabbath in the morning, the renovation of these cakes being a particular part of the worship of the day. There was also in the sanctuary the altar of incense; this was placed at the west end just upon the entrance into the most holy place, wherefore it is reckoned by the Apostle unto that part of the sanctuary, as we shall see in the next verse. This first part of the tabernacle was called " holy," that is, the " sanctuary."

V. 3.   *And after the second veil, the tabernacle which is called the Holiest of all.*

This veil, that separated the holy place from the most holy, was the second veil to them that entered the tabernacle; they had to pass through the whole length of the first part before they came to this, nor was there any other way of entrance into it. The first veil was the hanging at the door of the tabernacle. This second part is described as " the most holy," " the holiest of all." This that is thus called was most eminently typical of Christ, who is Himself called " the Most Holy " (Dan. ix. 24).

V. 4.   *Which had the golden censer, and the ark of the covenant overlaid round about with gold, wherein [was] the golden pot that had manna, and Aaron's rod that budded, and the tables of the covenant.*

" **Which had the golden censer.**" It doth not say that this censer was in this second part; but this second part " had " it. This "censer" may as well be the " altar of incense " overlaid with beaten gold; the Apostle speaks not of its *situation*, but of its *use*; the second part had the golden censer. The most holy place may well be said to have had this altar of incense, because the high priest could never enter into that place, nor perform any service in it, but he was to bring incense with him, taken in a censer from this altar. There was a twofold use of this altar; the one of the ordinary priests to burn incense in the sanctuary every day, and the other of the high priest to take incense from it when he entered the most holy place; the Apostle intending a comparison between the Lord Christ and the high priest only, he takes no notice of the ordinary daily use of the altar of incense, but only of that which respected the most holy place, and the entrance of the high priest thereinto, for he expressly applies it (v. 12). This incense burnt by the high priest on the day of expiation represents the mediatorial prayer of Christ Himself. Concerning it, we may observe that the time of it was after the sacrifice of the sin offering, and the incense was kindled by fire taken from the altar when the blood of the sacrifices was newly offered.

Let us observe, 1. That the mediatory intercession of Christ is a sweet savour unto God, and efficacious for the salvation of the Church. 2. The efficacy of Christ's intercession dependeth upon His oblation. It was fire from the burnt offering altar wherewith the incense was kindled. 3. We are always to reckon that the efficacy and prevalency of our prayers depends on the incense which is in the hand of our merciful High Priest. In themselves our prayers are weak and imperfect; it is hard to conceive how they can find acceptance with God. But the invaluable intercession of Christ gives them acceptance and prevalency.

"**And the ark of the covenant overlaid round about with gold.**" This ark with the mercy-seat wherewith it was covered was the most glorious and mysterious utensil of the tabernacle, and afterwards of the temple : the most eminent pledge of the divine presence, the most mysterious representation of the holy properties of His nature in Christ. The whole sanctuary was built for no other end but to be, as it were, a house and habitation for this ark. All flesh was excluded from the sight of the ark, the High Priest only excepted, who entered that holy place once a year, and that not without blood.

"**Wherein was the golden pot that had manna.**" God appointed that a pot holding an omer should be laid up before the Lord for their generations. It was miraculously preserved from putrefaction, whereas of itself it would not keep two days. The reason of the sacred preservation of this manna in the most holy place was because it was a type of Christ, as Himself declares (John vi. 48—51).

"**And Aaron's rod that budded.**" This rod was originally that wherewith Moses fed the sheep of his father-in-law—Jethro—in the wilderness, which he had in his hand when God called unto him out of the bush. God ordained it to be the token of the putting forth of His power in the working of miracles, having by a trial confirmed the faith of Moses concerning it (Ex. iv. 17). Hereby it became sacred, and when Aaron was called unto the office of a priest, it was delivered into his keeping. For on the budding of it, on the trial about the priesthood, it was laid up before the testimony, that is, the ark (Num. xvii. 10). This rod of Moses belonged unto the holy furniture of the tabernacle, because the spiritual Rock that followed them was to be smitten with the rod of the law, that it might give out the waters of life unto the Church.

"**And the tables of the covenant.**" The two tables of stone cut out by Moses, and written on with the finger of God, containing the ten commandments, which were the substance of God's covenant with the people. There have been many controversies as to the exact place of these various things ; I will give the true real position of them. In the closed ark there was nothing but the two tables of stone. Before it, or at the ends of it, were the pot of manna and the miracle-working rod. The word translated " in," " wherein was the golden pot," is frequently used in Scripture to signify adhesion, approximation of one thing unto another.

V. 5. *And over it the cherubim of glory shadowing the mercy-seat ; of which we cannot now speak particularly.*

These cherubim were of human shape, only with wings. Their faces were turned inward one towards another. This posture gave unto the whole work of the ark, mercy-seat, and cherubim the form of a seat, which represented the throne of God. They are hence called the cherubim of glory, for there the majestical presence of God did sit and reside. This place is the " mercy-seat," covering the ark.

"**Of which we cannot now speak particularly.**" He plainly intimates that all these utensils, every one of them in particular, were of singular consideration, as typical of the Lord Christ and His ministry. Only it seemed good to the Holy Ghost not to give unto the Church in this place a particular application of them, but He hath left it unto our humble diligence to seek after it out of the Scripture, according unto the analogy of faith, and such rules of interpretation as Himself giveth in the ensuing discourse. In all these things God did instruct His Church by the tabernacle, especially by this most holy place, the utensils, furniture and service of it. And the end of all was to give unto them a representation of the mystery of His grace in Christ Jesus, as was meet for the state of the Church before His actual exhibition in the flesh.

In His obedience unto God according to the law He is the *true ark*, wherein the law was kept inviolate, that is, was fulfilled, answered, and accomplished. He was the *mercy-seat*—the propitiation—and this was to cover the law under the eye of God. It was *His blood in figure* that was carried into the holy place to make atonement, and it is *His intercession* that is the cloud of incense which covers the ark and the mercy-seat.   It was He who took off the original curse of the law, whose first execution at the entrance to the garden of Eden was committed to the cherubim, who now has a ministry with respect unto the mercy-seat for the good of the "heirs of salvation."   He also was the *bread of life*, typed by the manna kept in the golden pot before the mercy-seat, for He alone is the nourishment of the spiritual life of men.   Thus was the Lord Christ all and in all from the beginning.

V. 6.   *Now when these things were thus ordained, the priests went always into the first tabernacle, accomplishing the service* [*of God*].

Only the priests entered the sanctuary; all these were of the posterity of Aaron, and they administered under the care of God and the directions of the high priest.   If the high priest ministered at any time in this part of the tabernacle, he did not as a high priest, but as a priest only, for all his peculiar services belonged unto the most holy place.   It was the great privilege of the priests under the old testament that they alone might and did enter the sanctuary; the body of the people might not so much as come nigh; it was forbidden them on pain of death, whereof they sadly complained.   This state of things is all changed under the gospel, it being one of the principal privileges of believers that, being made kings and priests unto God by Jesus Christ, this distinction as unto special access unto God is taken away.   The priests went into the first tabernacle only; they must go no further; they were not even to look into the most holy place, nor abide in the sanctuary when the high priest went into it, which the Apostle here hath a special respect unto.   They entered the sanctuary "always," there was no divine prohibition as there was with respect unto the high priest and the most holy place, which was allowed only once a year.   The object of their entrance into the sanctuary was to "accomplish the services."   There were daily services,—trimming the lamps, the service of the golden altar of incense; also the weekly service,—the change of bread on the table of shew-bread, &c.

V. 7.   *But into the second* [*went*] *the high priest alone once every year, not without blood, which he offered for himself, and* [*for*] *the errors of the people.*

No one but the high priest might enter the second place; this was the great truth which God in this ordinance taught the Church, namely, that there is no entrance into the gracious presence of God but by the high priest.   That the true High Priest should take all believers with Him, and give them admission with boldness unto the throne of grace, was, as the Apostle declares in the next verse, not as yet made known. The high priest *went into* this second place, a type both of Christ's entrance into heaven, and of our entrance by Him unto the throne of grace. The time of this service was only *once a year*, and that not a time as chosen by the high priest, but at the time appointed by God ; this time was the great day of atonement.

When it says " once every year," we are to understand on one day only every year, for it is evident that the high priest entered more than once on that particular day. As to the nature of the service accomplished by the high priest, it was " *not without blood*," showing us how impossible it was that there should be an entrance into the gracious presence of God without the blood and sacrifice of Christ. This blood the high priest " offered up " in the most holy place by sprinkling the blood, which was always consequential unto the offering or oblation properly so called. This blood he offered " for himself " first, and then for the errors of the people. The true High Priest was to offer His own blood, and that not for Himself at all but for others only.

V. 8. *The Holy Ghost this signifying, that the way into the holiest of all was not yet made manifest, while as the first tabernacle was yet standing.*

" **The Holy Ghost this signifying.** " He that by His words and works instructeth the Church is a Person, for He who by His authority and wisdom disposed of the worship of God under the old testament, so as it might typify and represent things afterwards to come to pass and to be revealed, can be no other. He ordained that the high priest should enter once a year with blood into the most holy place, thus plainly signifying that there would be an entrance, and that with boldness, in due time, unto the gracious presence of God Himself.

" **That the way into the holiest was not yet made manifest.** " The Apostle intends the " holy of holies,"—the second part of the sanctuary ; but he declares not what these things were, but what the Holy Ghost did signify by them. Wherefore, to enter " the holiest " is none other but an access with freedom, liberty, and boldness into the gracious presence of God, on the account of reconciliation and peace made with Him. The way into the holiest is no other but the sacrifice of Christ, the true High Priest of the Church of God. Until that sacrifice was offered, the way could not be opened into the holiest, which it was immediately after His death, and signified by the rending of the veil.

Under the old testament this way was not " *made manifest ;* " it was not actually existent though virtually so, and moreover there were many blessed privileges connected with the opening of this

way with which the Church of old were not acquainted. Three
things constituted the opening of the way: 1. The actual exhibition
of Christ in the flesh, and His sacrifice of Himself, making an
atonement for sin ; hereby the curse of the law was removed, and
a new and living way of access to God was consecrated for us.
2. The full, plain declaration of the nature of His Person and of
His mediation. The gospel is our sole direction how to make use
of this way, and how to enter by it into the most holy place.
3. The introduction and establishment of those privileges of gospel
worship whereby believers are led comfortably into the presence of
God.

" While as the first tabernacle was yet standing." The
Apostle includes in this " first tabernacle " the whole worship instituted together with it, and belonging to it, celebrated afterwards in
the temple according to the laws of the tabernacle. It had its state
and use in the Church of God, and that until the death of Christ,
and no longer. This was according unto the mind of God. *Declaratively* it remained till the day of Pentecost, for then in the coming
of the Holy Ghost was the foundation of the gospel church-state,
order, and worship solemnly laid, whereon a new way of worship
being established, the abrogation of the old was declared.

Actually it continued until the destruction of the temple, city,
and people, some years after. The Old Testament worship preserved its station and use in the Church by God's ordinance and
appointment unto the death of Christ. Then was the veil rent, and
the way into the holiest laid open. Then was peace with God
publicly confirmed by the blood of the cross, and the nature of the
way of access unto Him made known. The clear manifestation of
the way of redemption, of the expiation of sin, and of peace with
God therein, is the great privilege of the gospel ; for there is no
access unto the gracious presence of God but by the sacrifice of
Christ alone.

Vs. 9, 10.   *Which* [*was*] *a figure for the time then present,
in which were offered both gifts and sacrifices, that could
not make him that did the service perfect, as pertaining to
the conscience :* [*which stood*] *only in meats and drinks, and
divers washings, and carnal ordinances, imposed* [*on them*]
until the time of reformation.

"Which was a figure for the time then present." That
is, the tabernacle—not only the structure and fabric of it, but with
all its furniture, vessels, utensils, and services, as before described—
was but an obscure, parabolical, figurative instruction ; this was,
for that time, God's way of teaching the mysteries of His wisdom
and grace. The " *time then present* " was the state and condition of

the Church at the first setting up of the tabernacle. This kind of instruction was meet and fit for them to whom it was given, and it was a blessed means to ingenerate faith, love, and obedience in their hearts and lives to an eminent degree. And we may consider from hence what is required of us unto whom the clear revelation of the wisdom, grace, and love of God is made known from the bosom of the Father by the Son Himself.

"**In which were offered both gifts and sacrifices.**" In which time, during which season, God gave unto Moses laws and institutions for all the gifts and sacrifices of the people. The Apostle represents that as present which was long past ; he represents to the Hebrews the first tabernacle with all its services, as it was at its first institution. This he does that he may more fully declare the imperfection of this whole order of things, and its impotency unto the great end that might be expected from it; for these sacrifices and gifts could not make the worshippers perfect.

"**That could not make him that did the service perfect as pertaining to the conscience.**" They could not do it as unto the conscience of the sinner before God. What he intends here he doth more fully declare (chap. x. 2). There is a conscience condemning for sin ; this could not be taken away by those sacrifices, for they were not able to do it; for if they could have done so, the sinner would have had complete peace with God, and would have had no need to offer those sacrifices any more. To be made perfect as pertaining to the conscience is, through a sense of perfect atonement made for sin in the sight of God, to enjoy peace with God, with a sense of His love and favour in the conscience. This those sacrifices of the law could not effect. Neither priest who offered, or people who brought the offering, could obtain peace in their consciences by these sacrifices.

"**[Which stood] only in meats and drinks, and divers washings, and carnal ordinances.**" The argument of the Apostle is to prove the insufficiency of the gifts and sacrifices of the law unto the end mentioned of perfecting the conscience. There were laws as to those meats and drinks which were clean or unclean ; then there was the portion out of some of the sacrifices for the priests especially, what they were to eat in the holy place, as the portion of the sin-offering ; with many other ordinances that were to be observed with their gifts and sacrifices ; and this with " *divers washings.*" The Apostle hath special reference to the washings of the priests, and of the offerings in the court of the tabernacle before the altar ; for without these washings the gifts and sacrifices could not be offered rightly unto God. All these ceremonies and rites are here called " *carnal ordinances.*" This is to show still further the weakness of this service. All these carnal observances, consisting wholly in carnal things as meats, drinks, washings, and such like, could reach no further than the sanctification of the flesh ; and the faith of believers is rather weakened than confirmed by all such-like things, that divest the mind from an immediate respect unto and total dependence on the one sacrifice by Christ.

"Imposed on them until the time of reformation." These things were imposed on them as a burden that they might feel their weight, and groan under the burden of it. Of this bondage the Apostle treats at large in his epistle unto the Galatians. "The time of reformation" is the great time of the coming of the Messiah as the King, Prophet, and Priest of the Church, to order and alter things so as it might attain unto its perfect state.

V. 11. *But Christ being come an High Priest of good things to come, by a greater and more perfect tabernacle, not made with hands, that is to say, not of this building.*

" But Christ being come an High Priest of good things to come." By the word " come " no one single act is intended ; it is comprehensive of the whole accomplishment of the promise of God in sending Him, and His performance of the work whereunto He was called. He came an "High Priest ; " that is, in answer to and in the place of the high priest under the law. Those former priests were not priests of "good things," that is, things necessary to the purification, sanctification, and justification of the Church. So far as they were priests of good things, it was of things present, not of the good things promised. The *"good things to come"* are, in brief, all the good things in spiritual redemption and salvation which they looked for by the Messiah. Of these things, Christ was now come the High Priest ; He now entered upon the actual discharge of the duties of His office—these, in general, were His oblation and intercession. For although His intercession be continued in heaven, it began on earth ; as also His oblation was offered on earth, but is continued in heaven as unto the perpetual virtue of it.

" By a greater and more perfect tabernacle." This tabernacle whereby He became a Priest was His own human nature. The bodies of men are often called their tabernacle (2 Cor. v. 1 ; 2 Pet. i. 14). Christ called His own body His temple (John ii. 19). His flesh was the veil (chap. x. 20). And in His incarnation He is said to "pitch His tabernacle among us" (John i. 14). Herein dwelt the fulness of the Godhead bodily (Col. ii. 9). This taber-nacle was *" greater "* in worth and dignity than any material fabric such as the old tabernacle could be ; the human nature of Christ doth as far excel the Old Testament tabernacle as the sun doth the meanest star. It was not only greater, but *" more perfect."* It was more perfectly suited unto the use of a tabernacle, both for the inhabitation of the Divine nature and the means of exercising the priestly office in making atonement for sin, than the old tabernacle could be. So it is expressed (chap. x. 5) : " A body hast Thou prepared Me;" this was that which God accepted, wherewith He was well pleased, when He rejected the other as insufficient.

"Not made with hands, that is to say, not of this building." The Apostle elsewhere lays it down as a principle suited unto natural light, that "God who made all things could not dwell in temples made with hands" (Acts xvii. 24). Such was the tabernacle of old ; but such was not that in which our Lord Jesus administereth His office. Solomon openly affirms that the habitation of God could not be in the temple he had built, because it was made with hands. The constitution and production of the human nature of Christ was the immediate effect of the wisdom and power of God Himself. Nothing of human wisdom or contrivance, nothing of the skill or power of man, had the least influence or concurrence in the provision of this glorious tabernacle wherein the work of the redemption of the Church was effected. Neither is it "*of this building.*" It is so "not made with hands" like unto that tabernacle, as that it is not of the order of any other created thing, not of the same make and constitution with anything else in the whole creation here below. The substance of His human nature was of the same kind with ours, yet the production of it in the world was such an act of Divine power as excels all other Divine operations whatever.

V. 12. *Neither by the blood of goats and calves, but by His own blood He entered in once into the holy place, having obtained eternal redemption [for us].*

Christ "*entered in once into the holy place;*" that is, heaven itself, as the Apostle explains it (v. 24)—the glorious place—the residence of the presence or majesty of God, is that whereinto He entered. He entered into heaven upon His ascension in *regal* glory and triumph. Satan, the world, death, and hell being conquered and all power committed unto Him, He entered heaven triumphantly. He also entered *sacerdotally ;* peace and reconciliation being made by the blood of the cross, the covenant being confirmed, eternal redemption obtained. He entered as our High Priest into the holy place, the temple of God above, to make His sacrifice effectual unto the Church, and to apply the benefits of it thereunto. This He did "*once,*" only once for all.

The high priest of old went in once every year, and this repetition year by year proved its imperfection, seeing it could never accomplish perfection, as the Apostle argues in the next chapter. In opposition hereunto, our High Priest entered in *once only* into the holy place, a full demonstration that His one sacrifice had fully expiated the sins of the Church. Christ did not enter by the "*blood of goats and calves.*" The high priest entered in by the blood of goats and calves ; namely, by virtue of the sacrifice of their blood, which he had offered upon the altar. And so all things do correspond between the type and the antitype. For Christ entered in by "*His own blood.*" That is, He entered heaven by virtue of His own blood when it was shed, when He offered Himself unto God. This was that which gave Him the right unto the administration of His priestly office in heaven. This is the centre of all Gospel mysteries, the object of the admiration of angels and men unto all eternity. What heart can conceive, what tongue can tell, the wisdom, grace, and love that are contained therein? This alone is the stable foundation of faith in our access to God.

Two things present themselves unto us: 1. The unspeakable love of Christ in offering Himself and His own blood for us. There being no other way whereby our sins might be expiated, He, out of His infinite love and grace, condescended unto this way, whereby God might be glorified and His Church sanctified and saved. 2. The excellency and efficacy of this sacrifice is hereby demonstrated, that through Him our faith and hope might be in God. He who offered this sacrifice was "the only begotten of the Father "—the eternal Son of God. That which He offered was "His own blood." "God purchased the Church with His own blood." How unquestionable, how perfect, must the atonement be that was thus made! How glorious the redemption thus procured!

The effect of His bloodshedding was He "*obtained eternal redemption :*" He effectually obtained redemption by the price of His blood. All redemption respects a state of bondage and captivity, with all the events that do attend it. This redemption is effected in two ways: by price and by power. The price of redemption is two ways expressed. 1. By that which gave it its worth and value, that it might be a sufficient ransom for all; 2. By its especial nature. As to the first, it is the Person of Christ Himself—"He gave Himself;" "He offered Himself unto God;" "He gave Himself a ransom for all." This was that which made the ransom of infinite value, meet to redeem the whole Church.

As to the second, the especial nature of redemption, it was "*by His own blood.*" And this blood of Christ was a ransom, or price of redemption, partly from the invaluableness of that obedience which He yielded unto God in the shedding of it, and partly because this ransom was also to be an atonement, as it was offered unto God in sacrifice. For it is only by blood that an atonement can be made.

The cause—the *meritorious cause* of our need of redemption is sin, or our original apostacy from God ; the *supreme efficient cause* is God Himself, who as the Ruler and Judge of all men hath cast us all into a state of captivity and bondage ; the *instrumental cause* is the curse of the law, and the *external cause* is the power of Satan over the souls and consciences of men. In redemption out of this state there must be a ransom price paid, whereby the *guilt of sin is expiated;* there must be an *atonement made* to the satisfaction of divine justice; there must be removed the *curse of the law,* which could not be but by undergoing it; and there must be the *destroying of the power of Satan.* All this was done by Christ, who passed into heaven by His blood. This redemption is " *eternal ;* " in its effects and consequences it endures for ever and ever. This eternal redemption obtained by Christ was by *His blood;* He whose faith is most exercised and most conversant with this truth will be the most humble and fruitful Christian.

V. 13. *For if the blood of bulls and of goats, and the ashes of an heifer sprinkling the unclean, sanctifieth to the purifying of the flesh.*

"**For if the blood of bulls and goats ;** " this includes all the clean animals and beasts whose blood was given unto the people to make an atonement withal. It was by their blood, and that as offered at the altar, by which atonement was made. Purification was also made thereby, even by sprinkling of it.

"**And the ashes of an heifer.**" The institution, use, and end of this ordinance are described at large (Num. xix.). And an eminent type of Christ there was therein, both as unto His suffering and the continual cleansing efficacy of His blood in the Church.

1. It was to be a red heifer, without spot or blemish, whereon no yoke had ever come. Red is the colour of guilt (Isa. i. 18), yet there was no spot or blemish in the heifer ; so was the guilt of sin upon Christ, who in Himself was absolutely pure and holy. No yoke was upon the heifer ; nor was there any constraint on Christ, who offered Himself willingly through the eternal Spirit. 2. She was to be led forth without the camp, which the Apostle alludes to (c. xiii. 11), representing Christ going out of the city unto His suffering and oblation. 3. One did slay her before the face of the priest, and not the priest himself ; and so the hands of others, Jews and Gentiles, were used in the slaying of our sacrifice. 4. The blood of the slain heifer was sprinkled by the priest seven times directly before the tabernacle of the congregation, and so is the whole Church purified by the sprinkling of the blood of Christ. 5. The whole heifer was to be burned in the sight of the priest ; so was whole Christ, soul and body, offered up unto God in the fire of love, kindled in Him by the eternal Spirit. 6. Cedar wood, hyssop, and scarlet were to be cast into the burning heifer, to teach us that all spiritual virtue really and eternally was contained in the one offering of Christ. 7. Both the priest who sprinkled the blood, the men that slew the heifer, he that burned her, and he that gathered up the ashes, were all unclean until they were washed; so when Christ was made a sin-offering, all the legal uncleannesses,

that is, the guilt of the Church, were on Him, and He took them away.

But our Apostle calls special attention to the use of this ordinance. The "*ashes of the heifer*" were preserved, and, being mixed with pure water, they might be sprinkled on persons who were legally unclean. So with Christ; were it not that the blood of Christ in its purifying virtue is in a continual readiness unto faith, the worship of the Church could not be acceptable unto Him. In a constant application thereunto doth the exercise of faith much consist.

"**Sprinkling the unclean.**" Not only the act is intended, but the efficacy of it. It made the ceremonially unclean, clean. So with the blood of Christ; it is called the "blood of sprinkling" because of its efficacy unto our sanctification, as applied by faith unto our souls and consciences.

"**Sanctifieth to the purifying of the flesh.**" Every defiled person was excluded from the privilege of drawing near to God in solemn worship; but in his purification he was again separated to Him, and restored unto his sacred privilege. God ordained these ordinances as a representation of the "good things to come." With respect hereunto they were glorious, and of exceeding advantage unto the faith and obedience of the Church.

V. 14. *How much more shall the blood of Christ, who through the eternal Spirit offered Himself without spot to God, purge your conscience from dead works to serve the living God!*

"**How much more shall the blood of Christ.**" If those sacrifices and ordinances of the law were effectual unto the ends of legal expiation and purification, then is the blood of Christ assuredly so unto the spiritual and eternal effects designed thereby. There is a greater reason in the nature of things that "the blood of Christ should purge our consciences," than there is that "the blood of bulls and of goats should sanctify unto the purifying of the flesh." The faith of the Church of old was resolved into the mere sovereign pleasure of God as to the efficacy of their ordinances; nothing in the nature of the things themselves did tend unto their establishment. But in the dispensation of God by Christ, in the work of our redemption by Him, there is such an evidence of the wisdom and righteousness of God in the things themselves, as gives the highest security to faith. It is unbelief alone, made obstinate by prejudices insinuated by the devil, that hides those things from any, as the Apostle declares (2 Cor. iv. 3, 5). And hence will arise the great aggravation of the sin, and condemnation of them that perish.

Upon Christ being the Messiah depends the principal force of the present argument. It is the blood of Him who was promised of old to be the High Priest of the Church, and the sacrifice for their sins, in whom was the faith of all the saints of old, that by Him their sins should be expiated, that in Him they should be justified and glorified; Christ, the Son of God, in whose Person God purchased His Church. He who was "in the form of God, and thought it not robbery to be equal with God, took upon Him the form of a servant, and became obedient unto death." It was in the human nature He was a servant; nevertheless it was the Son of God, He who in His divine nature was in the form of God, who so served in office and yielded obedience. Wherefore He was so far a Mediator and Priest in both natures, as that whatever He did in discharge of these offices was the act of His entire Person, whereon the dignity and efficacy of all He did did depend.

The blood of Christ is not only that material blood which He shed, absolutely considered, when the work of our redemption is ascribed unto it that is intended, but there is a double consideration of it with respect unto its efficacy unto this end. 1. It was the pledge and the sign of the internal obedience and sufferings of the soul of Christ—of His Person. "He became obedient unto death, the death of the cross," whereon His blood was shed. This was the great instance of His obedience and of His sufferings, whereby He made reconciliation and atonement for sins. Hence the effects of His sufferings and of His obedience are ascribed unto His blood. 2. Respect is had unto the sacrifice and offering of blood under the law. The reason why God gave the people the blood to make atonement on the altar was because "the life of the flesh was in it." So was the life of Christ in His blood, by the shedding whereof He laid it down. Herein He made His soul an offering for sin.

"**Purge your conscience.**" There is here a two-fold effect of the blood of Christ, one in making atonement for our sins, answering unto the effect of the blood of bulls and goats being offered; the other in the sanctification of our persons, answering to the effect of the ashes of an heifer being sprinkled. There is nothing more destructive unto the whole faith of the gospel than by any means to evacuate the immediate efficacy of the blood of Christ: it overthrows the foundation of the gospel.

"**Who through the eternal Spirit offered Himself with=out spot to God.**" Christ offered Himself; the way of His offering was by the shedding of His blood. This offering of Himself was the act of His whole Person; both natures concurred in the offering, though one alone was offered. All that He did or suffered in His soul and body when His blood was shed is comprised in this offering of Himself. This offering of Christ was a real and proper sacrifice, 1. From the *office* whereof it was an act. He was made a Priest unto God for this end, that He might offer

Himself, and that this offering should be a sacrifice. 2. From the *nature* of it. For it consisted in the sacred giving up unto God the thing that was offered, in the present destruction or consumption of it. This is of the very nature of sacrifice, as we may see in the destruction by fire of the sacrifices of old. 3. From the *end* of it, which was assigned unto it in the wisdom and sovereignty of God, and in His own institution, which was to make atonement for sin. 4. In the *way and manner* of it. For He sanctified and dedicated Himself to be an offering; He accompanied His offering with prayers and supplications; there was an *altar* which sanctified the offering, which was His own divine nature; He kindled the sacrifice with the fire of divine love, acting itself by zeal for God's glory, and compassion for the souls of men. 5. He tendered all this unto God as an atonement for sin, as we shall see in the next words. This was the greatest expression of the inexpressible love of Christ, " He offered Himself."

Whatsoever might be effected by the glorious dignity of His divine Person, by His profound obedience, by His unspeakable sufferings, all offered as a sacrifice unto God in our behalf, is really accomplished. " *He offered Himself unto God;* " that is, unto the Father, " *by the eternal Spirit.*" The Deity of Christ and the eternal Spirit—the Holy Ghost—did both concur and were absolutely necessary unto the offering of Christ. The acting of His own eternal Spirit was as unto the *efficacy and effect* of His sacrifice ; and the acting of the Holy Ghost was as unto the *manner* of it.

The true sense of the words is, Christ offered Himself unto God through or by His own eternal Spirit, the divine nature acting in the Person of the Son ; for it was the act of His entire Person, wherein He discharged the office of a Priest when He offered Himself unto God. But it is no less certain that He offered Himself in His human nature by the Holy Ghost. He was filled with the Holy Ghost. That Christ should thus offer Himself unto God, and that by the eternal Spirit, is the centre of the mystery of the gospel. Unto the reason of some men it may be folly ; unto faith it is full of glory.

" *He offered Himself without spot.*" This respects the purity of His nature and the holiness of His life. He was the " Holy One of God," " holy, harmless, undefiled, separate from sinners," who " did no sin, neither was guile found in His mouth." There was nothing wanting in Him, and nothing in Him, that should any way hinder His sacrifice from being accepted with God. It may not be unuseful here to give a brief scheme of this great sacrifice of Christ, to fix the thoughts of faith more distinctly upon it.

1. God herein, in the Person of the Father, is considered as the Lawgiver, the Governor and Judge of all ; and that as on a throne

of judgment, the throne of grace not being yet erected. And two things do belong unto Him. First, a denunciation of the sentence of the law against mankind—" Cursed be everyone that continueth not in all things which are written in the book of the law to do them." And second, a refusal of all such ways of atonement, satisfaction, and reconciliation, as might be offered from anything that all or any creature could perform. " Sacrifice and offering and whole burnt offering for sin Thou wouldest not." He rejected them as insufficient to make an atonement for sin. 2. Satan appeared before His throne with his prisoners. He had " the power of death ; " and entered into judgment as unto his right and title, and therein was judged (John xvi. 11). And he put forth all his power and policy in opposition unto the deliverance of his prisoners and to the ways and means of it. 3. The Lord Christ, the Son of God, out of His infinite love and compassion, appears in our nature before the throne of God, and takes it on Himself to answer for the sins of all the elect, to make atonement for them, by doing and suffering whatever the holiness, righteousness, and wisdom of God required thereunto. " Then said He, Lo, I come to do Thy will, O God ; above when He said, Sacrifice and offering and burnt offering for sin Thou wouldest not, neither hadst pleasure therein, which are offered by the law ; then said He, Lo, I come to do Thy will, O God." 4. This stipulation and engagement of His, God accepteth of, and withal, as the sovereign Lord and Ruler of all, prescribeth the way and means whereby He should make an atonement for sin, and reconciliation with God thereon. And this was that " He should make His soul an offering for sin," and therein " bear their iniquities." 5. The Lord Christ was prepared with a sacrifice to offer unto God, unto this end. For whereas " every high priest was ordained to offer gifts and sacrifices, it was of necessity that He should also have somewhat to offer." This was to be " Himself." This body or human nature was prepared for Him and given unto Him for this very end, that He might have somewhat to offer. He took this, and assumed it unto Himself to be His own, for this very end, that He might be a sacrifice in it. He had full power and authority over His own body, His whole human nature, to dispose of it in any way unto the glory of God. " No man," saith He, " taketh My life from Me, but I lay it down of Myself. I have power to lay it down, and I have power to take it up again."

6. This therefore He gave up to do and suffer according unto the will of God ; and this He did, in the will, grace, and love of His divine nature; He offered Himself unto God through the eternal Spirit ; in the gracious holy actings of His human nature in the way of zeal, love, obedience, patience, and all other graces of the Holy Spirit which dwelt in Him without measure, acted unto their utmost glory and efficacy. Hereby He gave Himself up unto God to be a sacrifice for sin. This was the most glorious spectacle unto

God and His holy angels. Hereby He "set a crown of glory upon the head of the law," fulfilling its precepts in matter and manner unto the uttermost, and undergoing its penalty or curse, establishing the truth and righteousness of God in it. Hereby He glorified the holiness and justice of God, in the demonstration of their nature and by compliance with their demands. Hence issued the eternal counsels of God for the salvation of the Church, and way was made for the exercise of grace and mercy unto sinners.

7. Herein God was well pleased, satisfied, and reconciled unto sinners. Thus was He "in Christ reconciling the world unto Himself, not imputing our trespasses unto us," in that "He was made sin for us, that we might become the righteousness of God in Him." God was well pleased, delighted in His obedience; it was a "sacrifice unto Him of a sweet smelling savour." He was more glorified in that one instance of the obedience of His only Son, than He was dishonoured by the disobedience of Adam and all his posterity. All the demands of justice were satisfied unto His eternal glory.

8. Hereon Satan is judged, and destroyed as to his power over sinners who receive this atonement; all the occasions and grounds of it are hereby removed, his kingdom is overthrown, his usurpation and unjust dominion defeated, his goods spoiled, and captivity led captive. For of the anger of the Lord against sin it was that he obtained power over sinners, which he abused unto his own ends. This being atoned, the prince of this world was judged and cast out. 9. Hereon the poor condemned sinners are discharged. God says, Deliver them, for I have found a ransom. But we must return to the text.

"**Purge your conscience from dead works.**" The blood of Christ hath a double effect: *towards God*, in making atonement for sin; this was done once, and at once, and was now past. Herein "by one offering He for ever perfected them that are sanctified." Also *towards the consciences of men*, in the application of the virtue of it unto them. This is here intended. By "*dead works*," sins as to their guilt and defilement are intended; they are "*dead works*" because they proceed from a principle of spiritual death; because they are useless and fruitless, and because they deserve death and tend thereunto.

All these things are true, howbeit I judge there is a peculiar reason why the Apostle in this place calls them "dead works." There is here an allusion unto dead bodies and legal defilement by them. For he hath respect unto purification by the ashes of an heifer, and this respected principally uncleanness by the dead; so unless men are really purged from their moral defilements by the blood of Christ, they must perish for ever.

To purge the conscience from dead works is to purge that which is immediately affected by them; they bring a sense of

guilt, and with this a sense of fear and dread, whence
the sinner dares not approach into the presence of God.
The Apostle alludes to this in the next clause, " that ye may
serve the living God." To purge the conscience is to discharge
it from a sense of the guilt of sin and from its defilement. The
ground of the efficacy of the blood of Christ in thus purging
the conscience is that it was offered unto God; it was the
blood of Christ, the Son of God; the dignity of His Person gave
efficacy to His offering; He offered Himself by the eternal Spirit.
These things made the blood of Christ, as offered, meet and fit for
the accomplishment of this great effect.

Sin is not purged from the conscience unless the guilt of it be
so far removed, as that we may have peace with God and boldness
in access unto Him. In order to this, the blood must be sprinkled
on the conscience, in the communication of its sanctifying virtue
unto our souls.

" To serve the living God." In order to our serving the
living God; that is, we have the right and liberty so to do, being
no longer excluded from the privilege of it. I doubt not but that
in this word " serve " is included the whole life of faith in universal
obedience. That we may live unto the living God in all ways of
holy obedience. In order to this are required liberty and ability.
We must treat on the liberty when we come to chap. x. 19—21.
As to the ability, this respects all the supplies of the Holy Spirit in
grace and gifts. Observe, 1. The souls and consciences of men are
wholly polluted before they are purged by the blood of Christ.
And this pollution is such as excludes them from all right of access
unto God in His worship. 2. Even the best works of men, before
the purging of their consciences by the blood of Christ, are but
dead works. 3. Justification and sanctification are inseparably
joined in the design of God's grace by the blood of Christ.
4. Gospel worship is such, in its spirituality and holiness, as
becometh " the living God," and our duty it is always to consider
that with Him we have to do in all that we perform therein.

V. 15. *And for this cause He is the Mediator of the new
testament, that by means of death, for the redemption of the
transgressions [that were] under the first testament, they which
are called might receive the promise of eternal inheritance.*

There is a difficulty to be removed here. Why is the word
" testament " used here instead of covenant ? The word in the
original may be translated either covenant or testament. A
covenant implies the consent of both parties to it; the word testament signifies free grants and donations without any consent of one
of the parties, as not being necessary to it; and in this sense the

Apostle is about to speak of the disposal and communication of the good things unto us that God doth freely give. This hath more of the nature of a testament than a covenant.

It was the design of God that some should receive an "*eternal inheritance.*" It is altogether vain and foolish to seek for any other cause or reason for the gift of this inheritance unto any person, but only in the grace and bounty of God, His sovereign will and pleasure. What merit, what means of attaining it could be found in them who were considered under no other qualification but such as had wofully rejected the inheritance in which they were at the first instated? Observe, 1. The inheritance is *eternal,* and is so called in opposition unto that inheritance which, under the first covenant, God granted unto the Israelites in the land of Canaan. This eternal inheritance is communicated by Christ unto all believers ; He, as the great Testator, did in and by His death bequeath unto them all His goods as an eternal legacy. 2. The way God did communicate this inheritance was by promise : "*Might receive the promise of eternal inheritance*"—the promise is, "In thee and in thy seed shall all nations of the earth be blessed." The Apostle's design is to convince the Hebrews that neither by the law nor the sacrifices could they come unto the inheritance promised unto Abraham and His seed. It is conveyed by promise to evince the absolute freedom of the preparation and gift of it ; also to give security unto all the heirs of it unto whom it was designed ; also that the way of obtaining the inheritance on our part shall be by faith, and no otherwise ; for what God hath only promised doth necessarily require faith unto its reception. "It is of faith, that it may be by grace," and is thus evidenced to be of the mere grace of God in opposition unto all worth, works, and endeavours of our own. Freely it was provided, freely it is proposed, and freely it is received. 3. The persons unto whom this inheritance is designed, and who do receive the promise of it, are those "*that are called.*" It was the design of God in this whole dispensation that all the called should receive the promise; and if they do not do so, His counsel—and that in the greatest work of His wisdom, and power, and grace—is frustrated. These that are called, are they who are "called in Christ Jesus." 4. There was an obstacle in the way of actually receiving the promise, namely, "the transgressions that were under the first testament;" though God designed unto the elect an eternal inheritance, yet they cannot be made partakers of it but in such a way as was suited unto His glory. Whereas, therefore, they were all of them guilty of sin, their sins must be expiated and taken out of the way, or they cannot receive the promise of the inheritance. Transgressions under the first testament are all sins whatever, for there is no sin committed under the gospel but it is a sin against the law, which requires us to love the Lord our God with all our heart and all our strength. It was the work of God alone to contrive a way, and it was the effect of infinite wisdom and grace to provide a way, for the removal of sin, that it might not be an everlasting obstacle against the gift of an eternal inheritance to them that are called.

The means that God took and used for the removal of this hindrance, and the effectual accomplishment of His design, is the next thing to be considered. This, in general, was in the first place by the making of a " *new testament.*" The Apostle hath before fully proved that this could not be done by the old covenant ; and in order to secure its being done under the new testament, it had a Mediator : " *And for this cause He is the Mediator of the new testament.*" That Mediator is the Lord Christ, the Son of God.

In order to show in what sense He is here especially to be considered as a Mediator, the Apostle sets Him before us as a *Testator* dying, which belongs to His priestly office only. And the sole end which in this place he assigns unto His priestly office is His death —" *that by means of death.*" Whereas, therefore, expiation of sin is to be made by an act towards God, with whom alone atonement is to be made, so as that there may be pardon for the sinner, the mediation of Christ is here intended ; so that He by suffering death in our stead—in behalf of all that are called—He did make an atonement for sin.

By the obedience unto death of the Mediator, He purchased for them that are called this inheritance, and *bequeathed* it unto them. The provision of this Mediator is the centre of the eternal counsels of God ; in the womb of this one mercy all others are contained. Death was the means whereby the Mediator procured the effect mentioned. That which in the verse before is ascribed unto the blood of Christ, is here ascribed unto His death as a Mediator; these are really the same, only in the one *the thing itself* is expressed —" death ; " in the other the *manner of it*—by blood.

The Mediator died as a sacrifice : He was to die that death which was threatened unto transgressors against the first covenant ; that is, death under the curse of the law. There must, therefore, be some great cause and end why this Mediator—the only begotten of the Father—should thus die. The cause was this : " *for the redemption of transgressions.*" In the righteousness and faithfulness of God, sin lay in the way of the enjoyment of the inheritance which grace had prepared. Unless it were removed, the inheritance could not be received. The way it was removed was by *redemption*.

The "redemption of transgressions" is the deliverance of transgressors from all the evils they were subject to on their account, by the payment of a satisfactory price. This answers to " the purging of the conscience by the blood of Christ." He calls His life " a ransom," or price of redemption. Redemption belongs to the " new testament " alone ; and the glory and efficacy of the new testament, and the assurance of the communication of an eternal inheritance by virtue of it, depend hereon, that it was made a testament by the death of the Mediator, which is further proved in the next verses.

Vs. 16, 17. *For where a testament [is], there must also of necessity be the death of the testator. For a testament [is] of force after men are dead : otherwise it is of no strength at all while the testator liveth.*

This is to prove the necessity and use of the death of Christ, from the nature, ends, and use of the covenant whereof He was the Mediator; for it being a testament also, it was to be confirmed by the death of the Testator. This is proved in these verses from the notion of a testament, and the only use of it among men. A testament is the just determination of a man's will concerning what he will have done with his goods after his decease ; or it is the will of him that is dead. A testament is of no force while the testator liveth. For by what way soever a man disposeth of his goods so as that it shall take effect while he liveth, as by sale or gift, it is not a testament, nor hath anything of the nature of a testament about it.

Unto the confirmation and ratification of a *testament*, that it may be "sure and steadfast, and of force," there must be the " death of the testator." But there is no need that this should be by blood—the blood of the testator. But under the consideration of a *covenant*, blood—the blood of a sacrifice—was necessary, and death only consequentially, as that which should ensue on the blood being shed ; but there was no need that it should be the blood or death of him that made the covenant. Wherefore the Apostle, showing the necessity of the death of Christ, that it was really death and that by shedding of blood, evinceth that which was necessary unto a testament, and that which was necessary unto a covenant.

What is essential to a testament is the death of the testator ; and the excellency of a covenant is that it is confirmed by the blood of sacrifices, as the Apostle proves in the instance of the covenant made at Sinai (vs. 18—20). Christ was to die in the confirmation of the new covenant as a *testament*, He being the Testator of it; was to offer Himself as a sacrifice in His blood for the establishing of it in its nature as a *covenant*. The Apostle doth not here argue, as some imagine, merely from the signification of the word, as they say, that in the original is not exactly rendered. Those who have from this troubled themselves about the authority of the epistle, have nothing to thank for it but their own ignorance of the design of the Apostle, and the nature of his argument. How inextricable difficulties do appear sometimes in passages of the Scriptures, which when God is pleased to teach us, all are pleasant and easy !

A testament is made by a living man, but whilst he lives it is dead, of no use. That it may operate and become effectual, death must be brought into account—the death of the testator. Wherefore, if the new covenant hath the nature of a testament, it must have a testator, and that testator must die before it can come into force, which is what was to be proved.

"**For a testament is of force after men are dead, otherwise it is of no force at all while the testator liveth.**" We must consider wherein these things—a testament made by men and the new testament made by God—do agree, and wherein they differ. 1. They agree principally in the death of the testator; this is the fundamental agreement between them, whereon the Apostle insisteth. 2. They agree in that there are goods disposed of and bequeathed unto heirs or legatees which were the property of the testator. All the goods of grace and glory were the property, the inheritance of the Lord Christ, for " He was appointed heir of all things." But in His death as a testator He bequeathed them unto His elect, appointing them to be heirs of God, co-heirs with Himself.

3. They agree in that there is always in a testament an absolute grant made of the goods bequeathed, without condition or limitation. So is it in this new testament, and whatever there may be in the gospel that prescribes conditions, that exacts terms of obedience, it belongs unto it as it is a covenant, and not as a testament.

They differ in this : 1. A testator among men ceaseth to have any right in or use of the goods bequeathed by him, when once his testament comes into force. But our Testator divests Himself neither of right nor possession, nor of the use of any of His goods ; for " He lived again, and is alive for evermore "—hence all His goods are still in His possession, and also as in Him they are in the possession of them to whom they are bequeathed. 2. In the wills of men, if there be a bequeathment of goods made unto many, no one can enjoy the whole inheritance, but each one hath his own share. But in and by the *new testament* each one is made heir of the whole inheritance. All have the same, each one hath the whole; for God Himself thence becomes their portion, who is all unto all, and all unto each one. 3. In human testaments the goods bequeathed are only such as descended to the testators from their progenitors, or were acquired during their lives by their own industry. By their death they obtained no new right or title to anything. But our Testator, according unto an antecedent contract between God the Father and Him, purchased the whole inheritance by His own blood, " *obtaining for us eternal redemption.*" 4. They differ principally in this, that a testament among men is nothing more than a testament; but this testament is a covenant also. Hence it was not only necessary that He should die, but that He should offer Himself in sacrifice by the shedding of blood unto its confirmation.

Vs. 18—22. *Whereupon neither the first [testament] was dedicated without blood. For when Moses had spoken every precept to all the people according to the law, he took the blood of calves and of goats, with water, and scarlet wool, and hyssop, and sprinkled both the book, and all the people, saying, This [is] the blood of the testament which God hath enjoined unto you. Moreover he sprinkled likewise with blood both the tabernacle and all the vessels of the ministry. And almost all things are by the law purged with blood; and without shedding of blood is no remission.*

Sundry difficulties arise in the minds of some, as the account given by the Apostle of the dedication of the first covenant and of the tabernacle seems to differ in sundry things from that given by Moses. For the removal of all difficulties, let it be remembered, 1. That the Apostle wrote the epistle by divine inspiration; the whole and every part of it is animated by the wisdom and authority of its Author. 2. There is nothing that is affirmed here by the Apostle which hath the least appearance of contradiction unto anything that is recorded by Moses. 3. The Apostle doth not take his account of the things here put together by him from any one place in Moses, but gathers up what is declared in the law in several places unto various ends. He designs not only to prove the dedication of the covenant by blood, but to show the whole use of blood under the law as unto purification and remission of sin. This he doth to declare the virtue and efficacy of the blood of Christ under the new testament. We will now go through these verses one by one.

"Whereupon neither the first testament was dedi= cated without blood." This first testament, the covenant made on Mount Horeb, "was consecrated with blood." This dedication was by sprinkling of blood; the Apostle is not here speaking of the "confirmation" of the covenant by blood, but of its dedication by blood; this sprinkling of blood was the instrument of the peculiar Church relation between God and that people whereof the "Book" was the record. The meaning is this, That *first covenant* which God made with the people in the wilderness when He became their God, and they became His people, was dedicated unto sacred use by blood, in that it was sprinkled on the book and the people, after that same blood had been offered in sacrifice upon the altar. Hence it follows that this which so essentially belongs to the solemn dedication and confirmation of a covenant between God and the

Church, was necessary unto the dedication and confirmation of the
new covenant—which is that which is to be proved.

**"For when Moses had spoken every precept to all the
people according to the law, he took the blood of calves
and of goats, with water, and scarlet wool, and hyssop,
and sprinkled both the book, and all the people."** Moses
was the mediator between God and man in the giving of the law
(Gal. iii. 19). A mediator may be either only one who goes
between, a messenger, a daysman ; or also a surety and undertaker.
Of the first was the mediator of the old covenant ; of the latter
that of the new. Moses " spake every precept," that is, audibly ;
" he read it in the audience of the people," so as they might hear
and understand. The old covenant was one of " *precepts*," the new
is one of " *promises*." Moses spoke to " *all the people*," and he
sprinkled " *all the people*." These things were transacted with the
representatives of the people (for it was naturally impossible that
they could all hear Moses reading) ; yet I do believe that after
Moses told the elders " all the words of the Lord," means were
used by the elders to communicate the things, yea, to repeat the
words unto the people, that they might give their rational consent
unto them.

The warranty Moses had for this reading was from the law
itself ; he spoke " *according to the law*." He then took the blood of
the beasts that were offered ; the one half of it he sprinkled on the
altar, and the other half he sprinkled on the people. This two-fold
distribution of the blood signifies, that on the altar to make an atonement, that on the people to purify and sanctify ; or, in other words,
we have set before us justification and sanctification. The blood
being mixed with water to make it aspersible, Moses took a bunch
of hyssop bound up with scarlet wool, and dipping it into the
basons, sprinkled the blood, until it was all spent in that service.
This sprinkling was chosen of God as an expressive sign of the
effectual communication of the benefits of the covenant unto them
that were sprinkled.

The same blood was sprinkled both on the book and on the
people. Some may ask, how could it be necessary to purify " the
book ? " I answer, two things were necessary—atonement and
purification. The book was sprinkled as it lay upon the altar,
where atonement was made ; this was plainly to teach that atonement must be made for sins committed against that book, or the
law contained in it. The book in itself was pure and holy, but
unto us everything is impure and unclean that is not sprinkled
with the blood of Christ. So afterwards the tabernacle itself and
all its vessels were purified every year with blood, " because of the
uncleanness of the children of Israel, and because of their transgressions."

The principal truth asserted is confirmed by what Moses *said*,

as well as did, " **Saying, This is the blood of the testament
which God hath enjoined unto you.** " Hence the Apostle
proves that death, and the shedding of blood thereon, was necessary
unto the confirmation and establishment of the first testament.
This blood was a confirmatory *sign* of the covenant. 1. From
God's institution, He appointed it so to be. 2. From an implica-
tion of the interest of both parties in the blood of the sacrifice :
God unto whom it was offered, the people upon whom it was
sprinkled. 3. Typically, in that it represented the blood of Christ,
and fore-signified the necessity of it unto the confirmation of the
new covenant.

" **Moreover he sprinkled with blood both the tabernacle
and all the vessels of the ministry.** " Moses is said to do
what he appointed to be done. He sprinkled the tabernacle in that
by an everlasting ordinance he appointed that it should be done.
The next verse (22) declares that the Apostle speaks here, not of
dedication, but of expiation and purification. This sprinkling,
therefore, of the tabernacle and the vessels of it, was that which
was done annually on the day of atonement. For thereon, as the
Apostle speaks, " both the tabernacle and all the vessels of the
ministry were sprinkled with blood ; " as the ark, the mercy-seat,
the altar of incense, &c. And the end of it was to purge them
from the uncleannesses of the people.

" **And almost all things are by the law purged with
blood ; and without shedding of blood is no remission.** "
All things were purged with blood " according to the law," hence
the Apostle designs to prove the necessity of the death of Christ
and the efficacy of His blood for the purging of sin, whereof these
legal things were the types. The Apostle saith " almost all things."
Some things were purified " by fire " (see Num. xxxi. 23) and some
" by water," whereof there were many instances. All other puri-
fications were " by blood." The " almost all things," means that
absolutely all things which had any inward moral defilement " were
purged with blood," and directed unto the purging efficacy of the
blood of Christ.

And " *without the shedding of blood is no remission.*" The real
spiritual forgiveness of sins, and gracious acceptance with God,
were to be obtained alone by that which was signified by the blood ;
which was the sacrifice of Christ Himself. This is the great
demonstration of the demerit of sin, of the holiness, righteousness,
and grace of God. For such was the nature of sin and its demerit,
and such the righteousness of God, that without shedding of blood
sin could not be pardoned. And this must be the blood of the Son
of God. And herein are glorified both the love and the grace of
God, in that He spared not His only Son, but gave Him up to be a
bloody sacrifice in His death for us all.

V. 23. *[It was] therefore necessary that the patterns of things in the heavens should be purified with these ; but the heavenly things themselves with better sacrifices than these.*

" **It was therefore necessary that the patterns of things in the heavens should be purified with these.**" It was necessary from God's institution and appointment. The things intended are those which the Apostle hath discoursed of—the covenant, the book, the people, the tabernacle, the vessels of the ministry. The heavenly things themselves were framed, designed, and disposed in the mind of God in all their order, beauty, efficacy, and tendency unto His own glory. This was the whole mystery of the wisdom of God for the redemption and salvation of the Church by Jesus Christ. Of these things did God grant a typical resemblance, similitude, and pattern in the tabernacle and its services. They were "*patterns of things in the heavens,*" and these patterns were purified ; this was the annual sprinkling of the tabernacle and its vessels, because of the uncleanness of the people. They were purified "*with these*"—water, and scarlet wool, and hyssop, and the ashes of an heifer, were in some cases required thereunto.

"**But the heavenly things themselves with better sacrifices than these.**" These "heavenly things" must be all those, and only those, whereof the others were patterns ; some of these patterns were purified by *dedication*, some by *actual cleansing* from defilements. By "*heavenly things,*" then, I understand all the effects of the counsel of God in Christ, in the redemption, worship, salvation, and eternal glory of the Church ; that is, Christ Himself in all His offices, with all the spiritual and eternal effects of them on the souls and consciences of men, with all the worship of God by Him according unto the gospel.

I mention in particular, 1. Christ Himself and the sacrifice of Himself ; 2. All spiritual and eternal grace whereof the souls of men are made partakers by the mediation and sacrifice of Christ ; 3. The Church itself and its worship—it is God's heavenly kingdom ; 4. Heaven itself is comprised herein, not absolutely, but as it is the mansion of Christ and the redeemed in the presence of God for evermore. If the question be asked, How are these things said to be "purified" ?—for of real purification from uncleanness not one of them is capable, but only the Church, that is, the souls and consciences of men—I answer, There is a twofold sense of purification as we have already seen, namely, of *eternal* dedication and *internal* purging, both which are expressed in Scripture by the one word "sanctification."

These heavenly things are said to be purified "with better sacrifices than these." The one sacrifice of Christ is alone intended ; but because it answered all other sacrifices, exceeded them all in dignity, was of more use and efficacy than all of them, it is so expressed. Observe here, 1. Every eternal mercy, every spiritual privilege, is both purchased for us and sprinkled unto us by the blood of Christ; 2. There is such an uncleanness in our natures, our persons, our duties, and worship, that unless they and we are all sprinkled with the blood of Christ, neither we nor they can have any acceptance with God; 3. The sacrifice of Christ is the one, only, everlasting foundation and spring of all sanctification and sacred dedication, whereby the whole new creation is purified and dedicated unto God.

V. 24. *For Christ is not entered into the holy places made with hands, [which are] the figures of the true; but into heaven itself, now to appear in the presence of God for us.*

The places intended are the most holy place; it was built by the hands of men. These holy places Christ entered not into. They were the "*figures of the true;*" the true is not shadowy and typical like the holy places were. But Christ entered "*into heaven itself;*" this entrance was as a High Priest, and as such He entered the place of the peculiar residence, majesty and glory of God and of His throne, where all the blessed saints enjoy His presence, and all His holy angels minister unto Him. His entrance was into heaven as into the temple of God, wherein the chief thing to be considered is the "throne of grace." For it is that which answers unto and was signified by the entrance of the high priest into the most holy place of the tabernacle, and there was nothing therein but the ark and the mercy-seat, with the cherubim of glory overshadowing them; which, as we have declared, was a representation of the throne of grace. The end of this entrance into heaven as a High Priest is "*now to appear in the presence of God for us.*"

"Now" is expressive of the duration of time from the entrance of Christ into heaven unto the consummation of all things. The whole discharge of the remaining duties of His priestly office is comprised in the words "now to appear." Christ is in the real "presence" of God, before His face; and this expresseth His full assurance of His success in His undertaking, and His full discharge from the guilt of sin which He underwent. Had He not made an end of it, He could not have thus appeared in the presence of God.

This is said to be done "for us." "To appear . . . for us;" that is, to do all things with God for us at the throne of grace that we may be saved. Let us observe, 1. He appeareth as our High Priest. This is a part of His office, a duty in the discharge of it. 2. It is such an act of our High Priest as supposeth the offering Himself a sacrifice for sin antecedently thereunto; for it was with the blood of the expiatory sacrifice that He entered the holy place. 3. It supposeth the accomplishment of the work of redemption of the Church. He appeared not in the presence of God until He had finished the work His Father gave Him to do, and was ready in all things to give an account of it unto the eternal glory of God. 4. In this appearance He presents Himself unto God as a Lamb that had been slain. He is now alive and lives for ever. But there must, as unto efficacy in this appearance, be a representation of His sacrifice, His sufferings, His blood, His death—of Himself as a Lamb slain and offered unto God. 5. He thus appears *for us.* His appearance there is, as it were, a law appearance ; that of an advocate in the behalf of others. 6. This is the great testimony of the continuance of His love, care, and compassion toward the Church, now He is in the height of His glory. 7. This also compriseth His being our Advocate ; He is thereby in continual readiness to plead our cause against all accusations ; this is distinct from His intercession, whereby He procures supplies of grace and mercy for us. 8. This account of the appearance of Christ before God gives direction into a right apprehension of the way of the dispensation of all saving grace and mercy unto the Church. The actual application of all grace and mercy unto us depends on His appearance before God, and the intercession wherewith it is accompanied.

V. 25. *Nor yet that He should offer Himself often, as the high priest entereth into the holy place every year with blood of others.*

The repetition of sacrifices arose solely from their imperfection (chap. x. 1, 2) ; then how great must be the imperfection of the sacrifice of Christ, if it be not effectual to take away sin, and perfect them that are sanctified, unless it be repeated every day, and that, it may be, in a thousand places! Christ was once only offered, and could be so no more, from the glory of His Person, and the nature of the sacrifice itself. This sacrifice was accompanied by His bearing the curse of the law, and the punishment due unto sin, which were taken away thereby. If this sacrifice be despised in any way, or neglected, "there remaineth no more sacrifice for sin."

This one offering is always effectual unto the ends of it, even no less than it was in the day and hour when it was actually offered ; it needs nothing but renewed application by faith for the communication of its effects and fruits unto us. Wherefore the great call of the gospel is to guide faith, and keep it unto this one offering of Christ, as the spring of all grace and mercy. In the preaching of the word the Lord Christ is set forth as evidently crucified before our eyes; and in the ordinance of the Supper especially He is represented unto the peculiar exercise of faith.

The high priest, according to the law, entered the holy place once every year with the blood of others, that is, the blood of bulls

and goats offered in sacrifice. That which is denied of Christ, is
the repetition of this service, and that because of the perfection of
His sacrifice; the other being repeated because of its imperfection.
The entrance of the high priest once a year on the great day of
atonement into the most holy place, which act was the most glorious
solemnity of that dispensation, carried along with it the evidence
of its own imperfection, on account of its annual repetition.

V. 26. *For then must He often have suffered since the
foundation of the world: but now once in the end of the
world hath He appeared to put away sin by the sacrifice of
Himself.*

**"For then must He often have suffered since the
foundation of the world."** The suffering here intended is that
of His death and the shedding of His blood. "*Since the foundation of the world*," is from the first entrance of sin, and God's dispensation of grace in Christ thereon. The argument of the Apostle
against the repetition of the sacrifice of Christ, from the necessity
of His suffering therein, is full of light; His sufferings were inseparable from His sacrifice, because He Himself was both Priest and
sacrifice. The high priest of old offered often, but never suffered
therein; it was the lamb that was slain that suffered; but Christ
offered Himself, and this He could not do without suffering. Those
sufferings can never be repeated, therefore there can be no repetition of the sacrifice.

For, 1. It was *inconsistent* with the wisdom, goodness, grace,
and love of God that Christ should often suffer in that way which
was necessary unto the offering of Himself, namely, by death and
blood-shedding. 2. It was *impossible* from the dignity of His
Person. The faith of the Church was secured by the evident
demonstration of His divine glory, which in the resurrection
immediately ensued on His offering Himself. 3. It was altogether
needless; for as the Apostle demonstrates, " by one offering " of
Himself, and that *once offered*, " He put away sin," and " for ever
perfected them that are sanctified."

**"But now once in the end of the world hath He appeared
to put away sin by the sacrifice of Himself."** This latter
part of the verse contains the confirmation of the argument proposed in the former part. Not then, " but now; " not often, but
" once; " not from the foundation of the world, but in " the end "
of it. He appeared, He was "manifested in the flesh," that He
might suffer and offer Himself unto God. This He did to "*put
away sin;*" in its whole nature and effects, in its root and fruits,
in its guilt, power, and punishment, and that absolutely and
universally with respect unto the Church that is sanctified by His
blood, and dedicated unto God.

The putting away of sin is the destroying, annulling, disarming, taking away the force, power, and obligation of a law. The power of sin, as unto all its effects, whether sinful or penal, is called "the law of sin." Christ appeared to abrogate this law, that it should not condemn us any more, nor drive us over to punishment; He also destroyed sin's subjective power, purging our consciences from dead works, as we have seen. This He did "*by the sacrifice of Himself;*" of which we shall treat more fully in the next chapter.

Observe, 1. It is the prerogative of God to determine the times and seasons of the dispensation of Himself and His grace unto the Church. Hereon it depended that Christ appeared in the "end of the world," not sooner, not later. By delaying the appearance of Christ, God testified His displeasure against sin; He also did it to try and exercise the faith of the Church; also to prepare the Church for the reception of Him; also to give the world a full trial of what might be attained towards happiness and blessedness by the excellency of the things here below; and also to give Satan time to fix and establish his kingdom in the world, that his destruction might be more conspicuous and glorious. 2. God had a design of infinite wisdom and grace in His sending of Christ and His appearance in the world, which could not be frustrated; He appeared to put away sin, which had erected a tyranny over men as by a law. 3. No power of man, or of any mere creature, was able to abolish this law of sin, for the dissolution and destruction of it was the great end of the coming of Christ for the discharge of His priestly office in the sacrifice of Himself. 4. It is the glory of Christ, it is the safety of the Church, that by His one offering, by the sacrifice of Himself, once for all He hath abolished sin as unto the law and condemning power of it.

Vs. 27, 28. *And as it is appointed unto men once to die, but after this the judgment; so Christ was once offered to bear the sins of many: and unto them that look for Him shall He appear the second time without sin unto salvation.*

These verses put a close unto the heavenly discourse of the Apostle concerning the causes, nature, ends, and efficacy of the sacrifice of Christ, whereby the new covenant was dedicated and confirmed.

"**And as it is appointed unto men once to die, but after this the judgment.**" And inasmuch as it was so with mankind, it was necessary that Christ should suffer once for the expiation of sin and the salvation of sinners. Both death and judgment are equally from the appointment of God; this is appointed unto all men without exception; not as men only, but as sinful men. The sentence of death is continued towards all men, but the penal nature of death is removed in the case of some by Christ. And

after death " *the judgment.*"   " God hath appointed a day wherein
He will judge the world in righteousness."   As sure as men die, so
sure is it there is somewhat after death.   " As death leaves men, so
shall judgment find them."   The condemnation of sin follows after
death, in the righteous government of God, by the sentence of the
law.

And as Christ by His death doth not take away death absolutely,
but only as it is *penal ;* so on His second appearance He doth not
take away judgment absolutely, but only as it is a *condemnatory
sentence* with respect unto believers.   For we must all die, and must
all appear before His judgment seat (Rom. xiv. 10).   But as He
hath promised that those who believe in Him "shall not see death,"
for they are " passed from death unto life "—they shall not undergo
it *penally ;* so also, believers " shall not come into judgment "
(John v. 24)—they shall be freed from the condemnatory sentence
of the law.

" **So Christ was once offered to bear the sins of many.**"
Christ was offered is the same with " Christ suffered," Christ died.
This He did " once," which signifies an action or passion then past
and determined.   The end of His being offered was " *to bear the
sins of many.*"   The " many " are placed in contrast with the " all
men " of the former clause.   All men die ; but the relief granted
by Christ, though it be unto men indefinitely, yet it extends not to
all universally, but to " many " of them only.

" **And unto them that look for Him shall He appear the
second time without sin unto salvation.**"   The *first* coming
of Christ was when He " *came in the flesh ;* " the *second* is *in glory,*
unto the judgment of all, when He shall finish and complete the
salvation of the Church.   Any other personal appearance or coming
of Christ the Scripture knows not, and in this place expressly
excludes any imagination of it.   His first appearance is past, and
appear a second time He will not, until that judgment comes which
follows after death, and the salvation of the Church will be completed.   Afterward there will be no more appearance of Christ in
the discharge of His office, for " God shall be all in all."

It is the great exercise of faith to live on the invisible actings of
Christ on the behalf of the Church.   So also the foundation of it
doth consist in our infallible expectation of His second appearance,
when we shall see Him again (Acts i. 11).   And here is the faith
and patience of all sincere believers,—in the midst of all discouragements, reproaches, temptations, sufferings, they can relieve
and comfort their souls with this, that " their Redeemer liveth,"
and that " He will appear again the second time without sin unto
salvation ; " hence their continual prayer, as the fruit and expression of faith, is " Even so, come, Lord Jesus."

The present long-continued absence of Christ in heaven is the
great trial of the world.   God did give the world a trial by faith in

Christ, as He gave it a trial by obedience in Adam.   When Christ did appear, it was under such difficulties that it turned all un-believers from Him ; He appeared in the flesh, in a state of infirmity, reproach, and suffering.   Now He is in glory He appeareth not.   As many refused Him when He appeared because it was in outward weakness, so many refuse Him now He is in glory because He appeareth not.

But faith hath sufficient evidences of the return of Christ : in His faithful word of promise ; in the continual supplies of the Spirit which believers receive from Him ; and in the daily evidences of His glorious power, put forth in eminent acts of providence for the protection, preservation, and deliverance of His Church.   He will appear " *unto them that look for Him.*"   His second illustrious appearance shall fill the whole world with the beams of it, the whole rational creation of God shall see and behold Him.

But the Apostle treats here of His appearance unto the salva-tion of them unto whom He doth appear ; and these are they who " *look for Him.*"   This looking for the coming of Christ— also called waiting, expecting, longing, earnest expectation— consists in, 1. Steadfast faith of His coming and appearance. 2. Love unto it, as that which is most desirable ; they "love His appearing" (2 Tim. iv. 8).   3. Longing for it, or desires after it ; " Even so, come, Lord Jesus," that is, come quickly (Rev. xxii. 20). 4. Patient waiting for it amidst all discouragements.   These the world is filled with, and it is the great trial of faith (Jude 20, 21). 5. Preparation for it ; that we may be ready and meet for His reception (see Matt. xxv).

And He shall appear " *without sin.*"   As it respects Him, He shall appear perfectly free from all those sins that once were laid upon Him, as a conqueror over sin in all its causes, effects, and consequents.   As it respects the Church, He will then have made an utter end of sin in the whole Church for ever ; there shall not be the least remainder of it ; all its guilt, filth, power, and its effects in darkness, fear, and danger, shall be utterly abolished and done away.   Then will be the great distinction among mankind, when Christ shall appear unto the everlasting confusion of some, and the eternal salvation of others,—a thing the world loves not to hear of.

CHAPTER TEN

V. 1.   *For the law having a shadow of good things to come, [and] not the very image of the things, can never with those sacrifices which they offered year by year continually make the comers thereunto perfect.*

"**For the law having a shadow of good things to come.**" The law which the Apostle immediately intends is the sacrifices of the law, especially those which were offered yearly by a perpetual statute, as the words following plainly declare. The law, he says, had a "*shadow of good things to come.*" When we remember what the good things to come are, we shall better determine how the law was a shadow of them. They were good things to come whilst the law was in force. It is evident these good things are Christ with all the grace, mercy and privilege which the Church receiveth by His actual coming in the flesh, upon the discharge of His office. Christ was signally called "the coming One," "He who was to come." There is nothing good but what is made so by Christ and His grace. Now the law was a type of Christ—a shadow of Him. It was a "shadow of things to come," "but the body is of Christ." Take the significancy and representation of Christ, His offices and grace, out of the legal institutions, and you take from them all impressions of divine wisdom; but they are now no more a shadow, they are absolutely dead and useless.

"**And not the very image of the things.**" By not having the "very image" the Apostle means the law had not the very thing itself. The law had not "the body, which is Christ"; it had not the true and real sacrifice which expiates sin, hence its weakness and imperfection, so that by none of its sacrifices could it make the Church perfect.

"**Can never with those sacrifices which they offered year by year continually make the comers thereunto perfect.**" That which is affirmed of Christ and His sacrifice (vs. 12, 14) is here denied of the law. The meaning is that the law by its sacrifices could not perfect continually—for ever—the comers thereunto. All the sacrifices on the day of atonement year after year were the same in nature; and with "those sacrifices" none were made perfect. Those who offered these sacrifices year after year were the high priests; but though offered by them they failed to make the comers perfect.

Vs. 2, 3.   *For then would they not have ceased to be offered? because that the worshippers once purged should have had no more conscience of sins. But in those [sacrifices there is] a remembrance again [made] of sins every year.*

"**For then would they not have ceased to be offered?**" If those sacrifices could have made the worshippers perfect, God would have appointed them to be offered but once, and no more. Their constant repetition gave them no virtue to make an atonement for sin. If at any time they could have done so, they would then at once have ceased to be offered.

"**Because that the worshippers once purged should**

have had no more conscience of sins.'' If the law did not make them perfect (v. 1), then were they not purged. The word '' once '' doth not signify only the doing of a thing at one time, but the so doing of it that it can be never done again. That these worshippers were not purged is abundantly evidenced, for had they been purged their consciences would not continue to condemn them for guilt, and so deprive them of peace with God.

'' But in those sacrifices there is a remembrance again made of sins every year.'' In these sacrifices made year by year there was a remembrance of sins again, and that by virtue of their divine institution. God Himself appointed that every year they should make such an acknowledgment and confession of sin as should manifest that they stood in need of a further expiation than could be attained to by them. Their confession of sin was in order unto and preparatory for a new atonement to be made; this sufficiently proves the insufficiency of those that had gone before. It is an eminent difference between the spirit of bondage and that of liberty by Christ, that the one confesses sin as to make that very confession a part of atonement for it; the other is encouraged unto confession, because of atonement already made, as a means of coming unto a participation of the benefits of it.

V. 4.   *For [it is] not possible that the blood of bulls and of goats should take away sins.*

To what end, it may be asked, serve these sacrifices, if they cannot take away sins? By them the Church was taught to look continually unto and after that sacrifice which alone could really purge and take away sins. The Church knowing that these sacrifices did call sin to remembrance, representing the displeasure of God against it, and that they could not of themselves take away sin; it made them the more earnestly look after Him and His sacrifice, which should perfectly take away sin and make peace with God. They were also the principal direction of the faith of the saints to the way in which God could alone, consistently with His truth, holiness, and righteousness, take away sin. They were taught by these sacrifices that atonement must be made by the substitution of One who was no sinner in the room of sinners, so as to make satisfaction to the law and justice of God. It is the blood of Christ alone that cleanseth us from all sins, for He alone was the propitiation. Other ways men are apt to betake themselves unto for this end, but in vain. The declaration of the insufficiency of all other ways for the expiation of sin is an evidence of the holiness, righteousness, and severity of God against sin, with the unavoidable ruin of all unbelievers.

Vs. 5—10.   *Wherefore, when He cometh into the world,*

He saith, Sacrifice and offering Thou wouldest not, but a body hast Thou prepared Me; in burnt offerings and [sacrifices] for sin Thou hast had no pleasure.   Then said I, Lo, I come (in the volume of the book it is written of Me,) to do Thy will, O God.   Above when He said, Sacrifice and offering and burnt offerings and [offering] for sin Thou wouldest not, neither hadst pleasure [therein]; which are offered by the law; then said He, Lo, I come to do Thy will, O God.   He taketh away the first, that He may establish the second.   By the which will we are sanctified through the offering of the body of Jesus Christ once [for all].

The provision that God made to supply the defect and insufficiency of the legal sacrifices as unto the expiation of sin, peace of conscience with Himself, and the sanctification of the souls of the worshippers, is declared in these verses; for the words contain the blessed undertaking of our Lord Jesus Christ to do, fulfil, perform, and suffer all things required in the will, and by the wisdom, holiness, righteousness, and authority of God, unto the complete salvation of the Church.   A blessed and divine context this is, summarily representing unto us the love, grace, and wisdom of the Father; the love, obedience, and suffering of the Son; the federal agreement between the Father and the Son as unto the work of the salvation of the Church; with the blessed harmony between the Old and New Testament in the declaration of these things.   And it is our duty to enquire with diligence into the mind of the Holy Spirit herein.

"Wherefore, when He cometh into the world, He saith, Sacrifice and offering Thou wouldest not."   Because the law was insufficient, therefore God would remove it out of the way, and bring in that which was better—to do that which the law could never do.   The words here quoted were penned by David, inspired by the Holy Ghost, and uttered by our Lord Jesus Christ. We have here the solemn word of Christ, in the declaration He made of His willingness to undertake the work of the expiation of sin, proposed unto our faith, and engaged as a sure anchor of our souls.   By His coming into the world is intended, as all the best expositors, ancient and modern, are agreed, the *incarnation* of the Son of God.   It is the same with His " coming in the flesh," His being "made flesh," His being "manifest in the flesh;" for thereby and therein He came into the world.   The expression, " *cometh into the world*," hath respect unto all the solemn acts of the discharge of His mediatory office for the salvation of the Church.

By " *sacrifice and offering* " it is evident the Holy Ghost compriseth all the sacrifices of the law that had respect unto the expiation of sin.   " *Thou wouldest not;* " Thou tookest no pleasure in these sacrifices. This hath respect unto their *end :* they were insufficient, and therefore Jesus Christ undertook to do what they could not do. God never appointed them to make an atonement for sin, He never took pleasure in them with reference hereunto ; wherefore the sense is that God did not approve of them nor accept them for that end.

"**But a body hast Thou prepared Me.**" As sacrifices were those which God "*would not*" unto the expiation of sin, so this preparation of the body of Christ was that which He *would*, which He delighted in, and with which He was well pleased. But we must enquire into the Apostle's rendering these words out of the Psalmist. In the Hebrew they are, "Mine ears hast Thou digged." The words as given us by the Apostle in this place are those whereby he expressed the sense and meaning of the Holy Ghost in those used by the Psalmist; therefore it is certain that the sense intended by the Psalmist and expressed by the Apostle are the same ; and this is, that God the Father did so order things towards Jesus Christ, that He should have a nature wherein He might be free and able to yield obedience unto the will of God ; with an intimation of the quality of it in having ears to hear, which belong only unto a body.

By a "body" then is meant the human nature of Christ. The general end of His having a body was that He might therein and thereby yield obedience, or do the will of God ; and the especial end of it was, that He might have somewhat to offer in sacrifice unto God. Nor was the body alone offered, for He "made His soul an offering for sin," which was typified by the life that was in the blood of the sacrifice. Wherefore it is said, "He offered Himself unto God," that is, His whole entire human nature, soul and body, in their substance, in all their faculties and powers.

But the Apostle here and verse 10 mentions only the body, and that for these reasons : 1. To manifest that the offering of Christ was to be *by death,* as was that of the sacrifices of old. 2. Because, as the covenant was to be confirmed by this offering, it was to be *by blood,* which is contained in the body alone. 3. To testify that His sacrifice was *visible and substantial,* such as truly answered the real bloody sacrifices of the law. 4. To show the union between Him that *sanctifieth* by His offering and them that are *sanctified* thereby ; as "the children are partakers of flesh and blood, He also took part of the same," that He might taste death for them.

It is said that God "prepared" this body; the coming of Christ, the Son of God, into the world, His coming in the flesh by the assuming of our nature, was the effect of the mutual counsel of the Father and the Son. The Father proposed to His Son what was His will, what was His design, and what He would have done. This proposal the Son closeth with : "Lo," saith He, "I come." But all things being originally in the hand of the Father, the pro-

vision of things necessary unto the fulfilling of His will is left unto
Him.   The principal of these things was that the Son should have
a body prepared for Him, that so He might have somewhat of His
own to offer.   " *A body hast Thou prepared Me.*"

God prepared such a body for Christ as was fitted and adapted
unto all that He had to do in it.   Some instances thereof may be
mentioned.   1. He prepared such a body—such a human nature as
might be of the same nature with ours, for whom He was to
accomplish His work therein.   2. He so prepared it as that it
should no way be subject unto the pollution that came on our
whole nature by sin.   3. He prepared Him a body, consisting of
flesh and blood, which might be offered as a real substantial sacrifice, and wherein He might suffer for sin in His offering to make
atonement for it.   4. It was such a body as was animated with a
living, rational soul.   He was to offer Himself in obedience unto
the will of God, and all principles of obedience lie alone in the
powers and faculties of the soul.   5. This body and soul were
obnoxious unto all the sorrows and sufferings which our nature is
liable unto, and we had deserved, as they were penal, tending unto
death.   6. This body, or human nature of Christ, was exposed unto
all sorts of temptations from outward causes; but yet it was so
sanctified by the perfection of grace and fortified by the fulness of
the Spirit dwelling therein, as that it was not possible it should be
touched with the least taint or guilt of sin.   7. This body was
liable unto death, which being the sentence of the law with respect
unto the first and all following sin, was to be undergone actually by
Him who was to be our Deliverer.   8. As it was subject unto death,
and died actually, so it was meet to be raised again from the dead.
9. This body and soul being capable of a real separation, and being
actually separated by death, though not for any long continuance,
yet no less really and truly so than they who have been dead a
thousand years, a demonstration was given therein of an active
subsistence of the soul in a state of separation from the body.   He
was alive with God and unto God when His body was in the grave,
and so shall our souls be.   10. This body was visibly taken up to
heaven and there resides, which, considering the end thereof, is the
great encouragement of faith, and the life of our hope.   The last
thing to be noticed now is that the preparation of this body is
ascribed unto the Father.   The Father prepared it in the ordering
of all things; the Holy Ghost actually wrought it; and the Son
Himself assumed it.   In the same instant of time this body was
prepared by the Father, assumed by the Son, and wrought by the
Holy Ghost.

"**In burnt offerings and sacrifices for sin Thou hast
had no pleasure.**"   These sacrifices were not found out or
instituted by men; they were all " offered by the law " (v. 8);
they included the " burnt offerings," the smoke of which ascended

from their altar, a pledge of that sweet savour which should arise unto God above from the sacrifice of Christ here below ; also the offerings for sin, namely, all their sins of what sort soever, and the especial sins of particular persons. But in these sacrifices God " had no pleasure." In opposition hereunto God gives testimony from heaven concerning the Lord Christ and His undertaking : " This is My beloved Son, in whom I am well pleased."

" **Then said I, Lo, I come (in the volume of the book it is written of Me) to do Thy will, O God.**" There is no necessity that these very words should at any one time have been spoken by our Lord Jesus Christ. The meaning is, " This is My resolution, this is the frame of My mind and will." This undertaking of Christ is signalized by the word " Lo "—behold. A glorious spectacle it was to God, to angels, and to men. It is He who said, " I come " ; this He did by assuming the body prepared for Him.

The end for which He came was "*to do Thy will, O God.*" This will of God is the " good pleasure which He purposed in Himself;" that is, freely, without any cause or reason taken from us, to call, justify, sanctify, and save to the uttermost, or to bring them unto eternal glory. How this should be done was hid in the bosom of God from the beginning of the world (Eph. iii. 8, 9). Howbeit from the beginning He declared that such a work He had designed, and He gave in the first promise ; afterwards it pleased Him to make a representation of this whole work in the institutions of the law, especially in the sacrifices thereof. But the Church found by experience that these would never pacify the conscience, and that the strict observance of them was a yoke and burden.

In this state of things, when the fulness of the time was come, the glorious counsels of the Father, Son, and Holy Ghost brake forth with light, like the sun in its strength from under a cloud, in the tender made of Himself by Jesus Christ unto the Father : " Lo, I come to do Thy will, O God." This, this is the way, the only way, whereby the will of God might be accomplished. Jesus Christ fulfilled the will of God's purpose by obedience unto the will of His command.

" *In the volume of the book it is written of Me.*" The book itself was a roll ; at the head of it, the beginning of it, amongst the first things written in it, is this recorded concerning the coming of Christ to do the will of God. Now this can be no other than the first promise, which is recorded Gen. iii. 15. Then it was first declared, first written, that the Lord Christ, the Son of God, should be made of the seed of the woman, and in our nature come to do the will of God, even to deliver the Church out of that woful state whereinto it was brought by the craft of Satan. By directing us to the beginning of the volume we are directed unto the whole volume, which is nothing but a prediction of the coming of Christ.

"**Above when He said, Sacrifice and offering and burnt offering and offerings for sin Thou wouldest not, neither hadst pleasure therein, which are offered by the law; then said He, Lo, I come to do Thy will, O God. He taketh away the first that He may establish the second.**" "Above;" that is, in the first place, these things are recorded— His words and sayings are recorded in the first place. He emphasizes here that the sacrifices and offerings in which God had no pleasure were those offered "by the law"; and having stated this, "then said He, Lo, I come." "*He taketh away the first,*" that is evidently the sacrifices and offerings; and He took these away that He might "*establish the second,*" that is, the way of expiation of sin and the complete sanctification of the Church by the coming, mediation, and sacrifice of Christ; this God would establish, approve, confirm, and render unchangeable.

"**By the which will we are sanctified, through the offering of the body of Jesus Christ once for all.**" "We are sanctified," that is, all those believers whereof the gospel church-state was constituted, in opposition unto the church-state of the Hebrews, and those that did adhere unto it. This sanctification includes, 1. A complete dedication unto God. 2. A complete church-state for the celebration of the spiritual worship of God, by the administration of the Spirit. 3. Peace with God upon a full and perfect expiation of sin. 4. Real internal purification or sanctification of our natures and persons from all inward filth and defilement. 5. Hereunto belong the privileges of the gospel, in liberty, boldness, and immediate access unto God by Christ, our High Priest. These, with other things, are comprised in that "we are sanctified."

The whole fountain and principal cause of this state of grace is the "*will of God,*" even that will which our Saviour undertook to fulfil; and the means of the accomplishment of this will was the "offering of the body of Jesus Christ once." Whatever was prepared in the will of God for the good of the Church, it is all communicated unto us through the offering of the body of Christ, in such a way as tendeth unto the glory of God and the assured salvation of the Church. The *manner* of this offering was *once* for all—once only, and no more. This demonstrates the dignity and the efficacy of His one sacrifice.

V. 11. *And every priest standeth daily ministering and offering oftentimes the same sacrifices, which can never take away sins.*

By daily standing to minister and offer is signified the constant discharge of the priestly office day by day; and this is a high argument for the imperfection of their sacrifices, that they were never brought by them into that state as that they might cease from ministering, and enter into a condition of rest. They offered often-times " *the same sacrifices* "—sacrifices of the same kind and nature ; yet, though offered daily, monthly, and some of them yearly, yet they could " *never* take away sins."

V. 12. *But this man, after He had offered one sacrifice for sins for ever, sat down on the right hand of God.*

He—this man—Jesus Christ, the High Priest of the new testa-ment—offered for sin as the priests did ; but He offered only *one sacrifice*, not many ; this sacrifice was Himself. And it was but *once offered*. This sacrifice He offered before His exaltation in glory, or His sitting down " *on the right hand of God.*" His sitting down at the right hand of God is the highest pledge and assurance of two things, which are the pillars and principal foundations of the faith of the Church. 1. That God was absolutely pleased, satisfied, and highly glorified in and by the offering of Christ ; for had it not been so, Christ would not have been so highly exalted. 2. That He had by His offering perfectly expiated the sin of the world, so as that there is no need for ever for any other offering or sacrifice unto this end.

V. 13. *From henceforth expecting till His enemies be made His footstool.*

They were His enemies in a peculiar manner, whose blasphemies and contradictions He underwent, and with whom He had so many contests. I do judge that these are the enemies peculiarly intended, namely, the hardened, unbelieving Jews, who had obstinately rejected His ministry and opposed it unto the end. This act of vengeance on His enemies is peculiarly assigned unto God the Father. " I will make Thine enemies Thy footstool." But I will also open these words according to the generally received opinion. Christ hath had many enemies since His exalta-tion, and so shall have unto the consummation of all things, when they shall all be triumphed over. The head of this opposition is Antichrist, with all his adherents, and, in a special manner, all worldly power, rule, and authority acting themselves in subserviency to the Antichristian interest. Included in these enemies are all pernicious heresies against His Person and grace ; also all those who make profession of the gospel and live not as becomes the gospel. To these may be added sin, death, the grave, and hell. These all shall be deprived of their power, and brought into abso-lute subjection.

By Christ " *expecting* " is signified His rest and complacency in the faithfulness of God's promises, and His infinite wisdom as to the season of their accomplishment. From this interpretation

we may observe, 1. It was the entrance of sin which raised up all
our enemies against us. 2. The Lord Jesus Christ in His ineffable
love and grace put Himself between us and our enemies, so that
they became His enemies. 3. The Lord Jesus Christ by the offering of Himself, making peace with God, ruined all the enmity
against the Church, and all its enemies. For all their power arose
from the just displeasure of God, and the curse of His law. 4. It
is the foundation of all consolation to the Church, that the Lord
Christ, even now in heaven, takes all our enemies to be His, in
whose destruction He is infinitely more concerned than we are.
5. Let us never esteem anything, or person, to be our enemy, but
only so far and in what they are the enemies of Christ. 6. It is
our duty to conform ourselves to the Lord Christ, in quiet
expectancy of the ruin of all our spiritual adversaries. 7. Envy
not the condition of the most proud and cruel adversaries of the
Church, for they are absolutely in His power, and shall be cast
under His footstool at the appointed season.

V. 14. *For by one offering He hath perfected for ever*
them that are sanctified.

For by His " *one offering* " once offered—that is, the offering of
Himself—He effected what the priests never did or could do with
their many offerings of bulls and of goats often offered.

"He hath perfected for ever them that are sanctified."
This being perfected signifies, His bringing of the sanctified by
His one offering into a state and condition of that grace and
privileges which the priests, law, and sacrifices could never bring
them into.   By this one offering He wrought and procured for
them the complete pardon of sin, and peace before God thereon, so
that they should have no more need for the repetition of sacrifices ;
He freed them from the yoke of carnal ordinances, and the bondage
in which they were kept, prescribing unto them a holy worship to
be performed with boldness in the presence of God ; He brought
them into the last and best Church-state, the highest and nearest
relation unto God that the Church is capable of in this world, or
the glory of His wisdom and grace hath assigned unto it.   And
this He hath done " for ever," so as that there never shall be any
alteration in that estate whereunto He hath brought them, nor any
addition of privilege or advantage be made unto it.

Vs. 15—18. *[Whereof] the Holy Ghost also is a witness*
to us : for after that He had said before, This [is] the
covenant that I will make with them after those days, saith
the Lord, I will put My laws into their hearts, and in their
minds will I write them ; and their sins and iniquities will

I remember no more. Now where remission of these [is, there is] no more offering for sin.

The Author of this testimony is the Holy Ghost. Whatever is spoken in the Scripture is, and ought to be unto us, as the immediate word of the Holy Ghost. He is a witness to us,—to all who own the Scripture as the rule of our faith and obedience. His testimony is twofold : first, that which concerns the sanctification of the elect, by the communication of effectual grace unto them for their conversion and obedience. The second is concerning the complete pardon of their sins, and the casting them into everlasting oblivion. This covenant being confirmed and established, that is, in the blood and by the one sacrifice of Christ, there can be no more offering for sin.

And here we are come unto a full end of the dogmatical part of this epistle, a portion of Scripture filled with heavenly and glorious mysteries—the light of the Church of the Gentiles, the glory of the people Israel, the foundation and bulwark of faith evangelical. I do therefore here, with all humility and sense of my own weakness and utter disability for so great a work, thankfully own the guidance and assistance which have been given me in the interpretation of it, so far as it is or may be of use unto the Church, as a mere effect of sovereign and undeserved grace. From that alone it is, that having many and many a time been at an utter loss as to the mind of the Holy Ghost, and finding no relief in the worthy labours of others, He hath graciously answered my poor weak supplications in supplies of the light and evidence of truth.

Vs. 19—23. *Having therefore, brethren, boldness to enter into the holiest by the blood of Jesus, by a new and living way, which He hath consecrated for us, through the veil, that is to say, His flesh; and [having] an High Priest over the house of God ; let us draw near with a true heart, in full assurance of faith, having our hearts sprinkled from an evil conscience, and our bodies washed with pure water. Let us hold fast the profession of [our] faith without wavering; for He [is] faithful that promised.*

In these words the Apostle enters upon the last part of the epistle, which is almost entirely hortatory, there being only an occasional reference to the ground of the duties exhorted unto, of their necessity, and of the privilege which we have in being admitted unto them and accepted with them, all taken from the priesthood and sacrifice of Christ, with their effects and the benefits we derive thereby.

"Having therefore, brethren." He hath here a peculiar

respect unto those Hebrews who had received the gospel in sincerity ; the word " brethren " is used on the account of that spiritual relationship which was between them which " believe in God through Jesus Christ." In the word " therefore" there is a note of inference from the preceding discourse, declaring it to be the ground of the present exhortation. The design of the Apostle in the whole epistle is to call off the believing Hebrews from all adherence unto and conjunction in Mosaical institutions, for he knew the danger, both temporal and spiritual, which would arise from such an adherence, especially as it would weaken their faith in Christ, and give them a disregard of evangelical worship, which did indeed prove unto many of them a cause of that apostacy and final destruction which he so frequently warns them against.

"**Boldness to enter into the holiest, by the blood of Jesus.**" The privilege here intended is directly opposed unto the state of things under the law, and from the consideration of this state of things is the nature of the privilege to be learned. Under the law there was, 1. No entrance into the special presence of God, but only into a place made with hands, filled with some representations of things that could not be seen. 2. None might ever enter the holy place but the high priest alone, and that only once a year. 3. The body of the people—the whole congregation—were therefore jointly and severally utterly excluded from any entrance into it. 4. This prohibition of entrance belonged unto that bondage wherein they were kept under the law.

The privilege here mentioned being opposed to this state of things, it is certain that it doth concern the present worship of God under the gospel ; and so they are utterly mistaken who suppose the entrance into the most holy to be an entrance into heaven after this life for all believers. Believers under the old testament were not excluded from heaven any more than now ; so it is evident that the privilege mentioned is that which belongs unto the gospel Church in its perfect state in this world. There is then in these words a twofold opposition unto the state of the people under the law. 1. As to the spirit and frame of mind of the worshippers ; and, 2. As to the place of worship from which they were excluded and whereunto we are admitted.

The word " boldness " describes the state and frame of mind of the worshippers under the gospel state; they have the right, privilege, liberty, and confidence unto and in their access unto God. This is the liberty to enter into the immediate gracious presence of God Himself in Christ Jesus ; whatever was typically represented in the most holy place of old, we have access unto. This is the great fundamental privilege of the gospel, that all believers in all their holy worship have liberty, boldness, and confidence to enter into the gracious presence of God. They are not hindered by any prohibition, God hath set no bounds to Mount Zion as He once

did to Mount Sinai, when those who drew nigh were to be cut off;
but on the contrary those now who do not draw nigh shall be cut
off. Hence there is no dread, fear, or terror in their minds, hearts,
and consciences when they approach unto God. As the taking off
the prohibition gives us *liberty*, and the institution of this gospel
worship gives us *privilege*, so the consideration of the nature of that
presence of God whereunto we approach gives us *boldness*.

"**By the blood of Jesus.**" This is the procuring cause of
the boldness and privilege which we enjoy. His blood is here
placed in contrast with the blood of the sacrifices, which never gave
the privilege to the people of entering into the holiest; only to the
high priest, and that only on one day in the year. This "*blood of
Jesus*"—that is, the "sacrifice of Himself," removed and took
away all causes of distance between God and believers; it made
atonement for them, answered the law, removed the curse, broke
down the partition wall, or "the law of commandments contained
in ordinances," wherein were all the prohibitions of approaching
unto God with boldness.

These things being removed out of the way, by the blood of
the offering of Christ, peace being thereby made with God, He
procured Him to be reconciled unto us, inviting us to accept and
make use of that reconciliation by receiving the atonement. But
this "blood of Jesus" is the cause of boldness also with respect
unto the consciences of believers, in the application of it unto
their souls. The consciences of men, from a sense of the guilt of
sin, are filled with fear and dread of God, and durst not desire so
much as access unto Him. The efficacy of the blood of Christ,
being through believing communicated unto them, takes away all
this dread and fear, and in order to this He bestows on them the
Holy Spirit, who is a Spirit of liberty, as the Apostle shows (2 Cor.
iii).

"**By a new and living way which He hath consecrated
for us.**" The *preparation* of this way was by its consecration;
that is, this way was consecrated, dedicated, and set apart sacredly
for the use of believers, so that there neither is nor ever can be
any other way but by the blood of Jesus; and there is this also
implied, that this way was not extant before its consecration by the
blood of Jesus. It is called a "*new way;*" because it was newly
made, prepared, and consecrated; because it belongs unto the new
covenant; and because it admits of no decays, for it is always new
as unto its use and efficacy as in the days of its first preparation.
It is also said to be a *living way*, and that because of its opposition
unto the way into the holiest in the tabernacle, which was *by death*
—by the blood of the sacrifices, and entrance into it was death to
any who should make use of it, the high priest only excepted. It
is a living way as to its efficacy; it hath a spiritual, vital efficacy in
our access unto God; and it is a living way from its effects; it

leads to life, effectually brings us thereunto, and is the only way of entering into everlasting life.

"**Through the veil, that is to say, His flesh.**" What the veil between the holy place and the most holy place was to the high priest, on his entrance into this latter, that is the flesh of Christ unto us in our entrance into the presence of God. When the high priest entered the most holy place, the veil was turned aside, but immediately closed again, forbidding an entrance unto others. Wherefore there could be no entrance, unless the veil was rent and torn into pieces, so that it could close no more.

It came to pass on the death of the Lord Jesus that " the veil of the temple was rent from the top to the bottom." That which is signified thereby is this, that by virtue of the sacrifice of Christ, wherein His flesh was torn and rent, we have a full entrance into the holy place. That veil was an emblem, until it was rent in twain, of the hindrances which Christ hath taken out of our way by the sacrifice of Himself. This is the first encouragement unto the duty of coming boldly, from the benefit and privilege we have by the blood of Christ. Another to the same purpose follows.

"**And having an High Priest over the house of God.**" He is *our High Priest,* He exerciseth that office on our behalf, and our duty is in all things to be such as becometh this High Priest. What became Him that He might be our High Priest, as it is expressed (chap. vii. 26), shows what we ought to be in our measure that belong unto His care, and that we may say with boldness "*we have an High Priest ;*" which is another encouragement unto the diligent attendance to the duties unto which we are here exhorted.

Jesus, our High Priest, is a *great* High Priest ; He is great in His Person, God and man (chap. i. 2, 3) ; great in His glorious exaltation (chap. viii. 1, 2) ; great in His power and the efficacy of His office (chap. vii. 25) ; great in honour, dignity, and authority— the consideration whereof leads unto the confirmation of our faith, and the ingenerating of a due reverence in our hearts towards Him. For He is so great that He can save us unto the uttermost, or give us acceptance before God as unto our persons and our duties ; so He is so glorious that we ought to apply ourselves to Him with reverence and godly fear.

He is " *over the house of God.*" He now takes the oversight of the house of God, after He had first offered sacrifice for the people ; He orders all things unto the glory of God and the salvation of the Church. The house of God is the whole family of God in heaven and in earth. But it is with special reference to that part of the family on earth that this encouragement is given, and unto whom this motive of drawing nigh is proposed ; they " have an High Priest." The Lord Christ doth peculiarly preside over the persons, duties, and worship of believers ; in that their worship is of His appointment, and whatever is not so, belongs not to the .

house of God ; in that He assists the worshippers by His Spirit ; in that He makes their worship accepted with God ; and in that He makes their worship glorious by the administration of His Spirit, and effectual through the addition of the incense of His intercession.

" Let us draw near with a true heart in full assurance of faith." This drawing near containeth all the holy worship of the Church, both public and private,—all the ways of our access unto God by Christ. God requireth " truth in the inward parts " of the worshippers (John iv. 24). By this, all false worship is rejected, and all means of worship that are not of divine institution. Truth in the heart is intended, a sincerity opposed unto all hypocrisy. Without this sincerity of heart there can be neither boldness nor confidence in our access unto God ; the nature of God and of His worship requires this internal heart sincerity.

The manner of our access unto God is said to be " in full assurance of faith." He who hath this access unto God must be a true believer, for " without faith it is impossible to please God ; " and this faith must be in actual exercise in every particular duty of access. This " full assurance of faith " hath respect unto a firm and immoveable persuasion concerning the priesthood of Christ, whereby we have access unto God ; faith without wavering. Wherefore this " full assurance of faith " here respects not the assurance any have of their own salvation, nor any degree of such assurance ; it is only the full satisfaction of our souls and consciences in the reality and efficacy of the priesthood of Christ, to give us acceptance unto God, in opposition unto all other ways and means thereof, that is intended.

Let us here observe, 1. The actual exercise of faith is required in all our approaches unto God, in every particular act of worship. Without this no outward solemnity of worship will avail us. 2. It is faith in Christ alone that gives us boldness of access unto God. 3. The Person and office of Christ are to be rested in with full assurance in all our approaches to the throne of grace.

" Having our hearts sprinkled from an evil conscience." The way of removal of an evil conscience from our hearts is by " sprinkling ; " that is, by the efficacious application of the blood of atonement unto sanctification or inward purification. This sprinkling of our hearts is an act of the sanctifying power of the Holy Ghost, by virtue of the blood and sacrifice of Christ, in making that application of them unto our souls, wherein the blood of Christ, the Son of God, cleanseth us from all our sins. This sprinkling we need continually, in fresh applications of the blood of Christ, for the taking away of defilement by internal and actual sin. The Apostle hath special respect unto the necessity of this sprinkling ; for the want of it is the bane of public worship. Where this is lacking, there is no due reverence of God, no sanctification of His name, nor any benefit to be expected unto our souls.

"And our bodies washed with pure water." This hath respect unto all those sins which cleave unto our outward conversation, and their removal. This "pure water" is the assistance of the sanctifying Spirit by virtue of the sacrifice of Christ; we are sanctified thereby in our whole spirits, souls, and bodies. Our bodies are to be as those who, having wallowed in the mire, are now washed with pure water : for the body is placed as the instrument of the defilement of the soul in such sins.

"Let us hold fast the profession of our faith without wavering." Faith is here used in two senses,—the faith by which we believe, and the faith or doctrine which we believe. Of both which we make the same profession ; of one as the inward principle, of the other as the outward rule. This solemn profession of our faith is twofold : 1. Initial. 2. By way of continuation. The first is a solemn giving up of ourselves unto Christ in a professed subjection unto His gospel, and the ordinance of divine worship therein contained. This in the early days of the Church was done by all men on their first accession unto God, and it was accompanied with excellent graces and privileges ; God giving them great joy and exultation with peace in their own minds ; also such communications of His Spirit as was a seal unto them of the promised inheritance. Whatever there might be extraordinary in this, and not now to be looked for, yet if Christians in their initial dedication of themselves unto Christ did attend unto their duty in a due manner, and were affected with their privileges as they ought, they would have experience of this grace and advantage in ways suitable unto their own state and condition.

And second, the continuation of their profession first solemnly made in avowing the faith on all just occasions, in attendance on all duties of worship required in the gospel, in professing their faith in the promises of God by Christ, and thereon cheerfully undergoing afflictions, troubles, persecutions on the account thereof, is this " profession of our faith " that is exhorted unto.

By the exhortation to " *hold fast*" our profession, there is a supposition of great danger, difficulty, and opposition against this holding fast. To " hold fast " implies the putting forth our utmost strength and endeavours in the defence of our profession, and a constant perseverance in so doing. And this must be done " without wavering." The frame of mind thus expressed is opposed unto that spoken of by James, " one that is always disputing " (chap. i. 6), and tossed up and down with various thoughts in his mind, never coming to a fixed resolution. This state of mind, " *without wavering,*" is opposed unto " halting between two opinions," that is, to waver doctrinally ; also unto a weakness or irresolution of mind as unto a continuance in the profession of faith because of difficulties and oppositions ; also to a yielding in the way of compliance on any point of doctrine or worship, contrary unto or inconsistent with the faith we have professed ; also to final apostacy from the truth, which this wavering up and down brings unto, as the Apostle intimates in the following discourse.

"**For He is faithful that promised..**" The promises of God are of that nature in themselves as are suited unto the encouragement of all believers unto constancy and final perseverance in the profession of the faith. The efficacy of the promises unto this end depends upon the faithfulness of God who gives them. " The Strength of Israel will not lie nor repent." " Consider," saith the Apostle, " the promises of the gospel, their incomparable greatness and glory ; in their enjoyment consists our eternal blessedness, and they will, all of them, be in all things accomplished towards those who hold fast their profession, seeing He who hath promised them is absolutely faithful and unchangeable.

V. 24. *And let us consider one another to provoke unto love and to good works.*

The Apostle supposeth that those unto whom he wrote had a deep concernment in one another, their present temporal and future eternal state. Without this the mere consideration of one another would only be a fruitless effect of curiosity, and tend unto many evils ; also that they had communion one with another about those things, without which this duty could not be rightly discharged, for it was not then in the world as it is now, but all Christians who were joined in church societies did meet together for mutual communion in those things wherein their edification was concerned, as is declared in the next verse. And this they did " *to provoke unto love and good works.*" This is the great end of the communion of saints, to consider the circumstances, conditions, walkings, abilities for usefulness of one another, and thereby to excite one another unto love and good works. This was the way and practice of the Christians of old, but is now generally lost, with most of the principles of practical obedience, especially those which concern our mutual edification, as if they had never been prescribed in the gospel.

V. 25. *Not forsaking the assembling of ourselves together, as the manner of some [is]; but exhorting [one another]: and so much the more as ye see the day approaching.*

"**Not forsaking the assembling of ourselves together, as the manner of some is.**" The first thing spoken of is " *the assembling of ourselves together;* " the *end* of these assemblings was, first, the due performance of all solemn, stated, orderly, evangelical worship, in prayer, preaching of the word, singing of psalms, and the administration of the sacraments. Second, the exercise of dis-

cipline, or the watch of the Church over its members, with respect
unto their walk and conversation, that in all things it be such as
becometh the gospel and gives no offence ; so to admonish, exhort,
and provoke unto love and good works ; to comfort, establish, and
encourage them that were afflicted or persecuted, to relieve the
poor, &c.

Such assemblies were constantly observed in the first churches.
How they came to be lost is not unknown, though how they may
be revived, and ought to be, is difficult. Two things are evident
herein: First, that those assemblies were the only way whereby the
Church, as a Church, made its profession of subjection unto the
authority of Christ in the performance of all those duties of sacred
worship, whereby God was to be glorified under the gospel. And
second, that those assemblies were the life, the food, the nourishment of their souls, without which they could neither attend unto
the discipline of Christ, nor yield obedience unto His commands,
nor make profession of His name as they ought; whereas in the
due observance of them consisted the trial of their faith in the
sight of God and man.

The Apostle's charge concerning these assemblies is, that we
should "not forsake them," which may be done either *totally*, which
is the fruit and evidence of absolute apostacy ; or *partially*, in
want of diligence and conscientious care in a constant attendance
unto them. It is the latter that the Apostle refers to here ; of the
former he speaks in the following verses. This forsaking of the
assemblies mentioned here usually arises, 1. From *fear of suffering*.
The rule is peremptory against all such who, as to their lands,
possessions, houses, relations, liberty, life, prefer them before Christ
and the duties which they owe unto Him and His gospel, and therefore have no interest in gospel promises.

2. From *spiritual sloth*, with the occasions of this life—the
cause in many of this sinful neglect. If men stir not up themselves, and shake off the weight that lies upon them, they will fall
under a woful neglect as unto this and all other important duties.
Such persons as are influenced by them will make use of many
specious pleas, taken for the most part from their occasions and
necessities. Christ requires that we should attend unto these
assemblies diligently, as the principal way and means of doing and
observing that which He commands us—the certain rule of our
obedience unto Him. Where such neglect is frequent, and every
trivial diversion is embraced unto a neglect of this duty, the heart
is not upright before God—the man draws back unto perdition.

3. From *unbelief* working gradually towards the forsaking of
all profession. This is the first way, for the most part, whereby
"an evil heart of unbelief in departing from the living God" doth
evidence itself. It hath unquestionably put forth its power before,
within, and in a neglect of private duties, but hereby it first

evidenceth itself unto others. The Apostle declares that some had already fallen—"*as the manner of some is.*" During those early days some had begun to decline from their profession so as not to frequent the assemblies of the Church. It was not an occasional thing with those to whom the Apostle refers; it was their manner and custom so to do.

"**But exhorting one another.**" All the duties of these assemblies, especially those which are useful and needful to prevent backsliding, and preserve from apostasy, are proposed under this one, which is the head and chief of them all. This then is the duty of all professors of the gospel, to persuade, to encourage, to exhort one another unto a constancy in profession, with resolution and fortitude of mind, against difficulties, dangers, and oppositions,—a duty which persecution will teach them who intend not to learn anything of Christ. The motive for this exhorting is given.

" **And so much the more as ye see the day approaching.**" The "*day approaching*" is an eminent day. It is not the day of death, nor the day of future judgment absolutely that is intended, for these are common unto all equally, and at all times, and are a powerful motive in general unto the performance of gospel duties; but not an especial peculiar motive at some particular time unto peculiar diligence. Wherefore "the day" was no other but that fearful and tremendous day, a season for the destruction of Jerusalem, the temple, the city, the nation of the Jews, of which our Saviour had warned His disciples, and which they had in continual expectation.

From this we may learn that approaching judgments ought to influence unto especial diligence in all evangelical duties, the neglect of which is an evidence of inward decay of all graces; and they who neglect the use of the means we are here exhorted unto, will find themselves unable to stand in the day of trial. For such a day as is here intended hath fire in it to try every man's work of what sort it is, and every man's grace as to its sincerity and power. From which we observe,

1. If men will shut their eyes against evident signs and tokens of approaching judgments, they will never stir up themselves, nor engage unto the due performance of present duties. 2. In the approach of great and final judgments, God by His word and providence gives such intimations of their coming, as that wise men may discern them. 3. To see such a day approaching, and not to be diligent in the duties of divine worship, is a token of a backsliding frame, tending unto final apostasy.

Vs. 26, 27. *For if we sin wilfully after that we have received the knowledge of the truth, there remaineth no more sacrifice for sins, but a certain fearful looking for of judgment and fiery indignation, which shall devour the adversaries.*

" **For if we sin wilfully after that we have received the knowledge of the truth.**" The Apostle says, "*if we ;*" he puts himself among them, as is his manner in his threatenings, to show that there is no respect of persons in this matter, and that those who have equally sinned shall be equally punished. This sinning wilfully is after receiving the knowledge of the truth. There is no question but by "*the truth*" is intended the doctrine of the gospel, and the "*receiving*" of it is, upon the conviction of its being truth, to take upon us the outward profession of it. This therefore is the description of the persons concerning whom this sin is supposed. The gospel had been preached unto them, they had some conviction of its truth and sense of its power, and had taken upon them the public profession of it by the solemn dedication of themselves unto Christ, in and by their baptism, and by the solemn joining themselves unto the Church, and observance of its duties in its worship.

On this opening of the words, it is evident what sin it is that is intended, against which this heavy doom is denounced, and that on these two considerations : 1. That the preceding exhortation is, "that we should hold fast the profession of our faith without wavering" (v. 23), and the means of continuing in that profession (vs. 24, 25). Wherefore the sin is, the renouncing the profession of faith with all acts and duties belonging thereunto. 2. The state opposite unto this sin—it is, "*receiving the knowledge of the truth ;*" wherefore the sin is the renunciation of the truth of the gospel, and the promises thereof, after we have been convinced of its truth, and avowed its power and excellency. There is no more required but that this be done "wilfully"—willingly ; not upon a sudden surprisal and temptation, as when Peter denied Christ ; not on those compulsions and fears which may work a present dissimulation without an internal rejection of the gospel ; not through darkness, ignorance, making for a time an impression on the minds and reasonings of men, which things, though exceedingly evil and dangerous, may befall them who yet contract not the guilt of this sin.

It is required unto this sin, 1. That men by choice, and of their own accord and an evil heart of unbelief, depart from the living God. 2. That they do it by and with the preference of another way of religion before or above the gospel. 3. That they openly renounce the blood of the covenant with the atonement made thereby, and also the dispensation of the Spirit of grace. Such are they who fell from the gospel into Judaism in those days ; but I will say no more unto the sin at present, because I must treat of it under its aggravations on verse 29.

" **There remaineth no more sacrifice for sins.**" The Apostle chargeth this as an aggravation of the sin that it cannot be expiated. There is no repetition of sacrifices under the gospel ; that of Christ was offered "once for all," henceforth "He dieth no more," nor can there be any other sacrifice offered for ever.

" **But a certain fearful looking for of judgment and fiery indignation, which shall devour the adversaries.**" No sacrifice for sin remaineth, but there doth remain for such persons a fearful expectation of judgment. Let us observe, 1. That there is an inseparable connection between apostacy and eternal ruin. 2. God oftentimes visits the minds of apostates with dreadful expectations of approaching wrath. 3. When men have hardened themselves in sin, no fear of punishment will either rouse or stir them up to seek for relief. 4. A dreadful expectation of future wrath and judgment, without hope of relief, is an open entrance into hell itself.

The punishment and destruction of these sinners is described as "*fiery indignation.*" I doubt not that this hath respect unto the final judgment at the last day, and the eternal destruction of apostates. But yet it evidently includeth that sore and fiery judgment which God was bringing on the obstinate Jews in the total destruction of them and their Church-state by fire and sword ; and this is an eminent pledge of future judgment and the severity of God therein.

In the description of these men as "*adversaries*" we have a peculiar description of the unbelieving Jews of that time ; not only did they refuse the gospel through unbelief, but were acted by a principle of opposition thereunto, not only as to themselves but as unto others, even the whole world. So is their state described, "who both killed the Lord Jesus and their own prophets, and have persecuted us ; and they please not God, and are contrary unto all men, forbidding us to speak to the Gentiles that they might be saved, to fill up their sin alway ; for the wrath is come upon them to the uttermost."

Vs. 28, 29. *He that despised Moses' law died without mercy under two or three witnesses : of how much sorer punishment, suppose ye, shall he be thought worthy, who hath trodden under foot the Son of God, and hath counted the blood of the covenant, wherewith he was sanctified, an unholy thing, and hath done despite unto the Spirit of grace ?*

"**He that despised Moses' law died without mercy under two or three witnesses.**" The sin of apostacy is compared with that of despising Moses' law ; the punishment of which was death ; this refers then only to capital offences, such as murder, adultery, idolatry, &c., and to those who sinned presumptuously, or with an high hand. They who were guilty in these matters despised the law, by their contempt of the authority of it, or the authority of God in it. Such died "without mercy," for God had expressly forbidden that mercy or compassion should be shown.

There had to be two or three witnesses of the fact and crime, so that wicked and malicious persons should not have the opportunity of taking away the lives of the innocent.

"**Of how much sorer punishment, suppose ye, shall he be thought worthy who hath trodden under foot the Son of God.**" In the description of this sin, that which is first expressed is the Person of Christ—the Son of God. This is its first great aggravation, it is committed against the Son of God, and therein His goodness, authority, and love. To tread under foot is the highest expression of scorn, contempt, and malice. They utterly rejected Him and His authority, which at one time they did avow and submit themselves unto.

The second aggravation of their sin was, their opposition to the priestly office of Christ; they "**counted the blood of the covenant an unholy thing.**" They no longer esteemed it as that blood wherewith the new covenant was sealed, confirmed, and established; not of so much use unto the glory of God as the blood of bulls and goats in the legal sacrifices, which is the height of impiety. There are various degrees of this sin, some doctrinal, some practical, which, though they rise not to the degree here intended, yet are they perilous unto the souls of men. Practically there are but few who trust unto it for their justification, for pardon, righteousness, and acceptance with God; which is in a great measure to count it a common thing—not absolutely, but in comparison of that life, excellency, and efficacy that are indeed in it. But as Christ is precious to them that believe, so also is His blood wherewith they are redeemed.

The last aggravation of this sin with respect unto the blood of Christ is that it is that "*wherewith he was sanctified.*" This is not a real internal sanctification, but a separation and dedication unto God, in which sense the word is often used. Some have thought that this refers unto the person guilty of the sin here insisted on; but the design of the Apostle in the context leads plainly to another application of these words. It is Christ Himself who is spoken of, who was sanctified and dedicated unto God to be an eternal High Priest by the blood of the covenant which He offered unto God. That precious blood of Christ whereby He was sanctified and dedicated unto God they esteemed an "unholy thing," that is, such as would have no such effect as to consecrate Him unto God and to His office.

"**And hath done despite unto the Spirit of grace.**" This is the third aggravation of their sin, their opposition to the Spirit of Christ in that they do Him despite. There is a peculiar consideration of the Spirit, with respect whereunto He is sinned against, and that is this—He was peculiarly given and bestowed to bear witness unto the Person, doctrine, death, and sacrifice of Christ, with the glory that ensued thereon. By Him multitudes were converted unto God, the Scriptures opened to their understanding, and mighty works, wonders, signs, and miracles wrought, which accompanied the preachers of the gospel at the beginning.

Now all these things were owned, believed, and avowed to be the work of the Holy Spirit, and that by these very men who now had fallen away from their profession of the gospel. They did despise unto Him principally by calling in question the testimony He gave unto Christ in the gospel, and what greater despite and wrong could be done unto Him than to question the truth and the veracity of His testimony?

The Apostle asks, "*Of how much sorer punishment, suppose ye, shall he be thought worthy*" who thus falls into apostacy? Such apostates shall be punished with a sore, great, and evil punishment; it shall be a sorer punishment than that which was appointed for wilful transgressors of the law, which was death without mercy. They are worthy of punishment, and shall receive neither more nor less than their due.

Vs. 30, 31. *For we know Him that hath said, Vengeance [belongeth] unto Me, I will recompense, saith the Lord. And again, The Lord shall judge His people. [It is] a fearful thing to fall into the hands of the living God.*

"**For we know Him that hath said.**" It is as though the Apostle said, "If you will be convinced of the righteousness and certainty of this dreadful destruction of apostates, consider in the first place the Author of this judgment, the only Judge in this case."

"**Vengeance belongeth unto Me, I will recompense, saith the Lord.**" God in executing vengeance gives satisfaction unto His own infinite holiness and righteousness, which makes it holy and just; not only doth vengeance belong to the Lord, but in His own time He will execute it, when and how He pleaseth, and that this is certain the Apostle adds the words, "saith the Lord."

"**And again, The Lord shall judge His people.**" "And shall not the Judge of all the earth do right?" Shall not He who is Judge in a peculiar manner of those that profess themselves to be His people punish them for their iniquities, especially such as break off all covenant relation between Him and them?

"**[It is] a fearful thing to fall into the hands of the living God.**" God is called the "living God" in opposition unto all dead and dumb idols, those whom the heathen worshipped; also to impress our minds with a due sense of His glory and eternal power, whereby He is able to avenge the sins of men. He is the "God that liveth and seeth;" and as He seeth so He judgeth. To "*fall into His hands,*" as is here intended, is to be exposed to the power and judgment of God, when and where there is nothing in

God Himself, nothing in His word, promises, or institutions, that should oblige Him unto mercy or a mitigation of punishment. This the Apostle declares to be a "*fearful thing*."

Herein, by this general assertion, the Apostle sums up and closeth his blessed discourse concerning the greatest sin that men can make themselves guilty of, and the greatest punishment that the righteousness of God will inflict on any sinners. This is a passage of Scripture much to be considered, especially in these days wherein we live, when men are apt to grow cold and careless in their profession, and to decline gradually from what they had attained unto. And we live in days wherein the contempt of God, the despite of the Lord Christ and His Spirit are come to the full, so as to justify the truth that we have insisted on.

V. 32. *But call to remembrance the former days, in which, after ye were illuminated, ye endured a great fight of afflictions.*

"**But call to remembrance the former days.**" The " but " has respect unto the exhortation laid down (v. 25). The verses interposed contain a dehortation from the evil of which they are warned ; the Apostle now returns to the former exhortation unto the duties recommended unto them. He would have them " call to remembrance " what support they had received under their sufferings, what satisfaction in them, what deliverance from them, that they might not despond upon the approach of the like evils and trials on the same account. Those who call to mind with their sufferings the causes of them, and the presence of God with them therein, are encouraged, emboldened, and strengthened unto duty with zeal and constancy. A wise management of former experiences is a great direction and encouragement unto future obedience. The " former days " which he exhorts them to call to remembrance were those in which they first heard the gospel.

"**In which after ye were illuminated.**" Their enlightening did precede those days of their sufferings; it was their " translation out of darkness into His marvellous light." This spiritual change was presently followed with days of affliction, and trouble, and persecution. It was immediately after their first conversion to God ; and it is usual with Him thus to deal with His people in all ages. He no sooner calls them to Himself but He leads them into the wilderness. He no sooner plants them but He shakes them with storms, that they may be more firmly rooted. He doth this in order to take off their expectation from this world or anything therein ; for the trial of their faith ; for the glory and propagation of the gospel ; for the exercise of all graces ; and to bring us up in the military discipline of Christ, as He is the Captain of our salvation. They who pass through their first trials are Christ's veterans on new attempts.

"**Ye endured a great fight of afflictions.**" These afflictions, as it appears from what follows, were the persecutions which they suffered. God used them as His furnace "for the trial of their faith, which is more precious than gold." This word "afflictions" includes all the evils, troubles, hardships and distresses that may befall men upon the account of their profession of the truth of the gospel. Of these trials, afflictions, persecutions, they had a "*great fight.*" That labour and contention of spirit which they had in their profession with sin and sufferings is expressed by these words, which set forth the greatest, most earnest, vehement actings and endeavours that our nature can rise unto.

Three things are required hereunto: 1. That men prepare themselves for it (1 Cor. ix. 25). Self-denial and readiness for the cross, contempt for the world and the enjoyments of it, are this preparation; without this we shall never be able to go through with this conflict. 2. A vigorous acting of all graces in the conflict itself, in opposition unto and destruction of our spiritual and worldly adversaries (Eph. vi. 10—18; Heb. xii. 3). 3. That we endure the hardship and the evils of the conflict with patience and perseverance, which is that which the Apostle here specially intends. This is that which he commends in these Hebrews, with respect unto their first trials and sufferings; "*ye endured,*" and that patiently, so as not to faint or despond, or to turn away from their profession. The Apostle would have them remember this, that they might be encouraged and strengthened unto what yet remained of the same kind.

V. 33. *Partly, whilst ye were made a gazingstock both by reproaches and afflictions; and partly, whilst ye became companions of them that were so used.*

In this he distributes their sufferings under two heads; the first is what immediately concerned their own persons; the second, their concernment and participation in the sufferings of others.

"**Partly whilst ye were made a gazingstock, both by reproaches and afflictions.**" The first thing they suffered was "*reproaches,*" a great aggravation of suffering unto ingenuous minds. It is that kind of reproach which proceeds from malicious hatred, and is accompanied with contempt and scorn, and vents itself in all manner of obloquies and hard speeches such as those mentioned, Jude 15. Reproaches consist of false accusations, charging men falsely with vile and contemptible things, such as will expose them unto public scorn and rage. "They shall say all manner of evil against you falsely." So they reproached the Person of Jesus Christ Himself. Reproaches also consist in the contempt that is cast upon what is true, and what in itself is holy, just, good, and praiseworthy. They reproached them with their faith in Christ, with their worship of Him in owning His authority. This in itself was their honour and their crown.

Let us observe, 1. To take heed of so much softness and tenderness of nature that may give too deep a sense of reproach, scorn and shame, being such as will weaken in duties. 2. It is required that we do not put too much value on our names and reputation in the world. If we are not contented to be made " as the filth and offscouring of all things," it will greatly disadvantage us in the time of sufferings. 3. We must not think that any new thing befalls us when we are reproached ; no, not when the reproaches are new, and such as were never cast on any that went before. 4. Know that where reproach goes before, persecution will follow after, in the course of the world. It thunders in reproaches and falls in a storm of persecution. By these things they were " *made a gazingstock.*" They were publicly, and in the sight of all that had occasion or opportunity to observe them, exposed unto these things. This was a great addition to and aggravation of their sufferings. It requireth excellent actings of faith and spiritual courage to carry ingenuous persons above this public contest. The other part of their sufferings is said to be this:

" **And partly whilst ye became companions of them that were so used.**" I take it to mean that not all of those to whom he wrote did actually in their own persons suffer the things of which he speaks, but some of them did so suffer, and the rest of them were companions with them that suffered. All are not called forth unto the same actual sufferings ; some, in the providence of God and through the rage of men, are singled out for trials ; some are hid or do escape, at least for a season, and it may be are reserved for the same trials at another time. Hence some are companions of those who suffer; they are made companions by their common interest in the same cause for which only some suffered ; also by their apprehension that the same sufferings would reach unto themselves ; also by their sorrow, trouble, and compassion for the sufferings of the members of the same Head and body with them ; also by the duties of love and affection which they discharged in visiting them ; and by the communication of their goods and outward enjoyments unto them who had suffered the loss of their own ; so were they made companions.

V. 34. *For ye had compassion of me in my bonds, and took joyfully the spoiling of your goods, knowing in yourselves that ye have in heaven a better and an enduring substance.*

" **For ye had compassion of me in my bonds.**" The

Apostle first mentions his own case as an illustration of what he had just spoken concerning their being made companions of those that suffered. They had "compassion" on him, they suffered together with him. This they manifested by a real grief and trouble of mind for his bonds, as if they themselves were bound; by continual prayers for his relief; and by a ministration to him of such things as might be outwardly wanting. Then he reminds them of their own sufferings.

"**And took joyfully the spoiling of your goods.**" It was their outward substance with which they parted; houses, lands, possessions, also their money, corn, cattle, the very bread they should eat and the clothes they should wear. And this must needs be a sore trial unto men when not only themselves, but their relations also, their wives and children, some perhaps in their infant age, are reduced unto all extremities. Their goods were forcibly taken from them, and that not so much for their own advantage as for the satisfaction it gave them to vent their rage and malice in the ruin of the saints of Christ. But these Hebrews accepted all this "joyfully;"

"**Knowing in yourselves that ye have in heaven a better and an enduring substance.**" Faith gives us justification before God, access unto Him, and acceptance with Him, and therewithal gives joy and rejoicing unto the soul; and this it doth in an especial manner under sufferings and afflictions, enabling men to "take joyfully the spoiling of their goods;" for it stirreth up all graces into such a condition unto their due exercising, issuing in a blessed experience of the excellency of the love of God, and of His glory in Christ, with a firm and stable hope of future glory. This "substance" is better, more excellent, incomparably so, than the outward goods that are subject unto spoiling. It is not only better, but enduring, abiding, that which will not leave them in whom it is, and can never be taken from them. "My joy shall no man take from you." This substance, so far as it is "in heaven," compriseth the whole of the future state of blessedness; it is called "an inheritance," also "the eternal weight of glory," for in comparison with it all other things temporary have no substance in them. They had this substance; they knew in themselves that they had an undeniable title unto it, which none can deprive them of, but they shall certainly enjoy in the appointed season.

V. 35. *Cast not away therefore your confidence, which hath great recompence of reward.*

The inference of these words is plain,—Seeing you have suffered so many things in your persons and goods, seeing God by His grace hath carried you through with satisfaction and joy, do not now despond and faint upon the approach of the same difficulties, or those of a like nature. He exhorts them unto the preservation and continuance of their confidence. This confidence, whatever it be, was that which carried them through their sufferings. This confidence is a boldness of mind, with freedom from bondage and fear, in the duties of religion towards God and man, from a prevailing persuasion of our acceptance with God therein. Without this frame of mind it is impossible that we should undergo any great sufferings unto the glory of God or our own advantage. For if we are made diffident by unbelief, if the helps and succours tendered in the gospel and promises thereof be betrayed by fear, if the shame of outward sufferings and scorns do enfeeble the mind, if we have not an evidence of " better things " to lay in the balance against present evils, it is impossible to endure any " great fight of afflictions " in a due manner.

This " confidence " which had been of such use unto them, the Apostle exhorts them now " *not to cast away ;* " for where any graces have been stirred up unto their due exercise, they will not fail nor be lost without some positive act of the mind in rejecting of them. This rejection may be only as unto its actual exercise, not as to its radical inbeing in the soul. But sometimes failing in faith makes this confidence to fail ; and sometimes failing in confidence weakens and impairs the faith. The reason why we should be so careful of this confidence is because it " *hath great recompense of reward.*" This recompense of reward is the glory of heaven, proposed as a " crown " unto them that overcome in their sufferings for the gospel. Whoever abides in this exercise of not casting away his confidence shall be no loser in the issue. They are as sure in divine promises as in our own possession ; and although they are yet future, faith gives them a present subsistence in the soul as unto their power and efficacy.

V. 36. *For ye have need of patience, that after ye have done the will of God, ye might receive the promise.*

Patience is a bearing of evils with quietness and complacency of mind, without raging, fretting, despondency, or inclination unto compliance with undue ways of deliverance. " Confidence " will engage men into troubles and difficulty in a way of duty ; but if patience take not up the work and carry it on, confidence will flag and fail. They had need of the continual exercise of this grace of patience in the condition wherein they were, or whereinto they were entering. He that would abide faithful in difficult seasons must fortify his soul with an unconquerable patience. It is necessary to pray for it ; to give it its due exercise in the approaches of troubles ; to take care to keep faith vigorous and active, especially the exercise of faith unto a view of eternal things, which will engage the aid of hope and administer the food that patience lives upon.

There is no dismission from the discharge of this duty until we have done the whole *"will of God."* The will of God is that whereby our whole duty is presented unto us, as unto our faith, obedience, and worship. The whole of our duty is resolved unto the will of God, that is, the will of His command; and so to do the will of God is to abide constant in all the duties of faith and obedience, worship and profession, as He requireth of us. To *" receive the promise "* is to receive the things promised—all the grace and mercy of the covenant with the promise of eternal life and glory, which latter they had not yet received except in promise.

V. 37. *For yet a little while, and He that shall come will come, and will not tarry.*

As if the Apostle had said, " My brethren, faint not, be not wearied nor discouraged, keep up confidence and patience; you know what you wait for and expect, which will be an abundant recompense unto you for all your sufferings. And whatever appearances there may be of its tarrying or delay, whatever it may seem unto you, yet if you have but a prospect into eternity, be it what it will, it is but a very little while, and so to be esteemed by you." He that shall come is " the coming One," even Christ Himself. He is to come again in the power of His Spirit, and the exercise of His royal authority in the setting up and settling His Church in the world, and that by the assistance of His Spirit unto the ministers of the gospel ; also He is to come again for the punishment and destruction of His stubborn and inveterate adversaries. And then Christ will come at the last day unto judgment. This is known and confessed, and the business of His coming therein is the prayer of the whole Church.

V. 38. *Now the just shall live by faith: but if [any man] draw back, my soul shall have no pleasure in him.*

"Now the just shall live by faith." The just person here spoken of is one who is really made just—really and truly justified. What is principally intended here by a just man is that qualification which is opposed to haste and pride of spirit through unbelief, whereon men draw back from God in the profession of the gospel. This man "shall live by faith ; " faith is the means whereby a just man doth abide and persevere in his profession unto life. He shall live, he shall not die in or from his profession, he shall maintain a spiritual life, the life of God, as the Psalmist speaks, " I shall not die, but live and declare the lovingkindness of the Lord." He shall live and attain the promise of eternal life; he " shall believe unto the saving of the soul."

"**But if any man draw back.**" If any man who hath made or doth make profession of faith in Christ and of the gospel, upon the invasion and long continuance of trials, temptations, and sufferings for them, do, through want of submission unto and acquiescence in the will of God, withdraw himself from that profession, and from communion therein with them who persist faithful in it, " *My soul shall have no pleasure in him.*" This is the sentence pronounced against those who draw back.

" **My soul shall have no pleasure in him.**" The " soul " of God is God Himself, but He so speaks of Himself to affect us with a due apprehension of his concernment in what He so speaks, as we are with that which our souls are engaged in. To " have no pleasure " is to abhor, to despise, and in the end to utterly destroy.

V. 39. *But we are not of them who draw back unto perdition, but of them that believe to the saving of the soul.*

Drawing back unto perdition is here placed in opposition unto believing unto the saving of the soul. The former is denied of these Hebrews, and the latter is affirmed concerning them. Even in those early days there were those who fell into apostasy, and the end of their defection was " destruction." Gradual decays and declensions there may be among true believers, from which they may be recovered; but those here intended are such as fall into eternal ruin. It is our duty to evidence unto our own consciences and give evidence unto others that we are not of this sort or number, for nothing can free apostates from ruin. But these Hebrews were of " the faith," that is, true believers and heirs of the promises. We are, he says, of that faith which is effectual unto the saving of the soul. Sincere faith will carry men through all difficulties, hazards, and troubles unto the certain enjoyment of eternal blessedness.

CHAPTER ELEVEN

V. 1. *Now faith is the substance of things hoped for, the evidence of things not seen.*

This faith is that whereby the " just shall live; " that is, it is a divine, supernatural, justifying, saving faith, the faith of God's elect, the faith that is not of ourselves, but is of the operation of

God, wherewith all true believers are endowed from above. The " things hoped " and the " things not seen " are for the substance of them the same. They are the good things of the promises, as the Apostle declares in his ensuing discourse, where he makes the end and the effect of the faith which he doth so commend to be the enjoyment of the promises. Faith gives the things hoped for a real subsistence in the minds and souls of them that do believe. Faith mixes itself with the promises wherein the things hoped for are promised; faith gives unto the soul a taste of the goodness of the things promised; faith gives an experience of their power as unto all ends for which they are promised; faith really communicates to us the things promised and hoped for; and faith gives a representation of their beauty and glory unto the minds of them that believe, whereby they behold them as if they were present. So Abraham by faith saw the day of Christ and rejoiced, and the saints under the Old Testament saw the King in His beauty. Faith in its being " the evidence of things not seen " is the great means of the preservation of believers in constant, patient profession of the gospel, against all opposition, and under the fiercest persecutions; which is the thing the Apostle aims to demonstrate. It is faith alone that takes believers out of this world, whilst they are in it, that exalts them above it while they are under its rage, that enables them to live upon things future and invisible, giving such a real subsistence unto them and victorious evidence of their truth and reality, as secures its possessors from fainting under all oppositions, temptation, and persecutions whatever.

V. 2. *For by it the elders obtained a good report.*

Who these elders were is put beyond dispute by the ensuing discourse. All true believers from the foundation of the world, or the giving of the first promise, unto the end of the Old Testament dispensation are intended. This testimony was given unto them in the Scriptures; for it is the Holy Spirit in the Scripture that gives them this good testimony, for thereunto doth the Apostle appeal for the proof of his assertion. What was so testified of them is expressly declared,—it is, that they " pleased God " or were accepted with Him. And it was through faith they obtained this report; and though they were despised, vilified, and reproached n the world, yet having this faith they were accepted of God, and He gave them a good report.

V. 3. *Through faith we understand that the worlds were framed by the word of God ; so that things which are seen were not made of things which do appear.*

" Through faith we understand that the worlds were

framed by the word of God.'' By faith we understand, that is, we assent unto the divine revelation. If by faith we are assured of the creation of the world out of nothing, it will bear us out in the belief of other things that seem impossible unto reason, if so be they are revealed. In particular faith, well fixed on the original of all things as made out of nothing, will bear us out in the belief of the final restitution of our bodies at the resurrection, which the Apostle instanceth in as unto some of his worthies. By faith " *we understand* ; " understanding is opposed not only unto ignorance, but unto that dark and confused apprehension of the creation of the world which some, by the light of reason, attained unto.

We understand by faith " *that the worlds were framed by the word of God.*" The word " framed" means the ordering, disposing, fitting, perfecting, adorning of that which is produced ; it does not signify " created," although that is included herein ; for that which is framed must be first made or created ; but more is intended, namely, the disposal of all created things into that beautiful order which we do behold; all this is a demonstration of the eternal power of God. None ever knew anything of this framing of the world, or the reducing of the matter of it into perfect order, but by divine revelation only. The efficient cause of this framing of the worlds is " *the word of God ;* " that exertion of His mighty power which was expressed by His word, "Let it be," which was the sign of it, and the indication of its exercise. " He spake and it was made ; He commanded and it stood fast."

" So that things which are seen were not made of things which do appear." These things which are visible were made by those which are invisible, even the eternal power and wisdom of God. There is in these words, 1. A negation of any pre-existing material cause unto the creation of these worlds. 2. An assignation of the only efficient cause of it, which is the power of God, which things are rather supposed than asserted. 3. Respect unto the order of the creation of all things, in bringing them unto their perfection. All the things we now behold in their order, glory and beauty were made by the power of God out of that chaos, or confused mass of substance, which was itself first made and produced out of nothing, having no cause but the efficiency of divine power.

V. 4. *By faith Abel offered unto God a more excellent sacrifice than Cain, by which he obtained witness that he was righteous, God testifying of his gifts : and by it he, being dead, yet speaketh.*

" By faith Abel offered unto God." Abel, the first who suffered death in the cause of Christ and His worship. And this he did from his own brother, from one that joined with him in the outward acts of the worship of God; in this we have an example of the two churches, the suffering and the persecuting, to the end of the world. In Gen. iv. 3—5, it is declared *what time* Abel offered this sacrifice; it was "after the expiration of some time," namely, after he and Cain were settled in their distinct callings (v. 3). Until then they had been under the instruction of their parents; but now being fixed in their own callings, they made their distinct solemn profession of the worship of God.

Abel offered "the firstlings of his flock and of the fat thereof;" his offering was of *living creatures*, that is, creatures that had lived, and therefore was made by shedding of blood; it was of the *best of his flock*, the "firstlings;" and it was of the "*fat of them*," which God also claimed as His own. It appears, therefore, that the sacrifice of Abel was, as unto the matter of it, both in itself and in God's esteem, of the most precious and valuable things in the whole creation, subject unto man and his use. He offered this sacrifice "unto God;" this was, from the first institution of it, the highest and most peculiar way of owning and paying homage unto God. And he offered this sacrifice "*by faith.*" He did it by faith, because he had respect in what he did unto God's institution, which consists of a command and a promise, which faith hath regard unto. It was not a service invented by himself, for if it were he could not have performed it in faith. This faith was kindled in his heart by the Holy Spirit, before it was fired on the altar from heaven, for God gives no consequential approbation of any duties of believers, but where the principle of a living faith goes previously in their performance.

"A more excellent sacrifice than Cain." As to the matter of it, it was better, more valuable, more precious than that of Cain. But this is not a sufficient cause for ascribing such excellency unto it, as that on the account thereof Abel should obtain such acceptance with God, and a testimony from Him. The difference in the sacrifices arose from the faith of Abel; and there are two things to be noted here: First, That his person was justified in the sight of God antecedently unto his sacrifice, as we shall see immediately. Second, On the account thereof his sacrifice was grateful and acceptable unto God, as is to be observed from the ordering of the words, "The LORD had respect unto Abel and his offering."

But yet it is not evident where the great difference lay. For Cain also, no doubt, brought his offering in faith, for he believed in the being of God, as also in His government of the world with rewards and punishments, for all this he professed in the sacred offering he brought unto the Lord. It is certain that the faith of Cain and Abel differed, as in their special nature so in their acts and objects. For, 1. Cain considered God only as a Creator and Preserver, whereon he offered the fruits of the earth as an acknow-

ledgment that all these things were made, preserved, and bestowed
on man by Him ; but he had no respect unto sin or deliverance
from it as revealed in the first promise. The faith of Abel was
fixed on God not only as a Creator, but as a Redeemer; as Him
who in infinite wisdom and grace had appointed the way of redemption by sacrifice and atonement, intimated in the first promise.
Wherefore, his faith was accompanied with a sense of sin and
guilt, with his lost condition by the fall, and a trust in the way of
redemption and recovery which God had provided. And this he
testified in the kind of his sacrifice, which was by death and blood;
in the one owning the death which himself by reason of sin was
liable unto ; in the other the way of atonement, which was to be by
blood, the blood of the promised Seed. 2. They differed in their
especial nature and acts. For the faith of Abel was saving, justifying, a principle of holy obedience, an effect of the Holy Spirit in
his mind and heart; that of Cain was a naked, barren assent unto
the truths before mentioned, a common and a temporary faith,
which is evident from the event, in that God never accepted his
person or his offering. So, from the foundation of the world, there
was provision laid into warn the Church in all ages, that the performance of outward duties of divine worship is not the rule of the
acceptance of men's persons with God. The distinction is made
from the *inward principle* whence those duties do proceed. Yet will
not the world receive the warning unto this day. Many have no
greater quarrel at religion, than that God had respect unto Abel and
his offering, and not to Cain and his.

" By which he obtained witness that he was righteous."
This is the *first* consequent of the efficacy of faith in Abel. He
was " witnessed to " by God Himself. And this was so famous in
the Church, that our Saviour, in speaking of him, calls him " the
righteous Abel." But we do not find any such testimony in express
words given unto him in the Scripture. Wherefore the Apostle
proves his assertion by that wherein such a testimony is virtually
contained.

" God testifying of his gifts." God testified, in the approbation of his offering, that he had respect unto his person ; that
is, that He judged, esteemed, and accounted him righteous; for
otherwise God is no respecter of persons. Whomsoever God
accepts or respects, He testifieth him to be righteous, that is, to be
justified and freely accepted with Him. Abel was not made
righteous, he was not justified by his sacrifice ; but therein he
showed his faith by his works, and God by acceptance of his works
of obedience justified him, as Abraham was justified by works;
namely, declaratively, God declared him so to be. By what way
God gave this testimony unto the gifts or sacrifice of Abel is not
expressed. Most do judge that it was by causing fire to descend
from heaven to kindle and consume his sacrifice. Certain it is,

that by some such assured token and pledge his own faith was strengthened and Cain provoked. Thus both of them knew how things stood between God and them. As Esau knew that Jacob had got the blessing, which made him resolve to kill him ; so Cain knew that Abel and his offering were accepted with God ; whereon he slew him.

"**And by it he, being dead, yet speaketh.**" The second consequent of the efficacy of the faith of Abel was after his death. " The voice of thy brother's blood crieth unto Me from the ground." The Apostle in chap. xii. 24 directly ascribes this speaking unto the blood of Abel, as we shall see on that place, if God permit. There is a voice in all innocent blood shed by violence. There is an appeal in it from the injustice and cruelty of men unto God as the righteous Judge of all. But there is more in this speaking of the blood of Abel. God hath designed that it should be a type of the future persecutions and sufferings of the Church ; that it should be a pledge of the certain vengeance that God will take in due time on all murderous persecutors ; and that it might be instructive unto faith and patience in suffering, as an example approved of God, and giving evidence unto future rewards and punishments.

V. 5. *By faith Enoch was translated that he should not see death; and was not found, because God had translated him : for before his translation he had this testimony, that he pleased God.*

"**By faith Enoch was translated that he should not see death.**" There are but two states of good men, such as Enoch was, from first to last. 1. The state of faith and obedience here in this world in which Enoch lived for three hundred years ; he "walked with God," that is, he lived a life of faith in covenant obedience with God. 2. The other state is that of blessedness in the enjoyment of God. Wherefore Enoch, being translated from the one, was immediately instated in the other, as was Elijah afterwards. He did not " see death ; " this translation was not by death ; he was freed from death in a way of eminent grace and favour. This was a divine testimony that the body itself is capable of eternal life ; but whereas this evidence was confined to a body that never died, it could not be a convincing pledge of the resurrection of bodies over which death once had a dominion. This, therefore, was reserved for the resurrection of Christ."

"**And was not found because God had translated him.**" When he did no more appear, when he was not found, this was that which satisfied the godly that God had translated him ; there was sufficient evidence as a security for their faith, although at present we know not what it was in particular. Enoch was translated " *by faith;* " not *efficiently;* not *meritoriously,* but *instrumentally* only,

in that thereby he was brought into that state and condition, so
accepted with God as to be capable of so great grace and favour.
This is peculiar to these first two instances of faith; in the one it
led him unto a bloody death ; in the other it delivered him from
death, that he did not die at all.

"**For before his translation he had this testimony that
he pleased God.**" It is said of him that he walked with God three
hundred years, after which he was translated. That of "walking
with God" in Moses, the Apostle renders by "pleasing of God,"
for this alone is well-pleasing with Him. There being no direct
mention made of faith in the testimony given unto Enoch, but only
that by walking with God he pleased God, the Apostle in the next
verse proves from thence that it was by faith that he so pleased
God, and consequently that thereby he obtained his translation.

V. 6. *But without faith* [*it is*] *impossible to please*
[*Him*]*: for he that cometh to God must believe that He is,
and* [*that*] *He is a rewarder of them that diligently seek Him.*

"**But without faith it is impossible to please Him.**"
All pleasing of God is, and must be by faith, it being impossible
it should be otherwise. Three things are included in God's being
pleased. 1. That the person be accepted, that God be well pleased
with him. 2. That his duties do please God, that He is well pleased
with them as He was with the gifts of Abel and the obedience of
Enoch. 3. That such a person have *testimony* that he is righteous
—just or justified—as Abel and Enoch had, and as all true believers
have in the Scripture. Without faith it is *impossible* to please Him.
Many in all ages have tried it, and yet continue it. Cain began it.
All men in their worship profess a desire to please God, but most
of them seek it "not by faith," and therefore God rejects them
and their worship. The secret apprehension that God is to be
pleased with outward works and duties, is the foundation of all
superstition in divine worship. It is of the highest importance to
examine well into the sincerity of our faith, seeing thereon depends
the acceptance of our persons and all our duties.

"**For he that cometh to God must believe that He is.**"
This coming means, in particular, an access unto God in sacred
worship ; in order to this coming there is required a lost condition
in ourselves, by our distance from God ; also some encouragement
unto him that will come unto God, and that from God Himself ;
and this can be nothing but His free, gracious promise to receive
them that come unto Him by Christ, as the Scripture testifieth.
To come to God is to have access into His favour, to please Him,
as did Enoch ; so to come as to be accepted with Him. Such must
believe that "God is." This is such a believing of the being of

God as gives encouragement to come unto Him, that we who are sinners may be accepted.

"**And that He is a rewarder of them that diligently seek Him.**" " Fear not, Abram; I am thy shield, and thy exceeding great reward." God Himself is the reward of them that seek Him ; which eternally excludes all thoughts of merit in them that are so rewarded. This diligent seeking of Him consists in faith acting itself in prayer, patience, diligent attendance unto the ordinances of worship, &c. All faith is vain which doth not set men on a diligent inquiry after God.

V. 7. *By faith Noah, being warned of God of things not seen as yet, moved with fear, prepared an ark to the saving of his house; by the which he condemned the world, and became heir of the righteousness which is by faith.*

" **By faith Noah, being warned of God of things not seen as yet.**" Noah was one of those who " found grace in the eyes of the LORD " (Gen. vi. 8). Also he was "just, perfect in his generations, and walked with God" (v. 9). He was accepted with God, justified, and walked in acceptable obedience before he was thus divinely warned. He was a " preacher of righteousness " (2 Pet. ii. 5), that is, of the righteousness of God by faith, and of righteousness by repentance and obedience among men. There is no doubt that before, and whilst building the ark, he was urgent with men to call them to repentance, by declaring the promises and threatenings of God. Noah was warned of God,—a declaration of the purpose of God to destroy the whole world, and a direction from God to make an ark—" *of things not seen as yet,*" namely, the flood and the saving of himself in an ark. Wherefore it was an act of pure faith in Noah to believe that for which he had no evidence, but by divine revelation, especially as the thing itself was unto human reason every way incredible.

" **Moved with fear, prepared an ark to the saving of his house.**" By faith he was " *moved with fear;* " his believing the word of God had this effect on him. In the warning given him, he considered the greatness, holiness, and power of God, with the vengeance becoming those holy properties of His nature which He threatened to bring on the world ; he was filled with a reverential fear of Him. This fear, which arose from faith, was used by the same faith to stir him unto his duty. He " *prepared an ark;* " and a strange thing no doubt it was in the world, to see a man with so great an endeavour build an ark where there was no water near. During the preparation of the ark, he continued to preach righteousness and repentance unto the inhabitants of the world ; nor could it be avoided but that he must in what he did let them know in

what way they should be destroyed if they repented not. The
Scripture tells us they did not repent upon his preaching and the
striving of the Spirit of Christ with them therein, that they were
secure, not being moved by his threatenings till the last hour
(Matt. xxiv. 38, 39) ; and that they were scoffers, as is plainly intimated (2 Pet. iii. 3—6). The immediate effect of Noah's faith was
the saving of his family—his wife, his three sons and their wives.
This family God in sovereign grace and mercy would preserve,
principally to continue the conveyance of the promised Seed ; and
also for the continuation of the Church of God to be brought unto
God by that promise.

"By the which he condemned the world." He condemned it
by his doctrine, by his obedience, by his example, by his faith in
them all. Noah justified God in His threatenings and the execution of them ; he condemned the world by casting a weighty aggravation on their guilt in that he believed and obeyed when they
refused so to do ; he also condemned it by leaving it utterly without
excuse, he left them no pretence that they had not been warned
of their sin and approaching ruin.

**"And became heir of the righteousness which is by
faith."** This is gratuitous justification by the righteousness of
Christ imputed unto us by faith ; he was made the "heir" of this
righteousness ; that is, by gratuitous adoption. Whatever we
receive upon our adoption belongs unto our inheritance. The
righteousness of faith is the best inheritance, for thereby we are
manifested as "heirs of God, and joint heirs with Christ."

V. 8. *By faith Abraham, when he was called to go out
into a place which he should after receive for an inheritance,
obeyed ; and he went out, not knowing whither he went.*

" By faith Abraham, when he was called." Abraham
was called of God—by an immediate word of command from Him.
This call consisted of a command and a promise ; the command
was, " Get thee out of thy country." The promise was of a temporal blessing in the multiplication of his seed, and a spiritual
blessing in confining the promised Seed unto him and his family,
in whom all the families of the earth were to be blessed. Abraham
" obeyed " the command ; he was " called to go out," and he
" obeyed to go out." He was called from " out of thy country, and
from thy kindred, and from thy father's house ; " his call is a
pattern of the call of the Church, which consists of believers called
out of the world. **" To go out unto a place which he should
after receive for an inheritance ; "** he received it afterwards in
his posterity as is known. It was given to him by way of free gift,
and so he is said to receive it.

" Obeyed ; and he went out, not knowing whither he

went." This I look upon as a signal instance of the faith of Abraham; on the first call of God he engaged himself unto absolute obedience, without any prospect of what it might cost him, or what he was to undergo on account of it, or what was the reward proposed unto him. And the same is required of us.

V. 9. *By faith he sojourned in the land of promise, as [in] a strange country, dwelling in tabernacles with Isaac and Jacob, the heirs with him of the same promise.*

" **By faith he sojourned in the land of promise as in a strange country.**" To sojourn is to abide as a stranger, not as inheritor, for he had not a foot-breadth in that place (Acts vii. 5); not as a house-dweller, but as a stranger, moving up and down as he had occasion. This was in the "land of promise," that is, that which God had newly promised to give unto him, and wherein all the other promises were to be accomplished. He sojourned in it " as in a strange land." He built no house in it, purchased no inheritance, only a burying place.

" **Dwelling in tabernacles with Isaac and Jacob, the heirs with him of the same promise.**" These tabernacles—tents—were erected only with cords and stakes, so as they had no foundations in the earth; whereunto the Apostle in the next verse opposeth an house that hath foundations. He dwelt with Isaac and Jacob; it is evident that Abraham lived until Jacob was sixteen or eighteen years old; and they were heirs with him of the same promise, for not only did they inherit the promise as made unto Abraham, but God distinctly renewed it unto them both. So we see Abraham's life was one of faith; he had an internal principle of faith; and outwardly he sojourned as a stranger by faith; in both of which he lived in a constant resignation of himself unto the sovereign will of God, when he saw no way or means for the accomplishment of the promise. If we design to have an interest in the blessing of Abraham, we must walk in the steps of his faith. Firm trust in the promises of grace, mercy, and eternal salvation; trust in His providence, with a cheerful resignation of all our temporal and eternal concerns unto His disposal, are required hereunto. But the faith of most men is lame and halt in the principal parts and duties of it.

V. 10. *For he looked for a city which hath foundations, whose builder and maker [is] God.*

This city is the same as the "country" (v. 16); they are heavenly, and that in opposition unto Canaan, and Jerusalem, the metropolis thereof. It is plain that this was the ultimate object of the faith of Abraham, the sum and substance of what he looked

for from God on the account of His promise. This city is said to
have *"foundations;"* these give perpetuity, yea eternity, to the
superstructure, even all that are built thereon. These foundations
are the eternal power, the infinite wisdom, the immutable counsel
of God. Its *"builder and maker is God;"* that is, He built it for
His own habitation, with all that enjoy His presence. Abraham
"looked for " this city, that is, he believed in an eternal rest with
God in heaven, whereon he comfortably and constantly sustained
the trouble of his pilgrimage in this world,—a blessed fruit of faith,
and trust, and hope.

V. 11. *Through faith also Sara herself received strength
to conceive seed, and was delivered of a child when she was
past age, because she judged Him faithful who had promised.*

**"Through faith also Sara herself received strength to
conceive seed."** As Abraham was the father of the faithful, or
the Church, so was Sara the mother of it, so as that distinct
mention of her faith was necessary. By faith she received
strength which she had lost through age ; **"and was delivered
of a child when she was past age;"** she conceived, and
accordingly bare a son, when she was ninety years old (Gen. xvii.
17). And this was **"because she judged Him faithful who
had promised."** When she first heard the promise she considered only the thing promised, and was shaken in her faith by its
improbability ; but when she recollected herself, and took off her
mind from the thing promised to the Promiser, faith prevailed in
her. This is manifest in the especial object of her faith, *" Him
that promised."* She rested upon the veracity of God in the
accomplishment of His promises, which is the proper object of faith.

V. 12. *Therefore sprang there even of one, and him as
good as dead, [so many] as the stars of the sky in multitude,
and as the sand which is by the sea-shore innumerable.*

The blessing here declared is a numerous posterity ; it was a
special blessing, because the whole Church of God under the old
testament was confined to the posterity of Abraham. This blessing is variously set forth ; it was by " one " man ; this sets off the
greatness of the mercy, that so many should spring from one, and
" him as good as dead," being about an hundred years old ; they all
" sprang " from him, **" as the stars of the sky in multitude
and as the sand which is by the sea=shore innumerable."**

V. 13. *These all died in faith, not having received the
promises, but having seen them afar off, and were persuaded*

of [*them*], *and embraced* [*them*], *and confessed that they were strangers and pilgrims on the earth.*

"**These all died in faith.**" That is, Abraham, Sarah, Isaac, and Jacob ; they had all lived by faith, and now he adds that so they *died*. Their faith failed them not unto, nor in their last moments. They died in a firm belief of a future state of existence; also they resigned and trusted their departing souls unto God, with faith of the resurrection of their bodies after death ; and on their thus dying in faith, God after death " was not ashamed to be called their God" (c. xi. 16). Whence our Saviour proves the resurrection of the body (Matt. xxii. 31, 32).

"**Not having received the promises.**" This is none other than the actual exhibition of Christ in the flesh with all the privileges of the Church thereby. So in particular, Abraham's seeing the promises afar off and embracing them is interpreted by his seeing the day of Christ and rejoicing (John viii. 56).

"**But having seen them afar off.**" That is, the things promised ; the word " afar off " respects time, not place ; this kept the Church in a longing expectation and desire for the coming of this day, wherein the principal work of faith and love did consist. They did not see distinctly the whole of what was contained in the promises, but they understood them in general, and diligently inquired into the mind of God in them (1 Peter i. 11, 12).

"**And were persuaded of them.**" To confirm this persuasion God in infinite condescension confirmed His promise and His truth therein with His oath (Heb. vi. 12—18).

"**And embraced them ;** " that is, the heart's cleaving unto them with love, delight, and complacency, which is an inseparable fruit of faith. They knew the actual accomplishment of the promises was a long way off, howbeit they saw that of the Divine wisdom, goodness, and grace in it, that they thrust forth the arms of their love and faith to welcome, entertain, and embrace Him who was promised.

"**And confessed that they were strangers and pilgrims on the earth.**" On all occasions they avowedly professed that their interest was not in nor of this world, but they had such a satisfactory portion in the promises which they embraced, as that they publicly renounced a concernment in the world like that of other men, whose portion is in this life. This renunciation of all things beside Christ in the promise is an eminent act of faith, whereby we walk with God. This world is the home, the country, the city of habitation of most men ; but it is not so with believers; they are strangers and pilgrims, sojourners in the world for a season.

V. 14. *For they that say such things declare plainly that they seek a country.*

They declared plainly ; they made it manifest and evident unto all that they sought for a country, they diligently enquired after it; another country to that from which they came out, a " better " country, which could be none other but a heavenly.   Whereas these patriarchs did thus express their desire of a country, and diligently sought after it, it might be because, having lost their own country, their relations and enjoyments, meeting with the difficulties of a wandering life, they had a desire to return home again, where they might have quiet habitations.   This objection which, if of force, would overthrow his present design, the Apostle obviates and removes in the next verse.

V. 15. *And truly, if they had been mindful of that [country] from whence they came out, they might have had opportunity to have returned.*

That they had no desire to return is proved by the possibility and facility of such a return.   They had opportunity of returning. From the call of Abraham to the death of Jacob was two hundred years, so they had time enough for a return ; beside, it was no great distance ; Abraham sent his servant thither, and Jacob went the same journey with his staff.   It is evident that no opportunity could draw them to think of a return to their own country, and therefore it could not be that with respect whereunto they professed themselves to be strangers and pilgrims.

V. 16. *But now they desire a better [country], that is, an heavenly : wherefore God is not ashamed to be called their God; for He hath prepared for them a city.*

" **But now they desire a better country, that is, an heavenly.** "   They had an earnest, active desire, which put them on all due ways and means of attaining it.   This desire includes a sense of unsatisfiedness in things present ; a just apprehension of the worth of the things desired ; also a sight of the way whereby it may be attained.   Such a desire in any is an evidence of faith working in a due manner.   This better country they desired is heaven itself, or a habitation with God in the everlasting enjoyment of Him.   Heaven is the desire in the bottom of the sighs and groans of all believers, whatever outwardly may give occasion unto them.

" **Wherefore God is not ashamed to be called their God.** "   The privilege granted was that God should be called their God.   " I am the God of Abraham, the God of Isaac, and the God of Jacob; this is My name for ever, and this is My memorial unto all generations."   And this was the greatest honour that they could be made partakers of.   It is true He hath revealed Himself unto us by a more glorious name—"The God and Father of our Lord Jesus Christ;" howbeit by reason of His covenant made with them He is yet known by this name.　And whilst this name stands on record there is yet hope of the recovery of their posterity from their present forlorn, undone condition.　In His not being ashamed to be so called, we see a little of His infinite condescension.

"**For He hath prepared for them a city.**"　This is "the kingdom prepared for you from the foundation of the world;" that is, designated unto you in the eternal counsel of God.　By its being "prepared" is signified the fitting and suiting of that city unto them as the means of their eternal rest and blessedness.　So our blessed Saviour saith, "I go to prepare a place for you;" His entrance into heaven being a prerequisite unto that glorious state which is promised unto believers.　Eternal rest and glory are made sure for all believers in the eternal purpose of God, and His actual preparation of them by grace, which being embraced by faith is a sufficient support for them under all the trials, troubles, and dangers of this life.

V. 17.　*By faith Abraham, when he was tried, offered up Isaac: and he that had received the promises offered up his only-begotten* [*son*].

"**By faith Abraham, when he was tried, offered up Isaac.**"　This instance of faith is such as became him who was to be an example in believing to all that should succeed him; that whereon he was renowned and esteemed blessed in all generations; it is such as nothing under the old testament did equal, and nothing under the new can exceed.　This was that act of faith whereon he had that signal testimony and approbation from heaven: "Now I know," saith God, "that thou fearest Me;" it is enough, thou shalt be put to no more difficulties; walk now in assured peace unto the end of thy days.　God often reserves great trials for well exercised faith.　So this trial befel Abraham when his faith had been victorious in sundry other instances.　So He hath called many to lay down their lives by fire, blood, and torments in their old age.　True faith must be tried; and God proportions trials for the most part unto the strength of faith; and when true faith is tried it will in the issue be victorious.　The trial of Abraham's faith was the offering up of Isaac; the command was to "offer him for a burnt offering," which was first slain and then burnt.　Abraham did not actually offer up Isaac, but he did so in will, heart and affection, and God accepted the will for the deed.　He did as much for the trial of his faith as if his son had been actually slain.　In compliance with the command of God, he shut his eyes as it were against all difficulties and consequents, resolving to venture Isaac, posterity, truth of promises, all, upon the authority of God; wherein he is principally proposed as our example.

" **And he that had received the promises offered up his only begotten son.**" Isaac is called the " only begotten son," though Abraham had other sons, because he was the only son of Sarah who was concerned in all this affair between God and Abraham no less than himself. Abraham loved Isaac; and by the expression " only begotten son " is intimated the conflict he had with his own natural affections. Here then the power of faith manifested itself under all that storm of disorder which his affections were exposed unto; it preserved him against the power of temptations, in an entire resignation of himself and all his concernments unto the sovereign pleasure and will of God. " It is the Lord," prevented all murmurings, silenced all reasonings, and preserved his mind in a frame fit to approach unto God in holy worship. The excellency of the faith of Abraham is set forth by the consideration of his own circumstances with respect unto Isaac, for he had " *received the promises* " from God that " in Isaac shall thy seed be called." He had a promise not only that he should have a son by Sarah his wife, whence he was called the son or child of promise; but also the accomplishment of the promise was expressly confined to Isaac, and that by God Himself.

V. 18.   *Of whom it was said, That in Isaac shall thy seed be called.*

It was so said by God; literally, "In Isaac shall a Seed be called unto thee," that is, The seed promised unto thee from the beginning shall be given in him; and this Seed we know from the word of God was none other but Christ Himself. God promised Abraham a son; in process of time that son is born; and all the truth and benefit of the promised Seed did now absolutely depend on the life and posterity of Isaac; but as soon as he saw and enjoyed the assured means of the accomplishment of the promises, God commands him to take this Isaac, and offer him for a burnt offering. We are told in the next verse the especial working of faith in Abraham in this time of distress.

V. 19.   *Accounting that God [was] able to raise [him] up, even from the dead; from whence also he received him in a figure.*

The immediate object of Abraham's faith was the power of God. Abraham firmly believed not only the immortality of the souls of men, but also the resurrection from the dead, as we see clearly from what is said of him in this text. Abraham still firmly believed the accomplishment of the great promise, although he could not discern the way whereby it would be fulfilled. Abraham reasoned within himself as to how the power of God would fulfil the promise, and he accounted that if there were no other way, yet after he had slain Isaac, and burnt him to ashes, God could raise him again from the dead; "*from whence also he received him in a figure.*" Abraham had fully parted with Isaac: he was no more his than if he had been actually dead; he was devoted to God, and God gave him again unto Abraham.

Let us observe, 1. The privileges and advantages obtained by Abraham on this trial, exercise, and victory of his faith. He had the most illustrious immediate testimony from heaven of God's acceptance and approbation of him; the promise was solemnly confirmed unto him by the oath of God; he was constituted "heir of the world" and the "father of the faithful." 2. Faith obtaining the victory in great trials, and carrying us through difficult duties of obedience, shall have a reward even in this life. 3. Also that if we are the children of Abraham, we have no reason to expect exemption from the greatest trials, but should remember that faith of the same nature as Abraham's will carry us through them victoriously.

V. 20.   *By faith Isaac blessed Jacob and Esau concerning things to come.*

The whole story of Isaac and his wife, and their sons, represents unto us divine sovereignty, wisdom, and faithfulness, working effectually through the frailties, infirmities, and sins of all the persons concerned in the matter. It is certain that Isaac failed in two things: In his inordinate love unto Esau, whom he could not but know to be a profane person; also in not diligently enquiring into the mind of God in the oracle his wife received concerning their sons. As for Rebekah, there is no doubt that she was infallibly certain that Jacob should have the blessing; but her contrivance for obtaining it, when she ought to have committed the event unto the providence of God, cannot be approved.

As to Jacob, he had sufficient evidence that the birthright was conveyed unto him; yet although he followed his mother's instructions in getting his father's blessing, his own miscarriages therein, which are not a few, are not to be excused. Yet with all these mistakes and miscarriages, true faith acted in those that were concerned. We may see it in Isaac; he believed the promise was sure to his seed, and he instrumentally conveyed the blessing by his solemn benediction; though in his own intention he conveyed it to the wrong son, though in matter of fact to the right one. So true faith wrought in Rebekah and Jacob in that they believed the promises did belong to Jacob, though they miscarried in the way they took for obtaining a pledge of it in the paternal benediction.

Isaac's faith was fixed on the promise of the covenant, that God would be a God unto him and his seed, and that in his seed all nations of the earth should be blessed. Faith was acted by the promise, and was guided as to its object by God's providence. Isaac's blessing was "*concerning things to come ;*" and the principal part of it was the enclosure of the Church, the confinement of the covenant and the engagement of the promise of the blessed SEED unto him and his offspring. And it was for contempt hereof that Esau is stigmatized as a profane person.

V. 21. *By faith Jacob, when he was a dying, blessed both the sons of Joseph ; and worshipped, [leaning] upon the top of his staff.*

This act of faith in blessing the sons of Joseph is spoken of as a marked proof of Jacob's faith ; this act seems at first sight an inferior one to the time when he wrestled with the Angel and prevailed, but the thing needs to be looked into, for divine wisdom fixed on this instance of faith. Let us notice then, 1. It was the exercise of faith in old age ; his natural decay did not cause any abatement in his spiritual strength. 2. In this blessing of the sons of Joseph he did solemnly recognise, and plead, and assert the covenant made with Abraham: "God, before whom my fathers Abraham and Isaac walked." 3. He reflects on all the hazards, trials and evils that befel him : "He redeemed me from all evil." 4. In particular he remembered his wrestling with the Angel; "the Angel that redeemed me from all evil, bless the lads." 5. The discerning of the sons of Joseph one from another when he was blind ; the disposal of his hands on their heads, with their respective blessings, were evidences of the especial presence of God with him. From these and many other reasons it is evident that the Apostle for great and weighty reasons fixed on this instance of faith in Jacob, that he "*blessed both the sons of Joseph.*" The other instance of Jacob's faith is that "*he worshipped, leaning upon the top of his staff.*" By comparing the divine writers it is evident that Jacob bowed his head towards the head of his bed, leaning on his staff, indicating the infirmity of his body by reason of his great age, and the reverence of his spirit towards God in this solemn dying act of worship.

V. 22. *By faith Joseph, when he died, made mention of the departing of the children of Israel; and gave commandment concerning his bones.*

Joseph's faith had not forsaken him, it had accompanied him through all his afflictions and all his prosperity, not forsaking him now at his death. He had lived long in glory, power, and wealth,

but through all he preserved entire his faith in God. He by faith
made mention of the departing of the children of Israel out of
Egypt, with respect to that event being the fulfilment of the
promise made unto their fathers. He publicly confessed his faith
to his brethren, thereby discharging his own duty, and strengthening
their faith. He foresaw the bondage and oppression which they
were to undergo, but this did not weaken his faith in the accomplishment of the promise. He said, " God will surely visit you,
and bring you out of this land." And then another particular
instance of the faith of Joseph is this—"*he gave commandment concerning his bones.*" This command was that they should carry his
bones along with them into Canaan. Eventually his bones were
safely carried into the land of Canaan, and were buried in Shechem.
There are some things peculiar unto Joseph, which caused his faith
to act in this way about the disposal of his bones. For, 1. He had
been of great power, authority, and dignity among the Egyptians.
He might therefore have justly feared that if he had not thus
publicly renounced all alliance with them, he might have been
esteemed by posterity as an Egyptian, which he abhorred. Therefore he established this lasting monument of his being of the seed
and posterity of Abraham. 2. He did it plainly to encourage the
faith of his brethren and their posterity, as unto the certainty of
their future deliverance ; so also to take them off from all design-
ing to fix or plant themselves in Egypt, seeing he would not have
so much as his bones remain in that land. Hereby it is most
evident that this holy man lived and died in faith, being enabled
thereby to prefer the promise of God above all earthly enjoyments;
his mind is wholly on the promise, and thereby on the covenant
with Abraham.

V. 23. *By faith Moses, when he was born, was hid three
months of his parents, because they saw [he was] a proper
child ; and they were not afraid of the king's commandment.*

It is the faith of the parents of Moses that is here celebrated.
This birth of Moses fell out in the very height of the persecution
and fury of Pharaoh ; but in the wise disposal of Providence
Moses is preserved, who was to be the deliverer of the people. How
blind are poor, sinful mortals in all their contrivances against the
Church of God. By the faith of his parents, Moses "was hid three
months ; " they concealed as much as possible the birth of this male
child ; and no doubt but, during this season, their diligence was
accompanied with fervent cries unto God, and the exercise of trust
in Him. The outward act of hiding the child was but an indication of
the inward working of their faith. They hid him " *because they
saw he was a proper child ;* " holy Stephen expresseth the force of
the Hebrew word, "fair to God," or in the sight of God. I am per-

suaded that there was something about this child's countenance
that drew the parents into a deep consideration of him, and moved
their minds to endeavour all lawful ways for his preservation.

And more, " *by faith . . . they were not afraid of the king's
commandment.*" This edict of the king lay directly against the
accomplishment of the promise, for it aimed at the extirpation of
the whole race. But the parents of Moses did not fear this ; they
knew the promise of God for their preservation, multiplication, and
deliverance should take place, notwithstanding all the laws of men.
When the parents of Moses could no longer hide the child, they
committed him unto the providence of God in an ark, and waited
for the event of their so doing. And the issue did quickly prove
that they were led therein by a secret instinct and conduct of
divine providence. From which history we may learn that the
rage of men and the faith of the Church shall work out the
accomplishment of God's counsels and promises unto His glory,
from under all perplexities and difficulties that may arise in opposition unto it ; they did so in this instance in an eminent manner.

V. 24. *By faith Moses, when he was come to years,
refused to be called the son of Pharaoh's daughter.*

Moses is instanced as one of those who lived by faith, and an
eminent instance his life was ; none was ever more signalized by
Providence in his birth, education, and acts than he was. The
report and renown of his deeds and wisdom were famous among all
the nations of the earth ; yet this person lived, and acted, and did
all his works by faith. The work he undertook was a great one,
such as had never been wrought in the earth before, and especially
great as typical of the eternal redemption of the Church by Christ
Jesus. Moses was also the lawgiver to Israel, whence it is manifest that the law is not opposite to faith, seeing the lawgiver himself lived by faith. The time in his life that the Apostle now
refers to is " *when he was come to years ;* " in which expression he
calls our special attention to Moses's own way of acting, as in the
verse before he set before us the conduct of his parents, when he
had " become great," that is, fully grown up, and had attained to
the understanding of a man. It was then he " *refused to be called
the son of Pharaoh's daughter.*"

It is probable that, with the consent of her father, she
solemnly adopted Moses to be her son, and consequently the heir
of all her honour and riches. Hereon she gave him the name of
Moses, " Because I drew him out of the water," in which name
God gave him a perpetual remembrance of his deliverance, when
he was in a helpless condition. Moses learned from his nurse, who
was his mother, his Hebrew birth ; and we may be sure that his
parents took care to communicate unto him the principles of true

religion, with a detestation of Egyptian idolatries and superstition. It is a blessed thing to have the principles of true religion fixed in the minds of children before they are exposed to temptations from wealth, learning, and preferment. The negligence of most parents herein is a treachery which they must be accountable for. His refusal to be called the son of Pharaoh's daughter consisted in three things : 1. In the sedate resolution of his mind not to continue in that state whereunto he was brought by his adoption ; this was not attained to without great consideration, with the exercise of much prayer and faith in God. 2. There can be no doubt that as he had occasion he did converse and confer with his brethren, not only owning himself to be of their stock and race, but also of their faith and religion, and to belong unto the same covenant. 3. When there was no longer a consistency between his faith and profession to be continued with his station in the court, he openly and fully fell off from all respect unto his adoption, and joined himself unto the people of God, as we shall see.

V. 25. *Choosing rather to suffer affliction with the people of God, than to enjoy the pleasures of sin for a season.*

These " people of God " owed their relationship to Him entirely to His covenant with them, by which He became their God, and they became His people ; and all the people of God at that time were only a company of brickmakers under hard and cruel task-masters ; therefore let no man be offended at the low, mean, persecuted condition of the Church at any time. The sovereign wisdom of God in disposing the outward state and condition of His people in this world is to be submitted unto. It is certain there is something in this privilege of being the " people of God " infinitely above all earthly things, and which doth inexpressibly outbalance all the evils that are in it. For otherwise men might be losers by the nearest relation unto God, and He would not be an all-satis-factory reward. The Church in all its distresses is ten thousand times more honourable than any other society of men in the world ; they are " the people of God." And we may observe that their being so, and withal professing and avowing themselves so to be, is that which provokes the world against them. The world cannot endure to hear a company of poor despised persons, little better in their esteem than these brickmakers in Egypt, take to themselves this glorious title, " the people of God." Moses chose to suffer affliction with these people ; he chose to cast in his lot with the people of God, and left himself as to his own part and share of suffering unto the guidance of God. And this fell out in the danger of his life, his flight out of Egypt, his long poor condition in Midian, with all the evils that befell him afterwards.

He chose to suffer affliction, " *rather than to enjoy the pleasures of sin for a season*." The best that sin can pretend unto is but present, transitory pleasure. Moses considered the *worst* of the people of God, which is their affliction, and the *best* of the world, which is the temporary pleasure of sin, and preferred the worst of the one above the best of the other. This he did "*by faith*." These two states were divinely proposed unto him, and unto one of them—either the world or the Church—he must associate himself. Some think they may pass their time here without a relation to either of these societies; they will neither join the persecuted Church nor the persecuting world, as they suppose ; but they deceive themselves, for if they choose not the one they do belong unto the other. These two states are irreconcilable ; if Moses cleave to the "*treasures in Egypt*" he must renounce the "people of God;" if he join himself to the people of God, he must renounce all his interest in Egypt. The Apostle proceeds to give us the reason of his choice.

V. 26. *Esteeming the reproach of Christ greater riches than the treasures in Egypt : for he had respect unto the recompense of the reward.*

The thing which Moses chose is here called the "reproach of Christ,"—the same with the "afflictions of the people of God." All the persecutions and sufferings of the Church arose from the enmity between the two seeds which entered upon the promise of Christ. Again, Christ and His Church are esteemed as one body, so that what the one underwent the other is esteemed to undergo likewise. Hence it is said, "In all their afflictions He was afflicted." Again, the sufferings of the Church are called the "*reproach of Christ*," because it is for His sake alone that they undergo them, and it is He alone that they lay in the balance against them all. Again, they are called the "*reproach of Christ*," because the world cannot proceed to afflict the people of God till they profess their faith in Him ; then they are represented at once as heretics, schismatics, and seditious persons ; these reproaches are often the keenest part of their sufferings, hence the Psalmist in the name of Christ complains that "reproach had broken his heart." But this reproach of Christ was, in the esteem of Moses, "*greater treasure than the riches in Egypt;*" gold, silver, precious stones, with all the advantages and profits arising from their possession. He saw the state, glory, gallantry, and power of the court of Pharaoh, and by whom they were enjoyed. He saw also the poor, oppressed, scorned people of God bearing the reproach of Christ ; and faith preferred the latter before the former. Let us go and do likewise, for there is an all-satisfactory fulness in spiritual things, even when the enjoyment of them is under reproach and persecution, unto all the true ends of the blessedness of men.

In all this Moses " *had respect unto the recompense of the reward.*" This reward includes, yea, principally respects, the eternal reward of persecuted believers in heaven, and I doubt not there is also included in this the blessed peace, rest, and satisfaction to be obtained from a comfortable persuasion of covenant interest in God; in the keeping of His commandments there is a present great reward. Unto this reward Moses had respect; he believed it stedfastly upon the divine promise; he valued it as that which was to be preferred above all present things; and he brought it into the reckoning and account in the judgment he made concerning the reproach of Christ and the treasures of Egypt. And this was the victory whereby he overcame the world, even his faith.

V. 27.   *By faith he forsook Egypt, not fearing the wrath of the king: for he endured, as seeing Him who is invisible.*

The Apostle hath a peculiar respect unto what is recorded (Ex. x. 28, 29). " And Pharaoh said unto him, Get thee from me, take heed to thyself, see my face no more; for in that day that thou seest my face thou shalt die. And Moses said, Thou hast spoken well; I will see thy face again no more." Never was there an higher expression of faith, and spiritual courage thereon. Moses went out from Pharaoh " in a great anger ; " he had before him a bloody tyrant, armed with all the power of Egypt, threatening him with present death if he persisted in the work which God had committed unto him; but he was so far from being terrified that he professed his resolution to proceed, and denounced destruction to the tyrant himself.

" *He feared not the wrath of the king;* " and the reason of what he did, and the inward frame of his mind is expressed; " *He endured, as seeing Him who is invisible.*" He strengthened and confirmed his heart with spiritual courage and resolution to abide in his duty unto the end, without fear and despondency. That which preserved Moses in this frame of mind was—" *He saw Him who is invisible.*" Moses had a distinct apprehension of God in His omnipresence, power, and faithfulness; this gave him a fixed trust in Him, that He would protect him and be faithful to him in the discharge of His promise; which is the sum of the revelation He made of Himself unto Abraham (Gen. xv. 1 and xvii. 1). There is nothing insuperable to faith, whilst we can keep a clear view of the power of God and His faithfulness in His promises; from hence we may fetch revivings, renewals of strength, and consolations on all occasions, as the Scripture everywhere testifieth.

V. 28.   *Through faith he kept the passover, and the sprinkling of blood, lest He that destroyed the first-born should touch them.*

The word "*kept*" is of large signification; Moses performed the whole sacred duty of killing the passover, and sprinkling the blood. In so doing, his faith had respect unto its institution and perpetual observance at the command of God, and especially unto its typical signification. It will be well to consider some of those things wherein the passover was a type of Christ. It was a lamb, and in allusion thereto Christ is called "the Lamb of God;" it was taken out of the flock, so Christ was taken out of the flock of the Church of mankind; it was shut up separate from the flock, so Christ was separate from sinners; it was without blemish, so Christ is declared to be a "Lamb without blemish;" it was to be slain, so was Christ slain for us; it was a sacrifice, and so Christ our passover was sacrificed for us; it was to be roasted with fire, which signified the fiery wrath of God that Christ was to undergo; not a bone of it was to be broken, this is expressly declared to be the manner of the death of the Lord Christ; it was to be eaten wholly and entirely, and so Christ is the spiritual food of the Church in the communication of the fruits of His mediation unto us by faith.

And then by faith Moses kept "*the sprinkling of blood.*" This belonged unto the first celebration only of the passover; its use on the institution of the passover was, however, as to its signification, ever present unto the faith of believers. And unto this day we are taught by it that whatever is not sprinkled with the blood of Christ, the Lamb of God, who was slain and sacrificed for us, is exposed unto destruction from the anger and displeasure of God; and that it is this alone that gives us security from him that had the power of death. The end of this institution was "*that He who destroyed the firstborn might not touch them.*" They were all in their midnight sleep in Egypt when this messenger of death came amongst them, and destroyed the firstborn of man and beasts, and this was done at the same hour throughout the whole land of Egypt. But the blood on the houses was a token to Israel that, when the destroying angel went through the land and saw the blood on a house, he would pass over that house, and "not touch" the firstborn of Israel. By this expression we see the absolute security of Israel.

V. 29. *By faith they passed through the Red sea as by dry [land]: which the Egyptians assaying to do were drowned.*

Here we have the end and the issue of the long controversy between Egypt and Israel, a certain type and evidence of what will be the end of the long contest between the world and the Church. Almighty power divided the waters of the Red Sea, and by faith the people passed through; the faith of the few is spoken of as the faith of the whole; the whole passed through because of or by the faith of some. I doubt not but that Moses first entered at the head of the people; hence it is said that God led them through the sea by the right hand of Moses. The Egyptians, assaying to do the same thing, were drowned; it appears that Pharaoh himself, with all the nobility and power of his kingdom, were overthrown, and here came to an end the controversy between God and this proud tyrant. The account of their destruction is given us so gloriously in the triumphant song of Moses (Ex. xv.) that nothing need be added in its further illustration. This destruction of the Egyptians and deliverance of Israel was a type and a pledge of the victory and triumph which the Church shall have over her antichristian adversaries (Rev. xv. 2—4).

V. 30. *By faith the walls of Jericho fell down, after they were compassed about seven days.*

It was at the command of God and his promise of success that they now entered the land of Canaan; here they made their first experiment of the presence of God being with them in the accomplishment of the promise made unto Abraham. They showed their faith by obeying the command of God in compassing the walls of the city, a method of taking it that exposed them to the ridicule of their adversaries; also by the triumphant shout they gave before the walls moved or stirred. The walls were cast down by faith; and there are strongholds of sin in our minds, which nothing but faith can cast to the ground.

V. 31. *By faith the harlot Rahab perished not with them that believed not, when she had received the spies with peace.*

Rahab was a Gentile, an alien from the stock of Abraham; wherefore, as her conversion unto God was an act of free grace and mercy in a peculiar manner, so it was a type and a pledge of calling a Church from among the Gentiles. She was not only a Gentile, but an Amorite, of that seed and race which in general were devoted unto destruction; and she was an harlot; and herein we have a blessed instance of the sovereignty and power of God's grace. She was converted unto God before the coming of the spies, by what she had heard of Him and His mighty works and peculiar owning of the people of Israel. God had ordained that the report of these things should be an effectual ordinance, so as to terrify obstinate unbelievers, as also to call others unto conversion and repentance. Hence those who perished are said to be unbelievers; " She perished not with them that believed not," or " who were disobedient." Wherefore though their destruction was just, upon the account of their former sins, yet the next cause why they were not spared was because of their unbelief. If the inhabitants of

Jericho perished in their unbelief, because they believed not on the report that was brought unto them of the mighty works of God, what will the end be of them who live and die in unbelief under constant preaching of the gospel, the most glorious revelation of the mind and will of God for the salvation of men ? (Heb. ii. 3.)

Rahab, upon the first opportunity, made an excellent confession of her faith; this is recorded (Josh. ii. 9—11); she avows God to be the only " God in heaven above and in earth beneath," wherein she renounced all the idols which she had worshipped (v. 11).   She says moreover, " The Lord your God, He is God," in which she again confesses her faith in Him.   Believing in God, she separated herself from the cause and interest of her own people, and joined herself unto the cause and interest of the people of God.   She also manifested her faith by works ; she " *received the spies with peace.*" This work was accompanied with the utmost hazard and danger unto herself, and this makes her case exceeding apposite unto the purpose of the Apostle, which is to arm and encourage believers against the difficulties and dangers which they were to meet with in their profession.   The fruit of her faith was that she " *perished not.*" After the destruction of Jericho, she dwelt in Israel, and I am persuaded that from henceforth she was as eminent in faith and holiness as she had been in sin and folly ; for it was not for her wealth that she was afterwards married unto Salmon, the son of Naasson, a prince of the tribe of Judah, coming thereby to have a place in the genealogy of our blessed Saviour, and to be a type of the interest of the Gentiles in His incarnation.

V. 32.   *And what shall I more say ? for the time would fail me to tell of Gedeon, and [of] Barak, and [of] Samson, and [of] Jephthae; [of] David also, and Samuel, and [of] the prophets.*

He here intimates that he had already attested the truth by the examples already given, so that it needed no further confirmation. Yet that, if need were, he had in readiness many more examples of the same kind.   All these whom he here mentions were satisfied in their call from God, and so trusted in Him for His aid and assistance.   The work they had to do was the work of God, namely, the deliverance of the Church from trouble and oppression ; this work, therefore, they did with confidence commit to God by prayer.   And herein their faith wrought effectually.   They received many promises from God, some of them very particular and special ones ; and though at first they might be slow in believing them, as Gideon was ; or might be shaken in their minds, as David was, who feared that he would " one day fall by the hand of Saul," yet in the issue their faith was victorious, and they " obtained the promises," as in the next verse.   They are a meet example for our encouragement, for, 1. They were men of like passions with ourselves. 2. The faith whereby they wrought these great things was the same, as to its nature and kind, with that which is in every true believer. 3. Their faith was exercised in conflicting with and conquering the enemies of the Church, and we also are engaged in a warfare wherein we have no less powerful enemies to contend with than they had, though of another kind. 4. Most of these persons mentioned did fall into such sins and miscarriages as to manifest that they stood in need of pardoning grace and mercy as well as we.

V. 33. *Who through faith subdued kingdoms, wrought righteousness, obtained promises, stopped the mouths of lions.*

The Apostle proceeds to declare the things which were wrought by faith, all unto the same end—to encourage us to make use of the same grace on all occasions. It was at the command of God, and in accordance with His expressed will, that they "*subdued kingdoms.*" By obeying Him they accomplished His promises to them; the persons destroyed were devoted to that ruin for their own sins, and their overthrow was for the good of the Church. They also "*wrought righteousness;*" they executed the righteous judgments of God on the enemies of the Church; they also "denied ungodliness and worldly lust, and lived soberly, righteously and godly in this present world;" and they administered justice and judgment unto all that came under their rule, and this they did by faith. They also "*obtained promises;*" that is, they each obtained the things promised them; Joshua conquered Canaan, Gideon defeated the Midianites, and David became king of all Israel. And they "*stopped the mouths of lions.*" He that hinders them from devouring, may be said to stop their mouths. In this sense Samson stopped the mouth of the lion when he rent him to pieces; David also, as we read (1 Sam. xvii. 34, 35). And from this we may learn that the faith that hath stopped the mouths of lions can restrain, disappoint, and stop the rage of the most savage oppressors and persecutors of the Church.

Vs. 34, 35. *Quenched the violence of fire, escaped the edge of the sword, out of weakness were made strong, waxed valiant in fight, turned to flight the armies of the aliens Women received their dead raised to life again.*

"*Quenched the violence of fire,*" as we see in the history of the three companions of Daniel, who by faith so restrained the power of the fire that "not an hair of their head was singed." The faith of these men was considerable; it consisted in their committing themselves unto the omnipotency and sovereignty of God, not knowing what the issue might be. They "*escaped the edge of the*

sword;" it was so with David when he fled from the presence of
Saul ; so also Elijah when he was threatened to be slain by Jezebel.
It is the duty of faith to use all lawful means for escape from
danger ; not to do so, is not to trust in God, but to tempt Him.
" Out of weakness were made strong." It was so with Hezekiah,
" when he had been sick and was recovered of his sickness ; " for
this recovery was through faith, as is evident in the story. *" Waxed
valiant in fight ; "* and this may be applied to Joshua, Barak,
Gideon, Jephthah, and others ; David affirms that it was God who
" taught his hands to war, so as that a bow of steel was broken by
his arms." *" Turned to flight the armies of the aliens ; "* as we may
see in the victories of Jonathan against the Philistines; of Asa,
Jehoshaphat, and others, in all which there was an eminent exercise
of faith, as the history of them declares. *" Women received their
dead raised to life again."* There was the widow of Zarephath,
whose son Elijah received from the dead; also the Shunamite woman,
whose son was raised by Elisha. These ten instances did the
Apostle choose out to give of the great things that had been done
by faith, to assure the Hebrews, and us with them, that there is
nothing too hard or difficult for faith to effect, when it is set on
work and applied according to the mind of God.

V. 35.   *Others were tortured, not accepting deliverance ; that they might obtain a better resurrection.*

The Apostle passeth now unto them in whom faith exerted its
power in suffering ; for to *do the greatest things* and to *suffer the
hardest* is all one to faith ; it is equally ready for both as God shall
call, and equally effectual in both. *" Others were tortured ; "* there
never was any greater instance of the degeneracy of human nature
unto the image and likeness of the devil than this, that so many
men have been found—emperors, kings, judges, priests—who, not
satisfied to take away the lives of the true worshippers of God by
the sword, or such ways as they slew the worst malefactors, have
invented all kinds of hellish torture whereby to destroy them. But
God hath seen fit to permit this, in that patience whereby He
endures with much longsuffering "the vessels of wrath fitted for
destruction." These tortures can shut out no divine consolations
from the minds of them that suffer ; a little " precious faith "
will carry believers victoriously through the worst of them all.
These sufferers did evidence their faith in that they *" accepted no
deliverance ; "* that is, freedom from their tortures, which was offered
them in case they would forego their profession. Our martyrs in
England died on account of the sacrament of the Lord's Supper.
And if we begin at any time to suppose that to save our lives we
may comply with those things God hath forbidden (such as bowing
in the house of Rimmon) both faith and profession are lost. What

sustained these sufferers in their tortures was " *that they might obtain a better resurrection.*" This faith of the resurrection of the dead is the top stone of the whole structure, system, and building of religion ; it is that which gives life unto our obedience and suffering ; without it " we are of all men the most miserable."

V. 36. *And others had trial of [cruel] mockings and scourgings, yea, moreover of bonds and imprisonment.*

These others had experience of " Mockings," " Scourgings," " Bonds," and the " Prison;" they underwent these things, and their faith was tried with them. They were mocked—reproached— with their God, with their religion, with feigned crimes. Mockings are persecutors' triumphs. God may preserve His Church from blood and death, and yet by such things as those the Apostle mentions here, there may be sufficient trial of our faith.

V. 37. *They were stoned, they were sawn asunder, were tempted, were slain with the sword : they wandered about in sheep-skins and goat-skins ; being destitute, afflicted, tormented.*

" *They were stoned.*" Death by stoning was peculiar unto the Jews ; this punishment was appointed by the law for blasphemers, idolaters, profaners of the true religion ; but the impiety of the persecuting world reached such a height that they applied it unto the true professors of religion ; others were " *sawn asunder,*" evidencing the malice of the devil with the brutish rage and madness of persecutors.

They " *were tempted ;*" this may denote a distinct kind of suffering, or what befell them under their other sufferings. In either case, it lets us know how great a trial there is in temptations in a suffering season, and what vigour of faith is required to conflict against them.

" *Were slain with the sword ;*" many have been " beheaded for the testimony of Jesus;" Jezebel slew the prophets of the Lord with the sword ; multitudes of the true Church have perished in this way.

" *They wandered about in sheep-skins and goat-skins.*" These escaped in measure the rage of their adversaries, as unto death ; yet they gave their testimony unto the truth, and through faith bare that share in suffering which God called them unto. Their dress showed them to be poor, mean, and contemptible ; they were poor men wandering about in poor clothing. " *Being destitute, afflicted, tormented ;*" what is principally intended in this word "destitute" is, I judge, a want of friends, and all means of relief from or by them ; and this, as some know, is a severe ingredient in suffering.

This afflicted them, and brought them into real straits, in which state they were tormented, or rather evilly-entreated, all sorts of persons taking occasion to vex them and press them with all sorts of evils. He will be deceived who at any time, under a sincere profession of the gospel, looks for any other, any better treatment in the world.

V. 38. *(Of whom the world was not worthy:)* *they wandered in deserts, and [in] mountains, and [in] dens and caves of the earth.*

To tell the great, the mighty, the wealthy, the rulers of the world that they are not worthy of the society of such as in their days are poor, destitute, despised wanderers, whom they hurt and persecute as the "offscouring of all things," is that which fills them with indignation. Whatever the world may judge of the people of God, His esteem for them is never the less for their outward sufferings and calamities. The world did esteem Christ "stricken, smitten of God, and afflicted," as one rejected of God and man : and such is their judgment of His suffering followers ; nor will they have any other thought of them. But God is of another mind. These people of whom the world was not worthy wandered about in deserts and mountains, sheltering in dens and caves of the earth ; and from this we may learn that, though the world prevail to drive the Church into the wilderness, to the ruin of all public profession in their apprehension, yet it shall be there preserved unto the appointed season of its deliverance.

V. 39. *And these all, having obtàined a good report through faith, received not the promise.*

" *These all* " are all those who have been reckoned up and instanced from the beginning of the world, or the giving out of the first promise concerning the Saviour and Redeemer of the Church, with the destruction of the works of the devil. And all these were " well testified unto ; " God gave witness unto their faith. But none of these " *received the promise ;* " this was the state of the old testament believers ; they had the promise of Christ, the Son of God, in the flesh for the redemption of the Church ; this promise they received, saw afar off as to its accomplishment, were persuaded of the truth of it, and embraced it. The actual accomplishment of it they desired, looked for, and expected, inquiring diligently into the grace of God therein. Hereby they enjoyed the benefits of it even as we. Howbeit they received it not as unto its actual accomplishment in the coming of Christ.

V. 40. *God having provided some better thing for us, that they without us should not be made perfect.*

These " better things" provided by God are, without question, the incarnation of the Son of God, the coming of the promised Seed, with His accomplishment of the work of redemption of the Church, and all the privileges of the Church, in light, grace, liberty, spiritual worship, with boldness of access unto God that ensued thereon. Without these better things they "*could not be made perfect.*" That which the Apostle affirms is, that they were never brought into, never attained that perfect spiritual state which God had designed and prepared for His Church in the fulness of times, and which they foresaw would be granted unto others and not unto themselves. This verse is a plain epitome of the whole doctrinal part of the epistle ; and to close the chapter we may observe, 1. That the Apostle shuts up this discourse of the faith, obedience, sufferings, successes of the saints under the old testament, with a declaration that God had yet provided more excellent things for His Church than any they were made partakers of. 2. It was Christ alone who was to give perfection unto the Church. 3. All the outward glory of the old testament worship had no perfection in it ; and so no glory comparatively unto that which is brought in by the gospel. 4. All consummation, all perfection, is in Christ alone, " for in Him dwelleth all the fulness of the Godhead bodily, and we are complete in Him who is the Head of all principality and power."

CHAPTER TWELVE

V. 1.   *Wherefore, seeing we also are compassed about with so great a cloud of witnesses, let us lay aside every weight, and the sin which doth so easily beset [us], and let us run with patience the race that is set before us.*

" **Wherefore, seeing we also are compassed about with so great a cloud of witnesses.**" These witnesses testify to us that faith will carry believers safely through all that they may be called to do or suffer in the profession of the gospel ; which even we, therefore, ought with all patience to abide in. There may be also some reference to the departed saints looking on and encouraging us in our course ; both these senses are consistent, although I prefer the former. This great cloud of witnesses compass us round about ; they are placed in the Scripture for us to behold ; the recording of those witnesses in the Scripture is the actual compassing of us with them.

"**Let us lay aside every weight, and the sin which doth so easily beset us.**" To "lay aside" is the word wherewith our duty with respect unto all vicious habits of mind, especially such as are effectual hindrances in our Christian course, is described; no one thing is named, but every thing, of what kind soever it be, which would hinder us in our race. We cannot take up our cross to follow Christ unless we first deny ourselves. This laying aside includes a willingness, a readiness, a resolution, to part with any and every weight cheerfully, for the sake of Christ and the gospel, if called thereunto; also a daily mortification of our hearts and affections unto all things which would act as a weight or hindrance. Faith, prayer, mortification, a high valuation of things invisible and eternal, a continual preference of them unto all things present and seen, are enjoined in this word, "laying aside every weight."

"**And the sin which doth so easily beset us.**" I do judge that original sin is here intended, but only with respect unto an especial way of exerting its efficacy and unto a certain end; namely, as it works by unbelief to obstruct us in, and turn us away from the profession of the gospel. This instruction falls in with the rule given us in other places of the epistle, as c. iii. 12. "Take heed, brethren, lest there be in any of you an evil heart of unbelief in departing from the living God." Unbelief exposes us unto all sorts of temptations, gives advantage unto all disheartening, weakening, discouraging considerations, still aiming to make us faint, and so at length to depart from the living God. This sin easily "*besets us*," is ever present with us, and hath a peculiar readiness to oppose all the actings of grace in every faculty of the soul. "The flesh" always and in all things "lusteth against the Spirit." We may observe, 1. That universal mortification of sin is the best preparative, preservative, and security for constancy in profession in a time of trial and persecution. If unmortified sin in any prevalent degree do abide in us, we shall never be able to hold out in our race unto the end. 2. Whereas the nature of this sin is to work by unbelief in departing from the living God, or the relinquishment of the gospel and the profession of it, we ought to be continually on our watch against all its actings and arguings, whereby it clogs and hinders us in our constant course of obedience.

"**Let us run with patience the race that is set before us.**" This race is for a victory for our souls and lives, wherein the utmost of our strength and diligence is to be put forth. Sundry things are intimated by this metaphorical expression: 1. It is a matter of great difficulty, whereunto the utmost exercise of spiritual strength is required. 2. We are to consider the "Rewarder" of them who overcome in this race—which is Christ Himself; also the reward, which is an incorruptible crown of glory. 3. It being a race, it is of no advantage for anyone merely to begin or make an entrance on it. Everyone knows that all is lost in a race where a man does not hold out to the end. 4. This race is "set before us" by God Himself, and this is a source of great encouragement and assurance unto believers. 5. In order to running with success, there will be required strength in grace and diligence with exercise that we may "so run as that we may obtain." 6. We shall need patience; for the race is long, and we are sure to meet with difficulties, oppositions, and temptations in this race; but let us remember that the reward proposed at the end of the race is every way worthy of all the pains, diligence, and patience that are to be taken and exercised in the attainment of it.

V. 2. *Looking unto Jesus, the Author and Finisher of* [*our*] *faith; who for the joy that was set before Him endured the cross, despising the shame, and is set down at the right hand of the throne of God.*

"**Looking unto Jesus, the Author and Finisher of our faith.**" The Apostle leads us from our companions in believing unto the "*Author and Finisher of our faith.*" The Lord Jesus is not proposed unto us in these words as a *mere example* to be considered by us; but as Him in whom we place our faith, trust, and confidence, with all our hope of success in our Christian course. Without this faith in Him, we shall have no benefit by His example. By "*looking unto Jesus*" the Apostle intendeth a *looking off* from all other things which might be discouragements unto us, such as the cross, oppositions, persecutions, mockings, and many such like things. Jesus is the "*Author and Finisher of our faith;*" He is so, as the efficient cause of it; it is "given unto us on His account," He works it in us by His Spirit, in the beginning, and all increases of it from first to last. He is so, as the object of our faith; "grace and truth came by Him," and "by Him God hath spoken unto us in these last days." He is so, by His guidance, assistance, and directions. It is a mighty encouragement unto constancy and perseverance in believing that He in whom we believe is "the Author and Finisher of our faith;" He both begins it and carries it on unto perfection.

"**Who for the joy that was set before Him.**" This "joy" was the glory of God in the salvation of the Church. The glory of God herein is the centre and soul of all His glory; this the Lord Christ preferred before, above, and beyond all things; and that the exaltation of it was committed unto Him was a matter of transcendent joy to Him. And so His love unto the elect, with His desire of their eternal salvation, was inexpressible. These things were the matter of His joy. This joy was "*set before Him*" in the eternal constitution of God, that His sufferings and obedience should be the cause and means of the eternal glory of God in the salvation of the Church; also in the covenant of redemption between the Father and the Son, wherein these things were transacted and agreed; and also in the promises and prophecies, that were given out by divine revelation, from the beginning of the world.

"**Endured the cross, despising the shame.**" He patiently endured the sufferings of the cross; He neither reviled, reproached, nor threatened the Jews with that vengeance and destruction which it was in His power to bring upon them any moment, but He pitied them and prayed for them to the last, that if it were possible their sin might be forgiven them. The shame of this death He despised; that is, He did not faint because of it, He did not sink under it, He valued it not, in comparison of the blessed and glorious effect of His sufferings, which was always in His eye.

"**And is set down at the right hand of the throne of God;**" wherefore we should not think it strange nor fear if we have to suffer on account of our profession of the gospel, seeing the Lord Jesus has gone before us in the conflict with our enemies and conquest of them; and is now set down at His Father's right hand in equal authority, glory and power, in the rule and government of all. In the whole of this we have an exact delineation of our Christian course in times of persecution. 1. In the blessed example of it in the sufferings of Christ. 2. In the assured consequent, which is eternal glory. "If we suffer with Him, we shall also reign with Him." 3. In a direction for the right, successful discharge of our duty; which is the exercise of faith in Christ Himself for our assistance. 4. In an intimation of the great encouragement under all our sufferings, namely, the joy and glory that are set before us as the issue of them.

V. 3. *For consider Him that endured such contradiction of sinners against Himself, lest ye be wearied and faint in your minds.*

Consider this among yourselves, that if He, being so great, so excellent, so infinitely exalted above us, yet "endured such contradiction of sinners," ought not we so to do, if we are called thereunto? The object of this caution is, that "*ye be not wearied and faint in your minds.*" To abide and persevere in suffering, and labour for the name of Christ, is not to faint or be wearied. Wherefore to be wearied or faint is to be so pressed and discouraged with the length or greatness of our trials, as to draw back either partially or totally from the profession of the gospel. We ought to watch against nothing more diligently than the insensible, gradual prevailing of such a frame as this, if we intend to be faithful unto the end. There is spiritual vigour and strength required unto perseverance in profession in the time of persecution; hence we are commanded "to arm ourselves with the same mind that was in Christ;" " to take to ourselves the whole armour of God, that we may be able to stand ; " " to watch, to stand fast in the faith, to quit ourselves like men, to be strong." It is faith that stirs up and engageth spiritual courage, resolution, patience, perseverance, prayer,—all preserving graces and duties. Here lies the beginning of all spiritual declension, in the want of a due exercise of faith in all these graces and duties. The great means of our preservation from this evil frame of growing weary and fainting is the diligent consideration of the Person of Christ and His sufferings. He endured "*such contradiction of sinners against Himself;*" it was "*such*" contradiction; so bitter, so severe, so cruel; whatever the malicious wits of men or suggestions of Satan could invent, that was venomous and evil. It was the contradiction of "*sinners,*" especially the priests, and scribes, and pharisees, who boasted themselves to be just and righteous, and they alone were so, all others in comparison with them being sinners. Herewith they pleased themselves in the height of their contradiction to Jesus Christ. And so it hath been with their successors in the persecution of the Church ; but the constant consideration of Christ in His sufferings is the best means to keep our faith in due exercise in all our times of trial.

V. 4.   *Ye have not yet resisted unto blood, striving against sin.*

In these words the Apostle intimates what they might yet expect, and that is, "*blood ;*" this is the utmost persecution can rise unto. Men may kill the body ; but when they have done so, they can do no more. But I do not think the Apostle absolutely determines that these Hebrews would suffer unto " blood ; " but argues from hence, that as death by violence was part of the suffering prepared for the Church, they who were indulged and not yet called thereunto, ought to take care that they fainted not under those lesser sufferings whereunto they were exposed. It was "*sin*" they had to resist and strive against ; against the sin of their persecutors, for though they pretend other reasons for what they do, yet it is sin acting in malice, hatred of the truth, blind zeal, envy, bloody cruelty, that engageth, ruleth, and influenceth them in all they do. Again, believers have a contest with sin in themselves ; " fleshly lusts do war against the soul ; " and included in this is the sin of defection and apostacy. The opposition against sin in and for the preservation of our profession is described as " resisting " and " striving ; " these are military terms, and indicate there is no room for sloth or negligence in this conflict; and that they do but deceive themselves who hope to preserve their faith in times of trial, without the utmost, watchful diligence against the assaults of sin.

V. 5. *And ye have forgotten the exhortation which speaketh unto you as unto children, My son, despise not thou the chastening of the Lord, nor faint when thou art rebuked of Him.*

"And ye have forgotten the exhortation which speaketh unto you as unto children." What we mind not when we ought, and as we ought, we may justly be said to have forgotten. So it was with these Hebrews in some measure, whether we understand by the " exhortation " the divine words themselves as recorded in the Scripture, or the things exhorted unto. The neglect of a diligent consideration of the provision that God hath made in the Scriptures for our encouragement and comfort under difficulties, is a sinful forgetfulness, and of dangerous consequences unto our souls. The Scriptures are said to speak; which " speaketh unto you ; " in which there are sundry things very remarkable. 1. The Scripture is said to speak, so it is not a dumb and silent letter as some have blasphemed ; it hath a voice in it, the voice of God Himself ; and if we hear not the voice of God in it, it is because of our unbelief. 2. The word which was spoken so long before by Solomon is said to be spoken unto these Hebrews ; for the Holy Ghost is always present in the word of the Scripture, and speaks in it equally and alike unto the Church in all ages. He doth speak in it as immediately unto us, as if we were the first and only persons spoken unto ; and this should teach us to attend unto the Scriptures with reverence, it being the way and means whereby God Himself directly speaks unto us. 3. The word " speaketh " signifies that the Scripture argues, pleads with us, it maintains a holy conference with us. It presseth the mind and will of God upon us. 4. There is infinite condescension in this, that God speaketh unto us in the Scripture *" as unto sons."* This is the representation of the love and authority of God as a Father. And this, if anything, is meet to bind our minds unto a diligent compliance with His divine exhortation, namely, the infinite condescension and love of God, in owning of us as sons, in all our trials and afflictions. God sees us under our afflictions and sufferings, ready to fall into discomposures with excesses of one kind or another, and thereon applies Himself unto us with this endearing expression, " My children."

" My son, despise not thou the chastening of the Lord, nor faint when thou art rebuked of Him." We see in our sufferings, troubles, and persecutions for the gospel, nothing but the wrath and rage of men, thinking them causeless, and perhaps needless ; but they are indeed God's chastisements of us, for our education and instruction in His family. And we are cautioned not to despise these chastenings ; few may fall into the sin of openly despising and rejecting His chastisements, but not to esteem them as we ought, and not to comply with the will of God in them is

virtually to despise them. And we are also exhorted "*not to faint
when we are rebuked of Him.*" Fainting consists of despondency in
our own minds; heartless complaints to the discouragement of
others; omission of our necessary duty; and in judging amiss of
God's dealings with us, either as to the greatness of our trials or
their length, or His design in them.

V. 6. *For whom the Lord loveth He chasteneth, and
scourgeth every son whom He receiveth.*

"**For whom the Lord loveth He chasteneth.**" From
which we observe, 1. That He loves before He chastens; He
chastens whom He loves. 2. Chastening is an effect of love, it
springs from love; wherefore there is nothing penal in the chastisements of believers. 3. The consideration of a state of sin is
required unto all chastisement, for the end of it is to take away
sin, to subdue it, and to give an increase unto grace and holiness.
4. Divine love and chastening are inseparable; there are different
degrees, but none escape entirely. 5. Chastisement where it is not
penal is a broad seal unto our adoption. 6. This being the way of
God's dealings with His children, there is every reason why we
should acquiesce in His sovereign wisdom therein, and not faint
7. No particular person hath any reason to complain of his portion
in chastisement, seeing this is the way of God's dealing with all
His children.

"**And scourgeth every son whom He receiveth.**" There
is something, in my judgment, peculiar in this, which I shall
propose and leave it unto that of the reader. The word "*scourgeth*"
argues a peculiar degree and measure in chastisement above that
which is ordinary, and is never used but to express a high degree of
suffering. By the word "*receiveth*" I understand that some
special approbation is intended. Therefore "every son" is not to
be taken universally, for so every son is not scourged, but it is
restrained unto such sons as God doth specially accept. This
gives a distinct sense to the words, so that they are not a repetition
of the former clause. This truth is of great consolation unto many
of the children of God, for when all must take notice that they
are scourged in a peculiar manner, and suffer beyond most of the
children of God, they are ready to faint as Job was, and David and
Heman, and be utterly discouraged. But a due apprehension of
this, that God gives the severest trials to those whom He accepts
and delights in in a peculiar manner, will make them lift up their
heads and rejoice in all their tribulations.

V. 7. *If ye endure chastening, God dealeth with you as
with sons; for what son is he whom the father chasteneth
not?*

This patient endurance of chastisements is of great price in the sight of God, as well as of singular use and advantage unto the souls of them that do believe; for therein God proposeth Himself as a Father and acteth accordingly; not as an enemy, not as a judge, not as towards strangers, but as towards children. This way of dealing becomes the relation between God and believers, as Father and children; that He should chastise, and that they should take it patiently. The Apostle illustrates this by supposing that every son will stand in need of more or less chastisement; and that every wise, careful and tender father will in such cases chasten his son.

V. 8. *But if ye be without chastisement, whereof all are partakers, then are ye bastards, and not sons.*

Chastisement is for our learning and instruction, and this sort of chastisement some professors of religion may be without absolutely. None of their chastisements, if any, work for their good. But all sons are chastened; therefore if any be without it they cannot be sons, but are bastards; such have no right of inheritance by virtue of their sonship. If we can have no real participation in this inheritance without chastisement, it were a thing unwise and wicked to be weary of it or to faint under it.

Vs. 9, 10. *Furthermore we have had fathers of our flesh which corrected [us], and we gave [them] reverence: shall we not much rather be in subjection unto the Father of spirits, and live? For they verily for a few days chastened [us] after their own pleasure; but He for [our] profit, that [we] might be partakers of His holiness.*

As it is the duty of parents to chastise their children, if needs be, and of children to submit thereunto, so from hence may we be convinced of the equity and necessity of submission unto God in all our afflictions. For so these things are improved by the Apostle. He shows for our consideration the difference between divine and parental chastisements. He by whom we are chastised is the "*Father of spirits*," and that "*for our profit*;" what God designs by the chastisement shall surely come to pass. "Our profit" is "*that we might be partakers of His holiness*;" that is the holiness which He requires of us and approves of in us. This holiness consists of the mortification of our lusts and affections, the gradual renovation of our natures, and the sanctification of our souls; the carrying on and increase of these things is that which God designs in all chastisements. Next to our participation of Christ by the imputation of His righteousness unto us, this is the greatest privilege, honour, glory, and benefit that in this world we can be partakers of, so we have no reason to grow weary of His chastisements. What is required of us as children is that we be " *in subjection unto the Father of spirits* ; " the same which Peter calls " humbling ourselves under the mighty hand of God ; " and this consists of an acquiescency in His right to do as He will with His own ; an acknowledgment of His righteousness and wisdom in all His dealings with us ; a sense of His care and love, with a due apprehension of the end of His chastisements ; a diligent application of ourselves unto His mind and will ; keeping our souls by faith and patience from weariness and despondency ; and a full resignation of ourselves unto His will, as to the matter, manner, times, and continuance of our affliction. Such persons shall " *live* ; " the increase of spiritual life, and eternal life in the world to come, are the things here intended. The rebellious son, who would not submit himself to correction, was to die without mercy ; but they who are in subjection unto God in His chastisements shall live.

V. 11. *Now no chastening for the present seemeth to be joyous, but grievous : nevertheless afterward it yieldeth the peaceable fruit of righteousness unto them which are exercised thereby.*

" *For the present* ; " that is, whilst the chastisement is actually upon us ; whilst we suffer under it ; whilst the wound it gives unto the mind is fresh, before it be mollified by the ointment of faith and submission unto God. This chastening does not seem to be " *joyous but grievous;* " that is, whatever be the good spoken of chastisement, it represents itself otherwise unto us, and we cannot but make another judgment of it. It is not a sweet confection, but a bitter potion, as Peter says, " being afflicted with sorrow, through manifold temptations." But chastisement " yieldeth . . . fruit;" it is not a dead useless thing. When God purgeth His vine, it is that it may bring forth more fruit ; that is, the fruit that is born by righteousness ; none of our sufferings are the cause of our righteousness, but they promote it in us and increase its fruit ; such fruits as patience, submission to the will of God, weanedness from the world, mortification of sin, heavenly-mindedness, and the like. This fruit is said to be " *peaceable,*" and that because it is an evidence and pledge of our peace with God ; also because it brings peace into our own minds, and with respect unto men. " Follow peace with all men." The effect of chastisement may not appear at first, and so the Apostle saith, " but *afterward,*" that is, after we have been " *exercised thereby.*" Now, to be exercised by chastisement is to have all our spiritual strength, all our faith and patience, tried to the utmost, and acted in all things suitably to the mind of God.

Vs. 12, 13. *Wherefore lift up the hands which hang down, and the feeble knees: and make straight paths for your feet, lest that which is lame be turned out of the way; but let it rather be healed.*

" **Wherefore lift up the hands which hang down, and the feeble knees.**" In these hands hanging down and these feeble knees is a description of a man heartless, or slothful, or so fainting in the running of the race as to be ready to cast off all hope of success, and so to give over. Despondency of success and weariness of duty are sure to produce these very evils. This direction to "lift up" concerns others and not so much ourselves; it includes all the duties of exhortation, consolation, instruction, and prayer which are useful unto that end.

"**And make straight paths for your feet.**" To make straight paths is to walk uprightly in the paths of obedience; and so to walk in them that others may see and know that our paths are straight, for this is necessary unto the end proposed, namely, the preservation of others from being turned out of the way, or their recovery from their wandering. The duties especially enjoined in this precept are courage, resolution, constancy in profession, with a diligent watch against all crooked compliances or fearful relinquishment of duties. The enforcement of the duty required is the next thing in this verse. "**Lest that which is lame be turned out of the way, but let it rather be healed.**" The condition of lameness may be extended unto all those who are under the power of such vicious habits, inclinations, or neglects as weaken and hinder men in their spiritual progress. To be " *turned out of the way* " is to be turned off from the profession of the gospel, and this those we have just described are very liable unto. To " be healed " denotes the cure of him that is lame; see that you endeavour the removal of all causes of lameness which you see in others.

V. 14. *Follow peace with all* [*men*], *and holiness, without which no man shall see the Lord.*

"**Follow peace with all men.**" To "follow peace " is to earnestly pursue and seek after it; but we are not to do so by a compliance in evil with any, nor by a neglect of any duty, nor by anything that intrencheth on holiness toward God. We must eternally bid defiance unto that peace with men which is inconsistent with peace with God. That we may do our duty to follow peace with all men three things are required. 1. Righteousness; to wrong no man, to give every man his due, to do unto others as we would they should do unto us. 2. Usefulness; so that in our station and calling, according to our circumstances and abilities, we be useful unto all men in all duties of piety, charity, and beneficence. 3. Avoiding of just offence. The worst of men are not excepted from this rule; " *all men* " includes our enemies and persecutors; only let this be fixed in our mind, that in following peace with all we do nothing contrary to the Word of God.

" **And holiness, without which no man shall see the Lord.** " It is *universal holiness* which is here prescribed unto us, and this we are to follow diligently after, for without it " no man shall see the Lord." This future sight of the Lord doth depend peremptorily on our present holiness ; not as the meritorious cause of it, for be we never so holy, yet in respect of God " we are unprofitable servants ; " but it doth do so by an eternal, unchangeable divine constitution. God hath enacted, as an eternal law, that holiness shall be the way of our coming to blessedness; also holiness is a due preparation for blessedness, the soul being made meet by it to come to the sight of God. Let us observe, 1. They are much mistaken in the Lord Christ who hope to see Him hereafter in glory, and live and die in an unholy state. 2. If this doctrine be true, the case will be hard at last with a multitude of popes, cardinals, prelates, who pretend that they have the opening of the door unto His presence committed unto them. 3. We may follow peace with men, and not attain unto it ; but if we follow holiness we shall as assuredly see the Lord, as we shall come short of this without it.

V. 15. *Looking diligently lest any man fail of the grace of God; lest any root of bitterness springing up trouble* [*you*], *and thereby many be defiled.*

" **Looking diligently.** " This is the duty of all believers, it is an especial institution of Christ to be observed in His Church; the members of which are to watch over one another unto their edification, that spiritual good may be promoted, and spiritual and moral evil prevented. That the practice of this is so much lost in the Church is the shame, and almost ruin, of Christianity.

" **Lest any man fail of the grace of God.** " In the grace of God consists all spiritual mercies and privileges in adoption, justification, sanctification, and consolation. To "fail" of grace is to come short of it, not to obtain it, though we seem to be in the way thereunto. The Apostle here intimates that there were, or at least might be, in the Church those who, under the profession of the gospel, yet through their sloth, negligence, unbelief, or some other vicious habits of mind, might not attain unto the grace and favour of God, exhibited therein unto sincere believers. For this comes not to pass without their own guilt.

" **Lest any root of bitterness springing up trouble you;** " that is, lest any of you depart from the living God through an evil heart of unbelief (Heb. iii. 12—14). This "*root of bitterness*" is apostasy from the gospel, on one pretence or another. This will bring trouble upon you; for it is no small trouble unto them who have the bowels of Christian compassion to see men wilfully ruining their souls, as they do in this case. Such men trouble the Church by wrangling disputes, speaking perverse things, endeavouring to draw disciples after them, corrupting and deceiving, as is the way with all apostates.

"**And thereby many be defiled.**" Oft times whole churches have been ruined by one or more falling away from the truth; the ignorance, negligence, and especially the want of experience of the power of the truth of the gospel of many exposes them to be easily imposed on, and thereby defiled. Spiritual evils in churches are progressive; and church inspection is a blessed ordinance and duty designed by Christ Himself as a means to prevent these contagious evils. The neglect of this counsel is that which hath covered many churches with all manner of defilements.

V. 16.   *Lest there [be] any fornicator, or profane person, as Esau, who for one morsel of meat sold his birthright.*

"**Lest there be any fornicator.**" Look ye diligently that there be none such in your society; if there be any such, let them be removed from among you. The sin is evil unto them, but the communion of their persons is evil unto you. This sin is especially opposed unto that holiness, without which no man shall see the Lord, and it is a sin which men who forsake the gospel do usually fall into. The Apostle doth not here intend such as through temptation may be surprised into sin, but those who habitually live in it. Such are to be excluded from the Church as a certain pledge and assurance of their exclusion from heaven. Under this word fornication the Apostle doth include all sins of the same kind; and those who are given up to such sins are never, or very rarely, recovered from them. Whereas, therefore, the Church doth make a peculiar profession of separation and dedication unto God, in holiness, purity of heart and life, nothing can be a greater reproach unto it than that fornicators should be in its communion. Churches that tolerate in their communion men living in gross sins are utterly, as unto their discipline, departed from the rule of the gospel.

"**Or profane person as Esau.**" A profane person is one who despiseth, sets light by, contemneth sacred things; such mock at religion, lightly regard its promises and threatenings, despise and neglect its worship; and the world is filled with such. There are few in the Scripture concerning whom there are more evidences given of their being reprobates than Esau.

"**Who for one morsel of meat sold his birthright.**"

Esau sold the things that belonged unto him as the first-born; he sold the double portion of the paternal inheritance that belonged unto the eldest son; also the right of rule and government over the rest of the family, and so Isaac said of Jacob, " I have made him thy lord, and all his brethren have I given to him for servants." But especially there was the blessing that from Abraham ran in the patriarchal line, concerning the preservation of the promised Seed. So Esau complained that Jacob not only took away the birthright, but now "he hath taken away my blessing." And though this blessing was not annexed inseparably to the birthright, yet there was a just expectation that it would be conveyed according to primogeniture. It was not his by divine destination, as appears in the issue; nor had he made it his by obtaining an interest in the promise by faith, for he had it not; but in the ordinary course it was his, and in the purpose of his father it was his, and so in his own expectation; but God cut off the line of succession and gave it to Jacob. His profaneness is manifested by the ease and readiness with which he parted with his birthright and all that was annexed thereunto, in that he parted with it on so small an occasion, and sold it at so small a rate as " one mess of pottage " or " one morsel of meat; " in that, without further deliberation, he confirmed the sale with a solemn oath; and in his regardlessness of what he had done after the power of present temptation was over; " He did eat and drink, and rose up and went his way" as a man utterly unconcerned, whereon the Holy Ghost adds this censure, " Thus Esau despised his birthright; " he not only sold it but despised it, and this was his profaneness.

V. 17. *For ye know how that afterward, when he would have inherited the blessing, he was rejected: for he found no place of repentance, though he sought it carefully with tears.*

" You know all this from the Scripture, and therefore let it be of great weight and consideration with you."

" **For when he would have inherited the blessing he was rejected.**" He esteemed himself the heir-presumptive of the patriarchal blessing, and knew not that he had *virtually* renounced it and *meritoriously* lost it by selling his birthright. The event of this was " *he was rejected;*" the refusal of his father to give him " the blessing " is here intended.

" **He found no place of repentance, though he sought it carefully with tears.**" Some think the " it " that he sought carefully refers to the repentance of Isaac, others to the blessing; I incline to this latter, because his cry in the story was immediately for this blessing. This he sought when it was *too late*; he had long before forfeited his right, and had long lived in impenitency; not only so, his brother was solemnly invested with the blessing, which could not be recalled. Neither did he seek it in a *due manner*; he sought it not from God; he sought the end without using the right means of faith and repentance ; and herein lies the folly of most men, they would have the blessing of mercy and glory without the use of the means in faith, repentance, and obedience. Isaac could not, did not, might not change his mind or repent of what he had done in conferring the blessing on Jacob, an act which God approved of.

Vs. 18, 19. *For ye are not come unto the mount that might be touched, and that burned with fire, nor unto blackness, and darkness, and tempest, and the sound of a trumpet, and the voice of words ; which [voice] they that heard entreated that the word should not be spoken to them any more.*

The great privilege of the Israelites was their being taken into covenant with God at Mount Sinai, to be His peculiar people above all in the world ; but in this there was no evidence of God being reconciled unto them ; the whole representation of Him was as a Sovereign and a Judge, nothing declared Him as a Father, gracious and merciful ; there was no condescension from the exact severity required by the law ; there was no promise of grace ; it was a glorious ministration of death and condemnation. In the law God was revealed in all the outward demonstrations of holiness, justice, severity, and terrible majesty ; and men in their lowest condition of sin, misery, guilt, and death. As the Israelites stood under Mount Sinai and heard the law, they represented sinners under the sentence of it, not yet relieved by the gospel ; and this we may have respect unto in our following exposition. We have in these closing verses (18 to 29) a summing-up of the main argument throughout the epistle, which is the excellency, glory, and advantage of the gospel state whereunto they were called. He begins with this.

" For ye are not come unto the mount that might be touched." This was Mount Sinai, a visible, material mountain ; and the Apostle makes this observation to show how inferior the giving of the law was in comparison of the promulgation of the gospel, which was from heaven.

" And that burned with fire." This fire was a distinct token of God's presence, and a distinct means of filling the people's minds with dread and fear. Fire is the first thing men beheld when they came to the mount; and the first apprehensions that men have of God when brought under His law are those of His holiness and severity against sinners, with His anger and displeasure against sin. The law convinces them they are sinners, and in that law God appears to them as fire.

"Nor unto blackness, and darkness, and tempest."

This "*blackness*" that was mixed with the fire increased the dread of the people; it hindered them from clear views of the glory of God in this dispensation; it declared the dread sentence of the law in fire and utter darkness. So it is with the soul under a sense of God's fiery severity in His law; all things are covered with blackness and obscurity. To this is added "*darkness;*" the blackness produced this thick darkness; the glory of God could not be seen by the people; the subject-matter of the New Testament is to show us how this darkness is removed by the ministry of Christ and the gospel, and how the face of God as a Father—as a reconciled God, may be seen. "*And tempest;*" this includes the thundering, lightning, and earthquake that were then on and in the mount. And so does the law raise a tempest in the conscience, and this accompanied by blackness and darkness; but this is the place where Christ interposeth and cries unto sinners, "Behold Me, behold Me."

"**And the sound of a trumpet.**" It was not a real trumpet, but the sound of one, formed in the air by the ministry of angels, and it waxed louder and louder, to show the nearer approach of God. By this sound God summoned the people to appear before Him as their Lawgiver and Judge, for on the sound of the trumpet "Moses brought forth the people to meet with God." Under this dreadful summons of the law the gospel finds us, which exceedingly exalts the glory of the grace of God and of the blood of Christ in the consciences of believers, as the Apostle declares at large (Rom. iii. 19, 26).

"**And the voice of words.**" These words were the ten commandments, when all the people heard the voice of God, and then only. "These words the LORD spake unto all your assembly (speaking of the ten commandments) in the mount out of the midst of the fire, of the cloud, and of the thick darkness, with a great voice, and He added no more; and He wrote them in two tables of stone and delivered them unto me."

"**Which voice they that heard entreated that the word should not be spoken unto them any more.**" This voice heightened their fear and dread to the utmost; they said, "If we hear the voice of the LORD our God any more, then we shall die." So with the sinner now, when he finds God Himself speaking in and unto his conscience he can no longer bear it.

Vs. 20, 21. *(For they could not endure that which was commanded, And if so much as a beast touch the mountain, it shall be stoned, or thrust through with a dart: and so terrible was the sight, [that] Moses said, I exceedingly fear and quake.)*

That which was commanded, and which the people could not

endure, was nothing but the law itself; the interdict of touching the mount was given three days before the fear and dread of the people, and the words of Moses, " I exceedingly fear and quake," were spoken before the people had declared their dread and terror; so these two things are added only as aggravating circumstances of the insupportableness of that which was commanded. The people could not endure the law, and that because of the manner of its delivery, because of the nature of the law itself, and because there was administered with it a spirit of bondage and fear which aggravated the terror of it in their consciences. And these are the effects of the law in the conscience of a sinner. Thus far the law brings us, and here it leaves us ; here we are shut up. The terror of the law extended itself unto the meanest of beasts, and unto the best of men. What Moses said is not recorded in the story, but we are assured here by the Holy Ghost that he did say, " *I exceedingly fear and quake.*"

Vs. 22—24. *But ye are come unto mount Sion, and unto the city of the living God, the heavenly Jerusalem, and to an innumerable company of angels, to the general assembly and Church of the First-born, which are written in heaven, and to God the Judge of all, and to the spirits of just men made perfect, and to Jesus, the Mediator of the new covenant, and to the blood of sprinkling, that speaketh better things than [that of] Abel.*

This is the second part of the comparison, completing the foundation of the exhortation intended by the Apostle. In the former he gave an account of the state of the people and the Church under the law, from the giving of it, and the nature of its commands. In this he so declares the state whereinto they were called by the gospel, as to manifest it incomparably more excellent in itself and beneficial unto them. Whereas the Catholic Church is distributed into two parts, the militant and the triumphant, they are both comprehended in this description. In the exposition of these words we must have respect unto that which the Apostle intends, namely, a description of that state whereunto believers are called by the gospel.

" **But ye are come unto Mount Zion, and unto the city of the living God, the heavenly Jerusalem.**" The sum of the whole of this is that we are called unto a participation of all the glory which was ascribed or promised unto the Church under these names, in opposition unto what the people received in and by the law at Mount Sinai. The opposition between these two mounts was eminent ; for, 1. God came down for a season only on Mount Sinai, but in Zion He is said to dwell for ever. 2. He appeared in terror on Mount Sinai, but Zion was in Jerusalem a "vision of peace." 3. God gave the law on Mount Sinai, but the gospel proceeded from Zion. 4. He utterly forsook Sinai, and left it under bondage, but Zion is free for ever. 5. The people were burdened with the law at Mount Sinai, and were led with it unto Mount Zion, where they waited for deliverance from it.

Believers come to Mount Zion, that is, unto that state wherein they have an interest in and a right unto all the blessed and glorious things that are spoken in the Scriptures concerning Mount Zion,—the place of God's special gracious residence, of the throne of Christ in His reign, the subject of all graces, the object of all promises, as the Scriptures abundantly testify. Believers are said to come also " *unto the city of the living God, the heavenly Jerusalem.*" The state of the Church under the new testament hath the safety, beauty, and order of a city. It is the city of God, of the true and only God, who is omnipotent and able to keep and preserve His own city ; it is the heavenly Jerusalem, for it is not of this world, and no small part of its inhabitants are already actually instated in heaven. It is ten thousand times more glorious to be a citizen of this city than of the greatest city in the world.

"**And to an innumerable company of angels.**" This access unto angels is spiritual ; the access of the people unto the ministry of angels in Sinai was corporeal only, but ours is spiritual, which needs no local access. To them is committed a ministry of service to the Church (c. i. 14). There is a oneness in design and a communion in service between angels and us ; as we rejoice in their happiness, so they seek ours continually; their ascription of praise and glory to God is mingled with the praises of the Church, so as to compose an entire worship.

"**To the general assembly and Church of the First-born.**" There have been various opinions amongst good men as to what the Apostle especially intends by these words ; in my judgment it is most suitable unto his mind and his dealing in particular with the Hebrews, that the whole Church of elect believers then in the world, consisting of Jews and Gentiles, should be designed by him. The collection of the elect among Jews and Gentiles into one body, one general assembly, one Church, is that which he celebrates elsewhere as one of the greatest mysteries of divine wisdom, which was hid in God and not until then revealed. (See Eph. iii. 5—10.) So is this assembly described (Rev. v. 9, 10.), " Thou hast redeemed us to God by Thy blood out of every kindred, and tongue, and people, and nation ; and hast made us unto our God kings and priests,"—that is, one " *general assembly and Church of the First-born.*" This is that Church whereunto all the promises do belong, the Church " built on the Rock against which the gates of hell shall not prevail."

"**Which are written in heaven.**" The Church of God has

in Christ—the First-born—a right of inheritance in all that God
has provided in a way of grace and glory; and their names are
" written in heaven "—" in the Lamb's book of life." This includes
all the elect in all generations, yet believers come in a peculiar
manner unto them of whom the Church of God consists in the days
of their profession.

"**And to God the Judge of all.**" God is the supreme
head of this holy society; and believers have a peculiar access unto
God as the Judge of all, and this is often mentioned in Scripture as
an eminent privilege. They have access unto Him by their justification (Rom. v. 1, 2), and they have access unto Him and the throne
of His grace, with liberty and boldness in their worship of Him.
This none but believers have, and they have it no otherwise but by
Jesus Christ. Considering God as the supreme Judge, men desire
not, they dare not make use of, they cannot obtain, an admission into
His presence, but believers have this favour through Jesus Christ.
In order unto this access there are required the pardon of our sins,
the justification of our persons, and the sanctification of our
natures, without which no man can behold God as a Judge, but
unto his confusion. There is a double consideration of this
privilege of access unto God as a Judge. 1. That He will judge
the cause of the Church against the world, in that great contest
that is between them. It is a glorious prospect for believers that,
however much they may be cast in their cause here, yet God will
execute His righteous judgments on all their enemies. 2. That
God will, as the righteous Judge, give them their reward at the last
day; " There is laid up for me a crown of righteousness, which
the Lord, the righteous Judge, will give me at that day; " and
these are blessed privileges. This is a great part of the pre-eminence of the gospel state above that of the law, that whereas they
of old were severely forbidden to make any approach unto the outward signs of the presence of God, we now have access with
boldness unto His throne. The greatest misery of unbelievers is to
be brought into the presence of this Judge; it is one of the
greatest privileges of believers that they may come unto Him.

"**And to the spirits of just men made perfect.**" These
are they who are in the immediate presence of God the Judge of
all. From which we may observe, 1. That there are spirits of men
in a separate state and condition, capable of communion with God
and the Church. 2. That the spirits of just men departed are all
of them " made perfect." 3. The "just men" intended were all
those whose faith and the fruits of it he had declared in c. xi.,
with all others of the same sort with them from the foundation of
the world. I doubt not but especial respect is also had unto the
times now past of the gospel, and those who have departed in them;
for as they were most eminent in this world, most of the apostles
being now at rest in glory, so an access unto them is very expres-

sive of the privilege of the believing Hebrews who were yet alive.
4. These spirits of just men are "*made perfect;*" they had reached
the end of the race in which they had been engaged, enjoying a
perfect deliverance from all the sin, sorrow, trouble, labour and
temptations which in this life they were exposed unto; having
entered upon the enjoyment of the reward.   Though they are
"made perfect," yet they are no more than spirits; and here we
have a clear view into this part of the invisible world; for it is
declared that these spirits do subsist, acting their intelligent powers
and faculties; that they are in the presence of God; that they bear
a part in the communion of the Church catholic; and that they
are "made perfect." Their faith is heightened into vision, and all
their graces elevated into glory.

"**And to Jesus, the Mediator of the new covenant.**"
What this new covenant is, and how Jesus is the Mediator of it,
hath been declared in the exposition on c. ix. 15—17, as also in
other places, so that it is not necessary to take it up again here.
Jesus is mentioned here in opposition unto Moses, who was a
mediator between God and the people; but Moses was not the surety
of the covenant unto God on the part of the people; he did not
confirm the covenant by his death; neither did he offer himself in
sacrifice unto God.   In opposition to the people coming unto Moses,
—"they were all baptized into Moses in the cloud and in the sea"
—believers come to Jesus the Mediator; and their coming is such
as includes an interest in the new covenant, and all the benefits of
it.   In this then we are principally taught that the glory, the safety,
the pre-eminence of the state of believers under the gospel, consists
in this, that they come therein unto Jesus, the Mediator of the new
covenant.

"**And to the blood of sprinkling.**" The blood of Jesus
Christ is so called in allusion unto the various sprinklings of blood
by divine institution under the old testament.   No blood was offered
but what some part of it was sprinkled; and there were three
special instances of this. 1. The blood of the Passover Lamb.
2. The blood of the sacrifices wherewith the covenant was confirmed at Horeb. 3. The sprinkling of the blood of the great
anniversary sacrifice of atonement by the high priest in the most
holy place. All these were eminent types of the redemption,
justification, and sanctification of the Church by the blood of
Christ.   The blood of Christ is called the blood of sprinkling,
with respect unto the application of it unto believers, as unto all
the ends and effects for which it was offered in sacrifice unto God.

"**That speaketh better things than that of Abel.**" This
blood of Christ hath a voice; and it being the blood of a sacrifice
to God, it speaks unto God.   It speaks—cries, pleads for—to God
by virtue of the everlasting compact between the Father and the
Son, for the communication of all the good things in the covenant

in mercy, grace, and glory unto the Church. It did so when it was shed, and it continues to do so in that presentation of it in heaven and of His obedience therein, wherein His intercession doth consist. Concerning the blood of Abel, God Himself saith, " The voice of thy brother's blood crieth unto Me from the ground ; " but the blood of Christ pleadeth for pardon for sinners, and obtained it for many of them. This is the plain, obvious sense of the words. In this summary declaration of the two states of law and gospel with their difference, and the incomparable pre-eminence of the one over the other, we have three things presented unto us : 1. The miserable, woful condition of poor convinced sinners under the law. 2. The blessed state of believers in their deliverance from the law, and in the glorious privileges they obtain in the gospel. 3. A representation of the glory, beauty, and order of the invisible world. It only remains to consider how we " come " unto all these blessed things. And, 1. By the election of God the Father ; that is His book wherein He enrols the names of all angels and men that shall be of this society. 2. The only means of admission into this society is by Jesus Christ in His Person and mediation. 3. The means on our part whereby we come to this state and society is faith in Christ alone.

Vs. 25—27. *See that ye refuse not Him that speaketh : for if they escaped not who refused Him that spake on earth, much more [shall not] we [escape] if we turn away from Him that [speaketh] from heaven : whose voice then shook the earth ; but now He hath promised, saying, Yet once more I shake not the earth only, but also heaven. And this [word], Yet once more, signifieth the removing of those things that are shaken, as of things that are made, that those things which cannot be shaken may remain.*

These words have many difficulties in them which must be diligently inquired into ; there are four things in them in general : 1. The prescription of a duty, by way of inference from the preceding discourse. 2. An enforcement of the duty and inference from the consideration of Him with whom they had to do. 3. An illustration of that enforcement, from instances of the power and greatness of Him who speaketh, in what He had done and would yet do. 4. An inference from thence with respect unto the law and the gospel, with what belonged unto them.

" See that ye refuse not Him that speaketh." That is, " beware," " take heed ; " this caution is given to shake off all sloth and negligence, from the greatness of their concernment in what was enjoined them. To " *refuse not* " is so to hear as to believe, and yield obedience to what is heard. Whatever is less than this is a refusal, a despising of Him. Hence the Word is preached unto many, but it doth not profit them, because it is not mixed with faith. We must not refuse " *Him that speaketh ;* " the speaking of Christ Himself was now past; but He continued to speak by His Apostles and by His Spirit ; and in this caution to take heed, a rule is laid down that we are diligently to attend unto, and not to refuse any that speak unto us in the name of Christ; and this may be applied unto all the faithful preachers of the gospel, however they may be despised in this world. But here it is the Person of Christ Himself that is specially intended. God hath given command unto all men to hear, that is, to believe and obey His Son Jesus Christ ; this is the foundation of all gospel faith and obedience, and the formal reason of the condemnation of all unbelievers. By virtue thereof He hath given command unto others to preach the gospel unto all individuals. They who believe them, believe in Christ, and they who believe in Christ, through Him believe in God. And so they who refuse them do thereby refuse Christ Himself, and by so doing reject the authority of God, who hath given this command to hear Him, and hath taken on Himself to require it when it is neglected; which is the condemnation of all unbelievers. Unbelief under the preaching of the gospel is the great, and in some respects the only damning sin, as consisting in the last and utmost contempt of the authority of God.

"For if they escaped not who refused Him that spake on earth." He who spake on earth and gave those divine oracles was none other but the Son of God Himself. The Israelites' actual refusal of obedience unto Him that gave them the law began in their making the golden calf, from which sin they did not escape; God said concerning that sin, " In the day when I visit I will visit their sin upon them; and the Lord plagued the people." After this ensued sundry other rebellions, in all which they refused Him who spake on earth. Divine wrath and vengeance overtook them, and this is so fully set forth in 1 Cor. x. 5—10 that it needs no further illustration.

"Much more shall not we escape if we turn away from Him that speaketh from heaven." By comparing these words with John iii. 12, 13, and John vi. 33, 38, it is clear that what is intended here is the revelation of heavenly things by Jesus Christ. He came from heaven to make this revelation known, but yet whilst He did so He was still in heaven—" the Son of man who is in heaven." And now we must enquire what it is to turn away from Him. 1. In the declaration of the gospel by Jesus Christ from heaven there is a call, an invitation of sinners to draw nigh. " Come unto Me " was the life and the grace of the gospel; un-believers are said to " *turn away from Him ;* " which is the posture and action of them that refuse an invitation. 2. There is a dislike of the terms of the gospel proposed unto us. These terms are proposed to us, and such things as are required of us thereon. The former consist of the whole mystery of the salvation of sinners by Jesus Christ; the latter are faith, repentance, and new obedience. Unless we see that which is good and excellent in the terms proposed, we shall not think it worth while to endeavour after the latter. Herein then consists the turning away from Christ in the preaching of the gospel; men like not the terms of it; they account them weak and foolish—unbecoming the wisdom of God; all which the Apostle declares (1 Cor. i. 17—25). And there is no man who upon the call of Christ refuseth to believe and repent, but he doth it on this ground, that there is no such excellency in the terms of the gospel, and no such necessity for his compliance with them, as that it is his duty and wisdom to repent and believe that he may attain them. This is unbelief.

3. In this turning away there is a rejection of the authority of Christ; He spake in the name of Him that sent Him, so that all authority in heaven and in earth was in Him. When we consider the infinite condescension in the declaration of the gospel, by the way of a gracious, encouraging invitation, the glory of the terms proposed therein, with the divine authority of Him by whom the invitation and proposal is made, we need seek no further to justify the Apostle's "*How much more*" in the aggravation of the sin of unbelief as unto guilt and punishment above any sins whatever against the law. It is evident that human nature cannot more highly despise and provoke God than by this sin of unbelief.

4. In this turning away, an obstinacy of refusal is included; it is final and incurable; and such "*shall not escape.*" Let us here observe, 1. That it is the duty of ministers diligently to declare the nature of unbelief, with the heinousness of its guilt above all sins whatsoever. It is here laid in the balance with the guilt of sins against the law, and is here declared to have a weight of guilt incomparably above it. It is not more the duty of ministers to declare the nature of faith, and to invite men unto Christ in the gospel, than it is to make known the nature of unbelief, and the woful aggravation of it (Mark xvi. 16). 2. It is their duty to do so not only with respect of them that are open and avowed unbelievers, but unto all professors whatever; and to maintain an especial sense of it on their own spirits. 3. This is the issue whereunto things are brought between God and sinners, wherever the gospel is preached, whether they will hear the Lord Christ, or turn away from Him. If they hear Him, God puts an end to all the claim of the law against them on account of all their sins; but if they refuse so to do, they are left under the guilt of all their sins against the law, with the unspeakable aggravation of the contempt of Christ speaking to them from heaven for their relief. 4. The grace, goodness, and mercy of God will not be more illustrious and

glorious unto all eternity in the salvation of believers by Jesus Christ, than His justice, holiness, and severity will be in the condemnation of unbelievers.

" **Whose voice then shook the earth.**" The time wherein the Son of God put forth this mighty power was " *then,*"—that is, at the time of the giving of the law. The Mount Sinai was greatly shaken, did " quake greatly ; " and in this we have an illustrious evidence unto the divine nature of Christ, for it is unavoidable that He whose voice this was is no other but He that now speaks from heaven in the promulgation of the gospel.

" **But now He hath promised, saying, Yet once more I shake not the earth only, but also heaven.**" These words are from the prophet Haggai, and our principal enquiry is, what is the shaking of the heavens intended, and at what season was it to be done ? And for the clearance of this we must observe, 1. That the same thing and the same time are intended by the prophet and the Apostle : unless this be granted, there can be no force in this testimony unto his purpose. 2. These things are spoken in the prophet expressly with respect unto the first coming of Christ and the promulgation of the gospel. 3. The Apostle declares (v. 28) that believers do now actually receive what is the fruit and effect of the work here described, namely, " *a kingdom that cannot be moved* ; " before which the removal of the things that were shaken must precede ; which could only be in the coming of Christ and the promulgation of the gospel. The things whereof the Apostle doth discourse are spiritual things, such as end in that unshaken kingdom which believers do receive in this world. 4. Take the words in any sense, and they are applicable to the first coming of Christ ; they had a literal accomplishment in an eminent degree, in the announcement of His birth by an angel from heaven and celebrated by a multitude of the heavenly host ; the Holy Ghost descended on Him in the shape of a dove ; and God gave express testimony unto Him from heaven, " This is My beloved Son." 5. But this shaking of the earth and the heavens is descriptive of God's dealings with His Church, and the alterations He would make therein, concerning which the Apostle treats. It is therefore the heavens of Mosaical worship, with the earth of their political state belonging thereunto, that are here intended. These were so shaken at the coming of Christ as shortly after to be removed and taken away, for the introduction of the more heavenly worship of the gospel. This was the greatest commotion God ever made in the heaven and earth of the Church, and which was to be made once only. This was far more great and glorious than the shaking of the earth at the giving of the law.

" **And this word, Yet once more, signifieth the removing of those things that are shaken, as of things that are made, that those things which cannot be shaken may**

remain." This is the conclusion of the whole argument of the epistle, that all the ancient institutions of worship and the whole church-state of the old covenant were now to be removed and taken away, and that to make way for a better and more glorious state which would never be changed or altered. These things must be moved because they were "*made;*" they were made by the hands of men—the tabernacle, the ark, the cherubim—with all the means of divine service. All these were to be removed, so that things which cannot be shaken might be established. And then we shall yet further observe that although the removal of the Mosaical worship be principally intended, which was effected at the coming of Christ, and the promulgation of the gospel from heaven by Him, yet all other oppositions unto Him and His kingdom are included therein ; not only those that then were, but all that should ensue unto the end of the world. All things must give way ; all idolatry and antichristian darkness which at present seem in so many places to prevail, all things must yield unto the gospel and the kingdom of Christ therein.

Vs. 28, 29. *Wherefore, we receiving a kingdom which cannot be moved, let us have grace, whereby we may serve God acceptably with reverence and godly fear : for our God* [*is*] *a consuming fire.*

"**Wherefore, we receiving a kingdom which cannot be moved.**" Seeing it is so, that the state of believers under the gospel is such as we have described, and the gospel itself whereunto they are called so glorious and excellent, there is great force in the exhortation which is here addressed to them. This kingdom which believers receive, and which cannot be moved, is a heavenly spiritual state under the rule of Jesus Christ, whom God hath anointed and set as King upon His holy hill of Zion. It is that rule of Christ in and over the gospel state of the Church, which the Apostle hath proved to be more excellent than that of the law. Hereunto belong all the light, liberty, righteousness, and peace which by the gospel we are made partakers of, with all the privileges above the law insisted on by the Apostle. Christ is the King, the gospel is His law, all believers are His subjects, the Holy Spirit is its administrator, and all the divine treasures of grace and mercy are its revenue. The especial property of this kingdom is that it "*cannot be moved ;*" the gates of hell shall not prevail against it ; no internal decays shall ruin it ; the spring of it is in Him who lives for ever, and who hath the keys of hell and death. It shall never be exposed to such a shaking and removal as the church-state of the old testament suffered, for God Himself will never make any alteration in it, nor ever introduce another church-state or worship. Believers *receive* this kingdom ; they have it by gift, grant, or donation from

God their Father; " Fear not, little flock," saith Christ, " it is your
Father's good pleasure to give you the kingdom; " they receive it in
its doctrine, rule, and law, owning its truth and submitting unto its
authority; they receive it in the light, grace, mercy, and spiritual
benefits of it; for the kingdom of God is righteousness, and peace,
and joy in the Holy Ghost." All these do they receive in right,
title, and possession according to their various measures, and hereon are properly said to receive the kingdom itself. They receive it
by [an initiation into the sacred mysteries of it, the glory of its
spiritual worship, and their access unto God thereby. They receive
it in its outward rule and discipline; and in all these things they
receive it as a pledge of a future reign in glory.

"**Let us have grace, whereby we may serve God
acceptably.**" I judge that here peculiar respect is had unto the
worship of God according to the gospel, which was brought in upon
the removal of all those institutions of worship which were
appointed under the old testament. To serve God acceptably is
that we may be accepted of God in our worship; the principal
things required unto this acceptation are, 1. That the persons of
the worshippers be "accepted in the Beloved." God had respect
unto Abel and his offering. 2. That the worship itself, in all the
duties of it, and the whole of its performance, be of His own
appointment and approbation. 3. That the graces of faith, love,
fear, reverence, and delight be in actual exercise, for in and by them
alone, in all our duties, we give glory unto God.

To *have grace* may be taken for the free favour of God in Christ,
which we obtain by the gospel; also for the internal, sanctifying,
aiding, assisting grace of God, as set forth in the Scriptures in
places innumerable. To *have grace* is not to be in a bare possession
of it, but to retain it and hold it fast; thus the duty intended
should be perseverance in the faith of the gospel, whereby alone we
are able to serve God acceptably. This then is the great
apostolical canon for the due performance of divine worship,
namely, "Let us have grace to do it;" all others are needless and
superfluous."

"**With reverence and godly fear.**" The sense of these
words may be best learned from what they are opposed unto. Such
as, 1. Want of a due sense of the majesty and glory of God with
whom we have to do. 2. Want of a due sense of our own vileness. 3. Carnal boldness in a customary performance of sacred
duties, which God abhors. Wherefore *reverence* is a holy abasement
of soul in divine worship, in a sense of the majesty of God and our
own vileness. And *godly fear* is a religious awe in the soul in holy
duties, from a consideration of the great danger there is in sinful
miscarriages in the worship of God.

"**For our God is a consuming fire.**" The holiness and
purity of the nature of God, with His severity and vindictive

justice, are represented hereby. The holiness and jealousy of God, which are a cause of insupportable terror unto convinced sinners, driving them from Him, have towards believers only a gracious influence unto that fear and reverence which causes them to cleave more closely unto Him.

CHAPTER THIRTEEN

V. 1.   *Let brotherly love continue.*

All believers have one Father ; one elder Brother, who is not ashamed to call them brethren ; one Spirit, which being a Spirit of adoption interesteth them all in one family, whereby they become "joint heirs with Christ." This is the brotherhood principally intended in the duty of love here prescribed. This love is peculiar in its effects, some of which are pity, compassion, joy in prosperity, patience, forbearance, delight, readiness to suffer for and lay down our lives for each other. Next unto faith in Christ Jesus and the profession thereof, the life and beauty of Christian religion consist in the mutual love of them who are partakers of the same heavenly calling. And in vain shall men wrangle and contend about their differences in opinions, faith, and worship, pretending to design the advancement of religion by an imposition of their persuasions on others ; unless this holy love be again introduced among all those who profess the name of Christ, all the concerns of religion will more and more run into ruin. The very name of brotherhood among Christians is a matter of scorn and reproach, and all the consequents of such a relation are despised. The Apostle exhorts that this love continue,—take care that it be preserved. The *causes* of the decay of this love are self-love ; love of this present world ; abounding of lusts in the hearts of men ; ignorance of the true nature of grace and the exercise of it ; principally the loss of a concernment in the foundation of it, which is an interest in gratuitous adoption, the same new nature and life. The *occasions* of the decay of this love are : differences in opinion and practice about things in religion ; unsuitableness of natural tempers and inclinations ; readiness to receive a sense of appearing provocations; different secular interests; an abuse of spiritual gifts by pride on the one hand and envy on the other; attempts for domination; inconsistent in a fraternity; which all are to be watched against.

The continuance of the Church depends in the second place on the continuance of brotherly love. It doth so in the first place on faith in Christ, but in the second place on mutual love. Where this faith and love are not, there is no Church ; where they are, there is a Church.

V. 2. *Be not forgetful to entertain strangers: for thereby some have entertained angels unawares.*

There was a peculiar reason for this counsel, taken from the then present circumstances of the Church ; it was then in many places under great persecutions, whereby believers were driven from their own habitations and countries. In such cases God makes a double provision for His Church, namely, a refuge and hiding-place for them that are persecuted, and an opportunity for them that are at peace to exercise faith and love, yea, all gospel graces, in their helpful kindness towards them. To be " *not forgetful* " of this duty, is to remember to perform it; and this implies a conquest over those reasonings and pretences which will arise against the discharge of this duty, when we are tried with special instances. In doing this " *some have entertained angels unawares.*" This is usually referred unto Abraham and Lot ; yet I dare not ascribe it unto them exclusively.

V. 3. *Remember them that are in bonds, as bound with them ; [and] them which suffer adversity, as being yourselves also in the body.*

" **Remember them that are in bonds, as bound with them.**" Those who are in bonds are those who suffered for the gospel ; some were in prisons, and others troubled in their name, reputation, goods, and enjoyments. These that are in bonds are the " prisoners of Christ "—an honourable title. It is far better, more safe, more honourable, to be in bonds with and for Christ than to be at liberty with a brutish, raging, persecuting world. We are to *remember* these that are bound, from which it seems that those that are at liberty are apt to forget Christ's prisoners. This remembrance includes a care about their persons, compassion as if bound with them ; prayer ; assisting of them unto the utmost of our ability and opportunity ; visiting of them, which the Lord calls the visiting of Himself in prison. We are to remember them " *as bound with them* ; " this is a union of sympathy, of compassion, and of interest in the same cause.

" **And them which suffer adversity, as being yourselves also in the body.**" This " *adversity* " is to be restrained peculiarly to those evils which men undergo for the profession of the gospel. Believers are exempted from no sort of adversity, from nothing that is evil and grievous unto the outward man in this world ; and therefore ought we not to think it strange when we fall into them.　And whereas we are in the same natural state of life with them, equally exposed unto all the sufferings which they undergo, be they of what kind they will, and have no assurance that we shall be always exempted from them, this ought to be a motive unto us to be mindful of them in their present sufferings. When we are called to suffer, it will be a very severe self-reflection if we must charge ourselves with want of due compassion and fellow-suffering with those who were 'n that condition before us.

V. 4.　*Marriage [is] honourable in all, and the bed undefiled : but whoremongers and adulterers God will judge.*

There is no sort, order, or degree of men, by reason of any calling, work, or employment, but that marriage is an honourable state in them, and unto them, when they are lawfully called thereunto.　This is the plain sense of the words, as both their signification and occasion in this place do manifest.　The state of marriage being honourable in the sight of God Himself, it is the duty of them that enter thereinto duly to consider how they may approve their consciences unto God in what they do.　This state being of God's appointment, prayer for and expectation of His blessing on it, reverence of Him as the great witness of the marriage covenant, with wisdom to undergo the trials and temptations inseparable from it, are required of them that enter into it.　Violations of the seventh commandment in any of their various forms do expose men in a special way to the judgment of God : " *God will judge*," that is, execute divine vengeance upon them ; men living and dying impenitently in these sins shall eternally perish.

V. 5.　*[Let your] conversation [be] without covetousness ; [and be] content with such things as ye have : for He hath said, I will never leave thee, nor forsake thee.*

"Let your conversation be without covetousness."
" *Conversation* " here includes both the frame of our minds and the manner of our acting, as unto the morality of it, in all that we do about the things appertaining unto this life.　The order of our conversation aright in this matter is of great importance in our Christian profession.　Covetousness is an inordinate desire with a suitable endeavour after the enjoyment of more riches than we have, or than God is pleased to give unto us, proceeding from an undue valuation of them, or love unto them.　"Covetousness is idolatry " (Col. iii. 15) ; not only doth it fill the minds of men with perplexing anxieties, but it plungeth them into eternal perdition. Of this sin there may be various degrees ; where it is predominant it will exclude from life and salvation ; where it is present in believers it will be a subject of mortification all their days.

Covetousness in any degree is highly dangerous in a time of persecution or suffering for the gospel ; and it is with respect unto such seasons that we are here warned against it.

" **And be content with such things as ye have.** " This contentment is a gracious frame or disposition of mind, without complaining or repining at God's disposal of our outward concerns, and without envy at the more prosperous condition of others; also without fears and anxious cares about future supplies. " I have learned," saith the Apostle in one place, " in whatsoever state I am, therewith to be content." " Having food and raiment, let us therewith be content; " not that we are to allow discontent if we lack them, but these are a sufficiency unto a rational obligation to contentment. But among other evils that we may undergo for the gospel, we may be called unto " hunger and nakedness ; " and when we are so we are obliged to be therewithal content.

" **For He hath said, I will never leave thee nor forsake thee.** " All the efficacy, power, and comfort of divine promises arise from, and are resolved into, the excellencies of the divine nature. He hath said it who is Truth, and cannot deceive ; He who is Almighty, the supreme disposer of all things in heaven and earth, in whose hand and power are all the concerns of men. What He hath said is unto this purpose, " *I will never leave thee nor forsake thee.* " There is a vehement negation in this last clause, the design of which is to obviate all objections which fear and unbelief may raise against the assurance given. This promise was made to Solomon by David in the name of God (1 Chron. xxviii. 20) ; it was also expressly made to Joshua (Josh. i. 5). From the use made here of this promise we may learn, that all the promises made unto the Church, and every particular member of it, are made equally unto the whole Church and every member of it, in every age according as the mercy and grace of them is suited unto their state and condition. Faith sets every believer in the room or place of him or them to whom the promises were originally made. If " whatsoever things were written aforetime were written for our learning, that we through patience and comfort of the Scripture might have hope," much more are the promises recorded therein for our use and benefit. Herein lies the force of the Apostle's argument, that if God hath said to each of us what He said unto Joshua, that He will " *never leave* " us as to His presence, " *nor forsake* " us as to His assistance, we have sufficient ground to cast away all inordinate desires of earthly things, and to rest quiet and contented with His undertaking for us.

V. 6. *So that we may boldly say, The Lord* [*is*] *my helper, and I will not fear what man shall do unto me.*

These words are taken from Ps. cxviii. 6. " The Lord is on my side, I will not fear what man can do unto me." It is evident that David, in uttering these words, did use a more than ordinary boldness and confidence in God. We are to " say " what we believe, to profess it, yea, to glory and make our boast in God, against all opposition. The Word of God or the promises contained therein, which are common to all believers, was the ground of what David said and professed ; " In God will I praise His word." Believers, having the same grounds of it that he had, may use the same confidence that he did. The most effectual means to encourage our souls in all our sufferings is to compare the power of God, who will assist us, with that of man, who doth oppress us.

V. 7. *Remember them which have the rule over you, who have spoken unto you the word of God ; whose faith follow, considering the end of [their] conversation.*

" **Remember them which have the rule over you, who have spoken unto you the word of God.**" It is evident that the Apostle intends here all that had spoken or preached the word of God unto them, whether apostles, evangelists, or pastors, who had now finished their course ; and we are to remember them in what they did and taught, so as to follow them in their faith and conversation ; and this is a duty of no small advantage unto us. This ought to be the care of the guides of the Church, to leave such an example of faith and holiness, as that it may be the duty of the Church to remember them and follow their example. These their guides had spoken unto them the word of God ; this speaking may include the apostolical writings as well as their vocal preaching. What they wrote, what they taught by divine revelation, what others taught out of their writings and other Scriptures, is this word of God.

" **Whose faith follow, considering the end of their conversation.**" To follow their faith is to " imitate " it ; and this may be viewed *objectively*, for the faith which they taught, believed, and professed ; also *subjectively*, for the grace of faith in them whereby they believed the truth ; and it is in this latter sense the word is to be specially understood here. It was that faith whereby they glorified God in all that they did and suffered for the name of Jesus Christ. No mere man, not the best of men, is to be our pattern absolutely—this honour is due to Christ alone—but they may be so, and we ought to make them so, with respect unto those graces and duties wherein they were eminent. The motive given for following their faith is, the "*end of their conversation.*" They have finished their course in this world ; they had come to the end of it, and this is not merely " the end " that is intended, but an end accompanied with a deliverance from, and so a conquest over, the difficulties and dangers to which they had been exposed.

These guides are to be remembered, their faith followed, and the end of their conversation considered, and this by a repeated contemplation of the matter, with its causes and circumstances.

V. 8.   *Jesus Christ, the same yesterday, and to-day, and for ever.*

Jesus Christ hath many expressions in the Scripture concerning Him. "He was in the beginning; He was with God; He was God; His goings forth are from of old, from everlasting." By these and such expressions, and those used by the Apostle in this place, is denoted the eternity and immutability of Christ; to the same purpose He is said to be "He who is, and who was, and who is to come." He is, He ever was, all in all unto His Church. He is "*the same*," the author, the object, the finisher of faith, the preserver and rewarder of all them that believe, and that equally in all generations. As Jesus Christ had given a blessed end to them that had gone before, so would He give a blessed end to them who followed their faith and obedience; as though the Apostle said, "You shall find Christ unto you what He was unto them."

V. 9.   *Be not carried about with divers and strange doctrines.   For [it] is a good thing that the heart be established with grace; not with meats, which have not profited them that have been occupied therein.*

"**Be not carried about with divers and strange doctrines.**" These divers and strange doctrines were things foreign to the gospel, things that were opposed to the nature and genius of the gospel.   Such are all doctrines about religious ceremonies and the scrupulous observation of them, for "the kingdom of God is not meat and drink, but righteousness, joy, and peace in the Holy Ghost." Where such doctrines are entertained, they make men double-minded, unstable, turning from the truth, drawing them at length into perdition. The ruin of the Church in after ages arose from the neglect of this apostolical caution, in giving heed to divers and strange doctrines, which at length overthrew and excluded the fundamental doctrines of the gospel. And herein lies the safety of all believers and all churches, namely, to keep themselves precisely unto the first complete revelation of divine truth in the Word of God. Let men pretend what they will, and bluster what they please, in an adherence unto this principle we are safe; and if we depart from it, we shall be hurried and carried about through innumerable uncertainties unto ruin.

"**For it is a good thing that the heart be established with grace, not with meats, which have not profited them that have been occupied therein.**" To have the heart established, is to have it confirmed by a fixed persuasion in the truth, and that the heart through the truth do enjoy peace with God, which alone will establish it. The heart is thus "*established by grace*,"—the grace of God in Christ Jesus for the justification and sanctification of the Church as it is revealed in the gospel. Grace is to be considered here as in opposition unto the works of the law, and the observance of Mosaical rites. "*Not by meats*," by which word is intended the whole system of Mosaical institutions, but expressed by the word "meats" because of their immediate relation unto the altar, of which the Apostle designs to speak. The Jews laid great stress upon meats, upon the different kinds of meats, those that were lawful and those that were unlawful to eat; and these distinctions arose from the altar; for what was prohibited the altar was unclean, and the Jews would suffer the cruellest tortures rather than eat anything unclean. Hence we may see why they laid so much stress upon meats, because the taking away of all distinctions between meats did declare that their altar, which was the life and centre of their religion, was of no more use. So far as the Jews made these meats to be trusted in as a means of acceptance with God they did "*not profit them*," indeed they were pernicious unto them. They were insufficient to do for them what grace alone could do.

V. 10. *We have an altar, whereof they have no right to eat which serve the tabernacle.*

"*We have*," we who believe in Christ according to the gospel, and worship God in spirit and truth, we also "*have an altar;*" we have everything in the substance, whereof they of old had only the name and the shadow. The altar which we now have is Christ alone and His sacrifice, for He was Priest, altar and sacrifice, all in Himself. The Apostle doth declare who and what it is that he intends by the altar which we have, namely, that it is Jesus, who to sanctify the people with His blood, which was to be done at or on the altar, "suffered without the gate " (v. 12) ; and by Him, as our altar, we are to offer our sacrifices unto God (v. 15).

The sacrifices which we are obliged unto by virtue of this altar are such as have no respect unto any material altar, but are such as are to be offered unto God through Christ alone, namely, "the sacrifice of praise," which is the "fruit of our lips, confessing unto His name," which leads us off all thoughts and conceptions of any material altar. Sinners under a sense of guilt have in the gospel an altar of atonement, whereunto they have continual access for the expiation of their sins. HE is the Propitiation. There are some who are excluded from this altar, they are those who "*serve the tabernacle*." The priests under the old testament had the right to eat of the things of the temple, and they that wait at the

altar, partake with the altar. This right, or any other of an alike
nature, they had not, to eat of that altar which we have. He doth
not absolutely exclude such persons from ever attaining an interest
in our altar; but they had no such right by virtue of their office
and relation unto the tabernacle, and whilst they adhered unto
their privileges of the tabernacle and the use of meats thereby for
the establishment of their hearts in peace with God, they could
have no interest in this altar that "*we have.*"

V. 11. *For the bodies of those beasts, whose blood is
brought into the sanctuary by the high priest for sin, are
burnt without the camp.*

The sacrifice here intended is the sin-offering on the great day
of atonement, for it was the blood of that sacrifice alone that was
carried into the most holy place by the high priest; and the bodies
of the beasts whose blood was offered on that day were burned with
fire, without the camp. There are sundry things to be observed as
unto the design of the Apostle in this place. 1. This sin-offering
on the day of atonement was the principal type of Christ and His
sacrifice among all the sacrifices of the law. 2. That the matter
of this sacrifice was wholly devoted, as that which had all the sins
and uncleannesses of the Church upon it. 3. That in this sacrifice
there was no eating, no meats, or distinction of them or privilege
about them—all was consumed. Hence the Apostle proves that
meats did never contribute anything toward the establishment of
the heart before God. For there was no use of them in or about
that sacrifice whereby atonement was made for sin, whereon the
establishment of the heart doth depend.

V. 12. *Wherefore Jesus also, that He might sanctify the
people with His own blood, suffered without the gate.*

This is the altar we have, this is the sacrifice on the altar, and
this is the effect of it—the sanctification of the people. There are
sundry truths of great importance in these words, the consideration
of which will give us the true exposition of them. 1. That Jesus
did in His sufferings offer Himself unto God. 2. That He offered
Himself a sin-offering, in answer in a peculiar way to the sin-
offering on the day of atonement. 3. The end of this offering was
"that He might sanctify the people," that is, all the elect of God,
both Jews and Gentiles. 4. This sanctification of the people
Christ accomplished, when He made an atonement for their sins,
and obtained an acquitment from the defilement of it, as separating
from the favour of God, and a sacred dedication of them unto God.
5. And this He did "*with His own blood;*" in this we see His blood
placed in opposition to the blood of beasts; also an evidence of the

unspeakable worth and value of this offering, whereon all its efficacy doth depend; also a testimony of what it cost the Lord Jesus to sanctify the people, even His own blood.

The last thing in this text is the circumstance of His suffering "*without the gate.*" From which we may observe, 1. That He left the city and church-state of the Jews; whence He denounced their destruction as He went out of the gate (Luke xxiii. 28—30). 2. He put an end unto all sacrificing in the city and the temple as unto divine acceptation; all was now finishing. 3. He declared that His sacrifice and the benefits of it were extended to the whole world. 4. He declared that His suffering and death were not only a sacrifice, but a punishment for sin, for the sins of those that were to be sanctified by His blood. He went out of the city as a male-factor, and died the death which by divine institution was a sign of the curse. From these things we may learn that, when the Lord Jesus carried all the sins of His own people in His own body unto the tree, He left the city, as a type of all believers, under the wrath and curse of God; and going out of the city as a malefactor, He bore all the reproach that was due to the sins of the Church; which was a part of the curse.

V. 13. *Let us go forth therefore unto Him without the camp, bearing His reproach.*

To suffer "without the gate" and to be "without the camp," are one and the same place. To be in the camp, is to have a right unto all the privileges of the commonwealth of Israel and the service of the tabernacle. The Apostle now shows them that by the suffering of Christ without the camp, that they were called upon to forego, part with, and renounce all the privileges and advantages which are inconsistent with an interest in Christ and a participation of Him. This going forth after Him and unto Him denotes a relinquishment of all the privileges of the camp and city for His sake; a closing by faith with His sacrifice and sancti-fication thereby in opposition unto all the sacrifices of the law; also the owning of Him under all that reproach and contempt which were cast upon Him in His suffering without the gate, or a not being ashamed of His cross; also the betaking ourselves unto Him in His office as the King, Priest, and Prophet of the Church, as unto our acceptance with God and in His worship. In doing this we are to *bear His reproach*. This, in brief, is either the reproach that was cast on His person, or the reproach that is cast on our persons for His sake. In these things consist the first general duties of our Christian profession, which we are called and directed unto by His offering Himself and the manner of it, namely: 1. In a separation from all ways of religious worship not appointed by Himself. 2. In a relinquishment of all civil and political privileges which are inconsistent with the profession of the gospel. 3. In avowing the wisdom, grace, and power of God in the cross, notwithstanding the reproaches that are cast upon it. 4. In giving up ourselves unto Him in the discharge of His whole office towards the Church. 5. In conformity unto Him in self-denial and suffering. The sum of all which is that we must leave all to go forth unto a crucified Christ.

V. 14. *For here have we no continuing city, but we seek one to come.*

The Jews under the Mosaic dispensation had a city—Jerusalem, which was the seat of divine worship; but believers have no such city; they " *seek one to come;* " that city which is to be their eternal habitation. This city is prepared for them (chap. xi. 16), and is promised unto them, and the way to it is now laid open and made plain by Jesus Christ.

V. 15. *By Him therefore let us offer the sacrifice of praise to God continually, that is, the fruit of* [*our*] *lips giving thanks to His name.*

" **By Him therefore let us offer the sacrifice of praise to God continually ;** " Christ sanctifies and dedicates our persons unto God ; He " sanctifieth the people with His own blood; " and makes us " priests unto God,"—" an holy priesthood, to offer up spiritual sacrifices acceptable unto God by Him ; " He hath made a way for our access with boldness unto the holy place, where we may offer these sacrifices ; He " beareth the iniquity of our holy things," and makes our offerings acceptable through His merit and intercession. And it is " *by Him* " alone, and not by angels, or saints, or the Virgin Mary, for they are not our altar, neither did they sanctify us by their blood. These offerings are the "*sacrifice of praise;* " the Apostle describes it elsewhere as " presenting our bodies a living sacrifice, holy, acceptable unto God," as " our reasonable service." And this sacrifice is to be offered " *continually;* " from which word we learn that we have now freedom from appointed times, and seasons, and places ; also that we are to observe diligence and perseverance in attending to and abiding in such exercise.

" **That is, the fruit of our lips giving thanks to His name.** " This is the same duty as that described in Hos. xiv. 3, " the calves of our lips; " praise unto God is intended by both these expressions. The Apostle here declares that the vocal thanks-givings of believers in celebrating the praise of God shall succeed the vows and thank-offerings of calves and other beasts as insti-tuted by the law. " *Giving thanks to His name,*"—that is, confessing and making solemn acknowledgment of the wisdom, love, grace, and goodness of God in the redemption of the Church by Jesus Christ.

V. 16.   *But to do good and to communicate forget not; for with such sacrifices God is well pleased.*

Unto the former duties add this also.   To " *do good* " is " well doing," and concerns the whole course of our lives; " patient continuance in well doing " is the life of a believer, and this we are warned not to be weary of, nor faint in (Gal. vi. 9).   This " well doing " consists in a gracious readiness of mind to do good unto all; an acting of this inclination in all ways and things, spiritual and temporal, whereby we may be useful and helpful unto mankind; and the embracing of all opportunities for the exercise of pity, compassion, and lovingkindness in the earth.   To " *communicate* " is to distribute of the good things we enjoy unto others, as their necessities may require.   Thus the very world itself—even those who believe not—doth receive great advantage by the grace administered by the death of Christ and the fruits thereof.   And " *with such sacrifices God is well pleased;* " by this the Apostle doth confirm the cessation of all other sacrifices in the Church.   These works of faith are an especial pleasure unto God; and this being made known to us is the most effectual motive unto our diligence in them; for the promise of acceptance gives life to obedience. And from this we may learn that the works and duties which are peculiarly useful unto men are peculiarly acceptable unto God.

V. 17.   *Obey them that have the rule over you, and submit yourselves: for they watch for your souls, as they that must give account, that they may do it with joy, and not with grief: for that [is] unprofitable for you.*

" **Obey them that have rule over you, and submit your-selves.** "   Those who rule are those who guide, feed, or lead you with authority, or by virtue of their office.   It is with respect unto their teaching, preaching, or pastoral feeding, that they are commanded to obey them; to obey their doctrine, and submit to their rule.   It is not a blind, implicit obedience and subjection that is here prescribed; a pretence hereof hath been abused to the ruin of the souls of men.   If those who suppose themselves to be in office as guides of others do teach and enjoin things that belong not unto their office, there is no obedience due unto them by virtue of this command.   So is it with the guides of the Church of Rome, who, under a pretence of their office, give commands in secular things, no way belonging unto the ministry of the gospel.   It is our duty only to obey our guides whilst they teach the things which

the Lord Christ hath appointed them to teach, and to submit to
their rule whilst it is exercised in the name of Christ, according to
His institution and by the rule of His word. The ground of this
duty is taken from the office of these guides and rulers, " *they watch
for your souls, as they that must give account.*"

" *Obey them*   .   .   .   *for they watch.*"   The Apostle compresseth
herein the whole duty of the pastoral office, with the manner of its
discharge, and this latter is what he principally intends here ; they
watch with design, care, and diligence against troubles, dangers,
and oppositions, as those who " must give account."   Although
the last great account which all Church guides must give of their
stewardship may be intended, yet the present account which they
give every day to Jesus Christ of the work committed to them is
also included.   If the flock thrive and flourish and go on to perfection, this they give Him an account of, blessing Him for the work of
His Spirit and grace among them.   If they are diseased, unthrifty,
fallen into decays, or do any way miscarry themselves, therein also
they give an account unto Jesus Christ ; they spread it before Him,
mourning with grief and sorrow.

Much of the life of the ministry and benefit of the Church
depends on the continual giving an account unto Christ by prayer
and thanksgiving of the state of the Church and the success of
the Word therein.   It is a matter of the greatest joy unto pastors
when they find the souls of them committed unto their charge
thriving under their ministry.   It was so with the Apostles themselves.   " I have no greater joy than to hear that my children walk
in truth," saith one of them ; and another saith, " What is our
hope, or joy, or crown of rejoicing ?   Are not even ye in the
presence of our Lord Jesus Christ at His coming ?   For ye are our
glory and joy."   And when they give their account with praise, it
fills their hearts with joy in a peculiar manner ; and this on many
accounts is " *profitable* " for the Church, for they will quickly find
the effects of the joy of their guides by the cheerful discharge of
their ministry, and in tokens of Christ being well pleased with
them.   On the other hand, the sadness of ministers of the gospel
upon the unprofitableness of the people under their ministry, or
miscarriages of them with respect unto Church order and rule, is
not easy to be expressed.   With what sighing, groaning, and mourning their accounts unto Christ are accompanied He alone knows,
and the last day will manifest.

Vs. 18, 19.   *Pray for us : for we trust we have a good
conscience, in all things willing to live honestly.   But I
beseech* [*you*] *the rather to do this, that I may be restored to
you the sooner.*

The request for their prayers argues a confidence in their faith and mutual love, without which he would not have requested their prayers. And he grants that the prayers of the meanest saints. may be useful unto the greatest Apostle, both with respect unto his person and the discharge of his office. He tells them that he trusts he had a good conscience; not implying any doubt about it, but he speaks of himself with modesty and humility, even in things whereof he had the highest assurance. By a " *good conscience*" he means " a conscience void of offence toward God and man," as he expresseth himself elsewhere. A sense thereof gives a due confidence both in our persons and in our requests unto others for their prayers for us. The testimony of his conscience was that he was " *willing to live honestly.*" This honest living denotes a " beauty in conversation ; " this was the design of the Apostle in all things, and ought to be so for all ministers of the gospel, both for their own sakes, as also that they may be examples unto the people.

In this 19th verse some few things may be observed. 1. He had been with them formerly. 2. He desires to be restored unto them, that they might have the benefit of his ministry and he the comfort of their faith and obedience. 3. He is earnest in this desire, and therefore the more urgent in requesting their prayers. 4. He knew that the Lord Christ did dispense the affairs of the Church much according to their prayers, unto His own glory and their consolation. 5. It is uncertain whether ever this desire of his was accomplished or no, for this epistle was written after the close of the apostolical story in the Acts. 6. According to our present apprehensions of duty, we may lawfully have earnest desires after, and pray for such things as shall not come to pass, for the secret purposes of God are not the rule of our prayers.

Vs. 20, 21. *Now the God of peace, that brought again from the dead our Lord Jesus, that great Shepherd of the sheep, through the blood of the everlasting covenant, make you perfect in every good work to do His will, working in you that which is well-pleasing in His sight, through Jesus Christ ; to whom [be] glory for ever and ever. Amen.*

"**Now the God of peace.**" This title is often assigned to God by the Apostle; he useth it here in a way of prayer, as shutting up all the instructions given the Church in a prayer for a blessing from the God of peace. He is the Author of peace, He purposed, designed, and prepared it, in the eternal counsels of His own will; and He communicates peace by Jesus Christ.

"**That brought again from the dead our Lord Jesus, that great Shepherd of the sheep.**" He is *our* Lord Jesus, this is significant of His grace and relationship unto us ; all the work of God towards Jesus Christ respected Him as the Head of the Church, and thence we have an interest in all the grace of it. Jesus Christ is "*that* " great Shepherd ; He is the only Shepherd ; and He is the Shepherd only of the sheep. He is great in His Person, being the eternal Son of God ; He is great in power to preserve His flock ; He is great in His undertaking and the effectual accomplishment of it in the discharge of His office ; and He is great in His glory and exaltation. He is incomparably great and glorious. He is the " *Shepherd of the sheep* ; " He did not lay down His life for the whole of mankind, but for the flock that was given and committed unto Him by His Father. It is the God of peace that brought Him again from the dead, and herein He laid the foundation of the communication of grace and peace unto us. Christ, as the great Shepherd of the sheep, was brought into the state of death by the sentence of the law, and was thence led, recovered, and restored by the God of peace. The law being fulfilled and answered, the God of peace, to evidence that peace was now perfectly made, by an act of sovereign authority brings Him again into a state of life, in a complete deliverance from the charge of the law.

" **Through the blood of the everlasting covenant.**" This covenant is called " everlasting," in opposition to the covenant made at Sinai. The blood of this covenant is the blood of Christ Himself ; it was a sacrifice unto God, and by it the covenant was confirmed. By the blood of Christ, an end was put unto the old covenant with all its services and promises ; atonement was made for sin, the Church was sanctified or dedicated to God, the law was fulfilled, the threatenings of death executed, eternal redemption obtained, the promises of the covenant confirmed, and by one offering they who were sanctified are perfected for ever. The head and well-spring of the whole dispensation of grace lies in the bringing again of Christ from the dead. The death of Christ, if He had not risen, would not have completed our redemption, we should have been " yet in our sins." The bare resurrection of Christ would not have saved us ; but the " bringing again of Christ from the dead, through the blood of the everlasting covenant," is that which gives assurance of the complete redemption and salvation of the Church. There is then in this bringing again from the dead a blessed foundation laid for the communication of grace and mercy to the Church, unto the eternal glory of God.

" **Make you perfect in every good work to do His will, working in you that which is well-pleasing in His sight.**" It is not an absolute perfection that is intended, nor doth the word signify any such thing ; but it is to bring the faculties of the mind into that order, so to dispose, prepare, and enable them, that they may work accordingly. In general, the Apostle designs in this petition the application of the grace of God, through the mediation of Christ, unto our sanctification. And this adapting of us to do the will of God in every good work is by that habitual grace which is wrought in our souls. We are not sufficient of ourselves for such work in any one instance ; therefore, he prayeth that God would do it, work it, effect it, by an effectual *in-working* or working in them.

"**Through Jesus Christ, to whom be glory for ever and ever. Amen.**" All grace is from God, and through Jesus Christ, and so this ascription of glory may be taken as jointly to the Father and the Son. Amen. "So it is, so let it be, so it ought to be ; it is true, it is right and meet that so it should be." Amen.

And unto Him doth the poor unworthy author of this Exposition desire in all humility to ascribe and give eternal praise and glory, for all the mercy, grace, guidance and assistance, which he hath received from Him in his labours and endeavours therein. And if anything, word or expression, through weakness, ignorance and darkness, which he yet laboureth under, have passed from him, that doth not tend unto His glory, he doth here utterly condemn it. And he humbly prays that if through His assistance, and the guidance of His Holy Spirit of light and truth, anything have been spoken aright concerning Him, His office, His sacrifice, His grace, His whole mediation, any light or direction communicated unto the understanding of the mind of the Holy Ghost in this glorious Scripture, He would make it useful and acceptable unto His Church here and elsewhere. And he doth also humbly acknowledge His power, goodness and patience, in that beyond all his expectations He hath continued his life under many weaknesses, temptations, sorrows, tribulations, to bring this work unto its end. To Him be glory for ever and ever. Amen.

What follows in the epistle are certain postcripts which were usual in the other epistles of our Apostle ; and we shall briefly give an account of them.

V. 22. *And I beseech you, brethren, suffer the word of exhortation : for I have written a letter unto you in few words.*

By the term "*brethren*" he denotes his near relation unto them in nature and in grace ; his love unto them, and his common interest with them in the cause in hand. The "*word of exhortation*" is the truth and doctrine of the gospel applied unto the edification of believers, whether by way of exhortation or consolation, the one of these constantly including the other. In persuading them to "*suffer*" this word, he cautions them to take heed that no prejudices, no inveterate opinions, should provoke them against the word, render them impatient under it, and so cause them to lose the benefit of it. Out of love to them the Apostle wrote this epistle, which he calls here a "*letter in a few words*;" and when we consider the importance of the subject treated of in the epistle, the great contests there were among the Hebrews about these things, and the danger of their eternal ruin through a misapprehension of them; all that he hath written may be well esteemed a *"few words,"* and such as whereof none could have been spared.

V. 23.   *Know ye that [our] brother Timothy is set at liberty; with whom if he come shortly, I will see you.*

This Timothy was the companion of the Apostle in all his travels, labours, sufferings, "serving him as a son serveth his father;" unless when the Apostle sent him unto any especial work for the Church. The Apostle tells the Hebrews of Timothy's release out of prison, wherein he knew they would rejoice. He does not seem to have been present with the Apostle at the despatch of this epistle, but he believed it was in the mind of Timothy to visit them in Judea; and hereon the Apostle acquaints them with his resolution to give them a visit, which that he might do, he had before desired their prayers. What was the event of this resolution God only knows.

V. 24.   *Salute all them that have the rule over you, and all the saints. They of Italy salute you.*

This is given in charge unto them to whom this epistle was sent and committed. To salute in the name of another is to represent his kindness and affection unto them. Such rulers and such saints did constitute blessed churches. In Italy there were many Christians, both Jew and Gentile; some of these no doubt were with the Apostle, and knowing his design of sending a letter to the Hebrews, they desired to be remembered unto them; it being probable that many of them were their own countrymen and well known to them.

V. 25.   *Grace [be] with you all. Amen.*

This was the constant close of the epistles written by our Apostle. This he wrote with his own hand, and would have it esteemed as an assured token whereby an epistle might be known to be his (2 Thess. iii. 17, 18). By "grace," he intends the whole good-will of God by Jesus Christ, with all the blessed effects of it, for whose communication unto them he prays herein.

GLORY BE TO GOD.